S.
THEOLO(
1₁₁₁₁₁ıᴏʟ

MW01093792

Spinoza's *Theological-Political Treatise* was published anonymously in 1670 and immediately provoked huge debate. Its main goal was to claim that the freedom of philosophizing can be allowed in a free republic and that it cannot be abolished without also destroying the peace and piety of that republic. Spinoza criticizes the traditional claims of revelation and offers a social contract theory in which he praises democracy as the most natural form of government. This *Critical Guide* to the *Treatise* presents new essays by well-known scholars in the field and covers a broad range of topics, including the political theory and the metaphysics of the work, religious toleration, the reception of the text by other early modern philosophers, and the relation of the text to Jewish thought. It offers valuable new perspectives on this important and influential work.

YITZHAK Y. MELAMED is Associate Professor in the Philosophy Department at Johns Hopkins University. He is the author of *Spinoza's Metaphysics of Substance and Thought* (forthcoming), as well as several articles on early modern philosophy, German Idealism and metaphysics.

MICHAEL A. ROSENTHAL is Associate Professor of Philosophy at the University of Washington. He is the author of numerous articles on Spinoza and early modern philosophy, which have appeared in journals including *Archiv für Geschichte der Philosophie*, *Journal of the History of Philosophy*, and *Journal of Political Philosophy*.

SPINOZA'S
Theological-Political Treatise

A Critical Guide

EDITED BY

YITZHAK Y. MELAMED

Johns Hopkins University

AND

MICHAEL A. ROSENTHAL

University of Washington

CAMBRIDGE
UNIVERSITY PRESS

CAMBRIDGE UNIVERSITY PRESS
Cambridge, New York, Melbourne, Madrid, Cape Town,
Singapore, São Paulo, Delhi, Mexico City

Cambridge University Press
The Edinburgh Building, Cambridge CB2 8RU, UK

Published in the United States of America by Cambridge University Press, New York

www.cambridge.org
Information on this title: www.cambridge.org/9781107636927

© Cambridge University Press 2010

First published 2010
First paperback edition 2013

A catalogue record for this publication is available from the British Library

Library of Congress Cataloguing in Publication Data
Spinoza's 'theological-political treatise' : a critical guide / edited by Yitzhak Y. Melamed,
Michael A. Rosenthal.
p. cm. – (Cambridge critical guides)
Includes bibliographical references and index.
ISBN 978-0-521-88229-3 (hardback)
1. Spinoza, Benedictus de, 1632–1677. Tractatus theologico-politicus. 2. Philosophy and
religion – History – 17th century. 3. Free thought – History – 17th century. I. Melamed,
Yitzhak Y., 1968– II. Rosenthal, Michael A., 1962–
B3985.Z7S65 2010
199´.492 – dc22   2010033073

ISBN 978-0-521-88229-3 Hardback
ISBN 978-1-107-63692-7 Paperback

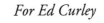

For Ed Curley

Contents

Contributors

EDWIN CURLEY is James B. and Grace J. Nelson Professor of Philosophy at the University of Michigan. He published the first volume of his edition of Spinoza's collected works in 1985 and is currently working on the second volume; he has also written two books on Spinoza (*Spinoza's Metaphysics*, 1969 and *Behind the Geometrical Method*, 1988) and is working on a third, which will focus on the *Theological-Political Treatise.*

MICHAEL DELLA ROCCA is Professor of Philosophy and Chair of the Philosophy Department at Yale University. He is the author of *Spinoza* (2008), of *Representation and the Mind-Body Problem in Spinoza* (1997), and of numerous articles in metaphysics and in early modern philosophy.

DON GARRETT is Professor of Philosophy at New York University. He is the author of *Cognition and Commitment in Hume's Philosophy* (1997) and editor of *The Cambridge Companion to Spinoza* (1996).

WARREN ZEV HARVEY is Chair of the Department of Jewish Thought at the Hebrew University of Jerusalem. He is the author of many studies on medieval and modern Jewish philosophy, including *Physics and Metaphysics in Hasdai Crescas* (1998).

JONATHAN ISRAEL is Professor of Modern History at the Institute for Advanced Study, Princeton. Prior to that he taught for twenty-seven years at University College London. He is the editor of the Cambridge English-language edition of Spinoza's *Tractatus Theologico-Politicus* (2007, translated by Michael Silverthorne).

SUSAN JAMES is Professor of Philosophy at Birkbeck College of the University of London. She is the author of several books, including *Passion and Action: The Emotions in Early Modern Philosophy* (1997), many papers on the history of philosophy, political philosophy, and feminism, as well as the editor of *The Political Writings of Margaret Cavendish* (Cambridge University Press, 2003). She is currently writing a book about Spinoza's political philosophy.

MOGENS LÆRKE is Lecturer at the University of Aberdeen, Scotland. He is the author of *Leibniz lecteur de Spinoza. La genèse d'une opposition complexe* (2008) and of numerous articles on early modern philosophy. He is editor of *The Use of Censorship in the Enlightenment* (2009) and co-editor (with M. Kulstad and D. Snyder) of *The Philosophy of the Young Leibniz* (2009).

DANIEL J. LASKER is the Norbert Blechner Professor of Jewish Values in the Goldstein-Goren Department of Jewish Thought at Israel's Ben-Gurion University of the Negev, in Beer Sheva. He is the author of five books, with additional editions, printings, and translations, and over 175 other publications. His areas of interest are medieval Jewish philosophy (including the thought of Rabbi Judah Halevi, Maimonides, and Rabbi Hasdai Crescas), the Jewish–Christian debate, Karaism and selected issues in Jewish theology and law.

YITZHAK Y. MELAMED is an Associate Professor in the Philosophy Department at Johns Hopkins University. He is the author of *Spinoza's Metaphysics of Substance and Thought* (forthcoming), as well as several articles on early modern philosophy, German Idealism, and metaphysics.

MICHAEL A. ROSENTHAL is Associate Professor of Philosophy at the University of Washington. He is the author of numerous articles on Spinoza and early modern philosophy, which have appeared in journals including *Archiv für Geschichte der Philosophie*, *Journal of the History of Philosophy*, and *Journal of Political Philosophy*. He is currently working on a book on the *Theological-Political Treatise*.

DONALD RUTHERFORD is Professor of Philosophy at the University of California, San Diego. He is the author of *Leibniz and the Rational Order of Nature* (Cambridge, 1995), editor and translator (with Brandon Look) of *The Leibniz–Des Bosses Correspondence* (2007), and editor of *The Cambridge Companion to Early Modern Philosophy* (2006).

PIET STEENBAKKERS is Lecturer in the History of Modern Philosophy at the University of Utrecht, and holder of the endowed chair of Spinoza studies at Erasmus University Rotterdam. He is a member of the international research team Groupe de recherches spinozistes, and he is currently involved in a research project on Biblical Criticism and Secularization in the Seventeenth Century.

JUSTIN STEINBERG is Assistant Professor of Philosophy at Brooklyn College, CUNY. His writings have appeared in the *Journal of the History of Philosophy*, *History of European Ideas*, and the *Stanford Encyclopedia of Philosophy*.

Acknowledgments

We wish to thank Hilary Gaskin and Joanna Garbutt from Cambridge University Press for their encouragement and help. Zach Gartenberg provided most valuable assistance in proofreading the book. Finally, we would like to acknowledge with love the support of our spouses, Janelle Taylor and Neta Stahl.

Abbreviations

C	*The Collected Works of Spinoza*, ed. Edwin Curley (Princeton: Princeton University Press, 1985–).
CGH	*Compendium Grammatices Linguae Hebraeae; Compendium of Hebrew Grammar*
CM	*Cogitata Metaphysica; Metaphysical Thoughts* (an appendix to *DPP*)
DPP	*Renati Des Cartes Principiorum Philosophiae, Pars I et II, More Geometrico demonstratae; Descartes' Principles of Philosophy*
E	*Ethica Ordine Geometrico demonstrata; Ethics*
Ep.	*Epistolae; Letters*
G	*Spinoza Opera*, ed. C. Gebhardt, 4 vols. (Heidelberg: Carl Winter Verlag, 1972 [Orig. 1925])
KV	*Korte Verhandeling van God de Mensch en deszelfs Welstand; Short Treatise on God, Man, and his Well-Being*
OP	*Opera Posthuma* (Amsterdam 1677)
Shirley	*Complete Works of Spinoza*, trans. Samuel Shirley (Indianapolis and Cambridge: Hackett, 2002).
Spinoza, *Letters*	Spinoza, *The Letters*, trans. Samuel Shirley (Indianapolis and Cambridge: Hackett, 1995)
TdIE	*Tractatus de Intellectus Emendatione; Treatise on the Emendation of the Intellect*
TP	*Tractatus Politicus; Political Treatise*
TTP	*Tractatus Theologico-Politicus; Theological-Political Treatise*

Passages in the *Ethics* and *DPP* will be referred to by means of the following abbreviations: a(-xiom), c(-orollary), p(-roposition), s(-cholium) and
app(-endix); "d" stands for either "definition" (when it appears immediately to the right of the part of the book), or "demonstration" (in all other
cases). Hence, E1d3 is the third definition of part 1 and E1p16d is the
demonstration of proposition 16 of part 1.

Introduction

Yitzhak Y. Melamed and Michael A. Rosenthal

Spinoza's *Theological-Political Treatise* was a notorious book in its own time both for what it attacked and for what it advocated. Spinoza did not hesitate to call into question traditional religious – and not only religious – pieties. He attacked the common understanding of prophecy as either a privileged and supernatural form of knowledge or a disguised mode of philosophizing. He denied that miracles, as violations of the Laws of Nature, were possible and claimed that belief in them demonstrated ignorance and undermined any adequate conception of God. Just as he hoped to demystify the content of Scripture, Spinoza sought to call into question its origin. Relying on historical and linguistic analysis, Spinoza argued that Scripture is itself a human artifact written and composed by several authors and editors over time. But Spinoza was not a skeptic about all things. He claimed that prophets used their vivid imaginations to advocate obedience to a social order in which justice and charity were paramount. He believed that the political model of the ancient Hebrews could be imitated in certain key respects. Spinoza's *Realpolitik* – his identification of right with might – led him to rather surprising conclusions. Unlike Hobbes, whose social contract theory justified absolute monarchy, Spinoza argued that democracy was a preferred form of government. And, finally, he thought that the state would be better off if it granted limited religious toleration and the freedom to philosophize.

These views ignited a firestorm of protest when the *TTP* was published anonymously in 1670. Some philosophers, like Leibniz, read it and felt compelled to reject its scandalous views. Others admired it, albeit with some qualifications. Thomas Hobbes was reported by his biographer to have said after reading it, "I durst not write so boldly." The authorities banned it, but its notoriety and depth of argument managed to secure an abiding interest and influence nonetheless. In our own time, its reception has been uneven. In Europe, especially in France, interest in the book remains strong. In the United States, since Edwin Curley wrote his "Notes

I

on a Neglected Masterpiece" in the late 1980s, there has been a resurgence of interest in the *TTP*, both among younger and more established scholars.

A possibly true, possibly fictitious story tells of a visit by the Italian fascist ambassador to France who, in the mid-1920s, paid a visit to the grave of Georges Sorel (1847–1922), the philosopher and prophet of modern political violence. On his way back from the tombstone, so goes the story, the Italian ambassador saw another diplomatic delegation approaching the grave. These were none other than the Russian-Bolshevik ambassador and his people, who had also come to pay their respect to Sorel's legacy. Just like Sorel, Spinoza's legacy has been claimed by a very wide variety of ideologies and intellectual streams. For many, Spinoza is the great atheist of modern philosophy, while for others he is considered an "acosmist," i.e., a radical religious thinker who denies the reality of anything *but* God. Some have considered him the herald of Marxist materialism, while others have suggested that Spinoza was the founder of the tradition of liberal political thought. Indeed, Spinoza has been taken to be the hero of many, perhaps too many, irreconcilable "-isms," from Zionism through Conservatism, Liberalism, Materialism, Idealism, Secularism, Federalism, etc. In the current collection, we would like to set aside these great ideological debates and try to read Spinoza on his own terms, without reducing his thought to any of the ideologies with which he shared some (admittedly interesting) ideas.

In our *Critical Guide* to Spinoza's *Theological-Political Treatise*, we would like to show the range of recent work being done on a variety of topics concerning the *TTP*. The goal is to call attention to the richness of the *TTP* in terms of both its historical influence and its philosophical contribution. We hope to do this through thirteen original essays, which do not present surveys of their various subjects, but rather represent some of the best current research in Spinoza scholarship. A particular motivation behind this collection is the desire to bring leading Spinoza scholars who have so far concentrated their work on Spinoza's major philosophical text, the *Ethics*, to a careful and rigorous examination of the *TTP*. The essays are predominantly from well-established scholars, but we have solicited work from some of the best younger scholars as well. We hope that this volume will serve to stimulate even more interest in the *TTP* among specialists in early modern philosophy, as well as among those more broadly interested in such topics as metaphysics and political philosophy.

The *TTP* is a particularly difficult book for the modern reader, especially the philosopher. First of all there is a great deal of discussion of two subjects, history and the Bible, both of which have been subsequently relegated to other experts in the modern university. Just as in the case of Hobbes's *Leviathan*, the sections on religion have more often than not been neglected in favor of those sections obviously dedicated to political theory, such as Chapter 16. In this collection, we have essays that treat the work as a whole and take us in several interpretive directions. Some show us how Spinoza's thought developed in relation to his intellectual context, whether in his engagement with Jewish thought or with other contemporary seventeenth-century thinkers. Many of the essays demonstrate in various ways the mutual relation of the *TTP* with Spinoza's philosophical *magnum opus*, the *Ethics*. Several demonstrate the ways in which the explicitly political arguments of the *TTP* are related to the earlier sections on prophecy and Scripture.

Edwin Curley has been one the leading scholars of Spinoza for decades, and his masterly studies and translations have done much to stimulate the resurgence of interest in the *TTP*, especially among American scholars. His essay in this volume examines Spinoza's correspondence with his former student Albert Burgh, which dates five years after the publication of the *TTP*, and contributes to our knowledge of Spinoza's relations with his immediate circle. Although the exchange is dated after the publication of the *TTP*, Curley shows how it relates to several of the key themes of the earlier work, in particular, the meaning and role of a universal religion. While other commentators have focused on the role of miracles in the exchange, Curley thinks that the debate over the status of the Catholic Church is more central. Whereas Burgh defends the Catholic Church as the only true representative of revelation, Spinoza claims that Catholicism and indeed all forms of Christianity are based on superstitious beliefs. Nonetheless, Curley argues that, according to Spinoza, even if a religion has superstitious beliefs, i.e., those that are contrary to reason, the state should tolerate it as long as it promotes beneficial conduct.

Because the text is so difficult the more we understand about the genesis and context of the *TTP*, the better we can understand the structure and point of its arguments. In "The text of Spinoza's *Tractatus Theologico-Politicus*," **Piet Steenbakkers** looks closely at several key questions: the origin of the *TTP* and its relation to a supposed earlier draft; the printing history of the text and the distinctions among the editions; the early translations of the Latin text; the annotations that Spinoza added in 1676 to the first edition of 1670; and later editions of the Latin text. These comments enrich our understanding of the composition of the text, its place within Spinoza's development, and its subsequent reception. With these details we can see just how widely and by whom the text was diffused. Modern scholars enjoy an unparalleled access to well-edited texts and Steenbakkers chronicles this process and explains how this was accomplished.

Much recent work has looked at Spinoza in the seventeenth-century context, emphasizing, for instance, his important intellectual ties to Descartes and Hobbes. But as H. A. Wolfson's pioneering, though flawed, study of 1934 made clear, Spinoza also owed a profound debt to medieval Jewish thinkers. Two of our essays throw some fresh light on Spinoza's relation to the Jewish philosophical tradition. **Warren Zev Harvey** has already made many important contributions to our knowledge of this relation. In "Spinoza on Ibn Ezra's 'secret of the twelve,'" he discusses the influence of the commentator Rabbi Abraham Ibn Ezra, who, besides Moses Maimonides, was the medieval author who had the most influence on Spinoza's treatise. Harvey focuses on Spinoza's discussion in *TTP*, Chapter 8 of Ibn Ezra's "secret of the twelve," whose meaning is open to several competing interpretations. Harvey locates Spinoza's use of Ibn Ezra in the context of medieval supercommentaries, i.e., the commentators on Ibn Ezra, in order to point out precisely where Spinoza's critical view on the Mosaic authorship of the Pentateuch is original.

In his chapter, "Reflections of the medieval Jewish–Christian debate in the *Theological-Political Treatise* and the *Epistles*," **Daniel J. Lasker** looks at a new and unexplored source in the Jewish tradition. While Wolfson cataloged possible parallels and influences on Spinoza from medieval Jewish philosophical tradition, Lasker examines medieval Jewish anti-Christian polemical literature. He demonstrates that this literature was available to Spinoza and that there are significant parallels in the content of the *TTP* and various works. The *TTP*, Lasker remarks, had a double critical intent – on the one hand, it criticized the religion of Spinoza's birth, and on the other hand, it questioned, distinctly more cautiously, some of Christianity's dogmas – and Spinoza drew on the polemical literature to help him accomplish both tasks. Spinoza did not intend to demolish religion, but rather to purge them of both Judaism's and Christianity's weakest claims and thereby make both suitable to play their role in society as promoters of charity and justice.

If the genesis and context of the *TTP* are important to our understanding of it, so too is its reception and subsequent influence. No one has contributed more to this field than **Jonathan Israel**, who, in his chapter, "The early Dutch and German reaction to the *Tractatus Theologico-Politicus*: foreshadowing the Enlightenment's more general Spinoza reception?," points out that, contrary to the views of some recent scholars, Spinoza was discussed more frequently and indeed was more central to the

Enlightenment than any other philosopher. In particular, he notes that no other book matches the *Tractatus* or the *Ethics* as a candidate for the honor of being the most analyzed, refuted, and – what counts most – obsessively pored over, wrestled with, and scrutinized text of the era 1670–1820." Israel examines the early Dutch and German responses and shows that these debates helped determine the axes along which the later Enlightenment discussions were organized. The German response, of Jakob Thomasius, for example, is notable for its emphasis on the supposedly pernicious implications of Spinoza's advocacy of freedom of speech and expression. He also looks at the response of particular intellectual circles, such as the Dutch Cartesians, the Lutherans, and Socinians.

While Jonathan Israel surveys the German reception of Spinoza, **Mogens Lærke** dedicates his chapter to a detailed analysis of "G. W. Leibniz's two readings of the *Tractatus Theologico-Politicus*." The point is to discover how a profound and influential philosophical reader shaped the meaning of the treatise in his time. Lærke provides a commentary on Leibniz's relation to each of the key religious (in particular the Socinian) and philosophical views that influenced his reading of the *TTP*. One of the most interesting aspects of the chapter has to do not with something Leibniz says about Spinoza but precisely with a subject on which he is silent. Lærke notes that while Leibniz discusses at some length Hobbes's social contract theory he barely mentions Spinoza's political theory of either the *TTP* or *TP* at all. Lærke suggests that the intersection of Spinoza's necessitarian metaphysics with his theory of natural rights made his views resistant to the strategy of conciliation Leibniz had employed in the case of Hobbes's theory.

Most scholarly attention has been focused on the critique of religion and the political theory of the *TTP*. Relatively little has been said about its metaphysics. As **Yitzhak Y. Melamed** shows in his chapter, "The metaphysics of the *Theological-Political Treatise*," that is unfortunate, because we can learn about the development of Spinoza's system and also about some key doctrines that are actually discussed in more depth than in the *Ethics*. Melamed first discusses two fundamental metaphysical principles that can be found in both works – the principle of sufficient reason and the ontological and epistemological priority of the infinite – and that are central to the critique of anthropomorphism in the *TTP*. He then goes on to analyze the positive conception of God and notes that in the *TTP* Spinoza makes the radical claim that God is identical with nature. Despite Spinoza's apparent disagreement with Maimonides's method of interpreting Scripture, Melamed explains that in fact, when it comes to the understanding of God's nature as revealed in their respective discussion of the Tetragrammaton, Spinoza concurs with his medieval predecessor in claiming that God's essence is nothing but his necessary existence. The *TTP* is certainly a polemical work and metaphysics was not its central concern. Although Spinoza did not cover every key doctrine (such as the distinction between substance and mode) in the *TTP*, Melamed shows that this work nonetheless provides us with some important insights into Spinoza's metaphysics.

Two chapters are notable for the ways in which they combine a deep analysis of the political doctrines of the *TTP* with careful attention to the metaphysical doctrines that are so central to Spinoza's philosophy. In "Spinoza's conception of law: metaphysics and ethics," **Donald Rutherford** gives us another, more specific path to link the *TTP* to the larger project of the *Ethics*. According to Rutherford, in the *TTP* Spinoza reinterprets the idea of law in the Hebrew Bible, in which God gives the law that the people are to obey, to one in which law is no longer a literal command but something individuals discover through reason and the investigation of human nature itself. Rutherford focuses on two central questions: How does the idea of a law bridge the natural and the normative? And how does the idea of the law ground the systematic unity of the ethical theory? Central to Rutherford's account is his reading of Chapter 4, where Spinoza distinguishes between two kinds of law, one that is descriptive and metaphysically basic, the other that is decreed by humans and is prescriptive. This distinction is particularly helpful in making sense of how Spinoza uses the notion of a "natural right" in Chapter 16 and the problem of state formation. Natural rights are understood in terms of descriptive laws of nature and they do not, as such, have a prescriptive or normative content. "Laws of human nature," on the other hand, are based on reason and apply to our particular situation. They teach us that for our own good (and not that of nature) we should transfer our natural right to the state, which then has the power to enforce the prescriptive laws of human nature. Rutherford notes, however, that this distinction is not always so clear-cut, and he explores the ambiguity in the idea of acting according to the dictates of reason. On the one hand, because we have the power of understanding, reason does define our nature to some extent and to act on its insights is simply to act in accordance with our nature. On the other hand, because we are only imperfectly rational, the laws of human nature appear to us as prescriptive to the extent that we recognize the intrinsic motivational force of their reasons. Rutherford also points out that divine laws have the same dual structure, a fact that helps explain the structure of the *Ethics*, where the first parts refer to divine law as descriptive, while the later parts use it prescriptively. The fact that prescriptive laws are ultimately based on descriptive ones also helps us understand the sense in which Spinoza can talk about making ethical decisions in a deterministic metaphysical system. Although the *Ethics* is always in the background, nonetheless, it is the *TTP* that offers the richest account of law in Spinoza's system, and Rutherford's analysis will be essential reading to those who seek to understand it.

Spinoza does not hesitate throughout his work to make strong moral judgments. He criticizes the emotions of indignation and pity, as well as practices such as lying or the pursuit of physical pleasure. What justifies these judgments is a doctrine of egoism and the ethics of self-interest based on it. However, as **Michael Della Rocca** notes, there are some problematic cases, such as lying, in which we are prohibited to do something that may very well be in our obvious self-interest. Likewise, in his political theory, it seems that it may be in the self-interest of citizens living under a despot to rebel, yet Spinoza forbids rebellion. Even more perplexing, perhaps, is that Spinoza condemns the successful rebel as well. To solve these problems Della Rocca goes back to the foundations of Spinoza's theory, which he finds in the principle of sufficient reason. What is wrong with most moral theories is that they ground their judgments in some *arbitrary* standard external to the object. What Spinoza is looking for is a standard of goodness that is intrinsic to the thing itself, which he finds in self-preservation. Della Rocca then invokes what is often thought of as another problematic claim in Spinoza's system – the notion that another person by being similar to me and acting rationally thus benefits me. He defends this claim in light of the principle of sufficient reason, and he demonstrates how it works in Spinoza's account of the social contract. An individual can be judged (non-arbitrarily) to have sought self-preservation when he joins others who are also rational (and thus similar to him) in the establishment of a state whose point is to aid their individual self-preservation. The rebel cannot be deemed to have met the normative standard of self-preservation either of himself or the state because the very act of rebellion violates the constraint of rational similarity. It is an arbitrary action and thus immoral in terms of Spinoza's egoism. One of the great virtues of this essay is that it shows persuasively how both the method and content of Spinoza's political theory relates to his broader epistemological and metaphysical project. It is that perspective that leads Della Rocca to question in conclusion whether from God's point of view there really is any moral judgment at all.

There are also some new contributions to the study of the central political ideas of the *TTP*. The core of Spinoza's political theory is found in Chapter 16 and it is clearly influenced by Hobbes's idea of a social contract. In his chapter, "'Promising Ideas': Hobbes and contract in Spinoza's political philosophy," **Don Garrett** reconsiders the relation of Spinoza to Hobbes's theory. He poses several puzzles that arise: Why does Spinoza say that he keeps the right of nature intact? Why does Spinoza write, "contrary to Hobbes, reason urges peace in all circumstances"? Why does Spinoza write, on the one hand, that violating a promise is sometimes permissible, and yet on the other that if all human beings were solely guided by reason, they would stand by their contracts completely? And why does Spinoza disagree with Hobbes, that one is obligated to keep a promise made with a robber? After having carefully discussed how the two philosophers each define related pairs of key philosophical terms – good and evil, reason and passion, faith and deception – Garrett explains the solution to the problems. Although it may seem that once Spinoza has identified natural right with power he has adopted a kind of "moral nihilism," Garrett points out that Spinoza has only rejected "the framework of *obligations and permissions* as a basis for drawing absolute moral distinctions." Spinoza can still make moral distinctions that are meaningful relative to a particular set of circumstances and laws. The same is true for politics as well. The result is that Garrett, just as he has done with Spinoza's moral philosophy, provides a nuanced philosophical account of the central concepts in the political philosophy.

Although Spinoza made it clear in the subtitle of the work that he would show that the state should allow freedom of philosophizing, the concluding chapters of the *TTP*, in which he ostensibly justifies this claim, have not always been carefully examined. They are sometimes praised as an early example of liberal toleration, or sometimes condemned for not offering enough of a principled argument, or they have simply been ignored. In "Spinoza's curious defense of toleration," **Justin Steinberg** goes a long way to redress these issues. His first step is to indicate what kind of argument Spinoza is not making. According to Steinberg, since Spinoza thinks that there is a *summum bonum* and a rational person can in principle know what it is, he is not offering an argument based on epistemic humility, in which these goods are not known. Steinberg also casts doubt on the claims of some scholars that Spinoza is making an argument based on pluralism. There are not a variety of central ways in which an individual life can flourish but a single model of the good. Finally, he also rejects the idea that Spinoza's defense of toleration is based on the notion of an inviolable individual right. Instead, Steinberg claims that Spinoza offers a two-pronged argument for toleration: while he gives a prudential argument – one in which attempts to legislate morality are shown to undermine their own goals – his account ultimately depends on a defense of a positive conception of freedom.

The final two essays demonstrate the inescapable relation between the political aspects of the *TTP* and its discussion of religion. Many readers of the *TTP* have assumed that Spinoza's thorough critique of religion led him to advocate a secular politics. In "Miracles, wonder, and the state in Spinoza's *Theological-Political Treatise*," **Michael A. Rosenthal** maintains that this view is mistaken and that religion still plays a role in Spinoza's political theory. He argues that Spinoza uses religion to solve some difficult collective action problems in his social contract theory. Of course religion must be stripped of its metaphysical pretensions. Once that has been done, religion is useful for the passions it produces, in particular those which evoke fear and awe. It may even be the case that, despite Spinoza's critique of them, miracles may still have some political function, precisely because they are a tried and true device to produce fear and awe. Rosenthal suggests that even if there is no explicit appeal to miracles and their attendant wonder, there is another way in which the structure of the miracle has been imported into Spinoza's political thinking at a key point. In other words, Rosenthal claims that Spinoza reestablishes the structure of the miracle in his account of the lawmaker's will. If this is true, then this point has interesting implications for modern social contract theory, in which the sovereign is authorized through the act of will of each citizen.

Susan James, in her essay, "Narrative as the means to freedom: Spinoza on the uses of imagination," investigates Spinoza's answer to the profound question of how individuals with their divergent interests can nonetheless be motivated to share in a meaningful collective life. She refers to two general ways in which this question has been answered in the history of ethics: one, the "universalist" approach, looks for general laws or principles that individuals can apply to their own situation; the other, the "particularist" approach, claims that we require a specific interpretation of ourselves, more often than not a thick description or narrative, that motivates us to act. In Spinoza's system, the universalist view of ethical and political self-understanding is expressed through "adequate ideas" or reason, while the particularist view is expressed through "inadequate ideas" or the imagination. James argues that Spinoza offers a distinct way to reconcile these two opposing views. On the one hand, narratives make it possible for us to become motivated by general principles. On the other, we can only apply the general principles if we embed them in a narrative related to our particular circumstances. James focuses on the first part of the reconciliation and convincingly shows us how the imagination can lead us to reason. She gives a reading of the *TTP* in which the useful, but flawed Mosaic narrative, based on the imagined laws of a retributive God, ought ultimately to be replaced by the rational precepts of Christ's moral teaching, in which we legislate for ourselves. The twist, of course, is that, given the fact that most men are not yet led by reason, Spinoza must use the particular to motivate the individual to search for the universal. James's paper is a fitting conclusion to the volume, for it is an example of how, through careful scholarship, Spinoza's views, both in the *Ethics* and in the *TTP*, can be brought into a productive dialogue with contemporary philosophical debates.

Spinoza's exchange with Albert Burgh

Edwin Curley

In September 1675 Albert Burgh, a young man who had been a close friend and admirer of Spinoza, sent him a long and passionate letter, imploring him to convert, as Burgh himself had recently done, to the Catholic faith. Spinoza was initially reluctant to reply, but when he did so, his response was generally temperate, concise, and tinged with sadness at his friend's conversion. In this chapter I propose to examine this correspondence, to see what it can tell us about the reception of the *Tractatus Theologico-Politicus*, and about Spinoza's philosophy as it appears in that work.

I've characterized Burgh's letter to Spinoza as passionate. It is also highly abusive. Although Burgh starts by saying how much he had previously admired Spinoza's acute and subtle intelligence, and by granting that Spinoza loves, and is even eager for, the truth, he quickly passes to saying that his friend has let himself be led astray by the Devil, the Prince of Wicked Spirits, and that his philosophy is a complete delusion.[1] Spinoza is "a wretched little man, a base little earthworm, indeed, ashes, food for worms."[2] Rash, insanely arrogant, puffed up with diabolic pride, Spinoza blasphemes by believing himself to be superior to Jesus.

This may not seem a very promising way to try to convert a friend to your new religion. Nevertheless, at the end of his letter Burgh insists that he has written it

---

[1] *Ep.* 67; *G* IV 281.

[2] I presented an earlier version of this essay to the Southeastern Seminar in Early Modern Philosophy, in Tampa, in November 2007. I'm indebted to the participants in the discussion for their comments, and especially indebted to Yitzhak Melamed, whose comments on the penultimate version of this chapter encouraged significant improvements in its argument. I am also indebted to the School of Historical Studies at the Institute for Advanced Study in Princeton, for the membership during which I completed the revision of this essay.

All translations from the *TTP* and the *Letters* are mine, from the current draft of my translations for Vol. II of the *Collected Works of Spinoza*, forthcoming from Princeton. When published, my translations will have the Gebhardt pagination in the margins. So in my references here I make use of the Gebhardt volume and page numbers. The passage quoted here comes from Vol. IV, p. 283. For citations of the *TTP* I also give chapter and Bruder paragraph numbers, which will be included in my edition.

with a truly Christian intention: first, that you may know the love I have for you, even though you are a Pagan; and second, that I might call upon you not to persist in corrupting others too . . . God wants to snatch your soul from eternal damnation, provided you are willing. Do not hesitate to obey the Lord, who has called you so often through others, and now calls you again, perhaps for the last time, through me, who, having attained this grace by the inexpressible mercy of God himself, pray wholeheartedly that you will attain the same grace.[3]

The Lord may work in mysterious ways, but in this case his instrument was not very effective. Spinoza did not convert to Christianity, much less to Catholic Christianity. In fact, Burgh's letter provoked Spinoza to be more openly critical of organized religion than he had been in the *TTP* itself, demonstrating that aggressive proselytization can backfire. At the end of his reply Spinoza characterizes Roman Catholic Christianity as a "pernicious superstition."[4] Though some of his grounds for that condemnation may be specific to the Roman Church, others would apply equally well to many other Christian denominations. Or so I shall argue. Spinoza also characterizes rabbinic Judaism and Islam as forms of superstition. Examining this correspondence should help us to clarify Spinoza's concept of superstition, suggest a theory about what might make a religion merit that label in Spinoza's eyes, and help to explain why Spinoza might nevertheless encourage state support of religions he regarded as superstitious.

So much for prologue. Recently Jonathan Israel has devoted several pages of his magisterial *Radical Enlightenment* to the correspondence between Burgh and Spinoza, in a chapter entitled "Miracles Denied."[5] I agree with Israel that Spinoza's denial of miracles was a major issue between him and Burgh, that this denial distressed many of Spinoza's readers, and that the questioning of miracles was a major theme in the Enlightenment to come. Still, Israel presents Spinoza as more innovative than he actually was. Hobbes, as Israel is aware, had also written quite skeptically about miracles, arguing that men were apt to give much too hasty credence to miracle stories. Hobbes's official position does concede that sometimes miracles really happen. Israel emphasizes that fact to characterize Hobbes as less radical than Spinoza on this issue. But I think Hobbes's concession is ironic, and that he essentially agrees with Spinoza in rejecting miracles. When Hobbes read Spinoza's *TTP*, he is reported to have said: "He has

[3] *G* IV 291.
[4] *G* IV 323a. The *a* here refers to the fact that of the two versions of Spinoza's reply in the Gebhardt edition, I cite the one in the upper half of the page, which appeared in Spinoza's *Opera Posthuma*. The version which Gebhardt reproduces in the lower half of the page is a copy made by Leibniz.
[5] See Israel, *Radical Enlightenment*, pp. 218–229.

outthrown me a bar's length; I durst not write so boldly."[6] The rejection of miracles is one way in which Spinoza is bolder – in spite of his motto, less cautious in his criticism of traditional religion.[7]

But I think we miss the most central disagreement between Burgh and Spinoza if we focus too exclusively on the issue of miracles. What Burgh is most concerned about is to convince Spinoza that

the Catholic Teaching is the wisest, and admirable in its profundity – in a word, that it surpasses all the other Teachings in the world . . . [it] teaches [men] the secure path to peace of mind in this life, and delivers the eternal salvation of the soul to be achieved after this.[8]

Spinoza not only rejects Burgh's claim for the Catholic Church, but does so in terms which imply a rejection of all forms of organized Christianity.

Burgh argues that the Christian religion is founded on historical facts, which "tens of thousands" of people accept, many thousands of whom "far

---

[6] This remark is often misquoted, because the standard edition of its source, Aubrey's life of Hobbes in his *Brief Lives*, misreads the ms. at this point. Clark reads: "He has *cut through* me a bar's length . . . ," which doesn't make much sense. Some Hobbes scholars have made the obscurity of the remark on that reading a ground for doubting that Hobbes ever said it. (See Hood, *Divine Politics*, and Pinto's emendation of the text, proposed in the *TLS* in September 1950.) Pinto explains that the reference is to a trial of strength in which players compete to see how far they can throw a bar.

I've compared Hobbes's position on miracles with Spinoza's in Curley, "Durst." There I argue also: (1) that if we compare the *TTP* with *Leviathan*, on several topics which they both discuss in the theological portions of their works – specifically, prophecy, miracles, and the authority of Scripture – we shall find much in Spinoza's work which Hobbes might have found to be bolder than what he had written on the same topics; (2) that where Spinoza's position is bolder, Hobbes's less radical position is often stated in a way suggesting irony; (3) that since irony often functions as a way of hinting at views it would be dangerous to express openly, Hobbes's use of it is evidence that he would have gone further than he did, if he thought he could have done so safely; (4) that it is entirely credible that Hobbes said what Aubrey says he said; and finally, (5) that Hobbes is properly viewed (with Spinoza) as a precursor of such Enlightenment figures as Voltaire and Hume. In spite of the surface deference he often shows to orthodox Christian doctrines, he is essentially a secular thinker, whose religious views are subversive of those held by most Europeans of his time. (This article, originally published in Bostrenghi's *Hobbes & Spinoza*, is available on my website: http://sitemaker.umich.edu/emcurley/hobbes.)

Since writing the article cited above, I have published an edition of *Leviathan* which notes the variations between the English edition of 1651 and Hobbes's Latin version, published in 1668 in the Netherlands. This was one of two editions of *Leviathan* Spinoza would have had available to him when he was writing the *TTP* (the other being a Dutch translation, published in 1667). On the interest in Hobbes in the Netherlands see Secretan, "La reception de Hobbes," in the special issue of *Studia Spinozana* devoted to *Spinoza and Hobbes*, Vol. 3, 1987.

[7] However, even Spinoza finds it prudent to veil his rejection of miracles in the ordinary sense of the term by allowing that we can define the term in a way which permits us to affirm that miracles occur: we can understand by a miracle, not an event contrary to the laws of nature, but "a work whose natural cause we cannot explain by the example of another customary thing, or at least which cannot be so explained by the one who writes or relates the miracle." See *TTP* Ch. 6, ¶¶ 6–15; G III 82–84. When miracles are equated with human ignorance in this way, they become far too common to provide a grounding for religious claims.

[8] G IV 289.

surpassed, and surpass, [Spinoza] in learning, in refinement, in true, precise solidity, and in perfection of life."⁹ Among the things this argument from consensus is supposed to prove are the facts that

Christ, the Son incarnate of the living God, suffered, was crucified, and died for the sins of the human race, that he was resurrected, transfigured, and reigns in the heavens, God with the eternal Father, in unity with the Holy Spirit, and the rest of the things which belong to this, the countless miracles which have been done in God's Church by the same Lord Jesus, and afterward, in his name, by the Apostles and the rest of the Saints.¹⁰

Miracles play an evidentiary role here, in so far as the miracles performed by Jesus and his followers attest to the truth of the religion he founded. But they are themselves events whose actual occurrence Burgh acknowledges must be proven. He does this by arguing that many, many people believe they really occurred, and that among these many, many people are many whose learning and moral character are excellent.

On Burgh's view, this consensus of the learned and virtuous is itself direct evidence for some of the historical facts which constitute the foundation of Christianity, facts not in themselves miraculous, such as the facts that Jesus suffered and was crucified. If we denied that events so widely accepted really happened, we would have no ground for accepting such secular events as Julius Caesar's transformation of the Roman Republic into a monarchy. Our belief in the undoubted occurrences of secular history rests on no better ground than the consensus of many thousands of people. A consistent skepticism about the historical claims of the Christian religion would have to be skeptical about all of secular history as well. "It is impossible that everyone who asserts such things . . . would either have deceived themselves, or have wanted to deceive others through the succession of so many ages."¹¹

In advancing this argument from consensus Burgh displays a deep skepticism about the evidence of the senses:

You can never be confident about whether the human mind possesses the ideas of all created things naturally, or whether external objects or the suggestion of good or evil spirits produce many, if not all, of them.¹²

Without consulting the testimonies of other men, how would Spinoza be able to tell whether there are, or can be, in nature, such things as divining rods, the alchemist's stone, the magic of incantations, sirens, gnomes, and any number of other supernatural phenomena? Burgh clearly believes in such things, and sees testimony as providing legitimate support for his

⁹ G IV 285.   ¹⁰ G IV 285.   ¹¹ G IV 286.   ¹² G IV 284.

beliefs. He does not seem to have paused to reflect that he needs to have some trust in the evidence of his senses in order to know that other men are testifying to the facts he takes their testimony as evidence for. Although it's certainly true that we do rely on testimony for justifying much of what we believe, testimony is hardly an independent source of knowledge, which can provide the justification for our reliance on the senses.

When Spinoza replies to Burgh, he does not address Burgh's skeptical arguments for reliance on testimony, except in so far as they seem to rely on the possibility of deception by a demon:

> you lament that I allow myself to be led astray by the Prince of wicked Spirits. But I beg you to be of good heart, and return to yourself. When you were in possession of your faculties, unless I'm mistaken, you worshiped an infinite God, by whose power absolutely all things happen and are preserved. But now you are dreaming of a Prince, an enemy of God, who, contrary to the will of God, leads astray and deceives most men – good men, in fact, are rare – and that for that reason God hands these men over to this master of wicked acts, to be tortured to eternity. The divine justice therefore allows the Devil to deceive men with impunity. But the men the Devil has wretchedly deceived and led astray are by no means without punishment.[13]

So the idea of deception by the Devil, which Burgh had used both to explain Spinoza's embrace of heresies and also as a general ground for skepticism about the senses, Spinoza rejects as incompatible with the idea of God as an infinite being. If God's power is infinite, the Devil cannot deceive men without God's permission. If God's justice is infinite, he would not punish men for being deceived by a Devil who was acting with God's permission.

Burgh's first argument, then, for the proposition that the teaching of the Catholic Church surpasses all other teachings, is simply that thousands upon thousands of people, many of whom are exemplary in their learning and virtue, believe this to be true. So far miracles are a part of the story, but a relatively small part of it. They are among the things which the consensus among the faithful warrants us in believing. And they are among the things which warrant other beliefs the faithful hold. But Burgh has several other arguments, none of which involves miracles.

Some of them seem to be arguments not so much for the superiority of Catholic teaching as for the superiority of Christianity in general, by comparison with other religions. His second argument, for example, invites Spinoza to reflect on the fact that

---

[13] *G* IV 319a.

from the beginning of the world to this day God's Church has been spread without interruption, and continues unchanged and solid, whereas all other religions, whether pagan or heretical, have at least had a later beginning, if they have not also already come to an end.[14]

There's a certain tension in this line of argument, of course. To make the Christian religion older than any other he has to treat it as having begun at the creation, that is, to treat Judaism as simply the first stage of the Christian religion. But this seems incompatible with his claim that the Christian religion has continued unchanged from the beginning of the world, since the work Christians call the "New Testament" is so-called because it introduces a new conception of the covenantal relationship between God and his people.

Burgh's third argument asks Spinoza to consider that the fact that Christianity spread because "unlearned men" were nevertheless able to convert most of the pagan world by teaching a doctrine which is "contrary to common sense, and exceeds and transcends all human reasoning."[15] In spreading the good news they "received no aid from the power of kings and earthly princes," who in fact persecuted them vigorously.

Consider that in this way Christ's Church spread throughout the world in a short period of time, and that finally, the Roman Emperor himself having been converted to the Christian faith, along with the kings and princes of Europe, the Church hierarchy increased its power to such an extent that it can be wondered at today. Consider that all this was brought about through love, gentleness, patience, trust in God, and all the other Christian virtues . . . [16]

---

[14] *G* IV 286–287.   [15] *G* IV 287.

[16] *G* IV 287. Burgh is by no means original in making this argument. A version of it appears in Aquinas's *Summa contra gentiles*, I, vi, 3, where Thomas argues for the reasonableness of Christian belief on the ground that "This wonderful conversion of the world to the Christian faith is the clearest witness of the signs given in the past; so that it is not necessary that they should be further repeated, since they appear most clearly in the effect. For it would be more wonderful than all signs if the world had been led by simple and humble men to believe such lofty truths, to accomplish such difficult actions, and to have such high hopes. Yet it is also a fact that, even in our own time, God does not cease to work miracles through His saints for the confirmation of the faith." Pegis edn., I, pp. 72–73. In the following section Thomas discounts the success of Islam by arguing that "those who believed in [Mohammed] were brutal men and desert wanderers, utterly ignorant of all divine teaching, through whose numbers Mohammed forced others to become his followers by the violence of his arms."

   In the seventeenth century Bayle gave this argument a special twist in his *Commentary*, when he argued against a common interpretation of the parable of the great dinner in Luke 14, that a literal interpretation of the parable, often used to justify forced conversion, would deprive Christianity of its principal claim to superiority over Islam (Book 1, Ch. vii). Whether Christianity is entitled to claim that it spread only by peaceful means, whereas Islam was largely spread by force, is doubtful, as the text will shortly make clear. I presume Bayle knew this. He certainly knew that in his own day Louis XIV was using force against the Huguenots, trying to make France wholly Catholic.

Of all of Burgh's arguments, this is the only one Spinoza will give any weight to. He does not directly challenge it, but contents himself with pointing out that "this argument supports not the Roman Church, but everyone who professes the name of Christ."[17]

Still, Spinoza shows he is unhappy even with this argument. For him it is no recommendation of the Christian religion that it requires belief in things which are contrary to common sense (*sensui communi repugnat*) and teaches things which "exceed human reasoning." The particular example he cites involves the Catholic doctrine of the Eucharist:

> O, young man bereft of understanding, who has bewitched you, so that you believe you are eating that highest and eternal being,[18] and have him in your intestines?[19] . . . Stop calling absurd errors mysteries . . . and do not shamefully confuse things which are unknown to us, or not yet discovered, with those which are demonstrated to be absurd, as are the horrible secrets of this Church. The more [these secrets/mysteries] are contrary to right reason, the more you believe they transcend the intellect.[20]

If unlearned men have been able to persuade thousands upon thousands of people to accept such absurdities, the proper conclusion to draw is, not that the absurdities are true, but that in the wretched despair which the uncertainty of human affairs produces, people can be made to believe almost anything which offers a way out of their difficulties. So Spinoza had argued in the opening paragraphs of the Preface to the *TTP*, in his discussion of the psychological basis for superstition.

Spinoza does not directly question the factual claims Burgh makes about the rapid rise of Christianity. But those claims are dubious, and unless we suppose that Spinoza was as ignorant as his correspondent, we must assume that he knew this. Christianity did, of course, spread rapidly in the first few centuries after the death of Jesus. At the beginning of the fourth century

---

He himself had fled France to escape persecution. When he used the comparative freedom of the Netherlands to publish a critique of a Catholic history of Calvinism, his brother, who had remained in France, was put in prison, where he soon died.

  Arguably, Islam has historically been more tolerant of religious minorities than Christianity has. See Cohen, *Crescent and Cross*. In his recent (and generally sympathetic) history of Christianity, Diarmaid MacCulloch claims that "For most of its existence, Christianity has been the most intolerant of world faiths, doing its best to eliminate all competitors, with Judaism a qualified exception, for which (thanks to some thoughts of Augustine of Hippo) it found space to serve its own theological and social purposes." MacCulloch, *Christianity*, p. 4.

[17] *G* IV 322a.   [18] *G* IV 319a.

[19] I learn from Professor Lasker's contribution to this volume that this was a common theme in Jewish polemics against Christianity. I learn from Hoffmann's "Anatomy" that it was also a common theme in Protestant polemics against Catholic Christianity.

[20] *G* IV 323a.

Christians seem to have still constituted a relatively small percentage of the population of the Empire as a whole: probably somewhere between 7 and 10 percent.[21] Considering how few followers Jesus must have had at the time of his death, that's impressive growth. Still, the transition from being a small (but significant) minority religion to being the majority religion occurred in the fourth century, when the emperors were predominantly Christians, who used their political power to advance the cause of their religion.[22] Between the accession of Constantine in 312 and the end of Theodosius's reign in 395, the number of Christians in the Empire seems to have grown from around 5 million to around 30 million.[23] But during that period, contrary to what Burgh assumes, those spreading the faith received considerable "aid from the power of kings and earthly princes."

The first Christian emperor, Constantine, did not persecute pagans in the way his predecessor, Diocletian, had persecuted Christians. He preferred the carrot to the stick. One of his first acts, after he rose to power in the western Empire, was to persuade his colleague in the east, Licinius, to join him in promulgating the Edict of Milan, which granted "both to Christians and to all men freedom to follow whatever religion one wished."[24] This commitment to religious liberty did not, however, mean that he would not favor his own religion. He did much to give Christianity a privileged position among Roman religions: first, by engaging in what Drake has described as "a massive redistribution of patronage resources to the bishops,"[25] but also, as Barnes notes, by giving "freely from the imperial treasury, both to build or enlarge churches, and to decorate them richly," stripping the pagan temples of their treasures, exempting the Christian clergy from taxation, and changing the laws regarding marriage and divorce, to bring them in line with Christian values.[26]

[21] I take this estimate from Drake, *Constantine*, p. 495 n. 2. It seems to be a consensus view. Though their numbers may have been small, Christians evidently exercised an influence out of proportion to their numbers. Cf. Barnes, *Constantine*, p. 191.

[22] The exception, of course, was Julian, called "the Apostate," who tried, during his brief reign (November 361–June 363), to restore paganism to what he thought its rightful place was.

[23] This is MacMullen's estimate, in *Christianizing*, p. 86. Stark, *Rise*, suggested that Christianity may have become the majority religion as early as the middle of the fourth century. He arrives at an estimated 56.5 percent of the population in 350 CE by assuming a base of 1,000 Christians in the year 40 CE, a growth rate of 40 percent per decade up till 350, and a population of the Empire in 350 of 60 million. He stresses that for over a century the Mormons have achieved a growth rate of this magnitude. He acknowledges that his starting figure of 1,000 Christians in 40 CE is somewhat arbitrary, but seems safe in his assumption that the number of Christians at that point must have been very small. More dubious, as he acknowledges, is his assumption of a constant rate of growth. If we suppose that the rate of growth may, at some periods, have been less than 40 percent, Christianity would not have achieved majority status quite so quickly.

[24] Drake, *Constantine*, p. 194.   [25] The quote is from Drake, "Constantine," p. 391.

[26] Barnes, *Constantine*, pp. 48–54, 246–247.

Though Constantine thought a Christian emperor should not persecute pagans, he did not hesitate to persecute Christians who dissented from the decisions of church councils. By using the power of the state to enforce orthodox belief among Christians, Drake has argued, he "erode[d] the long-held Christian principle that belief could not be coerced,"[27] thereby paving the way for his successors to persecute pagans. By the end of the fourth century the emperor was using his power vigorously, not only to favor Nicene Christianity in its competition with the Arian and Donatist heresies, but also to repress paganism:

Theodosius caused surviving pagan sacrifices at Alexandria and Rome to cease and proscribed domestic cults (16.10.10–11). The world-renowned Temple of Serapis at Alexandria was destroyed by monks led on by the local bishop, while Roman officials stood by. Riots by the Christian mobs, fueled by the promise of spoils, spread like wildfire.[28]

Contrary to what Burgh claims, not everything was done through love, gentleness, patience, and the other Christian virtues. I would not suggest that the support Christianity received from the state was anything like the sole cause for the dramatic increase in the numbers of Christians during the fourth century. To explain a phenomenon of this magnitude we would have to invoke many causes, as Gibbon did in Chapter xv of his classic *Decline and Fall of the Roman Empire*.[29] But it's hard to believe that it did not have some effect.

Spinoza does not have the advantage of modern scholarly knowledge of the ancient world. So he would not have been in a good position to make even the rough estimates of Christian numbers I have made in the last few paragraphs. The most he could have said with any justification would have been: Christians must have constituted a tiny minority of the population of the Empire during most of the first century; by the beginning of the fourth century, they were probably a significant minority, though still distinctly a minority; by the end of the fourth century, they were probably a majority. But he certainly would have been in a position to know that in its latter stages this growth did not occur without significant support from Constantine and his successors. That much he could have learned from Eusebius's *Life of Constantine* or Ammianus Marcellinus. That the subsequent spread of Christianity beyond the Roman Empire owed much to the sword, he would also have known from the history of the Jews and

---

[27] Drake, *Constantine*, p. 439.
[28] King, "Theodosius." For a more detailed account, see King, *Establishment*.
[29] To Gibbon's five causes we might now wish to add others, suggested by Stark, *Rise*.

Muslims in Iberia, and of Protestant Christians and indigenous peoples in the lands ruled by Spain in the sixteenth century.[30]

What Spinoza challenges, though, in his reply to Burgh is his contention that the Catholic Church is unique in its claim to antiquity, immutability, and perpetuity:

> What you add about the common agreement of many thousands of men, and about the uninterrupted succession of the Church, etc., is the same old song of the Pharisees. For with no less confidence than those devoted to the Roman Church, they display many thousands of witnesses, who report the things they have heard as things they have experienced . . . they trace their lineage all the way to Adam, and boast with equal arrogance that their Church has spread to this day, and remains unchanged and genuine, in spite of the hostility of the Pagans and the hatred of the Christians . . . What they are most proud of is that they count far more martyrs than any other nation, and that the number of those who have suffered for the faith they profess increases daily.[31]

Spinoza then tells the story of a certain Judah, called the faithful, a Christian noble in Spain who had converted to Judaism, and who died at the stake, singing a hymn to God in the midst of the flames. Though Burgh would prefer to ignore it, Christians have been both the persecuted and the persecutors. Their unfortunate belief that there is no salvation outside the Church, a belief Burgh explicitly endorses, gives them a perverse incentive to bring people to the faith, and keep them there, by whatever means they find necessary.

Nowadays we call the view that salvation awaits all and only those who accept a certain religion exclusivism.[32] Burgh is an exclusivist in that sense, and is arguing for the acceptance of a brand of Christianity which has long been exclusivist. The Second Vatican Council may have changed that. It would be pleasant to think so. But it remains to be seen how deep and lasting that council's distancing of Catholicism from exclusivism will be. Before he became pope, Benedict XVI seemed to be bent on returning the Church to its historical position on the relation between Catholic

---

[30] The best treatment of this I know is Fletcher, *Barbarian Conversion*.   [31] *G* IV 321a–322a.

[32] Or "soteriological exclusivism," as Quinn and Meeker call it, in the introduction to Quinn and Meeker, *Challenge*. Exclusivists are prone to find support for their position in such passages as John 3:16, 18: "For God so loved the world that he gave his only Son, so that everyone who believes in him may not perish, but may have eternal life . . . Those who believe in him are not condemned; but those who do not believe are condemned already, because they have not believed in the name of the only Son of God." Some authors use "exclusivism" in a different sense, to apply to religions which hold that there is only one God, and that worship of any other god is therefore inappropriate. Cf. Drake, *Constantine*, pp. 479–480. On this view monotheism is inherently exclusivist.

Christianity and other faiths.[33] Now conservatives in the Church appear to have the upper hand.

Exclusivism is often criticized as being arrogant. We can see one ground for that criticism in Burgh's arguments for the superior wisdom of Catholic teaching. One of the claims he makes for his faith is that Catholics are just better than other people from a moral point of view.

Countless Catholics of each sex . . . have lived wonderful and most holy lives . . . the most perfect Heretic or Philosopher who ever lived hardly deserves to be considered among the most imperfect Catholics.[34]

So it's not just that on average Catholics are morally superior to non-Catholics. Even the worst of Catholics is superior to even the best of non-Catholics.

In our more ecumenical times, when we are prone to acknowledge the existence of moral virtue in people of many different faiths, and even, occasionally, in the non-religious, this affirmation of the moral superiority of Catholic Christians may make Burgh seem both ridiculous and irrelevant. But there is a certain logic in his position. If religion is the foundation of morality, and if there is but one true religion, then it seems reasonable to suppose that the true religion ought to be more effective than other religions in making its adherents morally virtuous. If there is only one religion which can truly offer salvation, then it seems that if God is just, the adherents of that one salvific religion ought to be more deserving of an eternal reward than those outside the salvific religion. So we might expect an exclusivist to embrace the following set of propositions:

(1) There is exactly one true religion, acceptance of which is necessary and sufficient for salvation.
(2) God is just.
(3) The adherents of the one true religion are uniformly morally superior to the adherents of all other religions, and to those who have no religion.

The first of these propositions defines exclusivism, as I am here understanding that term. I take "acceptance of a religion" here to include at least

---

[33] See "Dominus Iesus," a Declaration by the Congregation for the Doctrine of the Faith, issued when the present Benedict XVI was still Cardinal Ratzinger, and Prefect of the Congregation. According to this document, those outside of Christianity are "in a gravely deficient situation" in comparison with Christians and non-Catholic Christians have "defects" in comparison with Catholic Christians. A Church which claims infallibility for the decrees of popes and ecumenical councils cannot easily admit that its previous teaching was wrong.

[34] *G* IV 289.

acceptance of its central teachings about God and its central moral teachings. The second proposition is widely accepted in monotheistic religions.[35]
The third proposition looks like it ought to follow from the first two. The
assumption here would be that in a world governed by a just God, if salvation is granted to all and only those who adhere to a particular religion,
then the adherents of that religion must be uniformly morally superior to
the adherents of other religions.

Some might object that this assumption ignores a fundamental Christian
teaching: that all men are sinners, and indeed, sufficiently sinful that what
they deserve is damnation. Paraphrasing Hamlet, we might say: "Use every
man after his desert and who should scape [not just whipping, but] hell?"
This seems to be the teaching of Paul:

There is no distinction, since all have sinned and fallen short of the glory of God,
they are now justified by his grace as a gift, through the redemption that is in
Christ Jesus . . . (Romans 3:22–24)

On this view if Christians and only Christians are saved, that is not because
of their superior virtue, but because of their faith, which is "reckoned" to
them as righteousness (Romans 3:28, 4:3). The fact that only Christians
will be saved is no reason to expect them to be better than other people.

That may be a more authentic interpretation of Christianity than
Burgh's. But it is not his interpretation of Christianity. And his particular
combination of views seems to open exclusivism up to empirical refutation. The simple fact is that there is no religion whose adherents have a
monopoly on moral virtue. Spinoza makes this point effectively when he
replies to Burgh. First, he points out, as politely as possible, that the leaders
of the Catholic Church have not always been paragons of virtue:

I shall not, as the opponents of the Roman Church usually do, relate the vices
of the Priests and Popes, to turn you away from them. For these stories are often
brought up maliciously, more to irritate than to instruct.[36]

Spinoza is reluctant to belabor the sins of the Church's leaders. He makes
his point clearly enough without engaging in a catalog of papal sins. But
he prefers to emphasize the positive, by granting that

in the Roman Church there are more men of great erudition, who have led
commendable lives, than in any other Christian Church.

---

[35] The scriptural traditions of the three major monotheistic religions make this a difficult proposition
to deny. Negative theologians like Maimonides may find it too anthropomorphic. But negative
theologians tend to get in trouble with their co-religionists.
[36] G IV 317a.

But this, he says, is because this church has more adherents than any other. So inevitably "there are more men of every condition in it." The crucial point, for Spinoza, is that

in every Church there are many very honorable men, who worship God with justice and loving-kindness. For we know many men of this kind among the Lutherans, the Reformed, the Mennonites, and the Enthusiasts,[37] and, not to mention others, your own ancestors, who in the time of the Duke of Alva, suffered all kinds of torture for the sake of religion, with equal constancy and freedom of mind.[38]

The Duke of Alva was a general whom Philip II sent to govern the Spanish Netherlands in the sixteenth century, who acquired the nickname "the Iron Duke" because of the brutality he used in suppressing the Protestant revolt. This is a gentle reminder that the Church did not sustain its position solely by the practice of Christian virtues.

Earlier I proposed what we might call the exclusivist syllogism and suggested that Burgh accepts all three propositions, while Spinoza rejects the third at least.

(1) There is exactly one true religion, acceptance of which is necessary and sufficient for salvation.

(2) God is just.

(3) The adherents of the one true religion are uniformly morally superior to the adherents of all other religions, and to those who have no religion.

If the third proposition does in fact follow from the first two, this raises the question which of the first two Spinoza would reject.

I think he would reject both of them. Although I've described the second proposition as an assumption widely accepted in monotheistic religions, I think Spinoza would regard it as too anthropomorphic to be accepted in its most natural interpretation. God is not like a king or prince proportioning rewards and punishment to merit and demerit.[39] But he would also reject the first proposition. There is not one true religion, acceptance of which is both necessary and sufficient for salvation. There are many paths to salvation. In that sense Spinoza is a pluralist.

Now some may object that, however much we in the twenty-first century might wish it were otherwise, Spinoza is no pluralist.[40] If this is not clear in the *TTP*, it becomes quite clear in the *Political Treatise*, where he

---

[37] A term generally applied in the seventeenth century to those Christians who believed themselves to be immediately inspired by God. Cf. Locke, *Essay*, Bk. IV, Ch. 19.

[38] *G* IV 317a–318a.

[39] Cf. *Ethics* E2p3s with *TTP* Ch. 4, ¶ 30; *G* III 64, where Spinoza explicitly rejects the attribution of justice (and compassion) to God.

[40] This is, essentially, an objection Yitzhak Melamed raised against an earlier version of this chapter.

prescribes that in an aristocracy it is essential for the rulers to agree in endorsing and practicing one national religion.[41] Other religions are to be allowed, but only subject to certain restrictions. They may build as many houses of worship as they wish, but these must be kept "small, modest, and somewhat dispersed," whereas the temples devoted to the national religion should be "large and magnificent." The rights Spinoza explicitly grants the civil authorities in the *TP* are implicit in the position he takes in the *TTP*, Chapter 19, where he insists that it is the prerogative of the civil authorities to determine in what way people are obliged to obey God and practice the externals of religious worship.[42]

All this is true, of course. But when we are considering Spinoza's advocacy of a national religion, whose practice is to be regulated by the sovereign, we must keep in mind his insistence that this national religion be the "universal religion" he described in Chapter 14 of the *TTP*.[43] That universal religion is clearly meant to represent what Spinoza takes to be the common core of the monotheistic religions which take their origin in the Jewish and Christian Scriptures. He equates its tenets with

the fundamental principles of the whole of Scripture, all of which . . . must tend to this point: that there is a supreme being, who loves Justice and Loving-kindness, whom everyone, if he is to be saved, is bound to obey and to worship by practicing Justice and Loving-kindness toward his neighbor.[44]

Spinoza goes on to enumerate seven doctrines which he claims follow from this foundation:

(i) that God exists, in the sense that there is a supremely just and merciful supreme being; (ii) that this supreme being is uniquely an appropriate object of devotion, admiration, and love; (iii) that he is present everywhere, and that everything is known to him; (iv) that he has the supreme right and dominion over all things, and does nothing because he is compelled by a law, but acts only from his absolute good pleasure and special grace; (v) that the proper worship of and obedience to this being consist only in justice and loving-kindness, *or* in the love of one's neighbor; (vi) that all and only those who obey God by living in this way are saved, the rest, who live under the control of the pleasures, being lost; and finally, (vii) that God pardons the sins of those who repent.[45]

---

[41]   *TP* Ch. 8, art. 46; *G* III 345.
[42]   See particularly *TTP* Ch. 19, ¶¶ 24–27; *G* III 232–233, but also Ch. 19, ¶ 3; *G* III 229, for Spinoza's insistence that the sovereign's power extends only to the external practice of religion.
[43]   Spinoza makes this clear in *TP* Ch. 8, art. 46. He describes the tenets of the universal religion in *TTP* Ch. 14, ¶¶ 24–34; *G* III 177–179.
[44]   *TTP* Ch. 14, ¶ 24; *G* III 177.
[45]   Here I paraphrase (closely) and abridge, rather than quote fully, Bruder ¶¶25–28; *G* III 177–178.

There are two things in particular which need to be noticed here. First, there is nothing specifically Christian about this universal religion, much less specifically Protestant or Catholic. In abridging this passage I did omit its only reference to Christ. But all Spinoza says when he does mention Christ – in his gloss on the proposition that God pardons the sins of those who repent – is that

whoever firmly believes that God, out of mercy and the grace by which he directs everything, pardons men's sins, and who for this reason is more inspired by the love of God, that person really knows Christ according to the Spirit, and Christ is in him.[46]

So if you believe in God's mercy, and if that belief inspires you to love God all the more, then you have the spirit of Christ in you, *whatever you may believe about the historical Jesus of Nazareth*, whether you think he was the son of God, or the Messiah, or a supremely wise moral teacher, or for that matter, merely an unusually charismatic preacher, who had some important moral insights, but may have erred in many ways (who did err, one might think, if he claimed to be the Messiah, or the son of God). You may have the spirit of Christ in you even if you have never heard of Jesus. So far as I can see, there is nothing in this which any Christian or any Jew need object to. Nor, I think, does this universal religion contain anything a Muslim would necessarily find objectionable.

The second point we need to notice is that though this "universal faith" is clearly intended to articulate a kind of lowest common denominator of the major monotheistic religions, it is couched in terms which Spinoza himself could not literally accept, and which no one who has accepted the teaching of the *TTP* prior to Chapter 14 could literally accept. It uses language Spinoza has previously devoted much space to rejecting as involving an inadequate, anthropomorphic conception of God. It is anthropomorphism to think of God as just, or merciful, or as a lawgiver to whom obedience is due. Spinoza makes provision for those who might agree with him in rejecting scriptural anthropomorphism when he adds, immediately after his enumeration of the tenets of this faith, that it does not matter how people interpret them, so long as they interpret them in a way consistent with the practice of justice and loving-kindness:

As for the rest – what God, *or* that model of true life, is, whether he is fire, spirit, light, thought, etc. – that does not matter as far as faith is concerned; nor does it matter in what way he is a model of true life, whether because he

---

[46] *TTP* Ch. 14, ¶ 28; *G* III 178.

has a just and merciful heart or because all things exist and act through him, and hence that we also understand through him, and see, through him, what is true, right, and good. It is all the same, whatever anyone maintains about these matters.

Again, it does not matter, as far as faith is concerned, whether someone believes that God is everywhere according to his essence or according to his power, or that he directs things from freedom or from a necessity of nature, or that he prescribes laws as a prince or teaches them as eternal truths, or that man obeys God from freedom of the will or from the necessity of the divine decree, or finally, that the reward of the good and punishment of the evil is natural or supernatural.

It does not matter, I say, as far as faith is concerned, how each person understands these and similar things, provided he does not conclude that he should take a greater license to sin, or that he should become less obedient to God.[47]

So Spinoza explicitly permits an interpretation of these tenets which would be consistent with his own philosophy. What matters for him, in the end, is simply conduct: whether a person is committed to loving God, however he may conceive of God, practicing justice, and loving his fellow man. This is very much in the spirit of modern pluralism, as advocated, for example, by John Hick.

But Spinoza is a pluralist with a difference. Unlike modern pluralists, he thinks that some of the religions in which we can be saved are forms of superstition. This is clear in the case of Roman Catholicism, which he explicitly characterizes as a "pernicious" superstition, even though he grants that there are many men who have lived commendable lives within that religion. How is this possible?

The answer, I think, lies in Spinoza's distinction between the theoretical aspect of religion and its practical aspect. Catholic Christianity involves theoretical beliefs, some of which are absurd, such as the belief that in the Eucharist the worshiper is literally eating the body of his God. That is sufficient to qualify Catholicism as a superstition. Perhaps there is no great harm in that particular belief. But Catholic Christianity also involves beliefs which can be very harmful, such as the belief that salvation is possible only within the Church, which provides an incentive to persecute non-believers, if not to convert them to belief, then at least to prevent them from corrupting the faithful.[48] That is sufficient to qualify Catholicism as a pernicious superstition. But within the Catholic Church there may be people who do not accept all the doctrines the Church hierarchy thinks they ought to accept, men like Rousseau's Savoyard vicar, who does not

---

[47] *TTP* Ch. 14, ¶¶ 30–32; *G* III 178.
[48] As, for example, in Aquinas, *Summa theologiae*, II-II, Qu. 10, art. 8.

care at all about theological niceties, and who is motivated by his belief in a personal, loving and just God to practice justice and loving-kindness himself, and to encourage the spread of those virtues. The beliefs of such a Catholic might still be superstitious, because of the anthropomorphism they involve. But they would not be pernicious. They would, in fact, be very beneficial, not only to the person so motivated, but also to the society in which he lives. That is one reason, I think, why Spinoza argues that the state may, and should, sponsor a suitably purified universal faith.

At the beginning of the chapter I suggested that Spinoza might characterize many of the Christian denominations of his day as forms of superstition. What might he think were legitimate grounds for that characterization? If the argument of this chapter is correct, it seems likely that Spinoza would reject as superstitious any religion which claimed that salvation was possible only within that religion. Exclusivism is a form of superstition. So is the advocacy of mysteries. The example most prominent in the letter to Burgh is the Catholic doctrine of the Eucharist. But any doctrine which a church proclaims as being beyond the power of human reason to understand seems a likely candidate. So the doctrine of the dual nature of Christ, that Jesus was both fully human and fully divine, would be another example. There were hints of this in the *TTP* itself, and the correspondence with Oldenburg confirms it.[49] Another example would be the Christian doctrine of hell, fear of which Spinoza calls "the sole cause of superstition."[50]

On his own principles, Spinoza exaggerates in saying this. The Preface to the *TTP* suggests a psychological account of superstition which relates it to more general causes in human nature than the fear of hell. Spinoza opens that Preface by writing that:

If men could manage all their affairs by a definite plan, or if fortune were always favorable to them, no one would be gripped by superstition. But often they are in such a tight spot that they cannot decide on any plan. Then they usually vacillate wretchedly between hope and fear, desiring immoderately the uncertain goods of fortune, and ready to believe anything whatever.[51]

The examples Spinoza goes on to give in that context involve pagans, who thought they could learn the future from reading the entrails of animals,

---

[49] So, for example, in *TTP* Ch. 1, ¶ 24; *G* III 21 Spinoza writes that he does not deny "the things certain churches maintain about Christ"; he simply does not understand them. In *Ep.* 73 he is more forthcoming: "As for what certain churches add to this [sc. that God's wisdom was manifested most through Jesus Christ] – that God assumed a human nature – I warned expressly that I don't know what they mean. Indeed, to confess the truth, they seem to me to speak no less absurdly than if someone were to say to me that a circle has assumed the nature of a square" (*G* IV 309a).
[50] *G* IV 323.   [51] *G* III 5.

and to some extent even control the future by getting the gods on their side. So he permits his Christian readers to suppose that only pagan beliefs are in question when he talks of superstition. One thing which is clear from the letter to Burgh is that this is not true, that much of the organized religion of his day is in question. What makes these religions forms of superstition is the illusion they cultivate that the world is governed by a supernatural being – or beings – who can and will intervene in its history to reward those they favor and punish those they dislike. That is common ground between paganism and Christianity.

The Preface to the *TTP* also suggests a further reason why Spinoza may have thought it desirable for the state to sponsor a religion he regarded as superstitious. It's not just that with suitable purification superstition can motivate us to do good. The causes of superstition lie deep in human nature. Even the most knowledgeable and powerful among us have very limited knowledge and power. We are all at the mercy of fortune, vulnerable to external causes which may help preserve us if we are lucky, or destroy us if we are not. Not knowing our fate, we cannot help but vacillate between hoping for the best and fearing the worst. It is natural for us to want to believe in the existence of powers who may protect us from what we fear, if only we can win their favor. Superstition is too deeply rooted in the human condition to be eradicated. But with good management it can be made less harmful, more beneficial. That is what Spinoza's universal religion seeks to achieve.

CHAPTER 2

The text of Spinoza's Tractatus Theologico-Politicus

Piet Steenbakkers

The issues in the textual history of the *Tractatus Theologico-Politicus* that deserve attention can be grouped under the following headings: the genesis of the work; the printing of the Latin text; the early translations; the "Annotations to the *Tractatus Theologico-Politicus*"; and the later modern editions of the text.

I GENESIS

The actual writing of the *TTP* must have occupied its author from the summer of 1665 to the final months of 1669. The earliest reference to the composition of a work that was eventually to be published as the *TTP* is to be found in Spinoza's *Ep.* 30 of the beginning of October 1665, to Henry Oldenburg. Spinoza had broached the subject in a preceding letter, written on September 4 (now lost). This can be inferred from Oldenburg's reply. After enumerating several scientific experiments conducted by Fellows of the Philosophical Society, Oldenburg (in what appears to be a somewhat skeptical vein) contrasts these with Spinoza's new project:

I see that you are not so much philosophising as theologising, if one may use that term, for you are recording your thoughts about angels, prophecy and miracles. But perhaps you are doing this in a philosophic way. Of whatever kind it be, I am sure that the work is worthy of you and will fulfil my most eager expectations. Since these difficult times are a bar to the freedom of intercourse, I do at least ask you please to indicate in your next letter your plan and object in this writing of yours.[1]

And this is precisely what Spinoza does in his answer:

I am now writing a treatise on my views regarding Scripture. The reasons that move me to do so are these:

---

[1] *Ep.* 29; Shirley 842.

29

(1) The prejudices of the theologians. For I know that these are the main obstacles which prevent men from giving their minds to philosophy. So I apply myself to exposing such prejudices and removing them from the minds of sensible people.

(2) The opinion of me held by the common people, who constantly accuse me of atheism. I am driven to avert this accusation, too, as far as I can.

(3) The freedom to philosophise and to say what we think. This I want to vindicate completely, for here it is in every way suppressed by the excessive authority and egotism of preachers.[2]

Thus we know fairly precisely when Spinoza began writing the book. He must have completed it late in 1669. On the title page, the year of publication given is 1670, and this is confirmed by the earliest responses. On April 8, 1670, the council of the Reformed Church in Utrecht expresses its dismay at the publication of a profane and sacrilegious book entitled "tractatus theologico-politicus de libertate philosophandi in republica,"[3] and in the same month the Utrecht theologian Frans Burman reports having read the book.[4] The *TTP* must therefore have been available early in 1670, perhaps even late in 1669:[5] it was not uncommon for publishers to antedate books that came out towards the end of the year.

In *Ep.* 30 to Oldenburg, Spinoza is explicit about his intentions: he wants the book to play a part in current debates on religion, philosophy, and politics. The topics dealt with in the *TTP*, however, are closely connected with issues that must already have had his attention in a much earlier stage of his development. The way he discusses the Hebrew text of the Bible, the history of Israel, and medieval Jewish philosophers like Ibn Ezra and Maimonides is obviously grounded in his own Jewish upbringing. It is also plausible that he developed his harsh views on Judaism in the period of his excommunication, i.e., around 1656. Though the evidence for the hypothesis that parts of the *TTP* had already been written well before 1665 is unconvincing, two pieces of information have tempted scholars to postulate the existence of some proto-*TTP*. The first is a report by Salomon van Til in 1694, according to whom Spinoza had given a justification for his apostasy from Judaism. In the preface to *Het voor-hof der heydenen*[6] Van Til wrote: "He had amassed objections of this sort against the Old

---

[2] *Ep.* 30; Shirley 844.

[3] Freudenthal, Walther, and Czelinski *Die Lebensgeschichte Spinozas*, 1, p. 278 (no. 88).

[4] In *Burmannorum pietas, gratissimae beati parentis memoriae communi nomine exhibita* (1700), p. 211, Burman's son Frans Burman the Younger quotes an entry to that effect from his father's diary.

[5] This is the range specified by Burman (p. 204: "aut exeunte anno LXIX, aut ineunte LXX"). The passage is quoted by Bamberger, "Early Editions," p. 29 n. 28.

[6] Dordrecht: Goris, 1694.

Testament in a Spanish treatise entitled *A vindication*[7] *of his dissent from Judaism.* He kept this back on the advice of friends, but then presumed to blend these things in a shrewder and more diluted manner into another work, that he published in 1670 under the name of *Tractatus theologico-politicus.*"[8] Van Til does not provide a source for this piece of information, nor is it confirmed by any independent witness: all references to Spinoza's presumed *Apology* (e.g., by Pierre Bayle in the *Dictionaire*) take their cue from Van Til.[9] Yet it would be rash to dismiss the story altogether. Salomon van Til, who in 1678 was a member of a committee in Leiden investigating whether Spinoza's works should be prohibited, apparently had access to documents that were subsequently lost. Elsewhere in his *Voor-hof* he cites a letter that gives an account of an interview with Spinoza.[10] What he reveals of the contents of this letter shows that it reported Spinoza's views on the vicissitudes of the books of the Hebrew Bible. The affinity with the *TTP* is obvious; yet the views imputed here to Spinoza do not occur in this form in the treatise.

Another document that has been interpreted as an indication for the existence of some proto-*TTP* is a letter from Adriaan Paets to Arnold Poelenburg of March 30, 1660. In it we read:

Please find enclosed a theologico-political treatise [*tractatum theologico-politicum*]; though its author will not be entirely unknown to you, his name should be kept silent for the moment. It contains an argument that is most useful for these times, and quite a few things one will not find elsewhere, especially the author's subtle and careful discussion of the difference between laws by institution and natural laws. . . . I beg you, dear Poelenburg, to deem this little book [*libellum*] worthy of a serious and careful examination, and to advise your learned colleagues to spend some of their spare time to reading it.[11]

The very phrase *tractatus theologico-politicus* of course immediately brings to mind Spinoza's work of that name. Yet there are several details that should give us pause. Paets describes a treatise on theology and politics, but he nowhere states that this is its title.[12] Moreover, the work at hand is a little book, the year is 1660,[13] and what is revealed of its contents – the

---

7 The Dutch word here is "verantwoordiging"; this is more accurately rendered by *vindication* than by *apology*. The latter, however, has established itself as the received name of this hypothetical text.
8 Freudenthal, Walther, and Czelinski, *Die Lebensgeschichte Spinozas*, I, p. 399.
9 Van der Wall, "Til, Salomon van," p. 982.
10 Freudenthal, Walther, and Czelinski, *Die Lebensgeschichte Spinozas*, I, p. 424.
11 Blom and Kerkhoven, "A Letter Concerning an Early Draft," p. 373 (my translation; "to advise" renders *author sis* rather than *author fis*).
12 As Mignini assumes: "un petit ouvrage intitulé: *Tractatus theologico-politicus (Tractatus theologico-politicus)*" (Mignini, "Données et problèmes," p. 9; same interpretation on p. 13).
13 Not 1670, as Meijer (*Aanteekeningen*, p. v n. 1) has it.

difference between laws by institution and natural laws – does not really match Spinoza's seminal discussion of law in the beginning of Chapter 4 of the *TTP*. I think I can now identify the theologico-political treatise cited in Paets's letter with considerable probability as a Dutch pamphlet published anonymously in 1660, *Ondersoeck of de Christelijcke overheydt eenigh quaedt in haer gebiedt mach toe laten* [An examination of the question whether Christian authorities may allow any evil in their territories].[14] Its author is Lambertus van Velthuysen, a radical Cartesian, who imported Hobbes's philosophy into the Netherlands and quarreled with Spinoza in 1671 about the *TTP*.[15] He was a very close friend of Adriaan Paets and an acquaintance of Arnold Poelenburg. The booklet – notwithstanding its 324 densely printed pages, a pocket-sized book in duodecimo – deals with the balance of power between religious and secular authorities, and presents a plea for religious toleration. Van Velthuysen himself calls it "Tractaet" in the Preface.[16] Chapter 1, some forty pages, elaborates the notions of instituted and natural law. Although the evidence is not yet conclusive, the *Ondersoeck* fits Paets's description quite well. It is at any rate a much more likely candidate than a putative proto-*TTP*, ten years before that book was published in its fully fledged shape.

The striking agreement between Paets's designation of the booklet as a *tractatus theologico-politicus* and Spinoza's later work of that name is, of course, an important reason for assuming that there must be some connection. This is, however, because we now associate this title immediately with Spinoza. In the 1660s a description of that kind will have brought to mind the debates on the powers of secular and religious authorities, i.e., precisely the sort of work that Van Velthuysen had written. In 1662, the Reformed minister Simon Oomius (1630–1706), under the pseudonym Simon van Heenvliedt, published a Dutch pamphlet against allowing Roman Catholics freedom of worship in the Dutch Republic. Its title was *Theologico-Politica Dissertatio, ofte Discours over dese Vrage: Of den Pausgesinden in dese vereenighde Nederlanden, niet en behoorde toe-gestaen te worden, d'openbare exercitiën van hare Religie* [Theologico-Politica Dissertatio, or a discourse on this question: whether the Roman Catholics in these United Netherlands should not be allowed public exercise of their

[14] Published in Middelburg by "Ian Effendewegh" (a pseudonym: "John Pave-the-way").
[15] Spinoza's correspondence, *Ep.* 42 and 43. They became friends afterwards, but that did not stop Van Velthuysen from attacking Spinoza again in two *Tractatus* (one *de cultu naturali*, the other *de articulis fidei fundamentalibus*), in his 1680 *Opera omnia* (see Van Bunge, "Velthuysen, Lambert van," p. 1019).
[16] He published several works, both in Latin and in Dutch, with *Tractatus/Tractaet* in the title, among them two *Tractatus medico-physici*.

religion].[17] Though Oomius never explicitly mentions Van Velthuysen, he obviously has pamphlets like the latter's *Ondersoeck* in mind when he counters arguments in favor of religious toleration. When Spinoza starts writing his *TTP* in 1665, he addresses similar issues. It seems more likely that his title was inspired by this specific political and religious context, than that the *tractatus theologico-politicus* mentioned by Paets should refer to a primordial version of his book.

2 PRINTING HISTORY: THE LATIN TEXT

The printing history of the original Latin text of the *TTP* has been well explored.[18] It was printed five times in the seventeenth century. The successive editions were labeled T.1 to T.5 (where T stands for *Tractatus theologico-politicus*) by Fritz Bamberger. Four of these (T.1–2, T.4–5) were in quarto, T.3 was an octavo volume. The quarto editions are so similar in appearance that the differences between them went unnoticed until 1865, when Graesse first pointed out their typographical distinctions. After that, the Dutch scholar and Spinoza editor J. P. N. Land charted the four editions in their chronological order.[19] Bamberger drew up the following list: T.1 1669/1670, T.2 1672, T.3 1673/1674, T.4 and T.5 after 1677.[20] Rather than providing a full technical description of the differences between them, I here list some features that may be helpful in distinguising the editions. In T.1 page 104 is numbered as 304; in T.2 (and its variant T.2a) page 42 is numbered as 24 and page 207 as 213; T.3 is an octavo volume which was distributed with five different fictitious title pages; in T.4, page 130 is numbered as 830; in T.5, page 192 is numbered as 92. Moreover, in both T.4 and T.5, the name of the fictitious publisher is spelt Künrath, whereas in T.1 and T.2 it appears as Künraht.[21]

The *TTP* first came out, in quarto, late in 1669 or early in 1670. Although there is only one genuine first edition, the other quarto editions also pretend that they were printed in the year 1670 (with one notable exception, which I shall deal with shortly). The reason for this is that the work was highly

---

17 The full title is too long to be quoted in its entirety. The book was published by Jacob Waterman in Utrecht. It is very rare: only three copies seem to have survived. A facsimile reprint came out in 2004, published by a Reformed institution ("Landelijke Stichting ter bevordering van de Staatkundig Gereformeerde beginselen," no place).

18 Land ("Over vier drukken"); Gebhardt, *Spinoza Opera*, vol. 3, 363–368; particularly Bamberger ("Early Editions"); Kingma and Offenberg, *Bibliography of Spinoza's Works*; Gerritsen ("Printing Spinoza").

19 Land, "Over vier drukken."   20 Bamberger, "Early Editions," 27.

21 For the details, see Bamberger, "Early Editions"; a convenient table is supplied by Kingma and Offenberg, *Bibliography of Spinoza's Works*, p. 7.

controversial: although formally banned only in 1674, it was considered illegal from its publication and there were attempts to have it repressed from the very start.[22] So the Amsterdam publisher, Jan Rieuwertsz, had to be careful. He did not reveal his identity on the title page (which carries a fictitious imprint: Henricus Künrath in Hamburg), and when there was a demand for reprints, it was important to make the books look like copies left over from the original 1670 issue, rather than newly printed ones. This would be true especially after the formal ban in 1674. The 1672 reprint is intriguing, since it came out in two variants, the only difference being the year of publication as mentioned on the title page: some copies have 1672, others 1670. According to Gerritsen, the 1670 variant (T.2a) is the original one: T.2 resulted from "the roman date 1670 having been press-altered to 1672 by the addition of two *I*'s."[23] The operation, then, seems deliberately planned; but for what reason is unclear. Kingma and Offenberg suggest that all quarto reprints, including T.2 and T.2a, may have come out after Spinoza died, because of the increasing number of errors.[24] Spinoza, however, does not seem to have taken an active interest in correcting proofs. It is true that he had wanted to add some clarifications later (see below, section 4), but he never showed any concern for proofs or typographical errors.[25]

In 1673, another reprint came out, this time in an octavo format (T.3 in Bamberger's chronological list), together with the reprint of a work by Spinoza's friend Lodewijk Meyer, *Philosophia S. Scripturae interpres*. The year of publication is given correctly as 1673, but the octavo edition came in as many as five disguises, all trying to mask its true contents under fancy titles. One of these presented it as a book on surgery by Villacorte (T.3V), another one as a collection of historical works by Daniel Heinsius (T.3H), yet another one as a medical treatise by Franciscus de le Boë Sylvius (T.3S) – Lodewijk Meyer's former teacher in Leiden. After the stratagem was discovered, the same edition was sold with title pages which did reveal its contents. The first of these, dated 1673, imitated the title page of the quarto editions (T.3T); the second one, dated 1674, was typeset in such a fashion that it looked as though the book had been printed in England (T.3E).[26]

---

[22] Israel, *Radical Enlightenment*, pp. 275–285. On its being illegal, see Freudenthal, Walther, and Czelinski, *Die Lebensgeschichte Spinozas*, 1, pp. 293–294 (resolution of the Court of Holland, April 16, 1671).

[23] Gerritsen "Printing Spinoza," p. 260.

[24] Kingma and Offenberg, *Bibliography of Spinoza's Works*, pp. 6, 8.

[25] See his *Ep.* 12A and 15, on the publishing of the *Renati Des Cartes Principia Philosophiae*.

[26] For the full story, which is even more complicated, see Bamberger, "Early Editions" and Kingma and Offenberg, *Bibliography of Spinoza's Works*.

Again, as in the case of the 1672 reprint, there is no indication whatsoever that Spinoza himself was in any way involved in bringing out the octavo edition. Rieuwertsz's policy will have been dictated by both commercial and political considerations: the *TTP* was controversial and therefore in demand, but the publisher had to operate very carefully so as not to provoke legal action. These circumstances were not conducive to quiet consultations between author and publisher about improvements for reprints. As Akkerman has shown, even the first printing of the *TTP* in 1670 was a hurried job, at any rate much more so than in the case of Spinoza's other works.[27] The printer of the *TTP* worked from a manuscript (possibly the author's autograph), which was hardly edited before it was typeset. The text shows irregularities and inconsistencies that may reflect Spinoza's own writing, as documented in the few autograph letters that have been preserved. Since the successive editions contain an increasing number of mistakes, we may safely assume that Spinoza did not intervene in preparing them for the press.

It may be useful to point out that so far the names of the printers who produced the early editions of the *TTP* remain unknown. The publisher of all Spinoza's works was Jan Rieuwertsz; "But alas, there is no good evidence that Jan Rieuwertsz at any time owned a press, and plenty that he commissioned others to do his printing for him."[28] In spite of the thorough research by Gerritsen, the identities of the printers have remained secret since the perilous times in which they multiplied Spinoza's high-risk treatise.

3 THE EARLY TRANSLATIONS

Already in the 1670s, the work was translated into Dutch, French, and English.[29] Spinoza wrote all of his works in Latin, but his Dutch friends were active in getting them translated, first and foremost for their own use, but also with an eye to publication. In the case of the *Short Treatise*, the Latin original is lost, and all we have is the contemporary Dutch translation. Spinoza's *Renati Des Cartes Principia philosophiae & Cogitata metaphysica* came out in Latin in 1663; a Dutch version was subsequently published in 1664. The *Opera Posthuma*, which contained the *Ethica*, was published simultaneously with its Dutch translation, *De nagelate schriften*, in 1677.

---

[27] Akkerman, ed., *Tractatus theologico-politicus*, pp. 21–22. For a detailed treatment of the particularities of the 1670 edition, see Akkerman, "Tractatus theologico-politicus," pp. 209–22.

[28] Gerritsen, "Printing Spinoza," p. 253.

[29] Not until 1787 did the first German version come out, translated by Schack Hermann Ewald, as the first volume of *Spinoza's philosophische Schriften.* It will not figure in this account.

Spinoza's correspondence contains several remarks on the practice of his friends to have his works translated. An important letter in this respect is that of June 1665, in which Spinoza asks Johannes Bouwmeester if he is willing to translate new installments of the *Ethica*. Eventually, it is not Bouwmeester, but the professional translator Jan Hendriksz Glazemaker who will supply all the Dutch texts for the *Nagelate schriften*.[30] How about the *TTP*? Spinoza himself took action in 1671 to prevent the publication of a Dutch version. In *Ep*. 44, he implores his friend Jarig Jelles to get the printing stopped. He feared a publication in the vernacular would arouse such a commotion that the *TTP* would be banned, both in Latin and in Dutch. It was not until 1693 that the translation, again produced by Glazemaker, was finally published, with the somewhat ironic title *De rechtzinnige theologant, of Godgeleerd staatkundige verhandelinge* [The orthodox theologian, or Theologico-political treatise]. Glazemaker apparently translated from a Latin manuscript, rather than from the printed 1677 text.[31] A year later, another Dutch rendering came out, called *Een rechtsinnige theologant, of Godgeleerde staatkunde*. Though it purports to be a reprint of the Glazemaker translation, it is in fact an entirely different translation. Who made it, and why it was published in this fashion, remains a mystery.[32] There is a third Dutch version of the *TTP*, which was never published, but it did survive in manuscript. It is bound with the oldest manuscript of the *Korte verhandeling* ("Short Treatise"). Akkerman has shown that this must be an edited copy of Glazemaker's translation, and that it once was in the hands of a typesetter: from pages 166 to 379, there are compositor's notes in the text and margins, and ink smudges. This must be the manuscript that was going to be printed in 1671, had Spinoza not intervened. When Jelles notified the publisher, the work was interrupted. This explains why only part of the manuscript shows traces of the typesetter's preparatory work.[33]

Spinoza's apparent ignorance of the plans to publish the *TTP* in Dutch, as expressed in *Ep*. 44, may seem puzzling. This is what he wrote to Jelles:

When Professor N.N. recently paid me a visit, he told me, among other things, that he had heard that my *Tractatus Theologico-Politicus* had been translated into Dutch, and that somebody, he did not know who, proposed to get it printed.[34]

---

[30] See Akkerman, "Studies," Chapter 5, especially pp. 101–153. Akkerman argues that it was probably Pieter Balling who translated the *Principia* and Parts I and II of the *Ethica*, and Glazemaker who translated the rest of the *Ethica*, as well as all the other texts contained in the *Nagelate Schriften*.

[31] Akkerman, "Tractatus theologico-politicus," p. 225.

[32] Akkerman, "Tractatus theologico-politicus," pp. 235–236.

[33] Akkerman, "Tractatus theologico-politicus," pp. 227–235. The editing of Glazemaker's translation may have been the work of Johannes Bouwmeester (pp. 233–234).

[34] Trans. Shirley. The anonymous professor may have been the Cartesian Theodor Kranen or Craanen, but according to Israel (*Radical Enlightenment*, p. 278), De Volder is a more likely candidate.

But in fact Spinoza only reports the anonymous professor's ignorance, without letting out what he himself knows about it. This letter has come down to us only in its printed form in *De nagelate schriften* and the *Opera Posthuma*. Originally it may well have contained more specific information, but it was the strategy of the editors of Spinoza's posthumous works to remove as much of this as they could from the printed text; leaving out the name of the professor is part of that strategy. What the letter in its transmitted reading comes down to is this: Spinoza warns Jelles that there is a rumor about a Dutch translation, and asks him to take action, because of the risks involved. This need not imply that Spinoza was unaware of the project until the professor told him about it. That would indeed have been most untypical, in view of the active interest he had shown in getting his other texts translated into Dutch.

Another early translation, and one that was soon published, is that into French. It is usually attributed to the French freethinker Gabriel de Saint-Glain or Saint-Glen (*c*.1620–1684), and it was published in 1678. It came out in two separate editions and at least eight variant issues, and under three different titles: *La Clef du santuaire* (or *sanctuaire*), *Reflexions curieuses d'un esprit des-interressé sur les matières les plus importantes au salut, tant public que particulier*, and *Traitté des ceremonies superstitieuses des juifs tant anciens que modernes.*[35] This was part of a deliberate publishing strategy:

The French translation of the *Tractatus theologico-politicus* in duodecimo published in 1678, in its different issues with the ctitious author's names, titles and addresses, seems to have been produced especially for a particular group of collectors: people whose main interest was not Spinoza's heritage but rather curious, dangerous or forbidden books.[36]

For the history of the text of the *TTP* itself, the Saint-Glain translation is of little interest, but it is important for the "Annotations to the *Tractatus Theologico-Politicus*," which were published here for the first time (see section 4, below).

The third early translation of the *TTP* was an English one. After the publication of the chapter on miracles in 1683, under the title *Miracles No Violations of the Laws of Nature*, commonly attributed to the English Deist Charles Blount,[37] a translation of the entire book came out in 1689: *A Treatise partly theological, and partly political*. According to the title page it was published in London; the publisher's name is withheld.[38] The translator

[35] Kingma and Offenberg, *Bibliography of Spinoza's Works*, pp. 16–21.
[36] Kingma "Spinoza Editions," p. 274.
[37] Popkin, "Deist Challenge," p. 206; Boucher, *Spinoza in English*, p. 7 (no. 33).
[38] Kingma and Offenberg *Bibliography of Spinoza's Works*, p. 22. A reprint appeared in 1737 (English Short Title Catalog, ESTC T175909). The book contains a preface ("The translator to the reader"),

is unknown, but Popkin suggested that it may have been Blount, too.[39] This is hardly more than an informed guess. The translation appears not to have attracted any sustained scholarly attention so far.

4 THE "ANNOTATIONS TO THE *TRACTATUS THEOLOGICO-POLITICUS*"

In two letters, written in the autumn of 1675, Spinoza brings up his plan to supply a number of explanatory notes to the *TTP*.[40] In the summer of 1676, half a year before his death, he donated a copy of the first edition (T.1) to Jacobus Statius Klefmann, with the following dedication on the title page: "The author donated [this book] to Mr. Jacobus Statius Klefmann, and adorned it with some notes and wrote these in his own hand, on 25 July 1676" [*Nobilissimo D° D°. Jacobo statio Klefmanno Dono D. Autor, et non-nullis notis illustravit illasque propria manu scripsit Die 25. Julii Anno 1676*]. In the margins of the text, Spinoza entered five annotations. In the early nineteenth century the Klefmann copy surfaced in Königsberg. In 1945 it was salvaged from the rubble in the streets of that city. It was donated in 1951 to Haifa University Library, where it is still kept.[41] The five annotations entered by Spinoza in his own hand constitute the authentic core of the so-called *Adnotationes ad Tractatum theologico-politicum*. Spinoza had entered these annotations originally in his own copy of the *TTP*,[42] and more annotated copies may have circulated, but the Königsberg copy is the only one that survived. Already in 1678, however, as many as thirty-one annotations were published in a French translation as an appendix to Saint-Glain's version of the *TTP*. In the course of time, several more collections of annotations came to light, in Latin, Dutch, and French. All of them contain the five seminal ones that Spinoza had entered in Klefmann's copy (*Adnotationes* 2, 6, 7, 13, and 14),[43] but the total number eventually rose to thirty-nine annotations. The transmission of these *Adnotationes* has been

---

but this does not reveal any information about the translator's identity. Selections from (apparently) the same translation were published in 1720, under the title *An account of the life and writings of Spinosa: To which is added, an abstract of his Theological political treatise* (London: printed for W. Boreham).

[39] Popkin, "Deist Challenge," p. 207; Israel, *Radical Enlightenment*, pp. 604–605.

[40] *Ep.* 68 to Oldenburg, September/October 1675; *Ep.* 69 to Van Velthuysen, Autumn 1675.

[41] For the dramatic vicissitudes of the "Königsberg copy" see Van der Werf, "Klefmanns exemplaar" (in English: Van der Werf, "Klefmann's Copy").

[42] The author's own copy was still extant in 1704, when Jan Rieuwertsz the Younger, the son of Spinoza's publisher, showed it to Hallmann (Freudenthal, Walther, and Czelinski, *Die Lebens-geschichte Spinozas*, 1, p. 89). It may still have been in the possession of the heirs of Rieuwertsz in 1757 (see Akkerman, "Tractatus theologico-politicus," p. 222).

[43] The numbering that is now generally used was first introduced by Boehmer in 1852 (see Akkerman, "Tractatus theologico-politicus," p. 214; Steenbakkers, "Les éditions de Spinoza," pp. 29–30).

thoroughly studied by Fokke Akkerman.[44] His findings are that all extant collections ultimately depend on Spinoza's lost copy, into which somebody else must have entered a number of additional notes, viz. Annotations 18, 33, 35, and 39. Several of the notes[45] are probably not authentic Spinoza texts at all: they rather look like reader's comments that were added subsequently.

Until the nineteenth century, the only Latin editions[46] of the *TTP* that were available were those printed in the seventeenth century.[47] As a result of the great German debates on Spinoza at the end of the eighteenth century, the so-called *Pantheismus-Streit*, there was a new demand for the philosopher's texts. The first complete edition of Spinoza's works (1802–1803), *Benedicti de Spinoza Opera Quae Supersunt Omnia* by H. E. G. Paulus, was in fact an uncritical reprint. Paulus, who did have the competence to make a scholarly edition, apparently only saw it as his task to make the texts available again in print; there is no critical apparatus, no justification of his editorial choices, no discussion of any textual problems. The great merit of his edition is that it made Spinoza's texts available to German philosophy at a crucial moment in its development: this is the edition read by Fichte, Schelling, Hegel, and Schopenhauer; and it formed the basis of many comments and translations. In 1830, A. F. Gfrörer published *Benedicti de Spinoza Opera Philosophica Omnia*. This is basically a corrected reprint of Paulus's edition and it suffers from the same weaknesses as its precursor. It seems that Gfrörer's edition only had a limited circulation. It was hardly noticed outside Germany. The most important edition in Germany in the nineteenth century, with a very wide circulation, was that of Karl Hermann Bruder: *Benedicti de Spinoza Opera Quae Supersunt Omnia* (three volumes, 1843–1846). It went through several reprints, even in the twentieth century, though all are dated 1843–1846. Bruder did go back to the original seventeenth-century texts but still

---

44 Akkerman, "Tractatus theologico-politicus," pp. 213–223. Cf. also Akkerman, ed., *Tractatus theologico-politicus*, pp. 28–37.

45 Viz. the numbers 15, 18, 20, 27–30, 33, 35, and 39.

46 In another article (Steenbakkers, "The Textual History of Spinoza's Ethics"), I deal with the textual history of Spinoza's *Ethica*. To the extent that the later editions of the works include both the *Tractatus theologico-politicus* and the *Ethica*, I reproduce the relevant passages from that article. For details on the German editions of the nineteenth century I refer to my study, "Les éditions de Spinoza."

47 There is one exception: a reprint of selections from Chapters 8 and 9 that came out in London in 1763. As far as I know, it is not mentioned in any of the Spinoza bibliographies. I found it in the Eighteenth Century Collections Online (Gale Group), English Short Title Catalogue Number ESTC T147491. Its title is *Tractatus de primis duodecim veteris testamenti libris*. The edition mentions neither the author's, nor the publisher's name.

reproduces some of Paulus's errors. Many commentators and translators worked from this *Opera* edition. An interesting feature of Bruder's edition is that he divided some texts into manageable, numbered sections. In referring to passages of the *Tractatus de intellectus emendatione*, Bruder's section numbers have since established themselves as the standard, but regrettably his numbering of the *TTP* did not catch on. In 1877 Hugo Ginsberg edited the Latin text as *Der theologisch-politische Tractat Spinoza's*, as the third volume of the collected works. Though this is, on the whole, an undistinguished edition, which relies heavily on Bruder, Ginsberg's treatment of the *TTP* does appear to be the result of independent editorial work.

With the publication of *Benedicti de Spinoza Opera Quotquot Reperta Sunt*, edited by J. van Vloten and J. P. N. Land in 1882–1883, Spinoza scholarship entered a new phase. Land was the first scholar to do serious philological research on Spinoza. Apart from his editorial work, he published several articles on textual issues.[48] They were the first editors to provide the texts with an (admittedly slender) apparatus and they took the original editions for their starting point. In the first printing, the presentation of the texts has been carefully executed. Unfortunately, the subsequent printings ([2]1895, [3]1914) are increasingly inferior, each adding new misprints to the ones copied from the preceding.

It is only with the monumental critical edition of Carl Gebhardt (1924, reprinted 1972) that Spinoza's texts are carefully presented again. Gebhardt was the first to base his edition rigorously on the genuine first edition. This is important, since the successive editions of the seventeenth century contain an increasing number of misprints: thus, several readings in Bruder's edition of the *TTP* reflect errors in the text that he used as his exemplar, a copy of the fifth printing (T.5). Yet Gebhardt's edition is also marred by the mistaken assumption that Spinoza kept rewriting his works incessantly. This is most notably the case in Gebhardt's treatment of the *Adnotationes*.

A new critical edition by Fokke Akkerman, accompanied for the first time by a full critical apparatus, a judicious account of the editorial choices and an examination of all the evidence now available, was published in 1999. Much of what I have offered in this chapter is based on Akkerman's thorough research. It is to be hoped that Spinoza scholars will avail themselves of the opportunity, and that Akkerman's authoritative text will henceforth be the starting-point of all new translations and commentaries. In this edition, the text is divided into numbered sections, to facilitate reference. As the Bruder numbering was never generally adopted, it would be useful if Akkerman's division of the text were to become the common standard.

---

[48] For the *Tractatus theologico-politicus*, see Land, "Over vier drukken."

CHAPTER 3

Spinoza on Ibn Ezra's "secret of the twelve"

Warren Zev Harvey

The renowned Spanish Bible commentator and philosopher, Rabbi Abraham ibn Ezra (1089–1164), is without doubt the medieval author who, with the exception of Maimonides, had the greatest influence on the *Theological-Political Treatise*.[1] Like Spinoza, he was a rare combination of metaphysician and grammarian – a man engaged by both the big questions about God and Nature and the small ones about conjugations and declensions. His influence may be detected in many places throughout the *TTP*. He is cited expressly by name in six different contexts.

In Chapter 1, Annotation 1, Spinoza endorses Rashi's interpretation of the word *nabi`* (prophet) as meaning originally "translator," and adds that Ibn Ezra criticized this interpretation but "did not know the Hebrew language so exactly."[2]

In Chapter 2, Spinoza writes that according to the Hebrews the "God of gods" ruled the land of Israel but allotted other lands to other gods. He cites Jacob's words to his family before they entered the land, "put away the foreign gods" (Gen. 35:2), and refers the reader to Ibn Ezra's comments on the verse. The reference, however, is mistaken, for Ibn Ezra rejects the interpretation advanced by Spinoza.[3]

---

[1] Cf. Strauss, *Persecution*, p. 181: "the only man to whom [Spinoza] almost explicitly refers in the *Treatise* as a predecessor regarding his technique of presentation is Abraham ibn Ezra, of whom he speaks with unconcealed respect."

[2] *TTP* Ch. 1, Annotation 1; *G* III 251. My quotations from the *TTP* will be based on Elwes, Shirley, Yaffe, and Silverthorne and Israel. Regarding the curious reference to Ibn Ezra's Hebrew, see my "Spinoza's Metaphysical Hebraism," 108–109.

[3] *TTP* Ch. 2; *G* III 39. See Ibn Ezra, *Perushe ha-Torah*, Gen. 35:2, p. 103, and Deut. 31:16, pp. 303–304. "Heaven forfend," he exclaims, "the prophet would sleep with women who worship foreign gods!" Rather, he writes, "God is One" but divine worship differs from place to place in accordance with the peculiar qualities of each place. Cf. on Exod. 20:3, p. 134: when Scripture mentions "other gods," it does not refer to real entities.

In Chapters 7 and 10, Spinoza cites approvingly Ibn Ezra's view that the Book of Job was translated into Hebrew from another language, but complains he did not prove it sufficiently.[4]

In Chapter 9, Annotation 14, Spinoza mentions an opinion, based on the Commentary of Ibn Ezra, that Jacob took eight to ten years to journey from Paddan-aram to Bethel (Gen. 31:17–35:6), and remarks that it "reeks of foolishness... *pace* Ibn Ezra."[5]

In Chapter 10, Spinoza cites Ibn Ezra as having observed correctly that the book containing the edicts of Queen Esther (Esther 9:29–32) is lost.[6]

However, by far the most significant mention of Ibn Ezra in the *TTP* occurs in Chapter 8 and concerns the "secret of the twelve."

I SPINOZA'S EXPOSITION

Chapter 8 of the *TTP* discusses the authorship of the Hebrew Bible, and begins with the Pentateuch. Spinoza argues that the Pentateuch was not written by Moses, as generally held in Jewish tradition, but by a historian who lived many years after him, and who he conjectures is Ezra the Scribe.[7] He then cites Rabbi Abraham ibn Ezra, whom he praises as "a man of very liberal disposition and no mean erudition" [*liberioris ingenii vir et non mediocris eruditionis*]. Ibn Ezra, he tells us, is the earliest writer he has read who held similarly critical views on the authorship of the Pentateuch. However, Spinoza continues, Ibn Ezra's ideas were so subversive to Jewish tradition that he dared not state them plainly but expressed them in a series of enigmatic hints. Spinoza then proclaims that he shall not fear to reveal Ibn Ezra's esoteric teaching about the authorship of the Pentateuch. This teaching involves a riddle known as the "secret of the twelve" (in Ibn Ezra's Hebrew: *sod ha-shenem-`asar*; in Spinoza's Latin: *mysterium duodecim*)."[8]

Spinoza begins his exposition of Ibn Ezra's esoteric doctrine by examining his comment on Deuteronomy 1:2. He quotes the comment *verbatim* in Hebrew and in his own Latin translation. According to him, the comment

---

[4] *TTP* Ch. 7; *G* III 110–111; *TTP* Ch. 10; *G* III 144. See Ibn Ezra on Job 2:11: "it is difficult to interpret, like every translated book."

[5] *TTP* Ch. 9, Annotation 14; *G* III 255. See Ibn Ezra on Gen. 33:20, p. 101, where it is suggested that Jacob dwelled "many years" in Shechem, and thus Dinah was not seven years old when raped, but presumably in her late teens.

[6] *TTP* Ch. 10; *G* III 145–146.   [7] *TTP* Ch. 8; *G* III 117–124, 126–128.

[8] *TTP* Ch. 8; *G* III 118. Cf. Jospe, "Biblical Exegesis as a Philosophic Literary Genre," pp. 118–128, 145–150; Lemler, "Abraham ibn Ezra et Moïse Maïmonide cités par Spinoza," esp. pp. 447–462.

teaches that "it was not Moses who wrote the Pentateuch but someone else who lived long after him, and that the book Moses wrote was a different one."[9] Ibn Ezra's comment reads as follows:

[1] "[These are the words which Moses spoke unto all Israel] beyond the Jordan" [Deut. 1:1]. If you understand [2] the secret of the twelve, and also [3] "And Moses wrote [the Law]" [Deut. 31:9], [4] "and the Canaanite was then in the land" [Gen. 12:6], [5] "on the mount of the Lord it shall be revealed" [Gen. 22:14], and [6] "behold, his bed was a bed of iron" [Deut. 3:11], then you will know the truth.[10]

Spinoza divides Ibn Ezra's comment into six units (which I have indicated by bracketed numerals), and discusses them in order. He explains Ibn Ezra's hints as follows:

(1) "The preface of Deuteronomy could not have been composed by Moses, who did not cross the Jordan." By "preface of Deuteronomy," Spinoza means its opening five verses, which refer to Moses in the third person (as opposed to Deut. 1:6–30:20, in which Moses speaks in the first person). The author of Deuteronomy 1:1–5 describes Moses as having been "beyond the Jordan." If Moses had been on the east bank, the author was on the west, and must have written these verses after the Israelites had crossed the river, i.e., after Moses' death.[11]

(2) The "secret of the twelve" refers to the fact that the entire Law of Moses was written "very distinctly" on the face of a single altar (Deut. 27:8; cf. Josh. 8:30–32), said by the Rabbis to consist of only twelve stones (BT *Sotah* 32a; cf. Josh. 4:9); and thus it may be gathered that the Law of Moses was much shorter than today's Pentateuch. This, states Spinoza, is in his opinion the meaning of Ibn Ezra's "secret of the twelve." However, he adds, there are other possibilities. The "secret of the twelve" may refer to the twelve curses recited by the Levites against those who do not observe the Law of Moses (Deut. 27:15–26), which curses are part of today's Pentateuch but do not seem to have been part of the original Law (which is presumed to be in existence in Deut. 27:8, before Moses instructs the Levites regarding the curses in Deut. 27:12–13; and cf. 27:26). Alternatively, the "secret of the

---

9 *TTP* Ch. 8; *G* III 118.

10 *TTP* Ch. 8; *G* III 118. See Ibn Ezra, Commentary on Deut. 1:2, pp. 214–215. Spinoza's Latin renderings are accurate, with three exceptions. (1) He translates "And Moses wrote the Law" (Deut. 31:9), where Ibn Ezra's Hebrew reads "And Moses wrote" (which could equally allude to Deut. 31:22). (2) He translates "mount of God," but the verse has "mount of the Lord." (3) He translates "it shall be revealed," but Ibn Ezra, judging from his comments elsewhere, understood the underlying Hebrew as meaning "one shall be seen (by God)" (see his Commentaries on Exod. 23:15, p. 160, and Deut. 16:16, p. 264; and cf. on Psalms 84:8).

11 *TTP* Ch. 8; *G* III 119.

twelve" might refer to the last twelve verses of the Book of Deuteronomy (34:1–12), which tell of the death of Moses, and thus would seem to have been written by someone who survived him.[12] Having given three possible explanations of the secret, Spinoza adds in evident exasperation: "But these, and what others have ariolated besides, there is no need to examine more carefully here."[13]

(3) The words "And Moses wrote the Law" (Deut. 31:9), written in the third person, "cannot be the words of Moses" but are those of "another writer who is narrating the acts and writings of Moses."[14]

(4) The words "and the Canaanite was *then* in the land" (Gen. 12:6) were evidently written at a time when the Canaanites were no longer in it, i.e., after the Israelite conquest of Canaan, long after Moses' death. Here Spinoza cites Ibn Ezra's reasoning in his commentary on Genesis 12:6: either Canaan, the grandson of Noah (Gen. 10:6), captured the land of Canaan from someone else (which Spinoza remarks is not supported by Genesis 10) and the word "then" has the force of "already," or there is here a "secret" (*sod*) and "one who understands it should be silent." The "secret" is that the words "and the Canaanite was then in the land" were not written by Moses.[15]

(5) The reference to Mount Moriah as "the mount of the Lord" (Gen. 22:14) had to have been written after the mountain had been chosen for the building of the Temple. This was not done in Moses' time, for Moses does not mention a particular place chosen for divine worship, but speaks of "the place which the Lord your God shall choose" (Deut. 12:5, 11, 14, 18, 21, 26, etc.).[16]

(6) The words concerning Og, king of the Bashan, namely, "behold, his bed was a bed of iron, is it not in Rabbah of the children of Ammon? – nine cubits was the length thereof and four cubits the breadth," etc. (Deut. 3:11), were written by someone who lived long after Moses. Spinoza adds that the *modus loquendi* is that of someone who refers to ancient times and points to a surviving relic in order to establish credibility. He infers that these words about King Og's bed were written during the days of King David, after the conquest of Rabbah (II Sam. 12:29–30).[17]

Thus, according to Spinoza, Ibn Ezra taught that the Pentateuch was not written by Moses, and that the historical "Law of Moses," which could be written on twelve stones, was much smaller than the Pentateuch.

---

[12] *TTP* Ch. 8; *G* III 119. [13] *TTP* Ch. 8; *G* III 119. [14] *TTP* Ch. 8; *G* III 119.
[15] *TTP* Ch. 8; *G* III 119. [16] *TTP* Ch. 8; *G* III 120. [17] *TTP* Ch. 8; *G* III 120.

2 REVIEW OF SPINOZA'S EXPOSITION

Did Spinoza understand Ibn Ezra's *mysterium* properly? Let us now examine his exposition of Ibn Ezra's comments, and try to determine to what extent it accurately renders their intent.

(1) Spinoza's opinion that Ibn Ezra's comment on Deuteronomy 1:1 indicates that "the preface to Deuteronomy" was written after the Israelites had crossed the Jordan seems correct. It should be mentioned that Ibn Ezra adumbrates his comment on Deuteronomy 1:1 in his Commentary on Genesis 22:14: "on the mount of the Lord it shall be revealed." He writes there: "the explanation of 'on the mount of the Lord it shall be revealed' will be given at [pericope] 'These are the words' [Deut. 1:1ff.]."[18]

(2) Spinoza's theory that the "secret of the twelve" refers to the Law's having been written on twelve stones (Deut. 27:8) is impossible. In the first place, and decisively, the problem of the lengthiness of the Law and the smallness of the altar is solved by Ibn Ezra in a different way. In his Commentary on Deut. 27:1, he endorses the view, advanced by Saadia Gaon, that the entire Law was not written on the stones of the altar but only a list of the commandments was written on them.[19] Secondly, all the other examples cited by Ibn Ezra refer to anachronisms that reveal the post-Mosaic date of the biblical author, but the problem presented by Deut. 27:8 is of a different sort. Thirdly, the number "twelve" is connected with Deut. 27:8 only by virtue of rabbinic exegesis; but Ibn Ezra, no less than Spinoza, was concerned about clarifying the simple meaning of the biblical text, not its Rabbinic interpretations.

Spinoza's second theory, that the "secret of the twelve" refers to the twelve curses (Deut. 27:15–26), is extremely unlikely. Ibn Ezra nowhere hints there is a problem concerning the curses and, moreover, the number twelve is not mentioned explicitly with regard to them.[20]

Spinoza's third theory is almost certainly correct: the "secret of the twelve" refers to the last twelve verses of the Pentateuch, apparently written

---

[18] Commentary on Gen. 22:14, p. 72. On "beyond the Jordan," cf. Rashbam, *Perush ha-Torah*, on Num. 22:1, p. 189, and Deut. 1:1, p. 198, who may have been influenced by Ibn Ezra. Another possible influence of Ibn Ezra on Rashbam is found at Exod. 3:15; cf. my "Judah Halevi's Interpretation," p. 130 (note also the reference to Spinoza there).

[19] Commentary on Deut. 27:1, p. 271. This solution of Ibn Ezra (in the name of Saadia) is cited and rejected by Moses Nahmanides, who writes: "Perhaps the stones were very big, or this was a miraculous act" (Commentary on Deut. 27:3).

[20] Nonetheless, Professor Uriel Simon has written me that there is in this second theory "something surprising and piquant"; for the twelve instances of the Hebrew *arur* (cursed) are indeed striking (Deut. 27:15–26), and the reference to "the Law" in the climactic twelfth curse is conspicuously problematic.

after the death of Moses. In his commentary on Deuteronomy 34:1–12, Ibn Ezra makes two separate significant comments about the post-Mosaic date of the narrator, the first on verse 1 and the second on verse 6:

"And Moses went up from the plains of Moab unto mount Nebo" [v. 1]. According to my opinion, from this verse on Joshua wrote [the Law of Moses]. For after Moses went up, he did not come down. He [Joshua] wrote it by way of prophecy. The proof [that he wrote it by way of prophecy] is "And the Lord showed him [all the land]" [v. 1], "And the Lord said unto him" [v. 4], and also "And he buried [him(self) in the valley]" [v. 6].[21]

"[And no man knoweth of his sepulcher] unto this day" [v. 6]. These are the words of Joshua. It is possible that he wrote this in his last days.[22]

Ibn Ezra asserts clearly that the last twelve verses of the Pentateuch (Deut. 34:1–12) could not have been written by Moses; for after having ascended the mountain, Moses disappeared. Joshua wrote the last lines of the Law of Moses "by way of prophecy." Only by way of prophecy could he have known that God showed Moses all the land of Israel, that God spoke to him about the promise to the Patriarchs, or that Moses buried himself.[23] It was important for Ibn Ezra to establish that Joshua wrote his verses "by way of prophecy," for otherwise the divine authority of those verses would be dubious.

The view that the last eight verses of the Law of Moses were written by Joshua is found already in classical rabbinic literature (*Sifre*, Deuteronomy, 357; BT *Baba Batra* 15a; BT *Makkot* 11a; BT *Menaḥot* 30a): it was debated there whether those verses relating Moses' death were written subsequently by Joshua or beforehand by Moses "with a tear." However, the view that the last twelve verses were written by Joshua seems to have been first suggested by Ibn Ezra.[24]

Ibn Ezra's remark that Joshua may have written the last twelve verses "in his last days" is significant. In shows that in his opinion many years separated Moses' death and the writing of the conclusion of the Pentateuch. The elapse of considerable time seems presumed by the phrase "unto this day."

---

[21] Commentary on Deut. 34:1, p. 328.   [22] Commentary on Deut. 34:6, p. 329.

[23] The subject of "buried" (Deut. 34:6) is unclear. According to some commentators, including Ibn Ezra, Moses buried himself; according to others, God buried him.

[24] The view is expounded also by the relatively obscure Greek scholar, Rabbi Meyuhas ben Elijah, in his Commentary on Deuteronomy: "'And Moses went up' [34:1]. There are those among our Rabbis who say that Joshua wrote the [final] eight verses from 'And Moses died there' [34:5]. However, I say: even from 'And Moses went up.' For once Moses went up, he did not come down again," etc. (*Perush le-Sefer Debarim*, pp. 200–201). Meyuhas, whose dates are unknown, is usually thought to have been influenced by Ibn Ezra; but the converse is not impossible.

(3) Spinoza's assertion that the words "And Moses wrote the Law" (Deut. 31:9) are those of "another writer who is narrating the acts and writings of Moses" is a convincing explanation of Ibn Ezra's intent. The suspicion that the words were not written by Moses is reinforced by the subsequent statements that Moses wrote down the entire Law "until its completion" and commanded the Levites to place it by the side of the ark of the covenant that it be "for a witness" after his death (Deut. 31:24–27). It would seem that all these verses, which tell about Moses writing the complete and final Law, could not themselves have been part of that Law.

(4) Spinoza's explanation of Ibn Ezra's allusion to the text "and the Canaanite was *then* in the land" (Gen. 12:6) is doubtless correct. It is based, after all, on Ibn Ezra's own words in his Commentary on Genesis.

(5) Similarly, Spinoza's explanation of Ibn Ezra's allusion to the text "as it is said today, 'on the mount of the Lord it shall be revealed'" (Gen. 22:14) seems clearly right. He convincingly contrasts the uniqueness of the future divine service at the Temple Mount in Jerusalem with Moses' recurring non-specific references to "the place which the Lord your God shall choose." The anachronism observed by Ibn Ezra is made acute by the biblical narrator's etiological use of the word "today": the saying about the Temple is familiar *today*, i.e., in the time of the narrator, when the Temple of Solomon has been built, but not in that of Abraham or in that of Moses.

(6) Finally, Spinoza's interpretation of Ibn Ezra's reference to King Og's bed (Deut. 3:11) is likewise compelling. The anachronism here is again clear: in the days of the narrator, who lived after King David defeated the Ammonites, the Israelites knew about King Og's bed in Rabbah, but they did not know about it in Moses' days.

Spinoza's interpretation of Ibn Ezra's esoteric teaching is thus mostly accurate. He does, however, exaggerate when he claims that Ibn Ezra denied the authorship of the Pentateuch to Moses. With one exception, Ibn Ezra's examples, as Spinoza himself interprets them, do not prove that Moses did not write the Pentateuch, but only that there are some passages in it not written by him. The one exception is Spinoza's erroneous interpretation of the "secret of the twelve" as referring to the "twelve stones." If Spinoza presumed the correctness of this interpretation (which was, after all, his preferred interpretation of the "secret of the twelve"), then his exaggerated assertion that Ibn Ezra denied the authorship of the Pentateuch to Moses may not be dismissed as having been made in bad faith. As for Ibn Ezra's true view, it might be argued plausibly that he had in mind only minor interpolations. Thus, with regard to Deuteronomy 1:1, he seems to have intended that only five verses were written after Moses' death. As for Deuteronomy 34:1–12, only twelve verses are involved. The allusion to Deuteronomy 31:9 may include most of the chapter. However, with regard to Genesis 12:6, 22:14, and Deuteronomy 3:11, it is possible that Ibn Ezra intended that only the short anachronistic phrases in question were inserted after Moses' death.[25]

3 INFLUENCES

Spinoza's interpretation of Ibn Ezra's cryptic comments on Deuteronomy 1:2 was not created *ex nihilo*. There was a remarkably rich supercommentary literature in Hebrew on Ibn Ezra's Bible commentaries. Scores of medieval supercommentaries were written. Many have survived – most only in manuscript, but some have been printed.[26] In addition, in his explication of Ibn Ezra's comments, Spinoza certainly found some help in the writings of Jews and Christians on the general topic of the authorship of the Pentateuch. In what follows, I shall briefly examine the discussions of Ibn Ezra's comments by two of his major medieval supercommentators, and then I shall say some words about Hobbes's discussion of the authorship of the Pentateuch and its relevance to Ibn Ezra's riddle.

4 SPINOZA AND RABBI JOSEPH BEN ELIEZER

One of the most important of the Ibn Ezra supercommentaries is Rabbi Joseph ben Eliezer of Saragossa's *Safenat Pa`neah* (cf. Gen. 41:45), written in Jerusalem in about 1385.[27] His work has been lauded by Ibn Ezra scholars. According to Michael Friedlander, it "may be considered as generally containing a correct interpretation of Ibn Ezra's opinions."[28] According

---

[25] Scholars have long criticized Spinoza for this exaggeration. See, e.g., Luzzatto, *Perush `al ha-Torah*, on Deut. 1:1: "Spinoza wrote a downright lie . . . The truth is that Rabbi Abraham ibn Ezra hinted secretly . . . that there are in the Pentateuch some texts added after Moses' death, but there is nothing in all his words or in all his hints that might lead one to think that he did not believe Moses wrote his book." Cf. Pick, "Spinoza and the Old Testament," p. 117: "it cannot be said that Ibn Ezra denies the Mosaic authorship of the Pentateuch, though it must be admitted that he believed in interpolations" (and see p. 118 n. 1). Cf. also Malcolm, *Aspects of Hobbes*, p. 404 n. 68. Interested in finding a precursor for his views, Spinoza did have a motive for intentionally exaggerating Ibn Ezra's opinion, but his erroneous first interpretation of the "secret of the twelve" provides a good defense against this charge. Evidence for the minimalist interpretation of Ibn Ezra is found in his Commentary on Gen. 36:31, p. 105; see Shapiro, *The Limits of Orthodox Theology*, pp. 109–110.

[26] See Friedlander, *Essays*, pp. 212–252; and Simon, "Interpreting the Interpreter." See also Shapiro, *The Limits of Orthodox Theology*, pp. 106–110; and Heschel, *Heavenly Torah*, Part 32, "The Beggar's Wisdom," pp. 633–638.

[27] Joseph ben Eliezer Bonfils, *Sofenat Pan`eah*. The surname "Bonfils" is erroneous (see Simon, "Interpreting the Interpretar," pp. 127–128 n. 49).

[28] Friedlander, *Essays*, p. 220.

to Uriel Simon, Joseph "excelled all his predecessors among Ibn Ezra's commentators, and, it seems, all those who followed him until the present day."[29] His work was printed (albeit abridged and expurgated) in Amsterdam in 1722, which fact increases the probability that a manuscript of it was available in that city in Spinoza's day. Whether or not Spinoza studied the *Safenat Pa`neah*, his interpretation of Ibn Ezra's comments on Deuteronomy 1:2 may be presumed to have been directly or indirectly influenced by the extensive supercommentary literature of which Joseph's work is exemplary. Spinoza refers to this literature when, in his discussion of the meaning of the "secret of the twelve," he mentions "what others have ariolated besides."[30] In order to put Spinoza's interpretation into perspective, it will be useful to summarize Joseph's interpretation.

Joseph elaborates on Ibn Ezra's comments on Deuteronomy 1:2.

(1) He asserts that Ibn Ezra's secret concerning the opening of the book of Deuteronomy can be solved if one understands the "secret of the twelve," as well as Deuteronomy 31:9, Genesis 12:6 and 22:14, and Deuteronomy 3:11. "If you understand the secret of these verses, which Moses did not write, then you will understand that the five verses at the beginning of this periscope [i.e., Deut. 1:1–5] . . . were not written by Moses but by one of the later prophets."[31]

(2) Regarding Ibn Ezra's "secret of the twelve," Joseph writes: "Know that the 'twelve' are the twelve verses at the end of the Law." He explains that Ibn Ezra was of the opinion that Joshua wrote those verses "by way of prophecy," for Moses could not have written them, since he ascended Mount Nebo and "did not come down." This interpretation, states Joseph, reflects the literal meaning of the text. Joseph mentions the rabbinical view that Moses wrote the last eight verses of the Law "with a tear" before his death, but reminds us that there is an alternative rabbinical view that is similar to Ibn Ezra's.[32]

(3) Regarding Ibn Ezra's allusion to "And Moses wrote," (Deut. 31:9), Joseph cites the verse more fully, "And Moses wrote this Law and delivered it to the priests," etc., and observes that the Law had thus been written and delivered "before this verse was written."[33]

(4) Regarding Ibn Ezra's allusion to "and the Canaanite was then in the land" (Gen. 12:6), Joseph explains: "It stands to reason that the word 'then'

[29] Simon, "Interpreting the Interpreter," p. 121.   [30] *TTP* Ch. 8; *G* III 119.

[31] *Safenat Pa`neah*, vol. II, pp. 65.25–66.1. The term used for "later prophets" (*nebi'im aharonim*) is the same one used to refer to the books of Isaiah, Jeremiah, Ezekiel, and the Twelve Minor Prophets.

[32] *Safenat Pa`neah*, vol. II, p. 65.7–15. Regarding the rabbinical views, see above, "Review of Spinoza's exposition."

[33] *Safenat Pa`neah*, vol. II, p. 65.15–17.

was written at a time when the Canaanite was not in the land. Now, we know that the Canaanite did not depart from the land until after Moses' death, when Joshua conquered it. Thus, it seems that Moses did not write this word [viz., "then"] here, but Joshua or another one of the prophets wrote it . . . Inasmuch as we must believe in the words of tradition and the words of prophecy, what difference is it to me if Moses wrote it or another prophet wrote it, since the words of them all are true and by prophecy?"[34]

(5) Regarding Ibn Ezra's allusion to "on the mount of the Lord one shall be seen" (Gen. 22:14), Joseph notes that the Temple Mount is identified with Mount Moriah in II Chronicles 3:1 but not in the Pentateuch. Moses referred to the Temple site only as "the place which the Lord your God shall choose" (Deut. 12:5, etc.), for he did not know the site since "God did not reveal it until the days of David." Similarly, Joseph adds, the phrase "as it is said *today*" (Gen. 22:14) clearly refers to words uttered during a time when pilgrimages are made to the Temple in Jerusalem (cf. Exod. 23:17; 34:23; Deut. 16:16); and so "Moses did not write this verse, but later prophets wrote it."[35]

(6) Regarding Ibn Ezra's allusion to King Og's bed in Rabbah of the children of Ammon (Deut. 3:11), Joseph observes that Moses never entered the land of the children of Ammon (Deut. 2:37) and the Israelites did not go there until the days of King David (II Samuel 12:26–31). "This is evidence that this verse was written in the Law afterwards [i.e., after the Davidic conquest], and it was not written by Moses but by one of the later prophets."[36]

A comparison of the analyses of Joseph ben Eliezer and Spinoza shows that there is nothing new in Spinoza's interpretation of Ibn Ezra's comments. Even peripheral insights that might otherwise have been taken as reflecting Spinoza's own keen Bible scholarship (e.g., Moses referred to the Temple site as "the place which the Lord your God shall choose" or Rabbah was not conquered until the time of King David) are found already in Joseph's commentary.

There is, however, one important point on which Spinoza, by his silence, breaks with Joseph and with the supercommentary literature in general. Joseph emphasized again and again that the additions to the Law of Moses were all inserted by prophets. By this emphasis, he preserved the divine authority of the entire Law. As he put it, "what difference is it to me if

[34] *Safenat Pa'neah*, vol. I, pp. 91.22–92.8. Joseph argues that interpolations in the Law of Moses are similar to the additions in the Book of Proverbs by the men of King Hezekiah (Prov. 25:1).
[35] *Safenat Pa'neah*, vol. I, p. 112.1–12.   [36] *Safenat Pa'neah*, vol. II, p. 65.19–25.

Moses wrote it or another prophet wrote it, since the words of them all are true and by prophecy?" Spinoza, who was not interested in preserving divine authority of the entire Law, does not stipulate that the additions were inserted by prophets.

5 SPINOZA AND RABBI ELEAZAR BEN MATTATHIAS

The highly convincing explanation of Ibn Ezra's "secret of the twelve," according to which it refers to the final twelve verses of Deuteronomy which were presumably written by Joshua and which thus are the paradigm case of a post-Mosaic Pentateuchal text, is found very frequently in the prolific supercommentary literature on Ibn Ezra. One thus cannot help wondering how it came about that Spinoza advocated his curious solution concerning the twelve stones, and mentioned the solution concerning the twelve verses only as a second afterthought.

It is possible that Spinoza made use of a supercommentary that was confused or ambiguous regarding the "secret of the twelve." Such uncertainty is found particularly in the early supercommentaries, written before the solution concerning the twelve verses became well known and routine. One such supercommentary is that of Rabbi Eleazar ben Mattathias, a learned and trenchant scholar who seems to have been born in France in about 1210, lived for a period in Egypt, and wrote his supercommentary in Byzantium between 1285 and 1295.[37]

Addressing Ibn Ezra's esoteric comments on Deuteronomy 1:2, Eleazar writes:

I searched among authors and books, and found none who has explained his words. Therefore, I will say what is in my heart.

It is known that when the exiles of Jeshurun were in Babylonia, the Law was forgotten, until there appeared Ezra the Priest, a ready scribe in the Law of the Lord [cf. Ezra 7:6], and recovered it for them. He did not change anything regarding all the commandments that the Lord had commanded Moses. However, regarding the narratives of events, where there is no harm in a little elaboration on them, like in the examples mentioned [by Ibn Ezra], the prophet [i.e., Ezra] was not concerned about additions; and it may be that it was by the word of the Lord that he added whatever he added . . .

The "twelve" are the sons of Jacob. It is written about them: "for the Lord hath looked upon my affliction" [Gen. 29:32], "for the Lord hath heard" [Gen. 29:33],

---

[37] See Simon, "Interpreting the Interpreter," pp. 106–110, 125–126. See further two recent doctoral dissertations: Visi, "The Early Ibn Ezra Supercommentaries," pp. 108–118, 279–283, and *passim*; and Shoshan, "Rabbi Eleazar ben Mattathias."

"this time will my husband be joined unto me" [Gen. 29:34], "this time will I praise" [Gen. 29:35], and similarly with regard to them all. It may certainly be that Moses knew by means of the holy spirit the intention of the Matriarchs, and elaborated on their words. Now, Ezra did the very same thing. Thus is written "And Moses wrote [the Law]" [Deut. 31:9] and not "And I wrote [the Law]"... So too "And Moses wrote this song" [Deut. 31:22], "And Moses died" [Deut. 34:5], and other similar texts are the words of the transcriber of the Law [i.e., Ezra]. Similarly, "The prayers of David the son of Jesse are ended" [Psalms 72:20] and "Blessed be the Lord forever more, amen and amen" [Psalms 89:53] are the words of the transcriber and collector of the psalms...

"And the Canaanite was then in the land" [Gen. 12:6]. I have seen regarding this text words of wind which need not be mentioned. My opinion on it is as follows. It is known that during Moses' days the Canaanite ruled over that land. Thus, why did Moses have a need to write "then"?... We say that these are the words of the transcriber of the Law [i.e., Ezra], and he had a need to say "then," for in the days of the transcriber the Canaanite did not rule over it but rather the king of Babylon. The transcriber wrote it as an elaboration.

Similarly, "[as it is said today,] 'on the mount of the Lord one shall be seen'" [Gen. 22:14]... If these are the words of Moses... why did he say "today"?... Is it not the case that in Moses' days there were no pilgrimage festivals? Rather, these are the words of the transcriber [i.e., Ezra], for in his days people did make pilgrimages on the festivals.

As for "behold, his bed was a bed of iron" [Deut. 3:11], if these are the words of Moses, why did he have a need to mention the immensity of the victory [over King Og] to people of his own generation, and give a proof from his bed... as if to say: "if you don't believe me, go to Ammon and see his bed!" Was not [King Og] killed "at that time" [Deut. 3:8] and in that year and all the people [of Moses' generation] had seen it. Rather, these are the words of the transcriber of the Law [i.e., Ezra].

Now, I have explained to you [Ibn Ezra's] secret, according to my understanding of it. He said, "[one who understands it] should be silent" in order not to weaken our Law in the eyes of the multitude.[38]

Eleazar's comments relate to Spinoza's discussion in three ways. First, like Spinoza, he was uncertain about the meaning of Ibn Ezra's "secret of the twelve." Second, like Spinoza, he dismissed disparagingly the attempts of previous scholars to explain Ibn Ezra's hints.[39] Third, like Spinoza, he named Ezra the Scribe as the post-Mosaic author. Unlike Spinoza, he held that Ezra wrote only some parts of the Law and not the entire book, and, moreover, such parts did not concern the commandments but only the narratives; and, again, unlike Spinoza, but like Rabbi Joseph ben Eliezer

---

[38] Ms. Vatican 54 (Institute of Microfilmed Hebrew Manuscripts, Jerusalem, no. 171), pp. 171b–172a.
[39] Spinoza's use (*TTP* Ch. 8; *G* III 119.) of the Latin *hariolantur* (ariolated, soothsaid, prophesied) may reflect Eleazar's use of *dibre ruah* (words of wind, words of spirit, nonsense; cf. Job 3:16).

and other supercommentators, he was careful to note that all post-Mosaic additions were made by a prophet (either on his own initiative or by the word of God).

Eleazar's explanation of the "secret of the twelve" is striking in its boldness and originality, but unabashedly conjectural. His explanation seems to run roughly as follows. In relating the pronouncements of the Matriarchs made when naming the twelve sons of Jacob, Moses quoted words he could not have known. He knew by prophecy the general intentions of the Matriarchs, but reconstructed their words on his own. So too Ezra narrated things about Moses that he could not have known. He knew by prophecy Moses' general comportment, but wrote on his own: "And Moses wrote [the Law]," (Deut. 31:9), "And Moses wrote this song" (Deut. 31:22), "And Moses died" (Deut. 34:5)," etc.

It might be imagined that Spinoza read Eleazar's supercommentary, was convinced by his general explication of Ibn Ezra's comments on Deut. 1:2, but dissatisfied with his forced explanation of the "secret of the twelve," and decided to offer an explanation of his own (the twelve stones).[40] Spinoza recognized that his own explanation was also forced, and thus offered an alternative one (the twelve curses). Subsequently, the generally accepted explanation (the twelve verses) was brought to his attention (perhaps he saw it in a different supercommentary), and he added it as a third possibility. Spinoza, it may be further imagined, borrowed from Eleazar the thesis that the post-Mosaic author was Ezra the Scribe. Indeed, this emphasis on the special editorial role of Ezra the Scribe seems to have been distinctive in Eleazar's supercommentary.[41] Eleazar and Spinoza's common focus on Ezra lends a modicum of plausibility to the notion that the thirteenth-century supercommentator did in fact influence the seventeenth-century philosopher directly or indirectly.

---

[40] It is possible Spinoza's explanation concerning the twelve stones was borrowed by him from one of the supercommentaries, but I have not seen it in the more than twenty I examined. A systematic study of the Ibn Ezra supercommentaries is a *desideratum*.

[41] The view that Ezra was the author of the Pentateuch (or its post-Mosaic portions) is found among critics of Judaism and Christianity, like the Greek Porphyry (d. 305?) and the Muslim Ibn Hazm (994–1064). It was not widespread among Jews and Christians. It is found in Hobbes (see below). Some Ibn Ezra supercommentators, perhaps influenced by Eleazar, mention Ezra as one of the glossators intended by Ibn Ezra. Thus, Rabbi Samuel ibn Motot (fourteenth century), addressing Ibn Ezra's comments at Deut. 1:2, writes: "his opinion is that all [the verses] he mentioned are an emendation that Joshua or Ezra the Scribe emended" (*Megillat Setarim*, p. 75b). On theories of Ezra's authorship of the Pentateuch, see Malcolm, *Aspects of Hobbes*, pp. 383–431; cf. the halakhocentric thesis of Halivni, *Peshat & Derash*, pp. 126–154, 213–226; and also the recent Hebrew study by Mayshar, *In His Image*, pp. 141–220.

6 SPINOZA AND HOBBES

Spinoza's discussion of Ibn Ezra's comments on Deuteronomy 1:2 should be compared also with Hobbes's discussion of the authorship of the Pentateuch in *Leviathan*, III, 33,[42] if only because Spinoza's philosophy was in several areas indebted to Hobbes. The *Leviathan* was published in English in 1651, almost two decades before the publication of Spinoza's *Theological-Political Treatise* in 1670; it appeared in Dutch in 1667 and Latin in 1668.[43] Hobbes did not read Hebrew and thus could not have studied Ibn Ezra directly, but may have seen references to his views in the Latin theological literature.[44] Whether or not he did, his discussion of the authorship of the Pentateuch may have been of assistance to Spinoza in his deciphering of Ibn Ezra's comments.

Arguing against the Mosaic authorship of the Law of Moses, Hobbes, like Ibn Ezra, cites Genesis 12:6 ("which must needs be the words of one who wrote when the Canaanite was not in the land; and, consequently, not Moses") and Deuteronomy 34 ("For it were a strange interpretation to say Moses spake of his own sepulcher . . . that it was not found to that day, wherein he was yet living").[45] Like Ibn Ezra, he mentions in this context also Deuteronomy 31:9 ("And Moses wrote the Law"), and explains that it refers to a portion of the Pentateuch that Moses himself did write.[46] In giving these examples, Hobbes may have been indirectly influenced by Ibn Ezra.

Regarding Spinoza's far-fetched conjecture that Ibn Ezra's "secret of the twelve" refers to the problem of writing the entire Pentateuch on the stones of the altar (Deut. 27:8), it is relevant to note that Hobbes too mentions these stones. He theorizes that what was written on them was not the entire Pentateuch but only Deuteronomy 11–27.[47] This theory might have influenced Spinoza's thinking about the "secret of the twelve."

[42] Hobbes, *Leviathan* (ed. Macpherson), pp. 417–418, 422.
[43] Spinoza's library had a copy of Hobbes's Latin *De Cive*, but not the *Leviathan*. However, according to Curley ("Kissinger, Spinoza, and Genghis Khan," p. 316 n. 5), "it [is] virtually certain that Spinoza knew *Leviathan* at least by the time he was composing the final draft of the *Theological-Political Treatise*." Moreover, Spinoza may have seen pages from the Dutch translation even before 1667, since the translator, Abraham van Berkel, seems to have been a member of his circle.
[44] On Hobbes's sources, see Malcolm, *Aspects of Hobbes*. Cf. Popkin, "Spinoza and Bible Scholarship," pp. 386–388: "[I]bn Ezra . . . was the favorite Jewish commentator . . . for Christian exegetes . . . Various late-sixteenth century commentators, using [I]bn Ezra, showed that there were difficulties in assuming the Mosaic authorship of the Pentateuch . . . The recognition of non-Mosaic lines [in the Pentateuch] only began to have . . . repercussions in the 1650s, in the writings of Thomas Hobbes, Isaac La Peyrère, Samuel Fisher, and then Spinoza."
[45] *Leviathan*, p. 417.   [46] *Leviathan*, p. 418.
[47] *Leviathan*, p. 418. Note also the reference there to Josh. 4:9.

Finally, the view held by Spinoza that Ezra the Scribe was the author of the Pentateuch had been adumbrated by Hobbes. However, unlike Spinoza, he cited in support of this view the apocryphal IV Ezra 14:21–22 *et seq.*[48]

In sum, Hobbes's discussion of the authorship of the Pentateuch may have contributed in an auxiliary way to Spinoza's understanding of Ibn Ezra's esoteric doctrine.

7 CONCLUDING REMARK

Spinoza was a profound and erudite student of Rabbi Abraham ibn Ezra's Bible Commentaries, and seems also to have been influenced by the medieval Hebrew supercommentary literature on them. In his critical approach to the Bible, he saw himself as continuing in the path paved by Ibn Ezra. His exposition of Ibn Ezra's esoteric comments on Deuteronomy 1:2 was not undertaken for its own sake and was not particularly original, but was intended primarily as a prolegomenon to his own biblical researches. After concluding his exposition, he states: "We have explained Ibn Ezra's opinion and the passages of the Pentateuch he cites to confirm it. However, he has not mentioned everything, nor the most important things; for many things remain to be noted of even greater moment in these books."[49] In a meaningful sense, Spinoza's project of Bible interpretation was an effort to pick up where Ibn Ezra had left off.

[48] *Leviathan*, 422.   [49] *TTP* Ch. 8; *G* III 120.

CHAPTER 4

Reflections of the medieval Jewish–Christian debate in the Theological-Political Treatise and the Epistles

Daniel J. Lasker

Modern research into the thought and writings of Baruch (Benedictus) Spinoza has revolved around many axes – historic, literary, philosophical, and others – using various tools, such as philosophical, philological, or political analysis. Two subjects which have occupied a number of researchers, especially Jewish ones, are (1) Spinoza's Jewish sources and, hence, the extent to which he belongs to the Jewish philosophical tradition;[1] and (2) his attitude towards his original religion, Judaism, especially in comparison to his relation to the majority religion, Christianity.[2] In light of these areas of research, it is of interest that scholars have yet to look at a body of Jewish writings that served as one of Spinoza's sources and, therefore, can illumine his attitude towards the two religions, namely medieval Jewish anti-Christian polemical literature (and its Christian counterpart).[3] This Jewish literature, which began in the ninth century in Islamic countries and continued uninterrupted to Spinoza's era and beyond, reflects the debate between the two religions, both the official confrontation as seen in public disputations, such as Paris, 1240, and Barcelona, 1263, and

---

I would like to thank Yitzhak Y. Melamed for his help and encouragement.

[1] The best example of a search for Spinoza's Jewish philosophical sources is Wolfson, *The Philosophy of Spinoza*. Other scholars have looked for influences in Kabbalistic literature, while others have understood Spinoza as someone who was influenced by the Converso milieu in Holland; see, e.g., Levy, "Al ha-Reqa'."

   Much has been written about Spinoza's Jewishness especially by Jewish scholars who have made an effort to include Spinoza in the list of Jewish philosophers; see, e.g., Ravven and Goodman, eds., *Jewish Themes*. The journal *Studia Spinozana*, 13 (1997; printed 2003) is devoted totally to the subject of Spinoza and Jewish identity. Most of the articles describe him as a Jewish thinker, but the article by Wiep van Bunge in the same volume disagrees with this conclusion.

[2] Frankel, "Piety of a Heretic"; Misrahi, "Spinoza and Christian Thought"; Leavitt, "Christian Philosophy."

[3] For instance, many scholars have discussed Hasdai Crescas's influence upon Spinoza, but they have looked only at his philosophical opus, *The Light of the Lord*, and not at his polemical composition, *The Refutation of the Christian Principles*. A researcher who has made reference to the polemical background of one detail in Spinoza's work is Shlomo Pines in his "Spinoza's *Tractatus Theologico-Politicus*," p. 513 (reprint, p. 726), but there is no overall treatment of the subject. Seidler, "Barukh Spinoza," does refer to the Christian background of Spinoza's concept of Judaism.

the informal daily debates between Jews and Christians. Part of this literature was written as a reaction to Christian attempts to convert Jews to Christianity, and part was written as a result of a Jewish initiative without reference to the Christian mission. These polemical compositions are not literary and intellectual creations of the highest rank, yet they were a very popular genre that greatly influenced developments in Judaism, such as Jewish self-definition.[4] A survey of Spinoza's use of this literature will enable us to broaden our knowledge concerning his Jewish sources as well as to evaluate his relation to the two religions, Judaism and Christianity.[5]

Let us look first at the possibility of Spinoza's exposure to the polemical literature. Was this genre of literature present in the libraries of the Jewish community of Amsterdam in which Spinoza grew up, and is it reasonable that he read it? The answers are positive. In Spinoza's time, Amsterdam was a center of Jewish–Christian polemics, especially as a result of the makeup of its Jewish population, namely former Conversos. The Jewish–Christian debate had been an essential feature of Iberian Jewish life until the expulsion in 1492, and even after the expulsion the debate continued. "Old Christians" were not convinced that the "New Christians" (the Marranos or the Conversos) were sincere in their new Christian faith. A good example of a polemical treatise of this type is the book by the Portuguese monk Francisco Machado, *The Mirror of the New Christians*, from the sixteenth century. This book, directed mainly at Conversos in Portugal, Spinoza's family's birthplace, concentrates on biblical and rabbinic proof texts that the Messiah had already come and that Jesus' life fulfilled the conditions of the Messiah. This composition, written in Portuguese, serves as a repository of traditional Christian arguments against Judaism, in addition to whatever few innovations of the author himself.[6]

The debate between Old and New Christians did not stop at the Iberian border. For instance, at the end of the sixteenth century a Jew, perhaps a former Converso, wrote an anti-Christian polemic in Ladino which was apparently meant for other Conversos, named *Fuente Clara* ("The Clear Fountain").[7] In the seventeenth century, many Conversos returned

---

[4] This literature has generally not been evaluated concerning its contribution to subjects other than the polemic itself; see Chazan, *Fashioning Jewish Identity*.

[5] For general surveys of the literature, see Krauss, *Jewish-Christian Controversy*; Berger, *Jewish-Christian Debate*; and Lasker, *Jewish Philosophical Polemics*.

[6] Vieira and Talmage, *Mirror*; for other Iberian polemics, see Talmage's introduction and Krauss, *Jewish-Christian Controversy*, p. 100.

[7] The treatise was published in Hebrew script in Salonica, 1595; for an English summary, see Romeu Ferré, "New Approach."

to Judaism after a period of over a hundred years in which their families lived as Christians. This transition was not smooth, and Christians tried to convince the Conversos not to return to Judaism. Sephardic Jewish authors, most of whom were from former Converso families, composed anti-Christian treatises in order to answer the arguments of those who opposed their return to Judaism. Two important Sephardic polemicists of the first half of the seventeenth century were Elijah Montalto[8] and Saul Morteira, one of the signatories of the ban of excommunication against Spinoza in 1656.[9] Other polemicists of the same period were Orobio de Castro[10] and Moses Rafael d'Aguilar.[11] Even if one were to claim that the writings of Abraham Cohen de Herrara and Manasseh Ben Israel of Amsterdam are characterized more by apologetics than by polemics,[12] one cannot deny that they confronted Christianity and Christians in one way or another. In addition, at the same time there were Christians in Amsterdam who wrote against Judaism, for instance Johann Stephanus Rittangel.[13] The classical Jewish polemical literature was written in Hebrew and the classical Christian polemical literature was written in Latin. The newer polemical treatises available in Holland were written in Spanish, Portuguese or Dutch. Hence, Spinoza was easily able to read most of this literature.[14]

It is possible that Spinoza himself was indirectly engaged in the Christian argument against Judaism by translating into Hebrew an appeal to the Jews

---

[8] Cooperman, "Elijah Montalto." There is a Dutch translation of Montalto's polemical treatise concerning Isaiah 53; see Rooden, "Dutch Adaptation."

[9] Kaplan, "Rabbi Saul Levi Morteira's Treatise"; for these two authors, see Melnick, *Polemics to Apologetics*, pp. 23–32; Krauss, *Jewish-Christian Controversy*, pp. 254–256.

[10] Kaplan, *Christianity to Judaism*; Krauss, *Jewish-Christian Controversy*, pp. 257–258.

[11] Krauss, *Jewish-Christian Controversy*, p. 249.

[12] This is Melnick's view, *Polemics to Apologetics*, pp. 43–54. It might also be pointed out that there were Conversos who were surprised to discover that normative Judaism was a religion based on the Talmud, a composition which was unknown to them, and not just a biblical religion which could be learned solely by reading the Bible. Therefore, at this time there was an extensive internal Jewish polemical literature defending the truth of the rabbinic Oral Torah; see, e.g., Petuchowski, *Theology*.

[13] Rittangel, who arrived in Amsterdam in 1641 in order to publish his edition and Latin translation of *Sefer Yezirah* (1642) and stayed there for about a year, corresponded with a Jew from the same city on the subject of Gen. 49:10 ("The staff will not depart from Judah"). This correspondence was published in Wagenseil, *Tela Ignea Satanae*, vol. 1, pp. 327–373 (English translation and commentary: Rankin, *Jewish Religious Polemic*, pp. 89–154); see also Krauss, *Jewish-Christian Controversy*, pp. 259–260. Rittangel was a Christian Hebraist, one of a group of Christian scholars in Western Europe who learned Hebrew, among other reasons, to try to convert Jews to Christianity more successfully; see Lasker, "Karaism and Christian Hebraism." The Christian Hebraist movement was particularly strong in Holland; see Rooden, *Theology*; Rooden, "Constantijn L'Empereur's Contacts."

[14] There were no polemical treatises found among the books in Spinoza's library at his death, but as Jacob Klazkin (*Barukh Spinoza*, p. 17) points out, the fact that a book was not in Spinoza's library does not mean that he had not read it.

by Margaret Fell. According to an assessment made by Richard Popkin and Michael Signer, Spinoza was the former Jew who translated a small composition named "A Loving Salutation," which was an attempt by Fell, an English Quaker, to convince the Jews to accept Christianity as part of the redemptive process. This Hebrew translation appeared in England in 1658, two years after the excommunication of Spinoza, at a time in which he apparently was interested in Quakerism.[15]

It is, therefore, quite reasonable to assume that polemical literature in its different languages was easily accessible to Spinoza in Amsterdam, and there is no *prima facie* reason to think that he was unable to use it. We will now see that, indeed, some of his arguments are identical or parallel with arguments found in this literature.

Spinoza's use of Jewish and Christian polemical literature was two-directional, namely he used Christian arguments against Judaism in order to undermine the religion in which he was born; but he also relied upon well-known Jewish arguments against Christianity in order to criticize the religion to which he refused to convert.

We may begin with Spinoza's criticism of Judaism. Although Christian arguments against Judaism were varied and related to diverse theological, exegetical, historical, and similar topics, there was one basic assumption at their core, namely that the Jewish religion is no longer valid because it had been superseded by Christianity. The commandments of the Torah were given to prepare the Jews for the coming of Jesus, who would give a new religion that would take the place of the old religion and that would spread throughout the world. The commands of the New Testament which Jesus brought are superior to the laws of the Old Testament of Moses, since the new commands are intended to purify the souls of the worshipers and not, like the old commandments, merely to discipline the Jews or to bring them civil order. The laws of Torah were also intended to punish the Jews for their being stiff-necked and to give the enemies of the Jews a means of identifying them (e.g., through circumcision). The Old Testament promised only physical rewards in this world, while the New Testament gives in addition spiritual pleasure after death in the world to come. The historical role of the People of Israel, to bring the redeemer to the world, justifies calling them God's chosen people, but today, with their rejection of Jesus and the consequent destruction of the Temple, this chosenness has passed to the Christians. Only the blindness of the Jews prevented them from

---

[15] See Popkin and Signer, eds., *Spinoza's Earliest Publication.*

understanding that at this time there is no more reason to hold on to the Torah of Moses and to observe its commandments.[16]

Spinoza did not accept Christian theology, and as we will see below, he even opposed some of its central doctrines. Nevertheless, his attitude towards Judaism is closely parallel to the Christian attitude towards it, and some of his arguments against Judaism are borrowed from the polemical literature. For Spinoza in the *Theological-Political Treatise*, both the observance of the commandments and the chosenness of Israel came to an end with the destruction of the Jewish state which once existed but was no more. The observance of the commandments, which were the societal laws of a historical, political entity, did not contribute to the improvement of Jewish ethical traits. These commandments were corporeal, and the only promises given by the Torah are also physical. In contrast, Christ's spiritual commandments are eternal and can give spiritual happiness. Therefore, there is no reason for the Jews to observe the commandments of the Torah of Moses, even if they have a slight value in contributing to national solidarity. Only the stubbornness of the "Pharisees," namely the rabbinic Jews, and their desire to oppose Christianity, causes them to continue to observe the commandments, which are no longer necessary.[17] Yet, "if the foundations of their religion did not make their hearts unmanly [*animos effoeminarent*[18]], I would absolutely believe that some day, given the opportunity, they would set up their state again, and that God would choose them anew, so changeable are human affairs."[19]

The Christians reinforced their claim that the commandments of the Torah were not intended to be observed forever by citations of selected passages from the Bible, which apparently criticized these commandments. For instance, well-known verses are those from Jeremiah 31:30–33,[20] in which the prophet said that in the future, God will make a new covenant (testament) with the People of Israel which will be written on their hearts, in contrast to the covenant he made with them when he took them out

---

[16] While the details of the Christian attitude towards Judaism took a while to develop, the idea of the annulment of the commandments, and the supersession of Judaism by Christianity, goes back to Paul's Epistle to the Romans. Paul agreed (Acts of the Apostles 15) that Jewish-Christians could continue to observe the commandments of the Torah, but rather quickly this position became heretical. Justin Martyr (middle of the second century) wrote that the commandments, such as circumcision, were given to the Jews to punish them.

[17] These themes are repeated throughout Spinoza, *TTP*, especially Chs. 3–5; G III 44–80. Translations will be from the forthcoming Edwin M. Curley translation.

[18] Citations in Latin will be taken from Gebhardt, *Spinoza Opera*, unless otherwise noted.

[19] *TTP*, end of Ch. 3; G III 47. Christians, of course, thought the destruction of the Jewish commonwealth was irreversible.

[20] 31:31–34 in the Christian versions.

of Egypt.[21] Another well-known verse is Ezekiel 20:25: "Moreover I gave them statutes that were not good and ordinances by which they could not live."[22] Spinoza adopted these verses as part of his argument that there was no need to continue to observe the commandments.[23]

As noted, Christians argued that the commandments of the Torah did not contribute to the believers' purity of the heart, since they relate only to their external actions. This Christian claim is reflected in medieval Jewish literature, for instance, in *The Book of Priniciples* of Joseph Albo (first half of the fifteenth century). Albo quoted a Christian who argued the following: "The law of Moses commands only right action, and says nothing about purity of heart; whereas the law of Jesus commands purity of heart, and thus saves man from the judgment of Hell."[24] Spinoza adopted this view as well when he wrote that even a prohibition such as "You shall not commit adultery," serves as a societal commandment and not as a spiritual one, in contrast to the words of Christ that it is forbidden to commit adultery even in one's heart (Matthew 5:28), and, therefore, Christ taught universal laws, not statutes intended solely for one people.[25]

There is similarity as well between other arguments used by Spinoza against the Hebrew Bible and the polemical literature. For instance, Christians claimed that one must interpret many biblical verses in an allegorical manner and not literally, especially in regards to particularistic references to Israel. Spinoza was of the same opinion, for instance, in his explanations of Psalms 15 and 24 ("your tent," "Your holy mountain," "His holy mountain") as happiness and tranquillity of the soul, and not as a physical place such as the Temple Mount or the sanctuary.[26] Neither Spinoza nor the Christians, however, gave clear instructions as to when one must use allegorical interpretation. In another passage, Spinoza attributed his own assertion that the whole purpose of the Bible is love of neighbor, and not the practical commandments, to Paul's Epistle to the Romans 13:8.[27] He could also have cited Jesus directly in Matthew 22:39 or Mark 12:21.[28]

In sum, Spinoza, like the Christian theologians who preceded him, agreed that there was no longer any reason to observe the laws of the Torah of Moses and that these commandments do not contribute to the

---

[21] These verses are already cited in Hebrews, 8:8–12; 10:16–17. For their use in the Middle Ages, see Berger, *Jewish-Christian Debate*, pp. 89–90; p. 271.

[22] See Berger, *Jewish-Christian Debate*, pp. 94, 272.

[23] For Jeremiah, see *TTP* Ch. 12; *G* III 159; Ezekiel, Ch. 17; *G* III 217. Shlomo Pines remarked that the verse from Ezekiel is cited in Christian polemical literature; see n. 3 above.

[24] Albo, *Book of Principles*, Vol. III, pp. 219–220 (with modifications in the translation).

[25] *TTP* Ch. 5; *G* III 70.   [26] *TTP* Ch. 5; *G* III 71–72.

[27] *TTP* Ch. 13; *G* III 168.   [28] Cf. *Ep.* 21; *G* IV 133.

soul's ultimate felicity. Although Spinoza's reasons for the invalidity of the Torah are different from those of the Christians, the arguments he used to advance his conclusions are parallel to those which can be found in Christian anti-Jewish polemical literature.

Although Spinoza did not engage in direct criticism of the New Testament to the extent to which he did concerning the Hebrew Bible (under the pretense that he was not sufficiently expert in the Greek language), his writings are full of implicit, and sometimes not merely implicit, criticism of this book and of the Christian religion. His arguments are often parallel to well-known Jewish arguments, and it would appear that their source lies in Jewish anti-Christian polemics.

Medieval Jewish authors argued that there are irreconcilable contradictions among the different Gospels, and, therefore, the stories about Jesus are not credible.[29] This assertion is reflected in Spinoza's statement in *TTP*, Chapter 12, that the Gospels tell different stories, thereby complementing each other, but only accidentally. Certainly, according to Spinoza, one would do just as well with fewer of them.[30] Jewish polemicists also pointed out contradictions between Jesus' statements and contemporary Christian praxis, especially in light of the statement in Matthew 5:17, that Jesus did not come to annul the Torah.[31] In *TTP*, Chapter 5, Spinoza also expressed doubt as to whether Jesus and the apostles were those who initiated Christian practices.[32] In Chapter 7, Spinoza stated that the morality that is implied in the verse: "If anyone strikes you on the right cheek, turn to him the other also" (Matthew 5:39) contradicts the Law of Moses. Since Christ said that he did not come to annul the Torah of Moses (v. 17), it follows that his intention in stating this moral directive was not to legislate a law, but rather to teach a lesson.[33] In essence, then, Spinoza argued, in the manner of Jewish polemicists before him, that Jesus did not establish his own new Torah in place of the Torah of Moses.

[29] Jewish criticism of the contradictions among the Gospels can already be found in the ninth century in a composition written in Judaeo-Arabic and which was ultimately translated into Hebrew as *The Book of Nestor the Priest*; see Lasker and Stroumsa, *Nestor*. This type of criticism is found in abundance in works such as *Nizzahon Yashan* (anonymous, thirteenth century) and *Hizzuq Emunah* by Isaac ben Abraham of Troki (end of the sixteenth century). *Hizzuq Emunah* was a very popular polemic in the seventeenth century and was translated into many languages, including Dutch. It should be noted that Jewish polemicists, unlike Spinoza, ignored possible contradictions in the Hebrew Bible.
[30] *TTP* Ch. 12; G III 164.
[31] This verse, which appears in almost every Jewish polemical work, was also cited in the Talmud, Shabbat 116b.
[32] *TTP* Ch. 5; G III 76.   [33] *TTP* Ch. 7; G III 103.

Spinoza's references to Christian doctrines, and his negative attitude towards them, had deep roots in the polemical literature as well. Let us take, for instance, the Jewish claim that the Christian belief that Jesus was the son of God, as the incarnation of the second Person of the Trinity, is both false and incoherent.[34] Spinoza wrote in *TTP*, Chapter 1, that in contrast to Jewish prophets, who prophesied by means of intermediaries and not directly from God, God revealed Himself to Christ "immediately – without words or visions" [*sine verbis, aut visionibus, sed immediate revelata sunt*]. Thus, it is possible to say: "God's Wisdom, that is, a Wisdom surpassing human wisdom, assumed a human nature in Christ, and that Christ was the way to salvation."[35] The non-careful reader might assume from this that Spinoza adopted the doctrine of incarnation, as reflected in the Gospel of John, 1:1–4, that the wisdom of God (the logos) took on flesh in the image of Jesus.

This conclusion, however, would not be correct, and Spinoza's view of Christ differs from that of the traditional Christian belief, for as soon as Spinoza wrote that Christ was the "spirit of God," he immediately added: "But I must warn here that I am not speaking in any way about the things certain Churches maintain about Christ. Not that I deny them. For I readily confess that I do not grasp them [*nam libenter fateor me ea non capere*]."[36] What is it that some churches teach which Spinoza did not understand? The answer can be found in Epistle 73 to Henry Oldenburg, in which Spinoza wrote:

As to the additional teaching of certain Churches, that God took upon himself human nature, I have expressly indicated that I do not understand what they say. Indeed, to tell the truth, they seem to me to speak no less absurdly than one who might tell me that circle has taken on the nature of a square [*imò, ut verum fatear, non minùs absurdè mihi loqui videntur, quàm si quis mihi diceret, quòd circulus naturam quadrati induerit*].[37]

Obviously, Spinoza could have refuted the incarnation without recourse to Jewish sources. The question of the status of Jesus was a central feature of theological disputes within Christianity itself. Nevertheless, what is interesting here is the comparison between the Christian doctrine of incarnation and a logical impossibility, the squaring of a circle. These types of comparisons are made in most of the Jewish philosophical polemics in Spain from the end of the fourteenth century and the fifteenth century.

---

[34] Sources for this claim are summarized by Lasker, *Jewish Philosophical Polemics*, pp. 105–134. Hasdai Crescas's philosophical arguments against incarnation are in *Refutation*, pp. 49–56.
[35] *TTP* Ch. 1; *G* III 21. [36] *TTP* Ch. 1; *G* III 21. [37] *G* IV 309.

The Jewish polemicists stated that a religion based upon logical contradictions, namely Christianity, could not be a true divine religion, whereas a religion based on supernatural miracles, namely Judaism, is a possible divine religion.[38] Spinoza's specific comparison between Christian beliefs and mathematical impossibilities can be found, for instance, in the words of Joseph Albo, in a proposition with which he prefaced his anti-Christian polemic in the *Book of Principles*, part 3, chapter 25:

> Anything that is the subject of belief must be conceivable by the mind, though it may be impossible so far as nature is concerned ... Such natural impossibilities as the dividing of the Red Sea, the turning of the rod into a serpent, and the other miracles mentioned in the Torah or in the Prophets can be conceived by the mind; hence we can believe that God has power to produce them. But a thing which the mind cannot conceive, for example that a thing should be and not be at the same time, or that a body should be in two places at the same time, or that one and the same number should be both odd and even, and so on, cannot be the subject of belief, and God cannot be conceived as being able to do it, as God cannot be conceived able to create another like Him in every respect, or to make a square whose diagonal is equal to its side, or to make now what has happened not to have happened. For since the mind cannot conceive it, God cannot do it, as it is inherently impossible.[39]

Albo distinguished between religious beliefs, which are naturally impossible, such as the splitting of the Red Sea, and those which are logically impossible, such as incarnation. Beliefs of the first type are rationally possible, and, therefore, a religion may teach them, but beliefs of the second type are rationally impossible and are, thus, disqualified. Although it would be difficult to imagine that Spinoza would accept that distinction, since he did not believe in supernatural miracles,[40] his comparison between incarnation and squaring the circle reflects the writings of Albo and other Jewish polemicists and demonstrates Spinoza's rejection of a central Christian tenet.[41]

Another anti-Christian argument can be found in Spinoza's Epistle 12a to Lodewijk Meyer. In this letter, Spinoza responded to a number of questions concerning the appendix "Metaphysical Thoughts" to his book *Principles of Cartesian Philosophy*, in which Spinoza wrote, among other comments, that "the Son of God" is equal to "the Father" [*filium dej*

---

[38] For a discussion of the issue of possibility in Jewish–Christian polemics, see my article "Averroistic Trends."

[39] *Book of Principles*, Vol. III, pp. 220–221; cf. *Book of Principles*, Part 1, Chapter 22 (Vol. 1), pp. 178–181.

[40] *TTP* Ch. 6; *G* III 81–96.

[41] On Albo, see my article "Theory of Verification"; I have discussed the problematics of the distinction between rational and natural impossibilities in "Imagination and Intellect."

esse ipsum patrem]. Apparently Meyer wished to understand what Spinoza meant by this phrase. Spinoza responded that the matter is clear: "Things which agree with a third thing agree with one another" [*quae in uno tertio convenient ea inter se convenient*]. Spinoza added that this statement was not particularly important to him, so if Meyer thought that his words would give offense to someone, he could omit them. Apparently, that is what Meyer did.[42]

Spinoza's argument, namely, if the father is God and the son is God, then clearly the father is the son, can be found, for instance, in the *Epistle Be Not Like Your Fathers* of Profiat Duran (late fourteenth century). Addressing his former friend in an ironic style, Duran wrote:

Be not like your fathers who were forced by their intellects to admit the truth of rational, physical, metaphysical, logical and mathematical principles; and the derivative principles, which were derived from them. On the basis of these principles, they built an arsenal on the mountains of the intellect. They used profound discussions in order to achieve the ways and orders of logic, distinguishing between a demonstrative syllogism and that which is not demonstrative . . . As for you, do not act in this manner. God forbid that you should believe that the conclusions of the first mood of the first figure of the figures of the syllogisms, which is the foundation of the whole science of logic, will follow from the conditional predicated on the universal. You will be led into a denial of the faith if you should say (A) The Father is God; (B) God is the Son; this should not generate the result that (C) The Father is the Son.

Joseph ben Shem Tov (mid-fifteenth century) presented this syllogism in a slightly different manner: (A) All of the Father, and everything predicated on God, is God; (B) All of God, and everything predicated on God, is the Son; but (C) The Father is predicated on God (from A); therefore (D) The Father is the Son.[43] This was a popular argument and can be found as well in the polemic of Judah Aryeh Modena from Venice.

Spinoza, then, made reference to the logical statement that two things equal to a third thing are equal to each other, while Duran and Joseph ben Shem Tov used more technical terms of Aristotelian logic, but the result was the same: if the Father is God and God is the Son, then the Father is the Son. The Christian belief that one can distinguish between the Father and the Son, although both of them are God, is incoherent.

---

[42] *Ep.* 12a. This epistle was not in the original editions of Spinoza's letters, having been discovered only thirty years ago; see Offenberg, "Letter" (which is the source of the Latin citations here). On the possible original location of this statement in *Metaphysical Thoughts*, see *C*, Vol. 1, 337.

[43] See Lasker, *Jewish Philosophical Polemics*, pp. 90–93, for the sources of these texts and explanations of the terminology.

Although Spinoza expressed an unwillingness to analyze the New Testament critically in the same manner in which he related to the Hebrew Bible, one can see that even here Spinoza did not accept the Christian narrative without qualification. In Epistle 78, Spinoza referred to the story in the New Testament that Jesus was tortured, died, was buried, and rose from the dead. Spinoza was willing to accept the torture, the death, and the burial as historically true, but he denied the resurrection. Already in the New Testament, Jews are described as doubting Jesus' resurrection, assuming that someone had moved his body out of his tomb.[44] Spinoza, for his part, wrote that apparently the resurrection was meant allegorically, but if the authors of the New Testament really believed in Jesus' resurrection, then they were mistaken, just as other prophets were liable to error.[45]

Spinoza's statement that Christ received divine revelation without an intermediary, and, hence, he is God's spirit, is not necessarily meant positively. Spinoza came to this conclusion on the basis of the fact that there are no references in the New Testament that God actually talked to Jesus. It is possible that there is a hint here to a Jewish criticism of the New Testament, namely, that it compares poorly to the Hebrew Bible, in which God spoke directly to the prophets, because God is never portrayed as speaking directly to Jesus. This argument can be found, for instance, in *The Book of Nestor the Priest*, a very popular composition in the Middle Ages.[46] It is true that Spinoza did not understand prophecy as the various religionists understood it, and he considered the prophets to be simple people, not sages. Nevertheless, the use of the Jewish argument that God did not speak with Jesus in the New Testament perhaps indicates that Spinoza was aware of the problematic nature of the claim that Christ was the spirit of God.[47]

Spinoza's most concentrated and continuous criticism of Christianity can be found in Epistle 76 addressed to Albert Burgh.[48] Burgh had converted from Protestantism to Catholicism and wrote a long letter to Spinoza (*Ep.* 67) with justification for his deed, in the hope of convincing Spinoza to

[44] E.g., Matthew 28:14–15.   [45] *G* IV 328.

[46] The polemic known as *The Book of Nestor the Priest* was originally written in Judaeo-Arabic; in that version of the work God is said to have spoken to Moses 570 times. The Hebrew version gives the number as 576; see Lasker and Stroumsa, *Nestor*, Vol. 1, pp. 88, 129–130.

In *TTP* Ch. 11; *G* III 151–158, Spinoza argued that the apostles of the New Testament were prophets even though they are not described as receiving God's word. In contrast, he also wrote that the apostles did not speak as prophets who claimed that God spoke with them directly but rather as teachers who spoke in their own names.

[47] This is in contrast to the general praise of Christ in Spinoza's works. The fact that Spinoza did not convert to Christianity, even to a form of liberal Christianity, would indicate that his respect for Christ and his teachings was not unambiguous.

[48] *G* IV 316–324.

convert to Christianity.[49] Spinoza started his response, which was intended
to explain why he refused to become a Catholic, with the statement that he
will not "recount the vices of priests and popes [*Sacerdotum, & Pontificum
vitia*]," as is often done by opponents of Catholicism who have "unworthy
motives." The accusations of immoral behavior on the part of the Catholic
clergy are included in medieval Jewish polemical compositions, beginning
with Joseph Kimhi's *Book of the Covenant* (*c.*1170) and including, especially,
Sefer Nizzahon Yashan, one of the most popular Jewish polemical works,
written by an anonymous author in the thirteenth century. In general, Jews
claimed that the declared celibacy of the priests, the monks, and the nuns
was fictitious, since they had sexual relations among themselves as well as
with the general Christian population.[50]

Spinoza continued the letter with a reference to the Eucharist, which
according to Catholic doctrine turns into the real body of Christ. The
status of the Eucharist was an important subject in the polemics between
Protestants, who generally understood the changeover from bread to body
in a non-literal fashion, and Catholics. In this context, Spinoza mentioned
an incident in which the consecrated Eucharist was thrown to the horses in
the city of Chastillon in 1635, without any disastrous consequences (which
one could assume there would have been if the disgraced bread were
actually the body of Christ). Spinoza compared the true, infinite eternal
God with the bread of the Eucharist, and called to his interlocutor: "O
youth deprived of understanding, who has bewitched you into believing
that you eat, and hold in your intestines, that which is supreme and
eternal?" [*O mente destitute juvenis, quis te fascinavit, ut summum illud,
& aeternum te devorare, & in intestinis habere credas?*] Here also Spinoza
can be seen as part of the tradition of the Jewish critique of Christianity,
in which there was no dearth of strong arguments against this Christian
belief.[51] One can also find references there to God's being in the intestines
of the believer, for instance in Profiat Duran's ironic words: "And you, o
brother, have saved your soul; eat and be satisfied since your savior is in
your innards. Hallow and sanctify God, since the Holy One of Israel is in
your midst."[52]

Spinoza made reference as well to Burgh's claim that the general consensus of Catholics concerning the doctrines of their faith, in addition to

---

[49] *G* IV 280–291.
[50] Kimhi, *Book of the Covenant*, p. 35; Berger, *Jewish-Christian Debate*, pp. 69–70, 205, 223–224.
[51] See Lasker, *Jewish Philosophical Polemics*, pp. 135–151. Crescas's discussion of this subject is in
     Refutation, pp. 57–61.
[52] Duran, *Epistle*, p. 77. The Hebrew translated here "your midst" (cf. Hosea 11:9) is the same as "your
     innards."

the number of Catholics who died as martyrs to their faith, strengthens the certainty that Catholics have concerning their religion. Spinoza responded that this argument is in essence a "Pharisaic" one, since they also use consensus and the death of martyrs as a reliable proof. Spinoza even mentioned a Jew named Judah who was burned as a martyr, continuing to proclaim his belief in Judaism to the very end. The claim that reliable, true tradition and Jewish readiness to die a martyr's death prove the truth of Judaism, one of whose main sources is Judah Halevi's *Kuzari*,[53] is adduced here in order to say that just as Judaism is not a true religion despite its tradition and its martyrs, so, too, is Catholicism not true. Spinoza continued by saying that Catholicism is contradicted by reason and relies upon superstitions. We see, therefore, that Spinoza's criticism of Catholicism integrates motifs taken from the Jewish critique of Christianity, with Protestant arguments against Catholicism, with rationalistic claims against religions in general.

If we take all these examples of Spinoza's arguments against Christianity, and compare them with the Jewish anti-Christian polemical literature, we can discern that Spinoza is definitely within this particular Jewish tradition. It is true that the polemicists not only attacked Christianity but also defended Judaism, something which Spinoza did not do, yet nevertheless it is clear that Spinoza utilized the same arguments as appear in Jewish polemical literature when he criticized Christianity.

It is possible that Spinoza's biblical exegesis, in which he cast doubt upon the trustworthiness and the authority of the Holy Scriptures, also was influenced by the medieval Jewish–Christian polemical literature. One of the central topics of that literature was scriptural exegesis. The two sides argued that a correct reading of the biblical text strengthened their religious claims. The Christian exegetes stressed the allegorical aspects of the Bible, namely, in order to find allusions to Jesus in the Hebrew Scriptures, they claimed that there was a need to read these works in a non-literal fashion. The Jewish polemicists answered that in general one must adopt the literal reading (the *peshat*) of the verses, namely to read Scriptures in their literal and historical context. There was also a long history of literalist Jewish biblical exegesis not necessarily connected with the polemic against Christianity, such as that of Rabbi Abraham ibn Ezra (1089–1164), whose

---

[53] Cf. Halevi, *Kuzari*, Book 1, sections 48, 86, 113; pp. 49–50, 60, 78. The relation to the *Kuzari* can be seen as well in Spinoza's statement in the same epistle that the Pharisees trace their lineage back to Adam; see *Kuzari*, Book 1, section 95; pp. 64–67.

commentaries were well known to Spinoza.[54] When looking at Jewish and Christian biblical exegetical strategies in the polemical literature, it would be fair to say that the nature of the exegesis followed theological needs, and each side cast doubt on the exegetical authority of the rival.

Since neither side was able to present a systematic methodology of exegesis, which would establish uniform criteria as to when to read a verse as literal and when as allegorical, the exegetical debate weakened the authority of the Bible. Spinoza exploited this weakness when he set himself to work at interpreting the Scriptures. He said explicitly that he was not willing to accept the exegetical authority of others, neither of "the Pharisees," nor of the pope.[55] He insisted that he would interpret the Bible solely in its context, i.e., in a manner close to the Jewish literalists, but without any particular sympathy for Jewish exegesis. Nevertheless, when Spinoza saw a need for it, he also read the Bible in an allegorical manner, every interpretation in place to advance his goals.[56]

Spinoza further claimed that sometimes it is impossible to interpret the Bible truly because one does not know for certain what the correct reading of the scriptural text is. The example he gave is taken from the polemical literature: there is a contradiction between the Massoretic reading of Genesis 47:31, and the citation of the same verse in Hebrews 11:21. The verse states that Jacob said at the head of the "m.t.h." According to the Masoretes, one is to read *mittah*, bed, but the Christian reading is *matteh*, staff, subsequently understood by Christians as the cross.[57]

The debate concerning this verse is found, for instance, in *Sefer Nizzahon Yashan*:

The apostates say: If "there is a mother to tradition," then one should consider the fact that in the verse, "Then Israel bowed at the head of the bed," the Hebrew word for bed [*mittah*] is written without a *yod* and can therefore be read *matteh*, which means staff. Consequently, it is probable that it was customary to place a cross at the head of dying men, and it was to the cross that Jacob bowed. One may answer them according to their own foolishness and say that Jacob was distraught as a result of his illness, and he therefore bowed to the cross. But when he came to his senses, he changed his mind and regretted what he had done, as it is written,

---

[54] Ibn Ezra is cited a number of times in *TTP*; in contrast, it is unlikely that Spinoza knew the Franco-German school of literalist biblical exegesis of which Samuel ben Meir (Rashbam) was the chief representative.

[55] *TTP* Ch. 7; *G* III 105.   [56] See, e.g., *Ep.* 21; *G* IV 132.

[57] *TTP* Ch. 7; *G* III 108; Spinoza seems to take the word to mean an actual staff used by an elderly person; in any event, he privileges the reading in Hebrews over the Masoretic vocalization.

"And he sat up on the bed (or staff)" [Gen. 48:2]. Thus, Jacob put it under his anus.[58]

For the Jewish polemicist, if the Christian insists that Jacob bowed to the cross, then they must also admit that ultimately he disgraced it when he sat on it. For Spinoza, the message was that if one cannot rely even upon the biblical text itself, then certainly the traditional exegesis of the two religions is unreliable.

Another possible influence of the medieval Jewish–Christian debate can be seen in Spinoza's discussion concerning how one can determine if a person claiming to be a prophet is actually a prophet. The topos of the signs of prophecy has its origins as far back as at least the ninth century in the three-way debate among Judaism, Christianity, and Islam in Islamic countries. Since Jews generally denied that Muhammad was a prophet (certainly in terms of prophecy for Jews) and also that Jesus had any claim to prophecy, let alone messiahship or divinity, it was important to clarify how one can determine whether someone is a prophet. In general, Jews claimed that miracles were not sufficient to establish a person's bona fides as a prophet; the content of the prophetic message is the most important determinant. Miracles were generally seen as a necessary, but not sufficient, condition for prophecy. This is a theme which runs from the works of Saadia Gaon in the tenth century to Joseph Albo in the fifteenth. Maimonides did not consider miracles as a necessary condition of prophecy; one had to investigate the message of the prophet as well as his morality to determine whether his claim of prophecy was legitimate.[59]

Spinoza was also concerned with establishing guidelines for determining the validity of claims of prophecy. Unlike Maimonides, who taught that prophets are distinguished by excellent intellectual and imaginative faculties, Spinoza believed that prophets had only vivid imaginations. He did write in addition, though, that the prophets must provide signs and that their hearts must be "inclined toward the right and the good."[60] For Spinoza, as for the medieval polemicists, the content of prophecy is

---

[58] Berger, *Jewish-Christian Debate*, p. 59; the expression "there is a mother to tradition," means that the text may be read according to the consonants without regards to the traditional vocalization; Berger gives Christian sources for identifying the staff with the cross; *Jewish-Christian Debate*, p. 248.

[59] The Islamic background is discussed by Stroumsa, "Signs of Prophecy." For Saadia, see *Beliefs and Opinions*, 3:8, pp. 163–164, and my "Saadia on Christianity and Islam"; for Albo, *Book of Principles*, 1:18, Vol. I, pp. 153–165. In Maimonides's *Guide of the Perplexed*, 2:40, miracles are not considered a necessary condition of prophecy, but they are considered a sign in his *Epistle to Yemen*. Maimonides's discussion is directed against Islam, Albo's against Christianity, and Saadia's against both.

[60] *TTP*, Ch. 15; G III 186–188 (the direct quotation is on p. 186).

its guarantee of validity, even if they differed as to what the content is. Furthermore, whereas the medievals' criteria were developed in order to refute the prophetic claims of Jesus (and Muhammad), Spinoza's reworking of those criteria allowed him to accept the New Testament as a work of prophecy.

The survey here of parallels between Baruch Spinoza's arguments and the medieval Jewish–Christian polemical literature not only expands the likely corpus of sources which were used by Spinoza and which shaped his world-view, but also allows us the possibility to reevaluate his relation to the two religions. In contrast to those who believe that Spinoza's attitude towards Judaism is much more negative than his attitude towards Christianity, because of his explicit criticism of the Hebrew Bible without a similar analysis of the New Testament, we see that the Christian religion received very critical treatment from Spinoza as well. Spinoza recognized the traditional Jewish arguments against Christianity and employed them in a controlled and careful manner. From hints in his *Theological-Political Treatise*, and from explicit statements in his *Letters*, we see that he had no more sympathy for Christianity than for Judaism. Both religions, from Spinoza's perspective, should have the same goal, namely bringing the masses to good behavior, but both have the same weaknesses, namely imaginative scriptural passages and irrational beliefs. If anything, Christian doctrines are considered more irrational than Jewish ones, which is the claim of the Jewish polemicists. In order for religion to play its proper role in society, it must be cleansed of its weaknesses. This is what Spinoza was attempting to do with his attacks on Judaism and Christianity. If Spinoza was more circumspect in his attacks on Christianity, saving them for private letters rather than published books, one can understand that in light of the historical context in which he wrote. In the final analysis, Spinoza adopted both the Jewish and the Christian polemical arguments, hoping thereby to produce a more progressive attitude towards religion in general. In contrast with the medievals, Spinoza did not think it was possible to defend one of the religions by attacking the other. For someone who knows how to interpret correctly the Holy Scriptures and who can use his God-given intellect, both religions are deficient.

CHAPTER 5

The early Dutch and German reaction to the Tractatus Theologico-Politicus: *foreshadowing the Enlightenment's more general Spinoza reception?*

Jonathan Israel

I THE EARLY EUROPEAN IMPACT

The old historiographical and philosophical *idée fixe* that during the century or so after his death Spinoza remained a scarcely studied and largely ignored figure whose philosophy played no substantial part in Enlightenment discussion down to the 1780s, dies hard. One scholar claimed in 1997 that Spinoza's position in the history of philosophy was a "strange one" since he was the "proponent of views which had no real effects in their time because they were overshadowed by the influence of Descartes and his successors."[1] Another historian of philosophy affirmed, in 2002, that the fact that Spinoza "in the two, even three generations that followed him had no historical-theoretical impact" [*in den zwei, ja drei Generationen, die auf ihn folgten, keine theoriegeschichtlich relevante Wirkung hatte*] was no accident as he was admired only by a tiny radical underground banished from respectable society and because his philosophy of religion is "incompatible with the programme of those enlighteners seeking to rationalize revealed religion or striving to reduce the latter to 'natural religion'" [*unvereinbar mit dem Programm derjenigen Aufklärer, die an einer Rationalisierung der Offenbarungsreligion arbeiteten oder ihre Reduktion auf eine "naturliche Religion" anstrebten*].[2]

One might ask whether anything could be more totally at variance with the facts than such still widely prevalent notions as these. For, in fact, it is impossible to name another philosopher whose impact on the entire range of intellectual debates of the Enlightenment was deeper or more far-reaching than Spinoza's or whose Bible criticism and theory of religion was more widely or obsessively wrestled with, philosophically, throughout Europe during the century after his death. If the great *Encyclopédie* of Diderot and d'Alembert allocates twenty-two columns of text to Spinoza,

---

[1] Mason, *The God of Spinoza*, p. 248.   [2] Schröder, "Die ungereimteste Meynung," pp. 136–137.

the longest entry for any modern philosopher, in its entry about him, as against the remarkably low figure of only four to Locke and three to Malebranche, in their corresponding entries, this was assuredly not because the editors of the *Encyclopédie* were so utterly unaware of what was relevant to their Enlightenment that they got their editorial priorities stupendously wrong or owing to some wholly inexplicable aberration that historians can in no way account for. The simple fact is – however much this runs counter to certain commonplace notions – that Spinoza was deemed by them to be of greater relevance to the core issues of the *Encyclopédie* not just than Locke and Malebranche but also Hobbes or Leibniz.

Both the *Opera Posthuma* (1678) containing the *Ethics* and the earlier *Tractatus Theologico-Politicus* (1670) had an immediate and huge Dutch, German, French, British, Scandinavian, and Italian impact. Indeed, the *TTP* of Spinoza undoubtedly figures among the most challenging and disconcerting books for its contemporaries ever published. Far from being ignored or marginal, it would be very difficult to cite any other book written in a European language, including English, more frequently discussed, refuted, and denounced, and, as part of this, scrutinized in detail, during the century and a half after its appearance. No doubt, Calvin's *Institutes* and Newton's *Principia* were venerated and held in far higher esteem by many; but these books were rarely discussed in detail by those who feared, rejected, or questioned their basic premises, so while these had countless admirers and some adversaries, they probably did not have large numbers of alert, close readers grappling long and meticulously with their every step with a view to seeking out every weak-point and invalidating their constituent arguments and basic logic.

One might perhaps cite Machiavelli's writings, Hobbes's *Leviathan*, Bayle's *Dictionnaire* or Locke's *Essay on the Human Understanding* as possible contenders with the *TTP* for wide notoriety combined with enduring intellectual impact in the form of debate and abrasive response. But even a cursory glance at the late seventeenth-century literature in Latin, French, German, Dutch, English, and Italian soon suffices to convince the impartial researcher that none of these matches the *TTP* or the *Ethics* as a candidate for the honor of being the most analyzed, refuted, and – what counts most – obsessively pored over, wrestled with, and scrutinized text of the era 1670–1820. Nor is this at all surprising if one recalls how most conventionally minded Enlightenment readers responded to reading these path-breaking books. For it seemed plainly evident that Spinoza was – as a prominent German adversary, Johann Musaeus, expressed it – not just "audacious, fanatical and contrary to all religion" [*homo perfrictor frontis,*

fanaticus, et a religione omni alienus] but also the surpassing "impostor
second to none" [*impostorem nulli secundum*].[3]

Due to the disruptive effect of the Third Anglo-Dutch War which for
some three years (1672–4) largely severed normal communication and commerce between the United Provinces and Britain, the initial impact of the
TTP in the English-speaking world was somewhat delayed by comparison with Holland and Germany. It was only in the mid and later 1670s
that Boyle, Hobbes, Oldenburg, Stillingfleet, Henry More, Cudworth, and
others – most probably including Locke – reacted to, wrestled with, and
sometimes, but not always, unreservedly condemned the *TTP*. While it is
not known exactly when Locke's (strictly internal and private) preoccupa-
tion with Spinoza began, it seems likely that the *TTP* seriously preoccupied
him from the fact that he had no less than three copies of the work in his
personal library.

Besides the delay the fact that the text circulated anonymously, and the
scarcity of first-hand knowledge in Britain about the circumstances of its
publication, created a degree of confusion and initial doubt as to who,
exactly, the author was and from what intellectual and cultural stables he
issued also after the war ended, in 1674.[4] The English Puritan minister,
John Wilson (dates unknown), for example, in his *The Scripture's Genuine
Interpreter asserted; or, a Discourse concerning the right Interpretation of
Scripture* (London, 1678), roundly denounces the *TTP*'s argument that
the "Prophets in their narrations, and in all matters of speculation (that is
whatsoever was not a matter of moral duty) disagreed among themselves;
and consequently that what is said by one, is not to be explained by
the words of another," a contention which, along with similar claims, it
seemed clear to Wilson, "does at once call in question the whole truth
and consequently the divine authority of the Scriptures."[5] But horrifying
though he considered this, he took little interest in the more philosophical
aspects of the text and was unperturbed by not knowing who the author
of this "piece of new divinity" was, referring to him merely as "a late
Belgick tractator." He supposed that he must be the same miscreant as
had anonymously published the *Philosophia S.Scripturae Interpres* (1666),
(actually, Lodewijk Meyer [1629–81]), an incorrect inference encouraged
by the fact that the edition of the *Philosophia* most commonly found in
the Anglo-Irish context, the 1674 octavo reprint, usually appeared bound

[3] Johann Musaeus, *Tractatus Theologico-Politicus*, preface.
[4] Israel, *Radical Enlightenment*, pp. 281, 283–284.
[5] Wilson, *The Scripture's Genuine Interpreter asserted*, p. 245.

together with the octavo edition of the *TTP* likewise clandestinely produced in the same year at Amsterdam.[6]

In France and Geneva, meanwhile, the *TTP*'s initial impact was delayed even longer owing to the severing of all commercial contact between the French monarchy and the Dutch Republic during the Franco-Dutch war of 1672–8.[7] Hence, although Huet and Justel found opportunities to examine the *TTP* somewhat earlier, it was not until the years 1679–80 that copies (both in Latin and French) reached the French-speaking world in any quantity and such prominent Catholic and Protestant figures as Arnauld, Bayle, Bossuet, and Le Clerc, began to study the text. The Geneva-born and raised Le Clerc, though he wrote nothing at this juncture, or later, directly in response was among the most profoundly affected by Spinoza's book. Both before and after his move to Holland in 1683, and his open conversion to the Remonstrant Church, he continued inwardly to wrestle with Spinoza's challenge. Nor was his an entirely tacit battle. In a letter to Bishop Kidder, in 1694, Le Clerc expressly affirms that many of the arguments he set out in his writings were in fact directed against Spinoza and his Bible criticism even though it was his practice, when engaging with him, not to mention Spinoza's name.[8]

The young Bayle, then teaching at Sedan, mentions Spinoza and his *TTP* for the first time in a letter dated Sedan, November 1677 where he refers to the "Theological-Political Treatise written by a Spaniard named Spinoza, if I am not mistaken" [*Tractatus Theologico-Politicus fait par un espagnol nommé Spinosa, si je ne me trompe*].[9] He had evidently heard more about Spinoza the next time he mentions him, in a letter of May 1679, where he assures his correspondent, Vincent Minutoli, that the anonymously published French translation of the *TTP* that had appeared the previous year under (among other false titles) the rubric, *Traité de cérémonies superstitieuses des Juifs* was certainly the book "most full of impious doctrines that I have ever read" [*le plus rempli de doctrines impies que j'aie jamais lu*].[10] From its content, it was not difficult for him to guess that "l'auteur est le fameux Spinosa" though Bayle appears not to have yet realized at that point that this text was simply a translation of the *TTP*, a work which, plainly, as yet, he did not know intimately.

---

[6] Bamberger, "Early Editions," pp. 20, 24; Israel, *Radical Enlightenment*, pp. 281, 283.

[7] Israel, *Radical Enlightenment*, pp. 284–285.

[8] See Jean Le Clerc to Richard Kidder, Amsterdam, Nov. 5, 1694 in Le Clerc, *Epistolario*, Vol. II, pp. 222–223; Israel, *Enlightenment Contested*, p. 35.

[9] Bayle, *Correspondance*, Vol. II, pp. 457, 459.   [10] Bayle, *Correspondance*, III, pp. 180–181.

By contrast, in Holland and Germany reaction was much more immediate and direct, dating from the early months of 1670 and, from the outset, and was far more specifically and purposely focused on the person and philosophy of Spinoza who, in any case, was considerably better known by the later 1660s in those countries than in France or Britain, owing to the previous success there of his 1663 commentary on the philosophy of Descartes, the only book published during his lifetime under his own name. By the mid-1660s, Spinoza was already a fairly well-known and respected as well as a rather controversial expositor of Cartesianism in the Lutheran and Dutch (and German-speaking Swiss) Reformed cultural contexts. Owing to these differences of timing and emphasis the early Dutch and German responses to the *TTP* were not just more consciously focused than were the early British and French reactions on the figure of Spinoza, and his philosophic endeavor, but also noticeably more concerned than the British and French responses with the relationship of Spinozism to Cartesianism and the general problem of how Cartesianism and the New Philosophy as a whole related to theology and university teaching.

2 THE EARLY DUTCH AND GERMAN RESPONSES

On the surface, at least, the early Dutch and German responses, like most of those that came later, look uniformly hostile and unreceptive. But here appearances are apt to be misleading. If one closely examines the "refutations," it becomes evident that some of the early response, like much of the later reaction in the early, mid and later eighteenth century, was by no means altogether unimpressed, unsympathetic, or unreceptive to Spinoza's general approach and arguments. While there was a great deal of outraged, highly rhetorical, and extremely hostile denunciation, there were also important instances, including Bayle's *Dictionnaire*, published at Rotterdam in 1697, and especially several of his later works, such as the *Continuation des Pensées diverses* (1704), where much of the denunciation was more pro forma than actual. In particular, it is both helpful and instructive to evaluate the initial reaction to the *TTP* in some degree as a set of early markers or signposts pointing out the lines of debates revolving around Spinoza's philosophy which in time led to some of the greatest, most prolonged, and most challenging philosophical engagements of the entire Enlightenment era.

One striking difference between the early Dutch and German reactions is that the latter seem in general to have been little noticed or discussed in the United Provinces, whereas in Germany the Dutch responses were among the best-known refutations in the period prior to the appearance of the long article on Spinoza published in 1697 in Bayle's *Dictionnaire.* This is evident, for instance, from Immanuel Weber's remark, in 1697: "in particular Spinoza has been refuted by Henry More, Mansvelt, Lambert van Velthuysen, Blyenbergh, Pierre Poiret, Abbadie, Christopher Wittichius, and Pierre Yvon" [*insonderheit haben den Spinozam* [in his *Tractatus*] *Henricus Morus, Mansveldus, Lambert Velthuysen, Blayenburgius, Petrus Poiret, Abbadius, Christoph Wittichius und Petrus Yvon widerleget*].[11] Among the best-known polemicists against atheism in Germany at the end of the seventeenth century, Weber was evidently more familiar with the Dutch than with the German rebuttals.

Although the *TTP* was clandestinely published in Amsterdam, falsely stating "Hamburg" on the title page, late in 1669 or early in 1670, it took some months before it was realized, in the Dutch universities, that its author was actually Spinoza, writer also of the well-known *De Principiis Philosophiae Cartesianae* (1663). The prominent Groningen professor, Samuel Maresius (Des Marets) (1599–1673), reports in a tract published later in 1670 that he had been making efforts to investigate the intellectual background of both the *Philosophia* and the *TTP* and discovered that the author of the latter was none other than "Spinoza, ex-Jew, blasphemer and formal atheist" whose "atrocious" views, despite the disclaimers of the Dutch Cartesians, derived, it seemed to him, precisely from Spinoza's Cartesian premises. In his opinion, this book represented as dire a threat to religion and theology as had ever been known. While Spinoza had also drawn on Hobbes and Machiavelli, he acknowledged, he attributes what he saw as his thoroughly pernicious arguments, including the principles of his Bible hermeneutics, chiefly to Cartesianism.[12]

Early in 1671, a theologian trained at Groningen under Maresius, Johannes Melchior (1646–89) seems actually to have been the first adversary of the *TTP* to publicly name and condemn its author, though owing either to a printing error or someone's confusion, his published rebuttal, namely J.M.V.D.M., *Epistola ad amicum, continens censuram libri cui titulus:* Tractatus Theologico-Politicus (Utrecht, 1671) utterly mangled Spinoza's name rendering it "Xinospa."[13] Melchior's *Epistola* focuses especially on Spinoza's refusal to regard the wording of Scripture as the word of God and his interpreting innumerable phrases and notions as only vague approximations to reality adjusted to the ideas of the common people or as products of

---

[11] Weber, *Beurtheilung Der Atheisterey*, pp. 140–141.   [12] Maresius, *Vindiciae dissertationis*, p. 4.
[13] J.M.V.D.M. [= Johannes Melchior], *Epistola Ad Amicum*, pp. 4–6.

the "imagination" of the prophets. The effect of Spinoza's *sophismata*, held Melchior, is to question the very reality of miracles, thereby usurping the will and decree of God, and misleading people into imagining that everything necessary for human salvation can be provided by natural reason and intellect alone. Behind Spinoza's Bible criticism, Melchior grasped, lurked an entire philosophy sustaining a purely secular conception of the universe and human life and one which leaves no room for supernatural agency, theology, or ecclesiastical authority. For Spinoza, he concluded, the will of God "is nothing other than the power of nature" [*non aliam esse quam naturae potentiam*]. Consequently, Spinoza's "false and absurd hypotheses" were far more likely, in his opinion, to destroy rather than stabilize the foundations of religion and the republic.[14]

Maresius and other leading Dutch theologians consciously and purposely linked Spinoza to what they saw as the menace of Cartesianism. Consequently, the response to the *TTP* in Holland remained from the outset heavily embattled and dual in character. Maresius and the strict Calvinist anti-Cartesians deliberately associated, or rather sought to smear, Cartesiansim with the *TTP* highlighting what they alleged was the peril inherent in Cartesianism as a way of countering what seemed on the verge of becoming the new philosophical consensus in the United Provinces. In this way, Spinoza, his philosophy, and his Bible criticism, became embroiled in a complex three-cornered fight. As Spinoza himself expressed the point in his letter to Henry Oldenburg, of September 1675, "the stupid Cartesians," in order to counter the suspicion under which they themselves labored "because they are thought to be on my side, ceased not everywhere to denounce my opinions and my writings, and still continue to do so."[15]

Leibniz, meanwhile, had encountered the anonymous *TTP* by September 1670 at the latest and had given it a first reading by October, making extensive marginal notes in the personal copy of the archbishop of Mainz, today at Erfurt, precious annotations discovered by Ursula Goldenbaum as recently as 1994. Thus, well before procuring his own copy from his regular bookseller in Frankfurt am Main, some months later, in October 1671, Leibniz already possessed a detailed knowledge of the text and had immediately begun to wrestle with the issues it raised.[16] In discussion with other learned men, he too denounced the book (as he had to) styling it a thoroughly pernicious work in various letters of 1670–2, including one to his former teacher, Jakob Thomasius (1622–84), a significant figure in the

---

[14] Melchior, *Epistola Ad Amicum*, pp. 33, 46–47.   [15] Spinoza, *The Letters*, p. 231.
[16] Otto, *Studien*, pp. 16–17; Lærke, "À la recherche," p. 387.

history of modern thought, professor of moral philosophy at Leipzig and the first true advocate of the study of the history of philosophy. Describing the Tractatus as "libellus intolerabiliter licentiosus" in this letter, of early October 1670,[17] Leibniz condemned it again in similar terms in a letter to Arnauld of late 1671. Yet, he made little secret of the fact that he also considered the book to be extremely formidable philosophically and its incisive author – whom he already knew something about earlier, for he had mentioned him in a previous letter to Thomasius, of 1669 – to be a thinker comparable to Bacon and Hobbes as one of the foremost of the moderns.[18] In the earlier letter, Leibniz maintains that none of Descartes's principal commentators whom he lists as "Clauberg, De Raey, Spinoza, Clerselier, Heereboord, Tobias Andreae and Henricus Regius" had added much of importance to Descartes's system.[19] But now he clearly felt he needed to grapple with the *TTP*'s far-reaching but complex implications not least in light of the huge furore the anonymous book was provoking in the Netherlands and Germany alike.

From his correspondent at Utrecht, the famous classicist Johannes Georg Graevius (1632–*c*.1705) (who was actually German), Leibniz heard as early as April 1671 that this newly appeared *liber pestilentissimus*, "following the Hobbesian path but going much further," had unquestionably been written by Spinoza.[20] In a second letter, Graevius assured him that Cartesianism was now becoming more and more dominant in the Dutch universities, Aristotelianism having been thrust utterly on the defensive although many of the preachers and much of the public remained extremely hostile to the New Philosophy. His friend and colleague, Regnerus van Mansvelt (1639–71), he added, was now the foremost champion of Cartesianism and the stoutest defender of its reputation in Holland and it was precisely because of the *TTP*'s pivotal importance in the intensifying struggle to establish the hegemony of Cartesianism that Van Mansvelt had decided, laying aside his other controversial battles, to concentrate his energies on a comprehensive refutation of Spinoza's "infamous and horrible book."

That Van Mansvelt did indeed lay aside other pressing tasks, in the midst of the escalating struggle between Cartesians and anti-Cartesians in the United Provinces, to martial his strength against the *TTP* is a point that needs to be stressed by scholars more than it has been. For while it is often

---

[17] Goldenbaum, "Der historische Ansatz," pp. 89–90.
[18] Goldenbaum, "Der historische Ansatz," p. 89; Friedmann, *Leibniz et Spinoza*, pp. 66–68.
[19] Friedmann, *Leibniz et Spinoza*, pp. 59–60; Bouveresse, *Spinoza et Leibniz*, pp. 220–221.
[20] Leibniz, *Sämtliche Schriften*, 1st series, Vol. I, p. 142. Graevius to Leibniz, Utrecht, April 22, 1671; Otto, *Studien*, p. 16.

implied that initial reaction to the *TTP* was indignant and loud but weak in comprehension and detailed debate, plainly Leibniz, Bayle, and Hobbes were not the only discerning early readers of the *TTP* who immediately grasped its philosophically formidable character, its wide ramifications, and the real nature of its message. There can be little doubt from their observations that not only Graevius and Van Mansvelt but also other early Cartesian readers such as Lambert van Velthuysen, the Danish Catholic convert, Nicholas Steno, and the Dutch Collegiant, Van Bredenburg likewise had an impressively accurate and penetrating grasp of what Spinoza was saying and what the underlying philosophical implications really were. The historical significance of this, as we shall see, is considerable.

Leibniz regarded the *TTP* as a challenge to be surmounted by honestly facing up to it, though this did not preclude his engaging in some of the usual vituperation at least pro forma. Regretting that a man of Spinoza's undoubted abilities "appears to have sunk so low," in his reply to Graevius, Leibniz agreed that Spinoza's Bible criticism has its roots in Hobbes's *Leviathan*. He also stressed the need for a formidable scholar to emerge who was Spinoza's equal in erudition, and knowledge of Hebrew while thoroughly differing from him in respecting the Christian religion, that is, someone capable of exposing his many paralogisms.[21] By the time Spinoza acknowledged in his one surviving letter to Leibniz, replying to Leibniz's first letter to him, early in 1672, that he was indeed the author of the *TTP*, offering to send him a copy from the Hague "if the *Tractatus theologico-Politicus* has not yet reached you," Leibniz had thus been studying and gathering information about the *TTP* for quite some time, in fact well over a year.[22] He also continued to wrestle with it in detail. At least one of his subsequently lost letters to Spinoza, sent in 1672 or soon afterwards, is known to have featured counter-arguments made in response to the *TTP*.[23]

The absence of an adequate refutation, and the necessity of coming up with one urgently and quickly, became the central theme of Leibniz's early concern with the *TTP*. Writing to Jakob Thomasius in 1672, albeit without revealing that he himself was now in correspondence with Spinoza and already knew quite a lot about the milieu in which that notorious text had been composed, Leibniz assured him that he considered the "anonymous" *theologico-politicus* to be a man of both exceptional intellectual acumen and unusual erudition. Thomasius, an anti-Cartesian Eclectic, had in fact

[21] Leibniz, *Sämtliche Schriften* 1st series, Vol. ii, p. 148. Leibniz to Graevius, Frankfurt, May 5, 1671; Friedmann, *Leibniz et Spinoza*, p. 64; Bouveresse, *Spinoza et Leibniz*, p. 221.
[22] Spinoza, *Ep. 46*.
[23] Friedmann, *Leibniz et Spinoza*, p. 66; Parkinson, "Leibniz's Paris Writings," p. 75.

already written against the *TTP*, and was indeed the first author, not just in Germany but anywhere in Europe, publicly to refute the book in print. He preceded the first Dutch refutation, that of Johannes Melchior, by many months. Having presented his text as a lecture at Leipzig, on May 8, 1670, a mere few weeks after the *TTP*'s appearance, Thomasius published the full version shortly afterwards under the title *Programma Adversus anonymum, de libertate philosophandi.*[24]

Condemning the anonymous tractate as highly damaging to religion, morality, and society, and explicitly linking the theological part of the work to Herbert of Cherbury and the political sections to Hobbes, Thomasius especially deplored its advocacy of full "freedom of thought and speech."[25] The worrying issues of freedom of thought and expression, here and elsewhere, seem to have been crucial to the initial German response to Spinoza's text and figured prominently in both German and Scandinavian Lutheran university theses throughout the early Enlightenment era. The prominence given to this aspect in Thomasius's refutation and in some of the other early German responses might well strike modern scholars as a feature sharply distinguishing German Lutheran reaction from the response in the Netherlands. Spinoza's Dutch detractors, it has been claimed, were apt to have fewer worries than their German counterparts regarding the *TTP*'s championing of the principle of free expression and *libertas philosophandi*; only the work's anti-scripturalism, it has been argued, seriously shocked Dutch readers.[26] However, this thesis, appealing to adherents of a now outmoded view of the Dutch Golden Age, is invalidated by the contemporary Dutch evidence. For Melchior's and Van Mansvelt's texts, and they were not alone in this, also express fierce criticism objecting not just to the principle of comprehensive toleration as enunciated by Spinoza but also to the extensive, albeit much lesser, degree of toleration then actually permitted in Amsterdam.[27]

Van Mansvelt rightly points out that "freedom to philosophize" as upheld by the Republic's leading Cartesian theologian-philosopher, Christopher Wittichius (1625–87), and other Dutch Cartesians, including himself, is in reality something quite distinct from Spinoza's "libertas philosophandi." What Cartesians understood by "libertas philosophandi," he explains, was broadly what had been legitimated by the States of Holland's decree on philosophy of 1656, namely, freedom to philosophize about everything that does not impinge directly on the interpretation of Scripture and central

[24] Freudenthal and Walther, *Die Lebensgeschichte Spinozas*, Vol. 1, p. 151.
[25] Walther, "Machina civilis," pp. 187–90.   [26] Van Gelder, *Getemperde vrijheid*, p. 270.
[27] Van Mansvelt, *Adversus Anonymum*, pp. 4, 362.

issues of theology.[28] What Spinoza meant by "libertas philosophandi" was something entirely different, being the right freely to overstep precisely those limits and favor "errors of every kind, that is to defend and propagate a profane license": "and, finally, he set out such principles which no sooner would they be admitted than all peace of the republic would necessarily be overthrown."[29]

The challenge Spinoza offered seemed to the Dutch no less than the Germans theological, philosophical, and political all at the same time. Leibniz, meanwhile, though likewise disinclined to embrace the standpoint of the Dutch Cartesians, was by no means ready to agree that his old teacher's intervention constituted a definitive or even approximately adequate response to Spinoza's arguments. Additional information about the Dutch reaction to the *TTP* reached him by letter from the Leiden Cartesian, Theodore Craanen (1621–90) who, in April 1672, assured him that Spinoza was now also rumored to have composed other works of like or even worse content than the *TTP* but which, owing to the general outcry against him, were expected to appear only after his death. Craanen readily agreed with Leibniz, in a further message, sent soon afterwards, that no adequate rebuttal of the *TTP* had as yet appeared, but unlike Leibniz confidently expected that the gap would soon be filled by Van Mansvelt's comprehensive text.

Leibniz evidently had something rather different in mind than either the Dutch Cartesians' or anti-Cartesians' predominantly theoretical, metaphysical, and dogmatic response and was seemingly no more impressed by these than he was by the refutation of Thomasius. Dismissing the latter's text, in a letter to his friend, the philologist and Lutheran Bible exegete, Gottlieb Spitzel, at Augsburg, of March 1672, as merely a "brief but elegant refutation" (while again concealing that he was corresponding with Spinoza), Leibniz sought to persuade Spitzel that what was needed to counter the *TTP* whose author "they say is a Jew" and who, with great learning as well as "much poison," had sought to overthrow the *antiquitatem*, *genuinitatem* and *auctoritatem* of Scripture, was a powerful and fully erudite refutation, one that eschewed not just all vituperation and rhetoric but also avoided the usual theological and metaphysical approaches (within which he doubtless included the Dutch Cartesian response) focusing instead squarely on the central hermeneutical and historical issues.[30]

---

[28] On this decree, see Israel, *Dutch Republic*, pp. 892–895.
[29] Van Mansvelt, *Adversus Anonymum*, p. 4.
[30] Lærke, "À la recherche," p. 390; Goldenbaum, "Der historische Ansatz," p. 94.

The author of a satisfactory rebuttal, Leibniz assured Spitzel, needed to be both intellectually incisive and highly erudite in Hebrew and other oriental languages "like you or someone like you." Spitzel failed to rise to the flattery, however, albeit in his next publication, he did devote several pages to resuming his attack on the *TTP* whose "fanatical" author had exploded all notion of Revelation, pulverized prophecy by reducing it to mere "imagination," and who perversely acknowledged no miracles or "opera supernaturalia."[31] Spitzel excused himself from such a difficult and exacting task as undertaking to compose a full-scale refutation of the *TTP*, by remarking that the "very learned Thomasius and his colleague Rappolt, at Leipzig" had already done so.[32] Friedrich Rappolt (1615–76), like Thomasius, had reacted at a very early stage to the *TTP*, in May 1670, and was likewise principally disturbed and appalled by what he saw as the adverse social consequences of the *TTP*'s arguments. He had especially deplored Spinoza's allocating the right to interpret Scripture for oneself to every individual and his subversively equating "religion" with justice and charity.[33] Outraged by the tract's attempt to redefine true "religion," maintaining that "adoration of God consists solely in justice and charity" [*cultum Dei in sola justitia et charitate consistere*],[34] Rappolt was equally incensed by the tract's wholesale elimination of ecclesiastical authority in favor of individual liberty of thought and expression.

A month later, Rappolt had resumed his polemic, producing a second and longer reply to the *TTP*, his *Oratio contra Naturalistas*. Here, he labels the *TTP* the worst and most virulent instance of *Naturalismus* to have thus far invaded German culture. Naturalism might be an ancient phenomenon reaching back to the ancient Greeks. But until it had been recently revived by the English "naturalist," Herbert of Cherbury, it had for centuries slept quietly posing no substantial threat. The situation had now changed and the most pernicious example of the new *Naturalismus* anchored in philosophy was undoubtedly the *TTP*, a devastating piece of philosophical corruption which he designated literally "soul-destroying" since neither the New Philosophy, nor any philosophy, can bring men to salvation – only religion and Revelation can accomplish that.[35]

---

[31] Spitzel, *Felix literatus*, pp. 143–145.
[32] Leibniz, *Sämtliche Schriften* 1st series, Vol. 1, pp. 193–195. Leibniz to Spitzel, March 8, 1672 and Spitzel to Leibniz, March 24, 1672; on Rappolt, see Freudenthal and Walther, *Die Lebensgeschichte Spinozas*, Vol. 1, p. 151 and Vol. 11, p. 75.
[33] Rappolt, *Opera theologica*, pp. 187–190 and Israel, *Radical Enlightenment*, p. 628.
[34] Rappolt, *Opera theologica*, pp. 2162–2163; Walther, "Machina civilis," p. 190.
[35] Rappolt, *Opera theologica*, pp. 1390–1391, 1404–1405; Friedmann, *Leibniz et Spinoza*, p. 62.

3 SPINOZA AND THE DUTCH ARMINIANS

Spitzel subsequently declined to combat Spinoza's hermeutics in detail and made no real effort to rescue miracles, on the latter front contenting himself with referring the interested reader to the Dutchman Batalier's *Vindiciae miraculorum, per quae divinae religionis et fidei Christianae veritas olim confirmata fuit, Adversus profanum auctorem* Tractatus Theologico-Politici (Amsterdam, 1673). Among the early reactions, Batalier's 103-page *Vindiciae miraculorum* was undoubtedly much more noticed than either Thomasius's tract or Melchior's *Epistola*, although neither of these was insignificant. Jacobus Batalier (1593–1672), a Remonstrant minister from The Hague, long at odds with the Dutch Reformed Church as well as with the Collegiant movement which adhered to more liberal theological principles than he could countenance, completed his vigorous defense of Christianity and the biblical miracles which has been designated the "second" Dutch refutation of the *TTP* only shortly before his death, in January 1672.[36]

Holding that the *TTP* outrageously distorts Scripture, not least by absurdly manipulating the story of King Solomon and presenting that monarch in a manner that is entirely unbiblical,[37] this text appears to have been the result of a concerted effort, almost an official Remonstrant group response, to the "Theologico-Politicus," in which, besides Batalier, Locke's future friend, Philippus van Limborch (1633–1712) played a substantial role.[38] At the heart of Batalier's critique is the idea that it is *stultissimum* (very stupid) to suppose that one man's philosophical reasoning could be supposed by anyone to carry greater weight than the direct experience of – and testimony to – the truth of miracles of all the apostles, evangelists, martyrs, and other doctors of the primitive Church since the first century AD. Were one to accept the *Theologico-Politicus*'s arguments, the reader would be obliged to conclude that in proclaiming miracles all these saintly figures were either absurdly confused or else infamous impostors.[39]

Almost from the outset, Van Limborch had taken it upon himself to alert like-minded theologians at home and abroad of the unparalleled danger and risks posed by the *TTP*. He appears to have been the first to announce the danger in England, sending a copy of the book to Oliver

---

[36] Van Bunge, *Johannes Bredenburg*, p. 143; Van Bunge, "On the Early Dutch Reception," p. 227.
[37] Batalier, *Vindiciae miraculorum*, pp. 36–39, 63.
[38] Van Bunge, "On the Early Dutch Reception," p. 227; Van Bunge, *Johannes Bredenburg*, pp. 143–144.
[39] Batalier, *Vindiciae miraculorum*, p. 97.

Doiley, on June 23, 1671, accompanied by a letter powerfully denouncing "this Theological-Political Discourse, whose author is believed to be
B. Spinoza, who from a Jew became a Deist if not an atheist" [*illum dis-
cursum Theologico-Politicum, cujus autor creditor Benedictus Spinoza, qui
ex judaeo factus est Deista, si non atheus*]. He assured Doiley, "I do not
remember ever having read a more pestilential book" [*Non memini me
pestilentiorem librum unquam legisse*].[40] Its author ridicules the prophets
and apostles, he observed, and denies miracles had ever occurred or ever
could. "There is a necessity to which God Himself is bound so that he
depicts God in such a way that he plainly appears to abolish Him" [*Datur
fatum, cui ipse Deus alligatus est; ita tamen Deum describit, ut eum plane
videatur tollere*].[41] Replying after reading the book some months later,
Doiley urged the need for *eruditi* in Holland, the land of origin of this virulent new pest of Hobbesian error, to refute its claims thoroughly, though
English writers such as Henry More and Richard Cumberland, he also
thought, being veteran opponents of Hobbes, could usefully contribute to
countering the "poison."

A decade later, in 1681, Van Limborch was to receive a letter from
his future close friend and ally, the young Jean Le Clerc (1657–1736), in
France, describing the powerful impact the *TTP* was then also having in the
French provinces. In his letter, Le Clerc asks whether the *TTP* had earlier
had a comparable effect in Holland. Van Limborch answered that "in our
country, the book has impregnated many minds, completely estranging
them from all religion."[42] He stuck to this view to the end of his life and
probably this had been his opinion all along.

The Batalier–Van Limborch response to the *TTP* was essentially an
Arminian theological reaction and, consequently, one which mostly avoids
the philosophical issues involved to concentrate on the challenge to scriptural authority. Perhaps the most formidable aspect of the *TTP*, viewed
from a historical perspective, however, was precisely that it set out a new
critical methodology and expertise in Hebrew philology resulting in a set
of extremely challenging propositions designed to curtail theology's sway
which are then pressed into the service of a general system and a body
of moral philosophy that is in turn integrally linked to a particular kind
of republican political thought. It was thus a work of criticism, theology,

---

[40] Van Limborch to Oliver Doiley, Amsterdam, June 23, 1671, printed in De Boer, "Spinoza in
Engeland," pp. 332–333.
[41] De Boer, "Spinoza in Engeland," 333.
[42] Le Clerc to Van Limborch, Grenoble, Dec. 6, 1681 and Van Limborch to Le Clerc, Amsterdam,
Jan. 23, 1682 printed in French translation in Meinsma, *Spinoza et son cercle*, pp. 523, 525.

philosophy, and political ideology all at the same time. Accordingly, it required a most unusual set of skills, going beyond what was available to Batalier and Van Limborch, to be able to grasp the full range of Spinoza's undertaking let alone adequately counter his incisive arguments.

4 VAN MANSVELT'S CARTESIAN REPLY

Given the broadly ascendant but still highly divisive role of Cartesianism in the Netherlands in the 1660s and 1670s, Maresius's insistence on linking Spinoza to Cartesianism was bound to be seen by many as a highly contentious and menacing challenge. Regnerus van Mansvelt (1639–71), professor at Utrecht and a fervent Cartesian, using the pseudonym "Petrus van Andlo" consequently produced a provisional riposte, or rather several ripostes, preceding his main refutation of the *TTP*, scathingly attacking Maresius who now in a theological alliance with the leading conservative Calvinist divine, Gijsbertus Voetius, the dominant figure at Utrecht University at the time. Above all, Van Mansvelt, a hardened controversialist as well as teacher of philosophy and key member of the Utrecht "Collegie van Scavanten," an association of Cartesians in that city, to which Graevius, Lambert van Velthuysen (1622–85), the well-known Reformed preacher and critic of Meyer, Louis Wolzogen (1633–90), and Frans Burman (1628–79) also belonged,[43] strove to discredit Maresius's and Voetius's efforts to interpret Spinoza as a thinker anchored in Cartesianism.

Van Mansvelt's main rebuttal of the *TTP* lay complete – apart from a final polishing up that he wanted to give it – at the time of his unexpected death, in 1671, and was publicly cited by Graevius, in the academic oration he delivered at his funeral. In his speech, Graevius praised Van Mansvelt's "most erudite" objections to that most detestable book the "*Discursus Theologico Politicus* [sic]" "than which none other is more pestilential or apt to overthrow the authority of sacred Scripture and every received idea about God" [*quo non alius pestilentior natus est ad auctoritatem sacri codicis et ominem de deo opinionem evertendam*].[44] In his refutation of the *TTP*, Van Mansvelt unrelentingly insists on the soundness of Cartesianism from a Christian standpoint, upholding its ability to accommodate all biblical categories of the supernatural and miraculous and pointing out that Cartesianism does not undermine belief in angels and other disembodied spirits in the way Spinoza's philosophy plainly does.

---

[43] Thijssen-Schoute, *Nederlands Cartesianisme*, pp. 444–445.
[44] Van Bunge, "On the Early Dutch Reception," p. 228.

Claiming never to have spoken to or laid eyes on Spinoza (unlike Grae-vius, Craanen, Van Limborch, Wittichius, and others) and to utterly loath his "absurd doctrines,"[45] Van Mansvelt stressed the overriding need, as he saw it, for a systematic differentiation of spirit and body and the advantages of Descartes's two-substance doctrine as a block against atheism and natu-ralism. Cartesianism, he contended, denouncing the anonymous author's "utterly absurd confusion of God with his creation, and body with spirit," was the one and only philosophy on the basis of which the essentials of Christianity could be fully safeguarded from Spinoza. Only Descartes's philosophy, he urged, could rescue the immortality of the soul and accom-modate the supernatural. Detesting Spinoza's metaphysics, Van Mansvelt was also greatly disturbed by the vision of a new kind of piety and morality encountered in the *TTP* and its wide-ranging implications for civil soci-ety. He countered by seeking to show that Spinoza's toleration, "piety," and recommended "peace of the republic" are all specious and in reality pernicious and socially damaging concepts.

Philosophically most corrosive of all, however, in his opinion, were the signs he detected in Spinoza's work of deliberate subversion of and appro-priation of Cartesian doctrines: "and seeing, how greatly were approved by the wisest the much sounder theses of recent philosophers daily discovered, by a legitimate method, from the principles most happily discovered by the most noble René Descartes, he substituted [for these] his most inept and most absurd chimaera which are completely alien to all truth and piety" [*et videns, quantum a sapientissimis probentur, Scholasticorum dictates, longe saniora recentiorum philosophorum dogmata, quae ex principiis a Nobiliss. Renato Des-Cartes felicissime detectis, legitimo methodo quotidie deteguntur, sub eorum nomine, ineptissima et absurdissima, ab omni veritate et pietate alienissima sua somnia, substituit*].[46]

Quoting numerous entire passages from the *TTP* as most of the early detractors did, Van Mansvelt totally repudiated his adversary's Bible crit-icism and especially his version of the "principle of accommodation," a notion first developed by his friend and colleague, Wittichius, a princi-ple which he does not dispute in itself but which he thinks his oppo-nent corrupts and abuses.[47] The "Theologico-Politicus" maintains that the "method of interpreting Scripture does not differ from the [correct] method of interpreting nature, but rather is wholly consonant with it" [*methodum*

[45] "Petrus van Andlo" [Regnerus van Mansvelt], *Animadversiones*, p. 7.
[46] Van Mansvelt, *Animadversiones*, p. 7.
[47] Van Mansvelt, *Animadversiones*, p. 163; Van Bunge, *From Stevin to Spinoza*, p. 50; see also Verbeek, *Spinoza's Theologico-Political Treatise*, pp. 95–97, 108, 119.

interpretandi Scripturem, haud differre a methodo interpretandi naturam, sed cum ea prorsus convenire].[48] But he presents this principle, objects Van Mansvelt, without first establishing the legitimacy of his method of studying nature. Even more dubious, he holds that knowledge of almost all things contained in Scripture is to be sought from Scripture itself, "just as is knowledge of nature from nature itself" [*sicuti cognitio naturae ab ipsa natura*]. This may be true of all revealed things in Scripture, contends Van Mansvelt, given that knowledge of Revelation can only be acquired from Scripture, especially with regard to such mysteries as the Holy Trinity, Incarnation, *justificatio per Christum*, etc., doctrines which have no equivalent in nature. But if what Spinoza means here is that almost nothing can be known about what is in Scripture, except from Scripture, then the principle is completely false.[49]

Here, as throughout his text, the "Anonymous" seeks by stealth to render reason and nature the sole valid and authoritative criteria for interpreting Scripture. He appears to concede that in separating theology from philosophy neither shall be ancillary to the other. But this, complains Van Mansvelt, is just a sleight of hand: the real consequence of his argument is that faith is completely subordinated to reason. Most intolerable of all is his final conclusion: "the good of the people is the highest law to which all laws both human and divine should be adapted" [*salutem populi summam esse legem, cui omnes tan humanae quam divinae accommodari debent*]. For quite the contrary, answers Van Mansvelt, "the people ought seek their salvation only in God and the observance of the divine laws, and all their human laws should be directed only to that goal whereby such observance should be promoted more and more in their lands and, finally, eternal salvation obtained by divine grace through Christ" [*populus non nisi in Deo et divinarum legum observancia suam salutem quaerare debet, et omnes suas humanas leges unice eo dirigere, ut magis magisque promeatur ea Dei in terris observantia, ac tandem divina gratia salus per Christum obtineatur aeterna*].[50]

Van Mansvelt's refutation was not a text that was quickly forgotten. Remarkably, as late as 1714, the Altdorf professor, Johannes Heinrich Müller (1671–1731), another who viewed Spinoza as the supreme "naturalist" of modern times, and who saw him as a philosopher who had striven not just to interpret the world but to change it, indeed the thinker who had gone furthest in setting the "natural" in fundamental conflict with the

---

[48] Israel, "Introduction" to Spinoza, *Theological-Political Treatise*, pp. xvi–xvii and Spinoza, *Theological-Political Treatise*, p. 98.
[49] Van Mansvelt, *Aversus Anonymum*, pp. 166–167.   [50] Van Mansvelt, *Aversus Anonymum*, p. 337.

"miraculous," selected Van Mansvelt's book in an academic lecture in which he read out several lengthy passages from the *TTP*, from all the vast and proliferating literature that had arisen in reply to it, as the most effective answer of all those available to students when viewed as a total system of thought, expressly preferring the work of this embattled, prematurely deceased young academic to Henry More's refutation and Frans Kuyper's far more widely criticized "Socinian" critique.[51]

The other major Dutch Cartesian refutation of the *Tractatus* published in 1674 was Van Blyenbergh's *De Waerheyt van de Chrstelijcke Gods-Dienst en de Autoriteyt der H.Schriften, Beweert Tegen de Argumenten der Ongodtsdienstige, of een wederlegginge van dat Godt-lasterlijcke Boeck genoemt* Tractatus Theologico-Politicus [The Truth of the Christian religion and Authority of Holy Scripture defended against the Arguments of the Irreligious, or a Refutation of that blasphemous Book entitled *Tractatus Theologico-Politicus*] (Leiden, 1674). Earlier a correspondent of Spinoza, the Dordrecht regent and merchant Willem van Blyenbergh (1632–96) wrote his refutation of the *TTP* as if he possessed no notion at all as to who its author was, proceeding in this fashion with the clear aim of exculpating Cartesianism (and himself) of any responsibility for Spinoza.[52] Van Blyenbergh's dedication of his book to the Dordrecht burgomasters was later scoffed at, in 1697, by the clandestine Spinozistic novel, the *Vervolg van 't Leven van Philopater* as if refuting the *TTP* was a worthy public service and appropriate concern of men of state.[53] Van Blyenbergh who in his refutation strove to be thorough, refuting Spinoza chapter by chapter, was dismissed by the *Vervolg*, not altogether unfairly, as a man of limited intellect incapable of distinguishing the sphere of reason from that of faith.

Of the early Dutch Cartesian reactions to the *TTP* that with which Spinoza himself chiefly engaged and the most interesting philosophically was that which emerged in 1671 initially as a letter from the pen of the Utrecht regent, Lambert Van Velthuysen (1622–85). The letter, dated Utrecht, January 24, 1671, about a year after the appearance of the *TTP*, was passed on to Spinoza by its recipient, the Rotterdam Collegiant Jacob Ostens, and later printed together with Spinoza's correspondence in the *Opera Posthuma* (1677), shortly after the philosopher's death. While Van Velthuysen totally rejects the theological implications of the *TTP*, and especially Spinoza's conception of God, counting him among those who, like Meyer, judge "philosophy to be the interpreter of Scripture" [*philosophiam*

---

[51] Müller, *Dissertatio*, pp. 15–17.   [52] Van Bunge, *From Stevin to Spinoza*, p. 115.
[53] Maréchal, ed., *Vervolg*, pp. 169, 171.

esse Scripturae interpretem],[54] he was by no means unsympathetic, it is important to note, to Spinoza's general separation of theology from philosophy (and politics), or his plea for *libertas philosophandi* (having himself been the frequent target of hard-line Calvinist polemical attacks).[55] Neither did he dislike the republican orientation of Spinoza's political thought. Like Leibniz's, Hobbes's and Bayle's evaluations, Van Velthuysen's was in several respects an ambiguous critique and, despite his lamenting in 1680 that the *TTP* had had a wide and pernicious effect, especially on young scholars, and other young people, an effect, he says, spread by Spinoza's disciples as well as by the book itself, his stance was one which continued to evolve from 1671 down to his restatement of his position in his *Tractatus de cultu naturali* (1680), in no small part, as he remarks at one point, through a series of long and arduous face-to-face discussions with Spinoza himself.[56]

5 THE LUTHERAN PERSPECTIVE

Cartesian, crypto-Socinian, liberal Reformed, and Arminian reactions to Spinoza, however important in the Dutch context and in the relatively small number of German Calvinist states, was of limited appeal in Germany more generally where at the time orthodox Lutheran scholars chiefly held sway in the intellectual sphere. Best known and regarded, and longest remembered, among the early German refutations was that published at Jena, with its preface dated April 1674, by Johann Musaeus (1613–91), a ninety-six-page tract, dedicated to Duke Johann Friedrich of Braunschweig-Lünenburg entitled *Tractatus Theologico-Politicus, Quo Auctor quidam Anonymus, conatu improbo, demonstratum ivit, Libertatem Philosophandi . . . Ad veritatis lancem examinatus*. Composed in the form of an academic dissertation, Musaeus's tract stands out less for its intellectual cogency than for the vivid way it alerts readers to the sweeping cultural, social, and intellectual implications of Spinoza's "freedom to philosophize" stressing what he saw as the great dangers lurking in the arguments Spinoza advances.

A zealous defender of (Lutheran) church power and authority and the princely court system prevalent at the time in Germany, Musaeus held that the *TTP* sought nothing less than to replace Christianity and the

---

[54] Blom, "Lambert van Velthuysen," pp. 203–204.
[55] Blom, "Lambert van Velthuysen," pp. 203–204.
[56] Blom, "Lambert van Velthuysen," p. 205; Klever, *Mannen rond Spinoza*, p. 204.

clergy who interpreted it for the people, with a new creed, denying the possibility of miracles and everything supernatural, a creed consisting of a comprehensive *Naturalismus*. Spinoza, he urges, replicating numerous lengthy quotations from the text of the *TTP*, is "second to none" as an advocate of a wide-ranging, comprehensive, and as he saw it, pernicious toleration, like that to be found in Amsterdam, one which will legitimize all strands of opinion and remove all barriers, including those presently operative against the Socinians and other anti-Trinitarians. This he regarded as a recipe for social disaster.

The *TTP* in effect proclaims the complete destruction of ecclesiastical authority and puts an end to the entwining of state and church power which the Church sanctions and maintains. What the author really means by "libertas philosophandi," argues Musaeus, is the right of every individual to investigate every aspect of truth and to have his own opinion about the state, religion, and morality, a conception rendering the laws of nature the sole and exclusive criterion of what is true and ending the Church's control over public morality.[57] "Who could be more troublesome in putting forward such depraved theses," asks Musaeus, "than this impostor born to work for the detriment of the Church and the republic" [*quam hic impostor, mango Ecclesiae malo, et reipublicae detrimento natus*]. Scripture does not concede to men liberty of thought and nor, quite rightly, holds Musaeus, does the princely state.[58] The real role of the Christian state, he contends, is by no means personal "freedom" as Spinoza maintans but rather to shepherd men in the right direction and towards the right beliefs, as well as to instill virtue whether by means of penalties or by exhortation and admonitions. Nothing is more apt to destroy the tranquillity of civil society and the state than the divisive freedom of thought and opinion advocated by the *Tractatus*. Philosophy is the weapon of this insidious assault on society and its subversive method is to pretend to demonstrate that "Holy Scripture is not the word of God" [*Scripturam sacram non esse verbum Dei*].[59]

Natural Law, in the hands of Spinoza, a "homo fanaticus" and a man alien to all religion, was apt to be reduced, he admonished, to mere appetite and the striving for power and self-expression of each individual. Like most German books of the time, Musaeus' text does not appear to have circulated much in the Netherlands although, ironically, according to Lutheran preacher Colerus, the philosopher's German biographer, at The Hague,

---

[57] Klever, *Mannen rond Spinoza*, p. 5.   [58] Musaeus, *Tractatus Theologico-Politicus*, p. 27.
[59] Musaeus, *Tractatus Theologico-Politicus*, p. 52.

and someone who held a high opinion of Musaeus, Spinoza himself must have read it, having possessed a copy of it in his own small library.

Two particular features of the early German responses to the *TTP* deserve to be highlighted and contrasted with the early Dutch responses. On the one hand, as Leibniz's intervention illustrates, and especially his letter to Spitzel, of 1672, the German reaction was less concerned with the underlying philosophical framework of Spinoza's book than challenging the hermeneutical principles which it enunciates and on which a large part of its argument is based. Obvious though it was that Spinoza "acknowledges no miracles or supernatural things in the Scriptures" [*miracula et opera supernaturalia in Scripturis agnoscit nulla*], as Musaeus puts it, the main thrust of the early German refutations lies in pointing out the social and institutional consequences of Spinoza's stance and, in particular, denouncing the comprehensive toleration, liberty of thought and expression, and general individualism which his text was clearly attempting to legitimate. There was also at least a hint of realization, notably in Musaeus, that this heretical philosopher's agenda represented a fundamental threat to a crucial pillar of princely and monarchical political thought and indeed to princely authority itself.

The Dutch denunciation of the *TTP*, by contrast, was led not by the public Church or theological exegetes seeking to challenge Spinoza's hermeneutics, but rather by Cartesians and Dissenters who were to a large extent in sympathy (even if by no means entirely so) with Spinoza's emphatic separation of philosophy from theology, and in some cases his plea for *libertas philosophandi* and freedom of expression, and even, in the latter case, elements of his portrayal of the Christ figure. The main attack in the Netherlands was undertaken by Cartesians and by fringe theologians, such as Batalier, Van Limborch, Bredenburg, and Kuyper, distinguished by an exceptionally strong commitment to the principle of toleration and freedom of conscience, albeit this freedom of thought and expression was adamantly set within clear limits in contrast to the comprehensive, unlimited freedom of thought advocated by Spinoza.

If Voetian hard-line Calvinists in the Dutch Republic reacted with no less indignation to the *TTP* than the Dissenters or the German Lutheran clergy, their response amounted less to a sustained attempt to answer the *TTP* than a rhetoric of denunciation and vituperation designed to discredit its separation of philosophy and theology which the Voetians saw as an attempt to destroy the theological way of viewing the universe and the human condition. This they did in part by decrying what they saw as the excessively elevated sense of itself which philosophy had acquired with the advent of Descartes and the Cartesians championing "freedom to philosophize," however mildly they did so by comparison with Spinoza. To this extent the ardently Cartesian physician, Cornelis Bontekoe, was certainly justified in his scathing retort to the reactionary Voetian, Doctor Helvetius, in the Hague, in a pamphlet published in 1680, in accusing the Dutch anti-Cartesians of avoiding the real fight. Helvetius had represented him as virtually a fellow-traveler of the Spinozists. Bontekoe replied that Spinoza's philosophy, contrary to what Helvetius was suggesting, actually diverges fundamentally from Cartesianism.

"What Cartesian," asks Bontekoe, "has ever said the Books of Moses are fabrications and that miracles are merely natural occurrences? No Cartesian ever uttered such blasphemy and you foul slanderer," he admonishes Helvetius, "will never provide even a single example." Furthermore, asserted Bontekoe, Spinoza's "abominable" teaching had been systematically refuted virtually only by Cartesians. "But despite all this you claim the Cartesians are 'Spinozists' even though they, and only they, I say, have refuted Spinoza namely via the pens of Professor Van Mansvelt and Blyenburgh, two well-known *Cartesianen*; indeed, other than Cartesians there has been no one among all the other philosophers and theologians, however much they always shriek against atheists who either dared or was willing to enter into combat with that monster. Yet despite this you claim that the Cartesians are *Spinosisten* although they and they alone, I say, have combated Spinoza!"[60]

The view that Cartesianism was the underlying culprit and should be made to carry the responsibility for the emergence of Spinozism remained a widespread tendency in Dutch culture and found some ready supporters elsewhere, not the least of whom was the Cambridge don, Henry More. "I was informed out of Holland, from a learned hand there," More assured Robert Boyle, in a letter of December 1676, having only recently discovered that "Spinoza, a Jew first, after a Cartesian, and now an atheist, is supposed the author of *Theologico-Politicus*," "that a considerable company of men appeared there, mere scoffers at religion, and atheistical, that professed themselves Cartesians: and that his [i.e., Descartes's] philosophy may naturally have such an influence as this, I can neither deny, nor could conceal in my preface to this book [i.e., his own refutation of the *Tractatus*]."[61]

[60] Bontekoe, *Brief Aen Johan Frederik Swetzer*, p. 38. (I am indebted to Annette Munt for drawing my attention to this rare tract in the Library at Wolfenbüttel.)
[61] Boyle, *Works*, Vol. v, p. 514. More to Boyle, Cambridge, Dec. 4, 1676; Cristofolini, *Cartesiani e Sociniani*, pp. 118–119.

6 THE SOCINIAN PREDICAMENT

To conclude this survey of early Dutch and German responses to the *TTP*, it is necessary to glance at two further Dutch refutations of the *TTP* which stand out in the one case for its overall grasp of Spinoza's intentions and tendency to merge Cartesianism and extreme Dissenting principles with unusual and striking effectiveness, preparing the ground for a Socinian alliance with Spinozism, and the other for laying down the lines of a Socinian anti-Spinozism. The former was the *Enervatio Tractatus Theologico-Politicus* (1675) by the Rotterdam Collegiant, Johannes Bredenburg (1643–91). Bredenburg was at this time uncompromising in defending the Cartesian conception of reason and seeking to render compatible a systematically philosophical view of the world with his Socinian-Collegiant conception of Christianity, an undertaking which subsequently embroiled him in serious conflict with his fellow Collegiant critics (and a task in which he later admitted to have failed, leading him to seek refuge in a form of double truth and finally pure fideism).[62]

Bredenburg lacked academic training. His *Enervatio* was translated for him into Latin, from his original Dutch, and he seems to have gained his knowledge of Descartes as well as of Hobbes, Meyer, and Spinoza entirely from reading the available translations in Dutch. Nevertheless, he is by no means unskilled or uninteresting as a philosopher. For Bredenburg saw few difficulties with Spinoza's sweeping plea on behalf of toleration and liberty of the press and was not particularly averse to his view of Christ as non-divine but rather a man uniquely inspired through some special communication with God. What Bredenburg did find difficult to accept was the unlimited sway of reason in Spinoza's argumentation, and the complete elimination of miracles and the sacred status of Revelation.

Bredenburg maintained, rightly enough, that the entire argument of the *TTP* relies not on its admittedly impressive display of hermeneutical skills which is in some degree merely an adornment and diversion, but rather on a formidable, undeclared, hidden philosophical system. In 1675, Spinoza's *Ethics* was, of course, still unknown and it has been argued by a number of scholars that Bredenburg could only have arrived at his relatively sophisticated grasp of Spinoza's system from reading an unpublished manuscript version of either the *Ethics* or the earlier *Korte Verhandeling*, which might have been made available to him by one of Spinoza's Socinian-Collegiant

---

[62] Kolakowski, *Chrétiens sans Église*, pp. 250–276.

allies such as Jarig Jelles.[63] But while it is true that Bredenburg could only have known of the distinction between *natura naturans* and *natura naturata* which he cites but is nowhere expressed in the *TTP*, from either conversation or else seeing an as yet unpublished text, his argument is in the main squarely based on the text of the *TTP* itself. Besides, other writers before him, such as Batalier, Van Limborch, Leibniz, and Musaeus, were also plainly aware of the philosophical identification of God and Nature in the text.

Bredenburg was alone, though, in maintaining in a sustained fashion, as the core of his counter-argument, that it is by identifying God with Nature that Spinoza constructs a metaphysics which abolishes divine providence and the judgments of a knowing God. The reason the *TTP* denies "the power of God to act over and beyond the laws of Nature," explains Bredenburg, lies in the anonymous author's "identifying Nature with God himself."[64] Bredenburg, then, was quite effective in demonstrating that the *TTP* is not based on biblical exegesis, as Spinoza claims, at all but is actually based on a concealed and "atheistic" system of philosophy. But he was much less effective at dismantling the basic premises of that semi-concealed system. His philosophical armory, essentially just Descartes's two-substance doctrine and his principle that the incorporeal, spiritual part of man, his soul, cannot be subject to physical laws in the same way as natural bodies are, proved inadequate for the task. It was doubtless in part because Bredenburg concentrates on the philosophical aspects of the *TTP* leaving largely intact its arguments for toleration and freedom of thought that Bayle later chose this book in particular, from among the large mass of earlier literature discussing Spinoza's system, for detailed scrutiny in his long article on Spinoza in his *Dictionnaire*,[65] though there was doubtless also another factor at work here. For what especially drew Bayle to Bredenburg's *Enervatio* was certainly the Collegiant's manifest inability to demolish Spinoza's arguments combined with his exceptional insight into how far they extended. While Bredenburg expresses a sincere antipathy to Spinoza's determinism, rejection of miracles, and equation of God with Nature in this book, it is nevertheless true that here too his refutation ends up being less a refutation than a heartfelt sigh at finding himself trapped in an agonizing philosophico-theological predicament.[66]

---

[63] Van Bunge, "Early Dutch Reception," pp. 229, 234; Van Bunge, "Johannes Bredenburg," pp. 322–326.

[64] Bredenburg, *Enervatio*, pp. 63–66; Wielema, *Filosofen*, p. 44.

[65] Bayle, *Écrits sur Spinoza*, p. 23.

[66] Scribano, "Johannes Bredenburg," pp. 67, 73; Van Bunge, *Johannes Bredenburg*, pp. 137–138.

The fact that Bredenburg himself later adopted a philosophical stance close to that of Spinoza and was denounced as a virtual "Spinozist" fitted perfectly with Bayle's deliberate tactic of underlining the formidable character of Spinoza's philosophy as part of his seditious campaign to further much the same separation of theology from philosophy, secularization of morality, and advancement of toleration, as was advocated by Spinoza himself. According to the Counter-Enlightenment writer and foe of Bayle, from Lorraine, Pierre Poiret (1646–1719), in his *Cogitationes rationales de Deo, anima, et malo* (1677), Bayle's praise of Bredenburg is just a strategem to draw the reader's attention to the latter's subsequent Spinozism and insinuate that Bredenburg (and Bayle) had the best insight into Spinoza while all along neither of them actually refuted Spinoza in earnest but were just throwing dust in readers' eyes in order surreptitiously to propagate Spinozism.[67]

Bredenburg's text was widely condemned but less severely criticized for furthering some of the same principles as Spinoza's than the slightly earlier *Arcana Atheismi revelata* (1676) of Frans Kuyper (1629–91). Kuyper, a Socinian Anabaptist fideist and "*anti-philosophe* avant la lettre," later emerged as Bredenburg's principal opponent during the Dutch Collegiant movement's bitter internal disputes and was the prime mover of the so-called "Bredenburgse twisten," a fierce controversy over Spinozism which virtually tore the Dutch Collegiant movement apart during the course of the 1680s.[68] Once a student at the Remonstrant seminarium in Amsterdam and even briefly a Remonstrant minister himself, until expelled from that church due to his opposing child baptism, in 1653, Kuyper was far from sharing the confidence in reason professed by the early Bredenburg or Arminian divines like Van Limborch, Batalier, and Le Clerc; rather he was a dogmatic anti-Trinitarian scriptural fundamentalist.

What is chiefly striking about Kuyper's forceful 304-page refutation of Spinoza's book is that practically all commentators, of whatever stripe, indignantly repudiated it. Like Van Limborch, Van Velthuysen, Bekker, the Jewish writer, Orobio de Castro, and many others, Kuyper held that there had been a sudden but widespread increase in the prevalence of "atheism" amongst the wisest and best minds in the 1670s, a shift attributable to nothing else, in his view, than the utter inadequacy of the arguments with which philosophical atheism was being combated as was evident from the flagging efforts to refute the *TTP*. Proceeding quite differently from

[67] Poiret, *Cogitationeum*, pp. 14–15.   [68] Fix, *Prophesy and Reason*, pp. 215–247.

Bredenburg, Batalier, Van Mansvelt, or Spinoza's other critics, Kuyper
fiercely repudiates Spinoza's hermeneutics by advancing an alternative set
of rules for interpreting Scripture, rather than launching any attack on the
reasoning underpinning his philosophy.[69] Opposing Spinoza's strictures
about the deficiencies of the biblical text as we have it and his rules of text
criticism, he pronounces Spinoza's claim that several books of Scripture,
such as Matthew's Gospel, Job, and the Letter to the Hebrews were originally composed in another language than that in which we have them, a
thesis which conflicts with the best available scholarly opinion.[70]

Scripture, for Kuyper, is God's direct decree and commandment to men.
But this cannot be proved by reason. Spinoza tries to prove that there are no
miracles since "there is nothing that vexes atheists more than miracles and
because there is no more effective argument for God's existence, omnipo-
tence and providence than miracles." But he is right in asserting that if
God is nothing more than just a "natural and necessary chain of causes,"
and reason provides no means to demonstrate otherwise, then there would
and could be no miracles. Nature's laws are manifestly God's decrees and
wishes, and reason on its own, he readily acknowledges, can yield no certainty as to whether these decrees are eternal and immutable.[71] Hence,
philosophy is a useless tool in the sphere of religion, morality, and men's
duties. Only felt, emotional, experienced, faith, a faith of weeping and
feeling,[72] can prove God's existence and providence and God's commands
for men. Fideism alone, and not philosophy, can prove Spinoza wrong. The
only other serious element of argument on which he grounds his rejection
of Spinoza's system in the *TTP* is a version of the argument from *consensus
gentium*. One has to accept, he grants, that philosophical reason on its own
cannot show us the truth about God and that nothing in Nature proves
that it was created by a benevolent divinity.[73] But the fact that all peoples
everywhere "with very few exceptions" [*paucissimis exceptis*], whatever the
hatreds and geographical distances that divide them, trace their origin, and
that of the world, to a God the Creator, demonstrates, he argues, that this
is known to all by a process of Revelation.

Kuyper was quite prepared to admit, then, that if one relies on philosophy, reason alone, then it is impossible to counter the anonymous
author's arguments, including his horrifying conclusion that "there is no

---

[69] Fix, *Prophesy and Reason*, pp. 282–283.   [70] Kuyper, *Arcana*, pp. 80–83.
[71] Kuyper, *Arcana*, p. 64; Kolakowski, *Chrétiens sans Église*, pp. 258, 263.
[72] Van Bunge, *Johannes Bredenburg*, p. 92.   [73] Kuyper, *Arcana*, pp. 264–265.

God other than Nature" [*nullus aliud Deus est praeter Naturam*].[74] Indeed, he insists that "no authority and no religion is known to us by natural reason alone" [*nullum Numen nec ullam religionem, ex solo naturali lumine nobis esse cognitam*].[75] This was Counter-Enlightenment in its purest form. Like Jacobi later, during the German *Pantheismusstreit*, Kuyper was in effect saying that those who chiefly prize reason and seek enlightenment or clarification in philosophy have no case against Spinoza and every jus-tification for being Spinozists. However, even if Spinoza's reasoning about metaphysics as such is correct, it does not follow that his moral philosophy is equally cogent: for it is incoherent, philosophically as well as theologi-cally, countered Kuyper, to hold that Man's "highest good lies in knowledge and love of the true God."[76] If Nature is our only God then the correct inference should be that Man's highest good lies in the "enjoyment" of nature in the here and now, that is in gaining as much worldly pleasure for himself as he can[77] [*Non consistit summum nostrum bonum, in Dei veri cognitione, sed in ejus fruitione*].[78]

Not surprisingly, both the Dutch Reformed Church and the States of Holland deemed Kuyper's *Arcana Atheismi* an exceptionally perni-cious book, hardly less damaging than the *TTP* itself, so that it had the rare distinction of being formally banned by States decree, in 1678, alongside Spinoza's *Opera Posthuma*, Meyer's *Philosophia* and Hobbes's *Leviathan*. The Dutch intellectual community, Reformed Cartesians and anti-Cartesians and Arminians alike, rejected this text more or less *en bloc* and *in toto*. Likewise, the Cambridge don, Henry More, in his refutation of 1679, labeled Kuyper's book altogether insidious and the great German polymath, Morhoff, judged that Kuyper's irreparable defect was to have rebutted Spinoza's *TTP* only *languide* [feebly].[79] From a strictly religious standpoint, one cannot question Kuyper's sincerity, the accusations of insin-cerity and hyprocrisy leveled against him at the time being impossible to square with the rest of his literary output and the undeniable consistency of his anti-philosophical stance. Yet, in practice many of his arguments could readily be used to support atheistic philosophies and Spinozism,[80] and his stance functioned rather like Bayle's "fideism" real or alleged, whether or not Bayle intended it so, as effectively a helpful prop to Spinozism.

---

74 Kuyper, *Arcana*, pp. 36–40; Wielema, *Filosofen*, pp. 51–52.
75 Kuyper, *Arcana*, p. 263.   76 Kuyper, *Arcana*, pp. 40–42.
77 Kuyper, *Arcana*, pp. 42–44.   78 Kuyper, *Arcana*, p. 44.
79 Henry More, *Ad V.C.Epistola altera*, p. 565; Weber, *Beurtheilung*, p. 55.
80 Van Bunge, *From Stevin to Spinoza*, p. 136; Wielama, *Filosofen*, p. 51.

Kuyper totally rejected Cartesianism, and the path of "philosophy" generally, alleging against Bredenburg – whose Cartesian strategy he deemed wholly disastrous – that knowledge of God and spiritual matters is attained only by embracing the truth of Revelation, miracles, and daemonology.[81] It was basic to his critique of Bredenburg and the Cartesians, as well as of Spinoza, that neither religious truth, nor right and wrong or any element of human morality, can be demonstrated by reason and that the morality essential for society derives from Revelation and God's direct decree alone.[82] If by reason we can determine neither that God exists or does not exist, nor that religion should or should not be observed, "from the natural light alone it is not possible to show that human actions are either good or bad" [*quamvis ex solo naturali lumine non ostendi possit, actiones humanas bonas vel malas esse*].[83] Here too, Kuyper tends to acknowledge rather than deny the force of Spinoza's critique of conventional moral teaching as well as of religion and miracles.

7 CONCLUSION

Many comments by intellectual historians and historians of philosophy about the early impact of Spinoza's thought suggest there prevailed more or less everywhere a fairly uniform pattern of rejection, denunciation, and repudiation. The almost universal claim in the modern scholarly literature is that prior to the 1780s Spinoza was not seriously engaged with. Closer scrutiny of the early reaction to the *TTP* quickly reveals that this is not actually so. Even the earliest reactions in Holland and Germany demonstrate a wide variety of conflicting responses which were indeed in part confessional, much depending on whether the critic was a Calvinist, Lutheran, Arminian, or Socinian Collegiant but which were even more varied from the standpoint of philosophy and the question of the status of reason. It is remarkable what a high proportion of the early antagonists were perfectly willing to embrace this or that slice of Spinoza's argument, sometimes his plea for toleration, sometimes his hermeneutical method, on occasion his firm separation of philosophy from theology, and in the Socinian case his view of Christ and the essential logic of his underlying philosophy as such. The primary lesson to emerge from this is that Spinoza, far from being an outsider or an isolated figure in the culture of his time was – and

[81] Van Bunge, *Johannes Bredenburg*, pp. 91–96.
[82] Van Bunge, *Johannes Bredenburg*, pp. 265, 267–268.
[83] Van Bunge, *Johannes Bredenburg*, p. 249; Wielema, *Filosofen*, pp. 54–55.

was also seen to be – a philosopher, however subversive and innovative, deeply embedded and enmeshed in the central issues of his cultural world. In the light of this, it is hardly surprising that the early Dutch and German reactions to the *TTP* turn out to have foreshadowed the wide variety of positions surrounding Spinoza's philosophical challenge characteristic of the Enlightenment as a whole.

CHAPTER 6

G. W. Leibniz's two readings of the Tractatus Theologico-Politicus

Mogens Lærke

I INTRODUCTION

Spinoza famously concluded the preface of the *Tractatus Theologico-Politicus* by requesting that "common people" should not read his book, because they would only "make trouble by interpreting it perversely," while insisting that its contents would be "extremely useful" for the "philosophical reader" [*philosophe lector*].[1] The question concerning the intended or, as it were, ideal or potential reader of the *TTP* has been extensively discussed by numerous commentators since Leo Strauss.[2] These discussions have been very helpful for clarifying the terms upon which Spinoza's reasoning relies and for understanding the motivations which led him to write the treatise. In order to complete such a historical, contextual approach to Spinoza's text, I believe, however, that we must also take into account the *actual* readers. The reception of the *TTP* constitutes an integral part of its historical meaning, whether this reception corresponds to Spinoza's intentions or not. This applies in particular when it comes to the reception of the book by readers that Spinoza would himself have found suitable. In the following, I will thus consider the question of how informed philosophical readers of Spinoza actually did understand him by examining one particular case, namely G. W. Leibniz.

One could object that Leibniz, who grew up in Leipzig in an intellectual milieu which was hardly open to modern philosophy but constituted one of the bastions of Lutheran orthodoxy, was not sufficiently free from such

The text is based on Part II of my *Leibniz lecteur de Spinoza. La genèse d'une opposition complexe.* I use the following abbreviations for the works of Leibniz: A = *Sämtliche Schriften und Briefe*, ed. Akademie Verlag. NB: the abbreviation A II-1² refers to the new, improved edition of the volume A II-1; GP = *Die philosophischen Schriften*, ed. C. I. Gerhardt; Dutens = *Opera Omnia*, ed. L. Dutens; Grua = *G. W. Leibniz. Textes inédits*, ed. G. Grua. Unless otherwise indicated, translations are my own.
[1] Cf. *TTP* Preface; *G* III 12.
[2] Cf. Strauss, *Persecution and the Art of Writing*, pp. 162–163; Smith, *Spinoza*, pp. 38–54.

prejudices as would disqualify him as a true *philosophe lector* in Spinoza's eyes. It is an objection easily countered. In fact, Spinoza himself explicitly admitted Leibniz into the circle of "philosophical readers." Thus, in 1671, he offered to send Leibniz a copy of the *TTP* (implying that he considered him fit to read it). Furthermore, in a letter to Hermann Schuller from 1675, Spinoza qualified the German philosopher as "a person of a liberal mind and well versed in every science."[3] There can be no doubt that Spinoza considered Leibniz to be a qualified reader of his book.[4]

First, I consider in some detail the historical and biographical context of Leibniz's reception of the *TTP*. He read the work twice, first around 1670 when he was living in Mainz, and then once again around the end of 1675 in Paris. Next, I will turn to a discussion of how Leibniz situated Spinoza and the *TTP* in the intellectual landscape of the time. I examine how Leibniz interpreted Spinoza's position in relation to the sect called Socinianism, in relation to the rationalistic biblical exegesis developed by Lodewijk Meyer and, finally, in relation to Thomas Hobbes's theory of natural right. The objective of these analyses is not to give an exhaustive account of Leibniz's own position on the issues discussed in the *TTP*. I have done that elsewhere.[5] The objective is only to see just how discerning a reader of Spinoza Leibniz was, i.e., to determine the extent to which he recognized the originality of Spinoza's position.

2 THE FIRST READING OF THE *TTP*

The *TTP* was published anonymously in 1670. It did not take long before Leibniz heard the first rumors about the book. As early as October 1670, he wrote from Mainz to his former professor in Leipzig, Jacob Thomasius:

---

[3] *Ep.* 72, *G* IV 305; Shirley 941.

[4] Spinoza did, however, refuse Schuller's suggestion that Leibniz should be allowed to consult Tschirn-haus's copy of the *Ethics*, arguing that it would be "imprudent," because he did "not understand why he, a councilor of Frankfurt, has gone to France," and that he would prefer to wait until Tschirnhaus had a "closer knowledge of his character" (*Ep.* 72, *G* IV 305; Shirley 941). It is not clear what prompted this refusal. Did Spinoza suspect Leibniz of being a spy? Maybe, but Spinoza had also requested Tschirnhaus not to speak about the *Ethics* with Christian Huygens, which suggests that his cautious attitude towards Leibniz stemmed from worries of a more general nature (cf. *Ep.* 70 and 72, *G* IV 301–302 and 304–305; Shirley 937–938 and 940–941). In fact, the change of the political situation in Holland in the years after the assassination of the brothers De Witt in 1672 had forced Spinoza to become more prudent about the people to whom he vented his opinions. Only a few months before writing to Schuller, in July 1675, he had been forced to abandon the publication of the *Ethics* because of rumors "that a certain book of mine about God was in the press, and in it I endeavour to show that there is no God" (*Ep.* 68; Shirley 935).

[5] Cf. Lærke, *Leibniz lecteur de Spinoza*, pp. 93–359.

I have recently seen a tract from Leipzig, no doubt written by you, where you have dealt with the intolerably licentious book on the liberty to philosophize in the way it deserved. It seems that the author follows closely not only the politics, but also the religion of Hobbes, as it has been sufficiently outlined in his *Leviathan*, a book as monstrous as the title suggests. For there is nothing in the wonderful critique of the Sacred Scripture put into effect by this audacious man [*homo audax*], the seeds of which have not been sowed by Hobbes in an entire chapter of the *Leviathan*.[6]

The "tract" [*programma*] in question was a dissertation by Thomasius entitled *Adversus anonymum de libertate philosophandi* which had been published on the occasion of a lecture he had delivered on May 8, 1670.[7] In this text, Thomasius rejected the "liberty to philosophize" defended by the anonymous author. He denounced him as a "naturalist" nourished by the "two most pestilential movements of the century," namely "libertin-ism" and "contractualism," and argued that, by eliminating the speculative elements of religion, Spinoza's conception of faith was, in fact, atheist. Furthermore, he compared Spinoza's position to the political philosophy contained in Hobbes's *Leviathan* (1651) and his conception of religion to the deism developed by Lord Edward Herbert of Cherbury in the *De veritate* (1624).

Leibniz himself had acquired the *TTP* around the end of 1670, quite probably before he knew the identity of the author. The marginal notes in his copy of the *TTP* indicate that he was interested in Spinoza's biblical exegesis, and in particular the question of the authorship of the Pentateuch.[8] In a letter to Lambert van Velthuysen written in June 1671, Leibniz criticizes Spinoza's hypothesis according to which it was Ezra who gathered and wrote down the books of the Old Testament: "I am not going to be easily persuaded that the sacred books of the Israelites are by Ezra alone."[9] Furthermore, Ursula Goldenbaum has argued that a text written by Leibniz around 1670 entitled *Commentatiuncula de judice controversiarum* contains traces of a refutation of Spinoza.[10] This text does indeed discuss questions similar to the ones addressed in the *TTP*, such as interpretive authority in relation to Scripture and the use of reason and history for biblical exegesis.

---

[6] A II-1², 106.
[7] Incidentally, this text is also the first known public refutation of the *TTP*. See the commentary by R. Bodéüs in *Leibniz-Thomasius*, pp. 265–269.
[8] Cf. Leibniz, "Leibniz' Marginalien."
[9] A II-1², 196. For Spinoza, see *TTP* Ch. 8; G III 125–126: "If now we attend to the connection and theme of all these books, we shall easily infer that they were all written by one and the same Historian [. . .] Who he was, I cannot show so clearly, but I suspect that he was Ezra."
[10] Cf. Goldenbaum, "Die *Commentatiuncula*." On the *Commentatiuncula*, see also Antognazza, *Leibniz on the Trinity*, pp. 50–59, 74–76.

It is indubitably a crucial text for understanding Leibniz's position vis-à-vis rationalist theology. It mentions both Lodewijk Meyer and Ludwig Wolzogen. It does not, however, mention Spinoza at all and, in my view, it is not certain that Leibniz wrote the text with the *TTP* in mind (although I agree that it might be the case).[11]

It is not entirely clear when Leibniz identified Spinoza as the author of the pernicious treaty. It may have been very shortly after he acquired the work in 1670. We do know, however, that Johann Georg Graevius, a Cartesian professor in Holland, gave Spinoza away in a letter to Leibniz written in April 1671, explaining that the author of this "pestilential book" was an excommunicated Jew named Spinoza.[12] Shortly after, Graevius wrote Leibniz once again, informing him that Voetius's successor in Utrecht, Regnerus Van Mansvelt, was working on a refutation of Spinoza's "horrible book."[13]

During the same period, Leibniz was exchanging letters with Jacob Thomasius. It is therefore somewhat surprising that it is only nine months after Graevius had informed him about the identity of the author of the *TTP*, namely in January 1672, that Leibniz passes on this important piece of information to his professor.[14] Why did Leibniz not disclose Spinoza's identity before, for example in the letter he wrote in the summer of 1671? My guess is that Leibniz was not yet sure that Graevius's information was reliable. In October 1671, Leibniz had, however, taken the initiative to contact Spinoza himself. He sent him a letter which did not mention the *TTP*, but only asked questions concerning optics. Leibniz also offered to send Spinoza a copy of the *Hypothesis physica nova*, a treatise that he

---

[11] Goldenbaum bases her argument on a passage where Leibniz explains that those who affirm the truth of the Christian mysteries without understanding their signification are like parrots who repeat words without grasping their meaning (cf. A VI-1, 551). According to her, Leibniz has taken up this argument from Chapter 13 of the *TTP*, where Spinoza writes on the subject of our understanding of God's attributes: "So someone who doesn't have demonstrations doesn't see anything at all in these matters. If they repeat something they have heard about such things, it no more touches or shows their mind than do the words of a parrot or an automaton, which speaks without a mind or without meaning" (*TTP* Ch. 13; G III 170). There exists another possible source for this "psittacist" argument. While discussing Leibniz's use of the notion of "psittacism" in the *Nouveaux essais*, the nineteenth-century French child psychologist Ludovic Dugas mentioned in a footnote of *Le Psittacisme* (1896) that the metaphor also exists in Girolamo Cardano's *De subtilitate libri XXI*. Thus, in a reflection concerning the simultaneity of thought and speech, Cardano writes: "And yet, if the force of language is developed first, since man is born with the ability to speak, what prevents that he refers to things as he heard them, but without understanding them, like the magpie and the parrot?" (orig. 1550; I have consulted the 1559 Lyon edition, Book XVIII, 677; cf. Dugas, *Le Psittacisme*, pp. 1–2, note). In the mid-seventeenth century, the *De subtilitate* was a commonly read philosophical treatise. Leibniz undoubtedly knew it. This is a good place to thank Andreas Blank for some stimulating discussions about parrots and Cardano.
[12] A I-1, 142.   [13] Cf. A I-1, 144, 202.   [14] A II-1², 320.

had recently completed and that he used to introduce himself to other scholars (he also sent it to the Academy of Sciences in Paris and the Royal Society in London). Shortly after, in early November 1671, Leibniz received a very friendly and open response from Spinoza. This reply explains the change of tone in Leibniz's letter to Thomasius from January 1672: the "audacious man" [*homo audax*] that he was denouncing only a year before is now presented as "a very cultivated man" [*homo omni literatura excultus*] and a "distinguished optician" [*insignis Opticus*].[15] But Spinoza's letter also confirmed Graevius's information about the authorship of the *TTP*, for, in a postscript, Spinoza offered to send Leibniz a copy of the book.[16] Shortly after, now certain that Spinoza was in fact the author, Leibniz unveiled his identity to Thomasius.

In my view, this affair bears witness to Leibniz's caution in these matters. He was keenly aware that identifying the author correctly was crucial, in so far as circulating incorrect information could have considerable consequences for the person thus wrongfully implicated in the affair. We will find further evidence of Leibniz's prudence in his letter to Albert von Holten from February 1672. Here he writes: "That Spinoza is the author of that book is, as far as I can see, not so certain. Therefore I prefer not to name him, especially in public."[17] In fact, at this point, Leibniz could no longer nurture any serious doubts about the identity of the author. So how should we interpret his secrecy? Must we consider it to be an expression of the "duplicity" that so many commentators have accused Leibniz of when it came to his relations with Spinoza?[18] There can be no doubt that we should interpret the reply to Von Holten as tactical. Leibniz always wrote – and not only when it concerned Spinoza – with great prudence, taking into account the nature of his interlocutors. But this does not necessarily have to be interpreted in terms of hypocrisy or duplicity. If we consider more closely Leibniz's correspondent, we get a more nuanced response to the question. Only a few months earlier, in November 1671, this same man, Albert von Holten, had written the following to Leibniz: "The Jew Spinoza, who bears a name which is a bad omen, and who has not been afraid to give the worst of examples, will be flogged by the learned as he deserves."[19] This letter, which refers to a well-known pun on Spinoza's name – the Latin adjective "spinosa" means "thorny" – can hardly be considered a cool, intellectual reaction to the *TTP*. Indeed, given Von Holten's violent reaction to the

---

[15] Cf. A II-1², 320.   [16] Cf. *Ep.* 46, G IV 234; Shirley 885.   [17] A II-1², 325.
[18] See, among other texts, Meinsma, *Spinoza et son cercle*, pp. 291, 360–361; Vernière, *Spinoza et la pensée française*, pp. 99, 108, 254; Friedmann, *Leibniz et Spinoza*, pp. 250, 273.
[19] A II, 1², 303.

TTP, I find it quite plausible to interpret Leibniz's "lie" as an attempt to protect his new acquaintance in Holland from the over-heated reactions of a member of the Republic of Letters quite clearly unwilling to partake in a serene debate.[20]

Leibniz thus received a great deal of information about the general reactions to Spinoza's book in both Germany and Holland. All this epistolary activity testifies to the fact that Leibniz was highly interested in Spinoza's work, and I fully agree with Paul Vernière when he states that "it is not exaggerated to say that during these two years [i.e., 1670–71], the publication of the *Tractatus* was for Leibniz the greatest intellectual event in Europe."[21] After this, Leibniz recognized in the Dutch Jew an exceptionally erudite adversary. Before the publication of the *TTP*, he considered Spinoza with some contempt as just another Cartesian. Thus, in a letter to Thomasius from 1669, he counted Spinoza as a member of a group of Cartesian "paraphrasers" which also included Johann Clauberg, Johannes de Raey, Claude Clerselier, Adrian Heereboord, Tobias Andreae, and Henry de Roy.[22] This changed after he had read the *TTP* and identified its author.

But how, in Leibniz's view, should one deal with the work of a man who, at the same time, was "intolerably licentious" and "very cultivated"? To suppress the book through the available means of censorship was a solution that one should adopt only with the utmost prudence (although Leibniz was not as such against acts of censorship, and certainly not a partisan of the liberty to philosophize).[23] The best would be to refute it effectively. Thus, Leibniz wrote to Von Holten: "as for the book itself, it should be refuted, and indeed I could wish for something more erudite and solid than vehement and harsh (for such a style renders even the best of causes suspect)."[24]

Leibniz never attempted to do this himself. Why not? According to Spinoza, in order to reconstruct correctly the meaning of the Bible, one must not only be in possession of extensive philological knowledge of the sacred text and its history, but one must first of all be intimately familiar with the language in which it was originally written, i.e., Hebrew.[25] Now,

[20] Even after he left Mainz to go to Paris in February 1672, Leibniz continued to receive information concerning the reactions to Spinoza's book. Cf. A I-1, 195, 200, 272.

[21] Vernière, *Spinoza et la pensée française*, p. 100.

[22] A II-1², 24. It is somewhat unclear, however, just how familiar Leibniz was with Spinoza's introduction to Descartes. In a letter from June 1671 to Velthuysen, he mentions that he has seen certain "Cartesian meditations" by Spinoza (cf. A II-1², 196). He thus had the volume in his hands as early as 1671. But I have found no traces of any attentive reading of the work before 1677 (cf. A VI-4, 2197–2198; A I-6, 478).

[23] Cf. Lærke, "Leibniz, la censure, et la libre pensée."   [24] A II-1², 325.

[25] Cf. *TTP* Ch. 7; G III 99–100.

what is true about an interpretation of the Bible is quite probably also true about any efficient refutation of this interpretation. Leibniz noted himself in 1677 in a letter to Johann Friedrich that "in order to examine [the *TTP*], one would have to go into more detail than is needed here, and it would require one to be exceptionally meticulous."[26] Only someone with a superior knowledge of the Hebrew language and culture would be able to refute the *TTP* in any convincing fashion: "If only we could persuade a man as erudite as Spinoza but [illegible word] towards Christianity, who could refute his many paralogisms and abuse of Oriental writings."[27] Leibniz himself did not possess the required philological knowledge, for he did not really know Hebrew.[28] He therefore chose to appeal to experts in such matters. The first person he approached was Gottlieb Spitzel:

> You have doubtlessly seen the book published in Holland entitled: The Freedom to Philosophize.... The author is said to be Jewish. It is in the interest of piety that he be refuted by some man thoroughly learned in oriental writings, like you or someone who has your qualifications.[29]

Spitzel had distinguished himself as a critic of atheism in 1666 by publishing the open letter *De atheismi radice*.[30] Moreover, he had shown himself favorable to Leibniz by publishing his *Confessio natura atheistas* in 1669.[31] Surely, Leibniz believed that he had a good chance of convincing this distinguished orientalist to pick up the glove. But Spitzel disappointed him: he showed no enthusiasm for the idea and simply referred Leibniz to the already existing refutations by Thomasius and Friedrich Rappolt.[32] Some years later, in a book published in 1676, Spitzel did make a few remarks about Spinoza, denouncing him as a "fanatic" and an "impious" man. But he never wrote any serious refutation.[33]

3 THE SECOND READING OF THE *TTP*

Probably towards the end of his stay in Paris, some time during the last two months of 1675 or the first months of 1676, Leibniz read the *TTP* a second time under the influence of the German nobleman Ehrenfried Walther von

---

[26] A II-1², 471.   [27] A I-1, 148.   [28] Cf. Goldenbaum, "Spinoza's Parrot," p. 568.
[29] A I-1, 193. See also A I-1, 85.   [30] Cf. A II-1², 37.
[31] At the time of its publication, Spitzel did not know that Leibniz was the author of the *Confessio naturae contra atheistas*. The text, written by Leibniz in some noisy guesthouse, was handed over to Philipp Jacob Spener by Leibniz's mentor, the Baron von Boinebourg. Spener subsequently transmitted it to Spitzel who published it anonymously in his *De atheismo eradicando . . . Epistola* from 1669 (cf. A II-1², 37–38; A I-9, 595).
[32] Cf. A I-1, 195.   [33] Cf. Israel, *Radical Enlightenment*, p. 504.

Tschirnhaus, a friend and (at least at the time) disciple of Spinoza whom Leibniz met around October 1675 and became close friends with. Leibniz made extensive excerpts from Spinoza's book.[34] As such, these excerpts are without great interest. Apart from one (significant) exception, Leibniz did not comment on Spinoza's text.[35] There are, however, other contemporary texts better able to inform us about Leibniz's stance towards the *TTP* in the late 1670s.

First, we must mention Leibniz's various exchanges with the French erudite Pierre-Daniel Huet in the period from 1673 to 1679. In the enormous work entitled *Demonstratio evangelica*, published in 1679, Huet attempted to refute, among others, the "author of the theologico-political treatise" and to establish the truth of Christian religion and the authority of Scripture on new foundations. Leibniz met Huet early on during his stay in Paris at the home of Henri Justel, a meeting place for intellectuals at the time. They corresponded from 1673 onwards.[36] At that time, Huet was already working on his *Demonstratio evangelica*. Leibniz got his hands on at least parts of the manuscript of the book before it was published and commented on it in his letters to the author.[37] Some texts suggest that Leibniz might have given some methodological advice to the French erudite.[38] Furthermore, as Paul Vernière has argued, it was probably not until he heard about it from Leibniz that Huet paid any attention at all to the *TTP*, or to the fact that he ought to refute this work in his grand treatise on the Christian religion.[39] Leibniz's advice and reactions to Huet's defense of Christianity provide important information about what he considered to be an efficient refutation of Spinoza. I have developed this question in some detail elsewhere.[40]

When Leibniz left Paris, he paid a visit to Henry Oldenburg in London, for some eleven days towards the end of October 1676. Sometime during this period, Oldenburg confided to Leibniz three letters he had recently

---

[34] Cf. A VI-3, 248–274.

[35] In the margins of his excerpts from Chapter 14, Leibniz noted that "God is not a mind, but the nature of things etc., of which I do not approve" (A VI-3, 269–270). The possible implications of this intriguing remark have been discussed in some detail by E. Curley and M. Kulstad in two papers delivered at the conference *Leibniz and Spinoza I*, organized at the *École Normale Supérieure – Lettres et sciences humaines* in Lyon in March 2007. The proceedings of the conference are forthcoming from ENS Éditions.

[36] Cf. A I-2, 455.   [37] Cf. GP III, 13; A II-1², 839–840; A I-2, 239.

[38] Cf. A I-2, 192; A II-1, 372–373.

[39] Cf. Vernière, *Spinoza et la pensée française*, pp. 106–108. Conversely, it was also through Leibniz that Spinoza learned that Huet was working on a refutation of the *TTP* (cf. *Ep.* 80, *G* IV 331; Shirley 955).

[40] Cf. Lærke, "À la recherche."

received from Spinoza, all concerning the *TTP* (*Ep.* 73, 75 and 78, written between November 1675 and January 1676). Leibniz's annotations to these three letters constitute an important source for understanding how he interpreted Spinoza's position on questions such as miracles and the Incarnation of Christ.[41] This is also the first text where Leibniz addressed the problem of Spinoza's necessitarianism. From his notes, it is it very clear that Leibniz did not find Spinoza's position philosophically or theologically sustainable. Thus, he objected that "one should not for a moment think that all things follow from the nature of God without any intervention of the will"[42] and that "if everything emanates from the divine nature with a certain necessity, and that all possibles exist, it will be equally easy [*facile*] for the good and for the bad. Therefore moral philosophy will be destroyed."[43]

We should also mention a letter to Johann Friedrich written by Leibniz in 1677, where he commented on Spinoza's letter to Albert Burgh, a text Leibniz had probably obtained from Hermann Schuller.[44] Burgh was a promising member of Spinoza's circle who, during a voyage to Italy in 1675, suddenly converted to Catholicism.[45] Shortly after, he sent Spinoza a fideistic and very aggressive exhortation to abandon his evil ways. He attacked what he saw as presumptuousness on Spinoza's part. How could he, Spinoza, know that his philosophy was the best if he did not know all other philosophies, including those to come?[46] Spinoza's reply to this argument is very famous: "I do not presume that I have found the best philosophy, but I know that what I understand is the true one."[47] Leibniz's comments on this exchange constitute one of the rare places where he placed himself unequivocally on the side of the Dutch Jew:

What [Spinoza] says about the certitude of philosophy and about demonstrations is good and incontestable. And I admit that those who always ask *How do you know that you are not mistaken, because so many others have different opinions?* are mocking us, or mocking themselves, for it is the same thing as if someone responded to my argument *How do you know that your conclusion is true?* while refusing to examine the premises.[48]

Leibniz's comments on the exchange with Burgh have often been compared to his comments on the open letter to Spinoza that Nicolas Steno

---

[41] Cf. A vi-3, 364–371.

[42] A vi-3, 364. For a detailed account of Leibniz's refutation of Spinoza's necessitarianism and its development, see Lærke, "Contingency, Necessity, and the Being of Possibility," pp. 40–62, and Lærke, "Quod non omnia possibilia ad existentiam perveniant."

[43] A vi-3, 365.   [44] Cf. A ii-1², 466–474.   [45] Cf. Israel, *Radical Enlightenment*, p. 507.

[46] Cf. *Ep.* 67, *G* iv 281; Shirley 922.   [47] *Ep.* 76, *G* iv 320; Shirley 949.   [48] A ii-1, 302.

had written in 1671 and published in Florence in 1675 under the title *De vera philosophia, ad novae philosophiae reformatorum*.[49] Leibniz read and commented on this work shortly after his arrival in Hanover in 1677,[50] probably in preparation for Steno's arrival at the Hanoverian court, where he took up a position as the apostolic envoy of the Pope in Scandinavia and the Protestant part of Germany.[51] Steno was, like Burgh, a former acquaintance of Spinoza who had abandoned a career as a scientist and converted to Catholicism during a voyage to Italy in 1666. Like Burgh, Steno insisted on the superiority of God's word over philosophical discourse and urged Spinoza to recognize the authority of the Church. In his comments, Leibniz very acutely noted the futility of Steno's enterprise:

Spinoza has not been particularly touched by Mr. Steno's exhortations because of the difference of their positions. And, indeed, it does seem to me that Mr. Steno presupposes too many things to persuade a man who believed so little . . . Spinoza would probably say that these are beautiful promises, but that he has sworn not to believe anything without proof.[52]

Leibniz's reactions to these two letters suggest some agreement between the two philosophers, at least when it came to their attitude towards fideist positions. Leibniz did insist, however, that if he considered Burgh to be an ignorant, he was "not happy about Spinoza's replies either, even though he does explain himself very neatly."[53] In my view, Leibniz's dissatisfaction with Burgh and Steno does not so much testify to his agreement with Spinoza as to his conviction that a refutation of Spinoza should be "more erudite and solid than vehement and harsh," as he wrote to Von Holten.[54]

4 LEIBNIZ ON SPINOZISM, NATURALISM, AND SOCINIANISM

Before the publication of the *TTP*, Leibniz was vaguely acquainted with Spinoza as the author of an introduction to Descartes, the *Principia Philosophiae Cartesianae* from 1663. But it never occurred to him to attempt a comparison between this text and the *TTP*. He did very briefly acknowledge the fact that the author was the same – first in a letter to Velthuysen from 1671 and again in a letter to Hermann Conring from 1678 – but at no point did he ever see the two works as related by anything else than the identity of their author.[55] Leibniz never compared the *TTP* with the

---

[49] Cf. *Ep. 67bis*, G iv 292–298; Shirley 929–935. Spinoza himself compared Burgh with Steno (cf. *Ep.* 76, G iv 317; Shirley 947).
[50] Cf. A vi-4, 2197–2202. See also A vi-1, 381; A ii-1, 377, 379.
[51] Cf. Israel, *Radical Enlightenment*, p. 507.   [52] A vi-4, 2198–2199.
[53] A ii-1², 468.   [54] A ii-1², 325.   [55] Cf. A ii-1², 196, 583.

Ethics either. In fact, the specificity of the underlying system of philosophy which governs Spinoza's argumentation in the *TTP* did not seem to interest him very much when he first read the text. It is clear that the *TTP* does contain important elements of the philosophical system also contained in the *Ethics*. Thus, in Chapters 4 and 17, we find statements which announce the necessitarianism developed in the *Ethics*.[56] We also find passages that suggest Spinoza's monist philosophy and identification of God with Nature.[57] But nowhere in the texts from around 1670–72 did Leibniz take any particular notice of these statements. Quite on the contrary, he seemed content to follow Thomasius's lead and simply place Spinoza in the somewhat vague category of "naturalists."[58]

But what does "naturalism" mean in this context? It is impossible to get any clear notion of this without taking a look at Leibniz's texts concerning natural and revealed religion at the time of his first reading of the *TTP*.

In the period from 1668 to 1671, Leibniz was working on the *Demonstrationes catholicae*, a grand theological project that he had conceived under the influence of his mentor and employer in Mainz, the Baron von Boinebourg. The project was never completed, but we do have numerous fragments, plans, and letters which relate to it. The *Demonstrationes catholicae* were first of all conceived as a contribution to the religious controversies of the time and most of Leibniz's adversaries must be found among theologians rather than among philosophers. Notably, according to Leibniz's *prospectus* of the project, Chapter 7 of the third part should contain a refutation of the *Socinians*.[59] The members of this originally Polish sect were often assimilated to the ancient group of heretics called the Arians, because of their common denial of the Trinity and refusal to acknowledge the divinity of Christ. At the outset, the Socinians had a "literalist" or "scriptualist"

---

[56] Cf. *TTP* Ch. 3; *G* III 46: "[T]he universal laws of nature, according to which all things happen and are determined, are nothing but the eternal decrees of God, which always involve eternal truth and necessity... no one does anything except according to the predetermined order of nature"; *TTP* Ch. 4; *G* III 58: "[E]verything is determined by the universal laws of nature to exist and produce effects in a certain and determinate way"; *TTP* Ch. 4; *G* III 65: "God really acts and guides all things only from the necessity of his own nature and perfection, and... his decrees and volitions are eternal truths, and always involve necessity"; *TTP* Ch. 6; *G* III 82: "[N]othing happens contrary to nature, but that it preserves a fixed and immutable eternal order"; *TTP* Ch. 6; *G* III 83: "Nothing... happens in nature which is contrary to its universal laws," etc.

[57] Cf. *TTP* Ch. 1; *G* III 28: "[T]he power of Nature is nothing but the power of God itself"; *TTP* Ch. 3; *G* III 46: "[T]he power of all natural things is nothing but the power of God"; *TTP* Ch. 6; *G* III 83: [N]ature's virtue and power is the very virtue and power of God"; *TTP* Ch. 16; *G* III 189; "[T]he power of nature is the very power of God," etc.

[58] Cf. A II-1², 37, 277. On Leibniz's critique of "naturalism," see also Lærke, "Leibniz et le libertinage," pp. 276–280.

[59] Cf. A VI-1, 495.

orientation, in so far as they were more concerned with the literal meaning of the biblical texts than with the philosophical implications of natural theology. Fausto Sozzini's *De Sacrae Scripturae autoritate* provides a representative example of this.[60] This was the form of Socinianism that Spinoza, for example, was acquainted with.[61] Later, however, Socinianism developed into a radical form of theological rationalism which rejected as false any dogma, or interpretation of dogma, that was contrary to reason. The standard example is the *Religio rationalis* published in 1685 by Fausto Sozzini's grandson, Andrej Wissowaty.[62]

Apart from these two forms of Socinianism proper we must discern yet a third, less well defined. It is the *image* of Socinianism developed by its adversaries. In his article on Sozzini in the *Dictionnaire historique et critique*, Pierre Bayle gave a marvelous description of what the figure of the Socinian represented in the second half of the seventeenth century. The "Polish brotherhood" was here depicted as a diffuse and subterranean movement, which was slowly gaining power because of its appeal to philosophers with rationalistic inclinations.[63] In other words, the "Socinian" embodied in the most general fashion the threat against Christian theology created by the success of rationalist philosophy, in particular the threat against the Christian mysteries. Hence, it is not surprising that in the intellectual jargon of late seventeenth- and early eighteenth-century philosophy, "Socinianism" and "Spinozism" were often used almost synonymously. Both terms represented a somewhat fuzzy category where a variety of heterodox, heretic, and atheist positions were grouped together. Hence, the collective condemnation of the *TTP*, Hobbes's *Leviathan*, Meyer's *De philosophia S. Scripturae interpres*, and Frans Kuyper's *Bibliotheca Fratrum Polonorum* by the States of Holland in 1674 was justified by means of the anti-Socinian legislation established in 1653. It would thus not be surprising if Leibniz had elaborated his critique of Spinozism within the same framework as he criticizes Socinianism and it has indeed been suggested that he did.[64] I believe, however, that such an approach is misleading both from the Spinozistic and Leibnizian point of view: Spinoza is certainly no Socinian and Leibniz never makes one of him either.

Spinoza was, of course, familiar with Socinian theology. At the time when he was frequenting Collegiant meetings in Amsterdam he had ample opportunity to learn about their opinions. There were people among Spinoza's

---

[60] Cf. Osier, *Faust Socin.*   [61] Cf. Moreau, *Spinoza et le spinozisme*, pp. 30–31.
[62] Cf. Lagrée, *La Raison ardente*, pp. 41, 59–60, 111, 115–116, 194–195.
[63] Cf. Bayle, *Dictionnaire*, vol. XIII, pp. 347, 418–419.   [64] Cf. Goldenbaum, "Spinoza's Parrot."

friends who sympathized with the Polish brotherhood. It appears that his editor, Jan Rieuwertsz, was organizing Socinian reunions at his home.[65] Spinoza's personal library included two editions of Christoph van den Sand's *Nucleus historiae ecclesiasticae* (from 1668 and 1676), a work which contains a history of Arianism and some reflections on the relations between Socinians and Remonstrants.[66] One could also see how Spinoza could be sympathetic to the two key points in Socinian theology, namely the denial of the Trinity and of the divinity of Christ. Thus, in a letter to Lodewijk Meyer, Spinoza rejected the notion of the Trinity under the pretext that it violates the principle of the excluded third.[67] In this same letter, Spinoza's dismissal of the notion of God's "personhood" [*personalitas*] does bring to mind Socinian opinions concerning the divinity of Christ.[68] But Spinoza makes no reference to, and certainly did not require, Socinian theology to establish his own position, but was perfectly capable of doing so by means of arguments of his own device. In fact, Spinoza only mentions the Socinians explicitly a single time, namely in a letter to Willem van Blyenbergh, where he explains that "except for the Socinians, I have never seen a Theologian so dense that he did not perceive that Sacred Scripture very often speaks of God in a human way and expresses its meaning in parables."[69] He thus only speaks of the Socinians in order to denounce their exegetical literalism as thick-headed. Consequently, it would be misleading to see anything Socinian in Spinoza.

Leibniz was perfectly aware of the tendency among scholars to confound Socinianism and certain forms of modern rationalistic philosophy. Thus, in a text written in October 1675, he noted that, in Holland, Cartesianism and Socinianism "are taken to be the same thing."[70] But did he himself adhere to this opinion? I think the answer to that question must be an unequivocal "no." Leibniz knew the doctrine of the Socinians too well and too early in his career to ever make such a mistake. Leibniz had already heard about certain Socinian writers before he left Leipzig, probably mainly from his professor Johann Adam Scherzer. But more importantly, in 1669–70, the Baron von Boinebourg was engaged in an exchange with Andrej

---

[65] Cf. Méchoulan, "Morteira et Spinoza," pp. 54–55. In 1675, Leibniz notes: "Mr. Tschirnhaus has told me that there is a publisher in Holland (in Amsterdam) who organizes conferences between Cartesians and Socinians at his home" (A VI-3, 282). It is highly likely that the "publisher" in question is Jan Rieuwertsz.

[66] Cf. Pautrat, ed., "Dossier: la bibliothèque," pp. 656, 680.

[67] *Ep.* 12A; *C* 206. This letter was not discovered until 1674 and is therefore not included in the Gebhardt edition. For the original Latin text, see Offenberg, ed., *Brief van Spinoza aan Lodewijk Meyer.*

[68] *Ep.* 12A; *C* 206.   [69] *Ep.* 21, G IV 132; *C* 381.   [70] A VI-3, 382.

Wissowaty whom Leibniz will, much later, qualify as the brightest among the theologians of the sect.[71] Boinebourg showed Leibniz the texts relating to this exchange. On that occasion, Leibniz wrote a series of commentaries on Wissowaty and on another Socinian, Daniel Zwicker.[72]

I will not discuss in any detail Leibniz's arguments against the Socinians. Maria Rosa Antognazza has done this in a splendid book on Leibniz's conception of the Trinity and the Incarnation.[73] What should be noted, however, is that, contrary to most of his contemporaries, Leibniz did not speak of Socinian theology with the venom so characteristic of much anti-Socinian literature from this period. In fact, he seemed to have a more eclectic, conciliatory attitude towards them. Already in the *Nova methodus discendae docendaeque jurisprudentiae* from 1667, he expressed a certain admiration for Fausto Sozzino who had made use of his knowledge of jurisprudence in his theology in such a clever manner, that it had required a man as extraordinarily gifted as Hugo Grotius to refute him efficiently.[74] And in November 1671, he wrote the following to Arnauld: "I have not avoided the subtleties of the Socinians either: nobody is better than them in what is good, and nobody is worse in what is bad."[75] But Leibniz never spoke about Spinoza in this particular context. Indeed, in the *Demonstrationes catholicae*, he seemed to reserve yet another chapter – namely Chapter 7 of the first part – to the refutation of the "paralogisms of the atheists." As examples, Leibniz mentions Giulio Cesare Vanini and the rumor concerning the notorious (and at the time most probably non-existent) *Tractatus de tribus impostoribus.*[76] But, after having read the *TTP*, he surely placed Spinoza in this category rather than in the Socinian one.

If Leibniz did not discuss Spinoza in the same context as he discusses the Socinians, it was doubtless because he had more sympathy for the Socinians on the theological level. If indeed he considered the Socinians to be lost sheep, Spinoza's doctrine was beyond heresy. Leibniz saw it as pure atheism, an extreme form of naturalism that thinkers much too imbued with modern philosophy were endorsing. Thus, in the letter that Leibniz sent to Antoine Arnauld in November 1671, Leibniz denounced the "horrible book" on "the liberty to philosophize" for the exact same reason as he criticized Bacon and Hobbes: they had all abused the principles of mechanical physics and of new philosophy to undermine the mysteries

---

[71] Cf. Grua, 72.   [72] A VI-I, 518–532.
[73] Cf. Antognazza, *Leibniz and the Trinity*, pp. 16–33, 150–160.
[74] Cf. A VI-I, 295.   [75] A II-I², 283.
[76] Cf. A VI-I, 494. On Leibniz, Vanini and the *Traité des trois imposteurs*, see Lærke, "Les sept foyers du libertinage," pp. 277–280, 284–287.

of faith, reducing them to simple allegories whose only objective was to impress the populace.[77] Leibniz continued:

Nothing is more efficient for confirming atheism, or at least the nascent naturalism, and for undermining the wavering faith in the foundations of the Christian religion of many great, but malevolent men than, on the one hand, to agree that the mysteries of faith have always been believed by all Christians and, on the other hand, to be convinced by assured demonstrations of right reason that they are utter nonsense. There are many enemies inside the church worse than the heretics themselves; and it can be feared that the last heresy may be, if not atheism, then at least public naturalism.[78]

This text sheds some light on exactly how Leibniz's critique of Spinoza's "naturalism" in the early 1670s relates to his controversy with the Socinians about the same time. For Leibniz, to refute the Socinians was properly speaking a problem of religious controversy: it was still a confrontation between two types of Christians. In this case, the governing principles of his approach were initial goodwill, conciliatory eclecticism, and engagement in argument, in conformity with the principle of charity which governed Leibniz's entire ecumenical project and speculations concerning practical theology.[79] In short, he engaged in a true argumentative exchange with the Socinian position. But if we consider the remarks from the letter to Arnauld quoted above, it appears that thinkers such as Spinoza (and Hobbes, in this context) fell outside the scope of this religious goodwill. Indeed, it appears that the "naturalism" that these thinkers were propounding was, for Leibniz, not simply *straying* from true theology (as in the case of the Socinians), but was positively *opposed* to true theology. For this reason, Leibniz did not combat the Socinians and the naturalists with the same weapons, because this would be a *strategic* error: the Socinians were sincere, but deeply lost Christians, who had to be *led back* to the true Church through religious controversy; the naturalists, on the contrary, in so far as they were truly and deliberately atheist, had to be *confronted*. Here, it was a question of creating a sort of *bulwark*, i.e., to establish and uphold the limits of the tolerable and to prevent the advancement of atheism and the "universal anarchy" such impiety leads to.[80]

5 LEIBNIZ ON SPINOZA AND MEYER

We will now turn to the second aspect of Leibniz's reading of the *TTP*, concerning the principles for interpreting Holy Scripture. In Chapter 7 of

---

[77] Cf. A II-1², 277.   [78] A II-1², 277.
[79] Cf. Lærke, "The Golden Rule"; "Apology for a *Credo Maximum*."   [80] Cf. A I 1, 85

the *TTP*, Spinoza developed an elaborate method of biblical exegesis. The *Leviathan* set aside, the most immediate context of Leibniz's reading of this chapter seems to have been the treatise of "rational theology" entitled *De philosophia S. Scripturae interpres* published in 1666 by Lodewijk Meyer.[81] The book had created a theological scandal comparable to that produced later by the *TTP*. Leibniz read Meyer's book shortly after its publication, and refers to it in his *Nova methodus* from 1667. At the time Meyer's book was first published, Leibniz seemed less inclined to condemn it than one could expect from a Lutheran. Thus, in a passage of the *Nova methodus*, where he discusses the idea of an *ars hermeneutica* containing "the rules for discovering the true sense" he speaks of Meyer in a rather laudatory fashion: this question has been developed "very carefully [*accurate admodum*] by the anonymous author, Arminian it seems, of *Philosophia Scripturae interpres*."[82] Leibniz was familiar with the repercussions of this book in the intellectual milieus in Holland. In particular, he knew the debates concerning Johann Ludwig Wolzogen's *De scripturarum interprete* (1668), which contained a refutation of Meyer that was generally – and not without justification – considered to be just as religiously problematic as the book it was refuting.[83] He also knew about the related debates between Samuel Maresius and Regnerus van Mansvelt, mainly through Johann Georg Graevius.[84]

When writing to Antoine Arnauld in November 1671, Leibniz pointed out that the *TTP* had provoked similar reactions among intellectuals and authorities as Meyer's book: "the author of the *Philosophia Scripturae interpres* [and] the author of the *De libertate philosophandi* [have] both recently created much commotion in Holland."[85] There is nothing surprising or unusual about the fact that Leibniz placed the *TTP* in the context of the polemics occasioned by the *Philosophia S. Scripturae interpres*. At the time, the authors of these two anonymous works were often assimilated. Even if the true identity of the author of the *TTP* was already established as early as the middle of 1670 – in Holland by Samuel Maresius and in Germany

---

[81] In the *Essais de théodicée*, Leibniz counts Meyer among the "théologiens rationaux."

[82] A VI-I, 338. It should be mentioned, however, that some thirty-three years later, in 1700, when Leibniz added an important number of notes to the *Nova methodus*, he partly retracted himself and insisted that Meyer should be read "with much caution" and that he "sometimes adopts perverse rules of interpretation" (cf. A VI-I, 338; on this, see also Antognazza, *Leibniz and the Trinity*, p. 202 n. 12. Antognazza does not, however, take into account the difference of dating).

[83] Leibniz addresses the Wolzogen disputes several times (cf. A VI-I, 552–553; A II-I², 196; GP VI, 58–59). He considered Spinoza's work to be both more ingenious and savant than Wolzogen's, but also considerably more dangerous (cf. A II-I², 196). On the Wolzogen controversies, see Israel, *Radical Enlightenment*, pp. 200–221.

[84] Cf. A I-I, 144.   [85] A II-I², 283.

by Friedrich Ludwig Mieg[86] – this did not prevent a considerable amount of false information from circulating. The false conjecture which identifies the authors of the *Philosophia S. Scripturae interpres* and the *TTP* would prove particularly difficult to eradicate, partly due to the fact that the two works were condemned at the same time, partly because some of the later editions gathered the two works in a single volume. Leibniz recalled all the confusion in the *Essais de theodicée*:

> As concerns what happened in my time, I remember that in 1666, when Louis Meyer, a medical doctor from Amsterdam, published, without indicating his name, a treatise entitled *Philosophia S. Scripturae interpres* (which many have mistakenly attributed to his friend Spinoza), there was an uproar among the theologians in Holland, and their writings against this book gave rise to much debate among them. There were many who thought that the Cartesians, when refuting the anonymous philosopher, were granting too much to philosophy.[87]

From a biographical point of view, it is understandable how it came about that Meyer and Spinoza were confounded. Meyer was among Spinoza's closest friends. In the early 1660s, Meyer had helped Spinoza with the publication of his introduction to Descartes: he had written a preface, corrected the Latin, even found a publisher. Spinoza had great respect for his friend and he followed most of his advice in relation to the text of the *Principia Philosophiae Cartesianae*. There can be no doubt that the two men were a constant source of inspiration for each other. There were, however, fundamental differences between their positions. Hence, Lambert van Velthuysen already noticed that Chapter 7 of the *TTP* did not at all express the same position as Meyer's, but should rather be seen as a critical response to the *De philosophia S. Scripturae interpres*.[88] Commentators as well-informed and perspicacious as Van Velthuysen were, however, rare. The question is whether we should count Leibniz among them.

We already know that Leibniz managed to establish Spinoza's authorship of the *TTP* very quickly after the publication of the book. He thus never made the mistake of actually confusing him for Meyer. But was he aware that they were theoretically distinct? The exact relations between Spinoza's and Meyer's positions have been the object of much debate among scholars.[89] There are at least two theoretical points where there seems to

---

[86] Cf. Israel, *Radical Enlightenment*, pp. 209–211, 629.

[87] Cf. GP VI, 58; Grua 71–72; A I-I, 202.   [88] Cf. *Ep.* 42, *G* IV 210; Shirley 871–872.

[89] An English translation by S. Shirley has been published in 2005 (cf. Meyer, *Philosophy as the Interpreter of Holy Scripture*). The volume contains a good introduction by L. Rice and F. Pastijn. For detailed studies, one can consult: Meyer, *La Philosophie interprète de l'Écriture sainte*; Lagrée and Moreau, "La lecture de la Bible"; Lagrée, "Louis Meyer et la *Philosophia S. Scripturae interpres*"; "Sens

be a clean-cut theoretical difference between their approaches to the interpretation of the Bible. Meyer clearly rejected that the Bible should be the
interpreter of itself, arguing that *reason* must be, to speak in seventeenth-
century jargon, the "judge of controversies" [*judex controversiarum*], i.e.
the authority which must decide between different possible interpretations
of Holy Scripture. His biblical exegesis relied on the idea that whatever
meaning is contained in the Bible must be true, i.e., in accordance with
reason, in so far as the Bible contains God's word and that God's word
must be true. In other words, his rationalistic principles of biblical exegesis
were grounded in a conviction that Holy Scripture was verbally inspired
by God. Spinoza, for his part, endorsed the idea that neither reason nor
any supernatural light should be the norm for interpreting the meaning
of Scripture, but that Scripture suffices for its own understanding. Thus,
Spinoza writes, "the knowledge of all these things, i.e., of almost everything in Scripture, must be sought only from Scripture itself, just as the
knowledge of nature must be sought from nature itself" and "the whole
knowledge of the Bible must be sought from the Bible alone."[90] The theory behind this at least nominal endorsement of the Protestant principle of
Sola Scriptura is quite complex, but the essential part relevant to Spinoza's
relationship to Meyer can be summarized as follows: According to Spinoza,
and contrary to Meyer, the Bible is a historical document. It is not God's
immediate word, but the prophets *adapted* the divine word to their own
understanding and to the collective mindset (*ingenium*) of the people to
whom they were explaining the divine law. But in so far as the prophets
were not philosophers, but only men who possessed a particularly vivid
imagination, there is no guarantee that their teachings are in accordance
with reason. Therefore reason cannot be the touchstone for interpreting the
meaning of Scripture, but it must be established on the basis of a historical
investigation of Scripture itself, i.e., of its historical origins and transmission through time (which is, granted, a very peculiar way of endorsing the
principle of *Sola Scriptura*).

   Meyer and Spinoza thus differed on two crucial points: the one believed
that reason alone can grasp the meaning of Scripture, the other believed
that the meaning of Scripture required a historical investigation of the text;
the one grounded his principles of interpretation in the conviction that
Holy Scripture is verbally inspired by God himself; the other maintained

et vérité"; "Louis Meyer et Spinoza devant la lecture de la Bible"; Klever, "L'erreur de Velthuysen
et des Velthuysiens"; Walther "Biblische Hermeneutik"; Bordoli, "Filosofia e teologia." Roberto
Bordoli has also written an entire book on the question: *Ragione e scrittura tra Descartes e Spinoza.*
[90] *TTP* Ch. 7; *G* III 99 and 101.

that the stories of Holy Scripture are historical adaptations of the divine word, grounded in the imagination of the prophets.

Was Leibniz aware of these fundamental differences? I think there is clear evidence that he was. We must here consult the letter that Leibniz wrote to Johann Friedrich in 1677 concerning Spinoza's epistolary exchange with Albert Burgh:

> I have nothing to say about the rest of it, until the place where he speaks of this fundamental principle taken from the *Tractatus theologico-politicus*: that Scripture is the interpreter of Scripture, that is to say, neither the Church, nor reason is this interpreter. The Church is not [the interpreter of Scripture], because he [i.e., Spinoza] does not recognize its infallibility; and reason is not either, because he imagines that the authors of the sacred books have often been wrong and that, consequently, someone who would want to explain them according to true philosophy, would not understand their true opinions very well.[91]

From this passage, it is clear that Leibniz did not consider Spinoza to be a rationalist comparable to Meyer, making reason the interpreter of Holy Scripture. Quite on the contrary, he points out why Spinoza rejected such a position: according to Spinoza, the true historical authors of the Bible do not explain themselves according to the principles of philosophy. What Leibniz also does, however, is to give an additional twist to Spinoza's theory of adaptation and presume that Spinoza defends the idea that the authors of the Bible were plain *wrong*.[92] Why would Leibniz radicalize Spinoza's actual position on this point, making it more "anti-religious" or "libertine" than it actually is?[93] I believe the crux of the matter is Spinoza's historical approach to the meaning of Scripture. In Leibniz's view, such an approach amounted to denying that the Scriptures contain the word of God, exactly because it involves denying the dogma of verbal inspiration that Leibniz, like Meyer but also like all members of the Lutheran church, saw as fundamental for the Christian religion.[94] Seen from this perspective, it is not surprising that, already in February 1672, Leibniz wrote to Spitzel that Spinoza "develops a critique which is indeed erudite, but also scattered with venom against the very antiquity, authenticity and authority of the sacred writings of the Old Testament."[95]

---

[91] A II-1², 470–471.
[92] We will find similarly biased interpretations of Spinoza's position in the annotations to the letters to Oldenburg. Cf. A VI-3, 366–367.
[93] On this, see also Lærke, "Les sept foyers du libertinage," p. 295.
[94] Cf. A VI-1, 338; A VI-4, 688; Dutens V, 145–146.
[95] A I-1, 193. See also Lærke, "La storia nell'esegesi biblica in Leibniz e in Spinoza."

6 LEIBNIZ ON SPINOZA AND HOBBES

In a letter to Thomasius from 1663, Leibniz already denounced the "Hobbesians" whose political philosophy he compares to Machiavelli's.[96] Five
years later, in the *Confessio naturae contra atheistas* from 1668, he condemned Hobbes's philosophy, arguing that it contributed to the mounting
"impiety."[97] He deplored the hypotheses of the *Leviathan* and complained
to Graevius that Hobbes had employed his "almost divine subtlety" to
make "abusive use of very harsh opinions."[98] Nevertheless, the young
Leibniz attempted twice to establish a correspondence with the English
philosopher, in two letters from 1670 and from 1674.[99] From the *De arte
combinatoria* (1666) onwards, Leibniz gladly cited the *De corpore* and one
will find many traces of Hobbesian logic in Leibniz's texts from the 1670s.
He explicitly acknowledged that Hobbes had been an inspiration for his
logic and clearly endorsed Hobbes's conception of demonstration.[100] In a
letter to Lambert van Velthuysen, Leibniz even exclaimed on the subject of
Hobbes that he is the philosopher that he "admires before any other of [his]
century."[101] Surely, it is a remark which must be considered in the light of
his interlocutor: Velthuysen was an enthusiastic follower of Hobbes. But it
is nonetheless an indication of the fact that Leibniz admired Hobbes just
as much as he deplored him. Leibniz's stance towards Hobbes was thus
constitutively ambiguous.

According to Edwin Curley, the way in which Leibniz read Spinoza was
analogous to the way in which he read Hobbes.[102] Indeed, Leibniz followed
Thomasius in considering that Spinoza's theory of natural right belonged
to the same "pestilential," "misanthropic," and "dangerous" contractualist
tradition. Also, this was by no means an uncommon conjecture to make.
One can find the same comparison in the texts of authors as different as
Johann Georg Graevius, a Dutch Cartesian, and in Pierre-Daniel Huet,
a French erudite close to the Jesuits.[103] Moreover, if the conjecture is not
uncommon, it is not unreasonable either. Spinoza's conceptions in the
TTP were very probably influenced by Hobbes's *De Cive* and by Dutch
Hobbesians such as Van Velthuysen, the brothers Pieter and Johann de
la Court, and the anonymous author known by the pseudonym Lucius
Antistius Constans.[104]

---

[96] Cf. A II-I², 5.   [97] Cf. A VI-I, 489.   [98] Cf. A II-I², 59.   [99] Cf. A II-I², 90–94, 383–386.
[100] Cf. A II-I², 153–154.   [101] A II-I², 63.   [102] Cf. Curley, "Homo Audax," pp. 282–283.
[103] For Graevius, see A I-I, 142. For Huet, see *Demonstratio evangelica*, p. 175.
[104] An edition of the *Leviathan* in a language known to Spinoza, namely Dutch, was not available
until 1667, and it is unclear how much it influenced Spinoza's position in the *TTP*. The 1647

The analogy between Leibniz's readings of Spinoza and Hobbes does, however, have its limitations. Leibniz's political thinking evolved in a constant critical dialogue with Hobbes. In spite of the inherent dangers of his position, Hobbes was "not to be scorned in relation to civil matters."[105] Thus, in a letter to Sebastien Kortholt, after having criticized John Locke and Samuel Pufendorf who "rarely penetrate to the foundations of their subject-matter," Leibniz granted that reading Hobbes is extremely useful for the intelligent reader who knows how to separate the profound ideas from the dangerous ones.[106] In fact, from the very early texts like the *Nova methodus* to much later texts such as the *Codex juris gentium diplomaticus* from 1693, Hobbes remained a privileged interlocutor in Leibniz's political philosophy, both as an inspiration and as a warning not to follow certain lines of reasoning too far: "Hobbes is full of good observations, but he usually exaggerates them."[107]

Spinoza's political philosophy is, on the contrary, completely absent from the horizon of Leibniz's political philosophy. We find some scarce and scattered remarks about it after his first reading, in particular in the letter to Thomasius quoted above where Leibniz establishes a relation between the *TTP* and the *Leviathan*. The excerpts from the reading of the *TTP* in 1675–76 testify to a close reading of the chapters concerning political philosophy: Leibniz copied out long passages from Chapter 16 where Spinoza lays down the foundations of his theory of natural right.[108] But Leibniz's excerpts contain no appreciation of Spinoza's theory. When Spinoza's *Opera Posthuma* were published in 1677, Leibniz also gained access to the *Tractatus Politicus*, but he simply ignored it. In fact, almost the only (known) references to the *TP* in Leibniz's work are in his comments on Johann Georg Wachter's *Elucidarius cabalisticus*, written around 1707–1709. The fact that Leibniz repeats some erroneous references made by Wachter does indicate, however, that he simply copied them from Wachter's book without ever checking the original edition or reading the passages in question in their proper context.[109]

---

edition of *De Cive* was present in Spinoza's library at his death, but it is unknown exactly when he read it. Spinoza alludes to the *Consideratie van Staat ofte Politike Weeg-schaal* published in 1660 by the De la Court brothers in the *Tractatus Politicus*, VIII, §31 (*G* II 338; Shirley 735). He also knew Van Velthuysen's *Epistolica dissertatio de principiis justi et decoris, continens apologiam pro tractatu clarissimi Hobbaei, De Cive* (1651) and Constans's *De jure ecclesiasticorum liber singularis* (1665). Spinoza mentioned Hobbes twice in texts written after the *TTP* was published (cf. *TTP*, Annotation 33; *Ep.* 50, *G* IV 238–239; Shirley 891–892).

[105] Cf. A IV-3, 257.   [106] Cf. Dutens V, 304.   [107] GP III, 419.

[108] Cf. Robinet, *Le Meilleur des mondes*, pp. 84–87.

[109] Cf. Leibniz, "J.-G. Wachteri de recondita Hebraeorum philosophia," p. 8. The reference to the *Tractatus Politicus*, III, §2, that we find here is, in fact, an erroneous reference to II, §2, that Leibniz

But why would Leibniz show such apparent indifference towards Spinoza's political philosophy? Obviously, it is not that he lacked a context for discussing it within his own philosophy. He was working on a theory of natural right during his entire life, from the *Nova methodus* (1667) and the *Elementa juris naturalis* (1670–71) in his youth to mature texts such as the preface to the *Codex juris gentium diplomaticus* (1693) or the famous *Monita quaedam ad Samuelis Pufendorfi Principia* (1700). In all these texts, we see how Leibniz continually confronted his own theories with those of the most prominent political philosophers of his time, from Hugo Grotius and Thomas Hobbes to Samuel Pufendorf and Christian Thomasius, *except* Spinoza.

One could give a historical or contextual explanation for this. Leibniz was not the only reader of Spinoza to completely ignore his political philosophy. Most of his contemporaries did exactly the same.[110] When it came to the *TTP*, contemporary commentators had a tendency to concentrate on themes which, without being unimportant, still appear somewhat marginal in relation to Spinoza's general argument concerning "the liberty to philosophize."[111] Thus, many contemporary critics concentrated on Spinoza's denial that the Pentateuch was written by Moses himself. They also made a collective outcry against Spinoza's theory of miracles which was considered, and rightly so, to be incompatible with Christian orthodoxy.[112] But when it came to Spinoza's political philosophy, his theory of natural right, and his conception of the liberty to philosophize – which unquestionably are central themes in his book – most of the seventeenth-century commentators seemed largely uninterested.

I am sure that such an observation concerning the general reception of Spinoza's treatise can indeed account for Leibniz's silence to a certain extent. He seemed to be mostly interested in the same questions as his contemporaries. Thus, the authorship of the Pentateuch was one of the problems that he focused on in his first annotations on the *TTP* from 1670–71 and in his letter to Van Velthuysen from April 1671.[113] As for the question of Spinoza's critique of miracles, he discussed this problem in

found in Wachter's *Elucidarius Cabalisticus*, p. 48, note c. In Leibniz's annotations, we also find a reference, this time correct, to *Tractatus Politicus*, II, §6 ("Wachteri de recondita Hebraeorum philosophia", p. 10), also taken from Wachter ("Wachteri de recondita Hebraeorum philosophia", p. 61). If these are "almost" the only references, it is because Leibniz repeats this last reference while discussing Wachter's book in the *Essais de théodicée*, §372, GP VI, 336.

110 Cf. Moreau, "Notice"; Vernière, *Spinoza et la pensée française*, p. 696.
111 Cf. *TTP* Preface; G III 7: "That freedom of opinion and worship is essential, not detrimental, to piety and the peace of the state is the main thing I resolved to demonstrate in this treatise."
112 Cf. Moreau, "Les principes de la lecture," pp. 122–123.   113 Cf. A II-1², 196.

some detail in his annotations to the Oldenburg letters, trying to prove that Spinoza's arguments against the Incarnation of Christ were flawed.

I am unconvinced, however, that it will prove sufficient. In the context of the first reading of the *TTP*, in 1670–71, it must be noted that one of the rare exceptions to this general tendency of ignoring Spinoza's politics described above was Jacob Thomasius. To the extent that Leibniz's first encounter with the *TTP* was through Thomasius's refutation, and that this text undoubtedly influenced his first reading, it is hard to believe that he should find the political question unimportant. Furthermore, in the context of the second reading, in 1675–76, it seems strange that Leibniz should read the "political" chapters of the book with such care if he was not interested in them at all.

We must thus look for deeper theoretical reasons for Leibniz's silence. In his *Philosophia practica, continuis tabellis in usum privatum comprehensa* (1661), a treatise that Leibniz quoted with much respect as late as 1710 in the *Essais de théodicée*, Jacob Thomasius argued from an Aristotelian standpoint that Hobbes reduced natural right to positive law and that he neglected to take into account man's natural propensity towards sociability.[114] On this point, Leibniz agreed: "[Hobbes] imagined the worst about his fellow man" as long as they were not "restrained by the power of the state."[115] From our sole community with God in whose image we are created, argued Leibniz, the state of nature is from the outset a civilized state: "by the existence of God all brute state of nature is suspended."[116] These two maxims – the natural sociability of man and his primordial community with God – testify to the Aristotelian and Augustinian roots of Leibniz's theory of natural right and form the foundation of his conception of "universal jurisprudence." Leibniz's primary objection to Hobbes's theory of natural right was that he subordinated wisdom to power: "*Stat pro ratione voluntas*... that is truly the motto of a tyrant."[117] According to Leibniz, Hobbes's political philosophy re-actualized the position of Thrasymachus, Socrates' adversary in the beginning of *The Republic*, according to whom "the just is that which is the most useful to the most powerful."[118]

However, Leibniz was not as clearly opposed to Hobbes's contractualism and theory of natural right as one might expect. Thus, in 1670, he wrote to Hermann Conring: "I suppose with Carneades (and Hobbes agrees) that [a conception of] justice which does not consider self-interest [*utilitate*

---

[114] Cf. GP VI, 249–250.   [115] A VI-I, 343, note.
[116] Leibniz cited in Robinet, *Le Meilleur des mondes*, p. 93.
[117] Leibniz, *Le Droit de la raison*, p. 108.
[118] Leibniz, *Le Droit de la raison*, pp. 109–110. See also A VI-I, 342–344; GP VI, 35.

propria] (either present or future) is the summit of folly."[119] Indeed, in the *Nova methodus*, Leibniz himself defined "justice" and "injustice" as that which is "publicly useful or harmful."[120] Simply, "public usefulness" does not here, as it would in Hobbes, signify everything which is in accordance with the interests of the civil Sovereign, but rather that which corresponds to the laws of the Universal Republic governed by God. Thus, Leibniz completely reinterpreted Thrasymachus' principle as the very principle of piety [*pietas*], i.e., the principle which governs God's actions and constitutes the "the ultimate foundations of natural right."[121] In a similar vein, in his letter to Hobbes himself from July 1671, Leibniz suggested that the principles of Hobbes did not apply to just any state, but only to some ideal state. He even suggested that this was in fact Hobbes's true intention.[122] It was thus not the reduction of the just to the useful that Leibniz reproached Hobbes for, but rather the reduction of the just to the useful for the civil Sovereign of some particular State. In fact, the just is what is most useful to God to whom we all – princes and kings included – are submitted. As Leibniz wrote to Jean Chapelain in 1670, the principle upon which Hobbes has based his theory must itself be grounded in a "much more universal" theorem.[123] This is far from saying that this principle is *false* and, as we have seen, Leibniz even suggested – wrongly, without any doubt – that Hobbes himself was inclining towards such a "Leibnizian" interpretation of Sovereignty.[124]

All this is a clear example of Leibniz's conciliatory eclecticism. Through this peculiar reading of Hobbes, he managed to integrate this radical contractualism into his own conception of universal jurisprudence. But Leibniz never attempted anything like this with Spinoza's political philosophy. Why not? In fact, it seems that Leibniz considered Spinoza's philosophy not only to be inspired by Hobbes, but to be a particularly dangerous form of Hobbesianism. Indeed, there is reason to believe that the more radical nature of Spinoza's conception of natural right made his theory impenetrable to reinterpretations such as the one Leibniz submitted Hobbes's political philosophy to.

In the *Essais de théodicée*, Leibniz wrote about Spinoza's relation to Hobbes: "Spinoza has gone *even further*."[125] This remark refers specifically to the question of necessitarianism, but it is likely that Leibniz was of the same opinion when it came to Spinoza's theories about theology and

[119] A II-I², 47.   [120] A VI-I, 300–301.   [121] A VI-I, 344.   [122] Cf. A II-I², 91.
[123] A II-I², 88.   [124] On this, see also Lærke, "Les sept foyers du libertinage," pp. 287–291.
[125] GP VI, 217.

politics, exactly because Spinoza's conception of natural right is grounded in a necessitarian conception of nature, as is clear from Chapter 16 of the *TTP*. Spinoza writes for example: "Whatever each thing does according to the laws of its own nature, it does with supreme right, because it acts as it has been determined to do according to nature, and cannot do otherwise."[126] At the time of his second reading at least, Leibniz was aware of the importance of this necessitarian element in Spinoza's conception of natural right, for he copied out this exact passage in his 1675 excerpts from the *TTP*.[127]

In his conciliatory reading of Hobbes's theory of natural right, Leibniz construed the *Leviathan* as being none but God himself, and thus depicted God as a "good tyrant" or absolute monarch, as good and knowledgeable as he is powerful, whose understanding and will are, as it were, working in unison to determine the exercise of his power. There are a number of complex reasons why Spinoza's position must remain closed to a conciliatory reading of this type. Spinoza's necessitarianism is one of the most important ones. Within a necessitarian framework such as Spinoza's, God cannot be considered to be such a "good tyrant," whose understanding and will are necessarily equivalent to his power, because Spinoza denied that will and intellect pertain to God's essence at all.[128] In other words, there is an inherent theoretical resistance in Spinoza's political philosophy to the conciliatory reading strategy Leibniz employed in Hobbes's case, in so far as the conception of natural right upon which Spinoza's theory rests is grounded in a necessitarian metaphysics.

I believe this can partly explain Leibniz's curious silence on the subject of the *TTP* after his second reading. It was exactly at the time around 1675–76 when he noticed the necessitarian elements in Spinoza's theory of natural right in the *TTP*, and that he acknowledged the catastrophic theological and moral consequences of Spinoza's necessitarianism by reading the Oldenburg letters, that Leibniz no longer commented on the *TTP*. What I believe Leibniz discovered at that time was that Spinoza's treatise was impenetrable to his conciliatory reading strategies and that he could extract nothing from it useful for his own project, in fact rather the contrary. Moreover, he had acknowledged already in 1671 that he did not possess the qualifications to write an efficient refutation himself. He

---

[126] Cf. *TTP* Ch. 16; G III 189.   [127] Cf. A VI-3, 270.
[128] It is an objection against Spinoza that Leibniz very often made. See for example A II-1², 592, 593; Grua 24; GP VI, 217.

therefore chose not to work on the text anymore. In 1668, in the *Confessio naturae contra atheistas*, the young Leibniz wrote that the "very subtle Hobbes [. . .] would deserve for his discoveries to not even be mentioned by name," here doubtless referring to the political philosophy developed in *Leviathan*.[129] But in reality Leibniz never stopped mentioning Hobbes and his political philosophy. It seems that it was rather Spinoza who was granted this dubious honor.

7 CONCLUSION

When Spinoza's *Opera Posthuma* was published in 1677 it contained, much to Leibniz's dismay, the two letters they had exchanged in 1671 on the subject of optics. There is some evidence, however, that Leibniz sent Spinoza at least one more letter, this time concerning the *TTP*.[130] There are no indications to the effect that Spinoza ever responded to this or these letters. But might he have? Considered generally, Leibniz's reactions to *TTP* were those of someone who clearly did not belong to "Spinoza's circle" as K. O. Meinsma called it. Leibniz was intellectually very far removed from the group of heterodox freethinkers who took part in Spinoza's close intellectual milieu. But, contrary to what is sometimes asserted, Spinoza was far from unwilling to accept critique from qualified adversaries or to engage in debates with them about his work. When Oldenburg expressed some concern about the orthodoxy of the *TTP*, Spinoza asked him to explain in detail exactly what the problematic points were and, in his subsequent letters, responded to them one by one without concealing his true opinions in any way.[131] Similarly, Spinoza responded in length to Lambert van Velthuysen's very critical, but insightful letter to Jacob van Osten concerning the *TTP* and, later, requested permission from Velthuysen to include their exchange as an appendix to the second edition of the *TTP* he was planning to publish at the time.[132] What I have argued above is that Leibniz was a qualified adversary of the *TTP* comparable to Oldenburg and Velthuysen. Even

---

[129] A VI-1, 489.
[130] In 1675, Schuller wrote the following to Spinoza: "This same Leibniz thinks highly of the *Tractatus Theologico-politicus*, on which subject he once wrote you a letter" (*Ep.*70, *G* IV 303; Shirley 939). To this, Spinoza responded: "I believe I know Leibniz, of whom he writes, through correspondence [. . .] As far as I can judge from his letters [*epistolis*], he seemed to me a person of liberal mind [. . .]" (*Ep.*72, *G* IV 305; Shirley 941, translation modified).
[131] *Ep.* 68, *G* IV 292; Shirley 935–936. See also their subsequent exchange, i.e., *Ep.* 71, 73, 74, 75, 77, 78, 79.
[132] Cf. *Ep.* 69, *G* IV 300; Shirley 936.

though Leibniz took a very critical stance towards the book, he was capable of placing Spinoza in his true intellectual context, while still being sensitive to the specificity of his position. This would surely have been apparent from his lost letter(s) to Spinoza on the *TTP*. It is thus far from unlikely that Spinoza would have responded in earnest to Leibniz's letter(s) in the early 1670s – a conclusion which leaves us with one, nagging question: if Spinoza did indeed respond, what happened to those letters?

CHAPTER 7

The metaphysics of the Theological-Political Treatise

Yitzhak Y. Melamed

"[The common people] love the relics of time more than eternity itself."

(*Theological-Political Treatise*, Preface [*G* III 10])

I INTRODUCTION

In a certain, seemingly possible world in which Spinoza's *Ethics* had not been published, the *Theological-Political Treatise* would have become Spinoza's major *oeuvre* for generations to come. How likely such a world would have been – an issue which is primarily a function of the determination and capacities of Spinoza's circle of friends, as well as those of the Dutch authorities – is not for us to tell. But given the possibility, one might be tempted to consider the following question: had it been the case that the *Ethics* did not survive, what would we know about the metaphysical views of Spinoza? Unfortunately, this counterfactual exercise is virtually impossible to carry out, for we cannot un-know what we know about Spinoza's late views in the *Ethics*, nor can we truly avoid reading the *TTP* with an eye towards the *Ethics*.

For these reasons, it is not surprising that, with a few exceptions,[1] the existing literature on the *TTP* pays little attention to the metaphysical doctrines of the book, while on the other hand, studies of Spinoza's metaphysics commonly make little use of the *TTP*. These complementary attitudes, while understandable, seem to be mistaken for two reasons. First, a study of the *TTP* can tell us quite a bit about the development of Spinoza's metaphysical views. Second, and more importantly, on *some* metaphysical

I am indebted to Zach Gartenberg, Zeev Harvey, Michael Rosenthal, and Oded Schechter for their most helpful comments on earlier drafts of this chapter.
[1] Two notable exceptions are Curley's "Notes on a Neglected Masterpiece" and Miquel Beltrán's "The God of the *Tractatus Theologico-Politicus*."

issues, Spinoza's discussion in the *TTP* is more elaborate than the equivalent discussion of the same topic in the *Ethics*. One obvious case in point is the identity of God's essence and existence.

In this chapter I will attempt to reconstruct and draw an outline of the metaphysics of the *TTP*. I will begin with a brief overview of two methodological principles that play a central role in motivating Spinoza's metaphysics, and then delve into the issues of Spinoza's alleged pantheism, the identity of God's essence and existence, substance and attributes, and finally, the *conatus*.

Before we begin, let me briefly address one notable worry. It is commonly argued that many of Spinoza's claims in the *TTP* are veiled due to political circumstances and Spinoza's caution. This is not a groundless worry, yet I think it has been somewhat overstated since Spinoza usually gives very clear indications – far *too* clear, in fact, since many of his orthodox readers were immediately alarmed by them – as to his true views. We will encounter several examples of this practice.

2 METAPHYSICAL PRINCIPLES: THE PRINCIPLE OF SUFFICIENT REASON AND THE PRIORITY OF THE INFINITE

In E1p11d, Spinoza stipulates:

For each thing there must be assigned a cause or reason, both for its existence and for its non-existence.[2]

This strict demand for universal explicability and the rejection of any brute facts has been termed in recent literature – adequately to my mind – Spinoza's own version of the Principle of Sufficient Reason.[3] Since similar statements of the Principle of Sufficient Reason can be found in Spinoza's earliest works,[4] one may wonder what role, if any, the principle plays in the *TTP*.

At the end of Chapter 15 of the *TTP*, concluding his discussion of the relation between reason and theology, Spinoza makes the following quite extraordinary announcement:

[W]hat altar of refuge can a man find for himself when he commits treason against the majesty of reason [*nam quam aram sibi parare potest, qui rationis majestatem lædit*].[5]

---

[2] Cf. E1p8s2; *G* II 50/28. E1a2, which states that all things are conceived (and hence explained), could also be read as a statement of the Principle of Sufficient Reason.

[3] See Della Rocca, *Spinoza*, pp. 4–9, and Della Rocca, "A Rationalist Manifesto."

[4] *DPP*, 1a11; *G* I 158/3.   [5] *G* III 188.

There is much to be said about this image of reason, which ascribes to reason the same exhaustiveness, dominance, and omnipresence that traditional theologies ascribe to God. This passage leaves no room for anything that is beyond, or against, reason. Similarly, in the page preceding the above-mentioned announcement, Spinoza argues:

No one who is not without hope or insane would want to abolish reason completely and . . . deny [*negare*] the certainty of reason.[6]

Yet in spite of these bold statements, as well as Spinoza's severe critique of the commoner's tendency to prefer the imagination over the intellect,[7] it is not easy to find a clear statement in the *TTP* to the effect that *every* fact demands an explanation. The closest that Spinoza comes to making such a statement is, unsurprisingly, in his discussion of miracles. Let us have a close look at the following passage:

But since miracles were produced according to the capacity of the common people who were completely ignorant of the principles of natural things, plainly the ancients took for a miracle whatever they were unable to explain in the manner the common people normally explained natural things, namely by seeking to recall something similar which can be imagined without amazement. *For the common people suppose they have satisfactorily explained something as soon as it no longer astounds them.*[8]

What precisely went wrong in the *vulgus'* attempt (and failure) to explain miracles? Obviously they erred, according to Spinoza, by "being ignorant of the principles of natural things"; but why did they stay ignorant in spite of their genuine attempt to trace the causes of miracles? Why did they not look for the natural explanations of miracles? The *vulgus* were definitely not wrong in trying to find a causal explanation for miracles; Spinoza openly argues that we ought to try to explain things through their proximate causes.[9] What went wrong in the method of the "common people" was that they did not go far *enough* in their attempt to explain the nature of things. Instead of stubbornly seeking the complete causal chain for each fact, they felt content once an extraordinary fact was shown to be the result of a familiar phenomenon, while paying no attention to the need to explain the familiar. In a way, they were rudimentary common-sense philosophers who asked for an explanation for what appears to be against common sense, and were completely reassured once the unfamiliar turned out to be a result of the common. For Spinoza, our familiarity with a phenomenon does not render it intelligible, and the familiar, just like the extraordinary, demands

[6] *G* III 187.   [7] *TTP* Ch. 5; *G* III 77 and *TTP* Ch. 6; *G* III 81.
[8] *G* III 84; emphasis mine.   [9] *TTP* Ch. 4; *G* III 58/19–20.

a clear causal explanation. Indeed, it is precisely at this point that the thoroughness of one's commitment to the Principle of Sufficient Reason is tested. Few people would deny the need to explain unusual phenomena (e.g., flying hippos), but fewer would demand an explanation for what is common and ordinary (e.g., time), and it is precisely here where the task of the philosopher begins, first in making us de-familiarize ourselves with, and question the nature of, the ordinary, and then in attempting to explain it.

The other major metaphysical principle which motivates much of the metaphysics of both the *Ethics* and the *TTP* is *the ontological, as well as epistemological, priority of the infinite.*[10] In one of his boldest moves in the *Ethics* (and Spinoza's philosophical temper was never too mild), Spinoza criticizes his predecessors who

did not observe the [proper] order of Philosophizing. For they believed that the divine nature, which they should have contemplated before all else (because it is prior both in knowledge and in nature) is last in the order of knowledge, and that the things that are called objects of the senses are prior to all. That is why, when they contemplated natural things, they thought of nothing less than they did of the divine nature; and when afterwards they directed their minds to contemplating the divine nature, they could think of nothing less than of their first fictions, on which they had built the knowledge of natural things, because these could not assist knowledge of the divine nature.[11]

One may debate the precise target of this criticism (Descartes is clearly one of the targets), but as far as I can see, it is clear that this criticism is at least applicable to the Platonic path of epistemological ascent from the knowledge of beautiful bodies, through knowledge of beauty in the soul and the sciences, and which culminates in contemplation of "the very soul of the beauty . . . which neither flowers nor fades."[12] But Spinoza, unlike Socrates, does not seem to be impressed by Diotima's speech. If you begin with the beauty of Callias, you will end up with the purified beauty of Callias, which (at least for Spinoza) is still all too human. If you arrive at God at the end of the process you are likely to have a conception of God cast in the image of the things with which you began your journey. That is, I think, the meaning of Spinoza's claim that "when afterwards they directed their minds to contemplating the divine nature, they could think of nothing less than of their first fictions." But, for Spinoza, the Platonic path furthermore does not allow us to know finite things, since all things are to be known through their causes.[13] Hence, one *must* begin with the

[10] This paragraph is modified from my recent review of Michael Ayers, ed., *Rationalism, Platonism, and God.*
[11] E2p10s.   [12] Plato, *Symposium*, 210–211.   [13] E1a4.

knowledge of the infinite, the cause of all things, before turning to the knowledge of finite things ("when they contemplated natural things, they thought of nothing less than they did of the divine nature"). The immediate result of this epistemological revolution which makes the knowledge of any thing dependent upon our having a prior knowledge of God's essence (the ultimate cause of all things), is the trivialization of the knowledge of God's essence by making the knowledge of God's essence something one *cannot fail to have* – "God's infinite essence and his eternity are known to all"[14] – if one is to know anything at all.

In the *TTP* we find a very similar view, though it is never explicated in any systematic way and is presented in a manner that invites association with more traditional, primarily Christian, views. In Chapter 2 of the *TTP*, Spinoza scolds "those who freely admit that they do not possess the idea of God and know him only through created things (whose causes they are ignorant of), and do not hesitate to accuse philosophers of atheism."[15] Like the adversaries he takes to task in E2p10s, Spinoza criticizes here those who invert the order of philosophizing by trying to understand the infinite through created things, and as result fail to know both God and finite things.

The dependence of all knowledge on the prior knowledge of God is stated explicitly in Chapter 3:

[A]ll our knowledge and the certainty which truly takes away all doubt depends on a knowledge of God alone, and . . . without God nothing can exist or be conceived, . . . we are in doubt about everything as long as we have no clear and distinct idea of God.[16]

In several places in the *TTP* Spinoza also alludes to the view that the knowledge of God's essence is most common and unavoidable. In Chapter 1 Spinoza makes the apparently enigmatic claim that God communicates his essence to our minds *directly* "without the use of any physical means,"[17] and later, in the same chapter, he adds that we have "natural knowledge" that is "common to all" and by which "God's mind and his eternal thoughts [*æternæ sententiæ*] are indeed ascribed on our minds."[18] According to Spinoza, for God to speak to us "directly without the use of any physical means" is just to conceive things as eternal truths [*æternas veritates*].[19] Hence, we can conclude that God's "eternal thoughts," which are common

---

[14] E2p47s.   [15] *G* III 30.

[16] *G* III 59–60. For the dependence of all knowledge on our knowledge of God see further Annotation 6 to the *TTP* (*G* III 252).

[17] *G* III 20.   [18] *G* III 27.   [19] *G* III 63.

to all, are nothing but the eternal truth. Indeed later, in Chapter 16, Spinoza notes that eternal truths are such that "no one can fail to know."[20] Similarly, in Chapter 4 of the *TTP*, Spinoza suggests an interesting interpretation of Paul's announcement that all are without escape and cannot be excused by ignorance, by arguing that "assuredly they could have been excused were [Paul] talking about supernatural inspiration, the suffering of Christ in the flesh, the resurrection, etc."[21] Unlike the case of these supernatural beliefs, men could not be excused, says Spinoza, for failing to know God's eternity and power, which "each man fully understands by the natural light of reason."[22] Given Spinoza's claim in the *Ethics* that God's power is his essence,[23] and that eternity pertains to the nature or essence of God,[24] it is clear, I think, that in the last passage Spinoza alludes to the doctrine of the unavoidability of the knowledge of God's essence.

As I suggested above, Spinoza's main reason for demanding that the proper order of philosophizing is to begin with God is primarily the need to avoid an anthropomorphic conception of God. The critique of anthropomorphic and anthropocentric thinking is clearly one of the major underlying themes of the *TTP*.[25]

3 THE GOD OF THE *TTP*: GOD AND NATURE

In *Ep.* 6, addressed to Henry Oldenburg, Spinoza announces openly:

I do not separate God from nature as everyone known to me has done.[26]

This explicit admission of the novel nature of Spinoza's conception of God turns into a much more cautious expression in his late correspondence. Following the publication of the *TTP*, some of its readers detected the same view in the book. Lambert van Velthuysen charged Spinoza with "asserting that all things emanate from God's nature and that the universe itself is God,"[27] and Oldenburg noted that many readers of the *TTP* thought that Spinoza "confused" God with nature.[28] Spinoza does not really respond to Velthuysen's charge. He notes briefly that he does not wish to inquire "why it is the same, or not very different, to assert that all things emanate necessarily from God's nature and that the universe is

---

[20] *G* III 192.   [21] *G* III 68.   [22] *G* III 68.   [23] E1p34.   [24] E1p19d.
[25] See Spinoza's critique of those who "consider nature to be so limited that they believe men are its most important part" and believe "that they are dearer to God than others and are the ultimate reason for God's creation and continual governance of all things" (*TTP* Ch. 6; *G* III 82). Cf. *G* III 88, and *TTP* Ch. 16 (*G* III 190–191).
[26] *G* IV 36/24.   [27] *Ep.* 42; *Letters*, p. 227.   [28] *Ep.* 71; *Letters*, p. 329.

God,"[29] and moves on to another issue. In response to Oldenburg's query, he first states that his views are not really anything new since Paul, "the Ancient Hebrews,"[30] and "perhaps all ancient philosophers" all shared the same view of God's relation to nature. Spinoza's attempt to present his views of God and nature as being traditional and in contrast only with the innovations of the "modern Christians"[31] is a sharp change of strategy from his presentation of the same views in *Ep.* 6. Spinoza's second line of defense against Oldenburg's query is to claim that those who thought that the *TTP* "rests on the identification of God with Nature . . . are quite mistaken"; and then he adds in brackets that this is so if "by the latter of which [Nature] they understand a kind of mass or corporeal matter."[32] The clear implication of the provision in brackets is that under a different understanding of nature (i.e., one which does not identify nature with "mass or corporeal matter"[33]), God *is* identical with nature.

But where in the *TTP* does Spinoza assert or allude to the identity of God and nature? We have seen that Spinoza understands (or perhaps pretends to understand) Velthuysen as ascribing to him the identification of God and the universe on the basis of Spinoza's alleged claim that "all things emanate necessarily from God's nature." However, I am not aware of any place in the *TTP* in which Spinoza makes the latter claim. Spinoza perhaps comes close to this by suggesting that the laws of nature "follow [*sequuntur*] from the necessity and perfection of the divine nature,"[34] but this does not have to be read as a pantheistic claim. Nor should Spinoza's claim that "the power of Nature is nothing other than the power of God itself"[35] have to be read as an endorsement of pantheism.[36] Yet, there are at least two passages in the *TTP* which strongly suggest a pantheistic view.

Spinoza begins the passage below with the rather weak claim that by knowing nature we improve our knowledge of God, the creator, or cause, of all things.[37] Yet, in the second half of the passage he makes the much stronger claim that our knowledge not only depends on the knowledge of

---

[29] *Ep.* 43; *Letters*, p. 239.
[30] On the identity of the "Ancient Hebrews," see my "Spinoza's Metaphysics of Substance," p. 40 n. 72, and "From the 'Gates of Heaven'" (unpublished manuscript).
[31] *Ep.* 73; *Letters*, p. 332.   [32] *Ep.* 63; *Letters*, p. 332.
[33] See Spinoza's footnote in *TTP* Ch. 6; *G* III 83, where he says that by "nature" he means "not only matter and its affections, but other infinite things besides matter." See section 5 below.
[34] *G* III 82–83.   [35] *G* III 28.
[36] Nature could be independent of, and yet caused by, God, and then in its turn, cause other things. In such a scenario the causal power of nature will be ultimately traced to God, but without identifying the two.
[37] This weaker claim appears quite commonly in the *TTP*. See, for example, Ch. 6; *G* III 86.

God, but "consists altogether [*omnino consistit*]" in the knowledge of God, clearly implying that there is nothing "outside" God.

Further (since knowledge of an effect through a cause is simply to know some property of the cause [*causæ proprietatem aliquam congnoscere*]) the more we learn about natural things, the more perfectly we come to know the essence of God (which is the cause of all things); and thus *all our knowledge*, that is, our highest good, *not only depends on a knowledge of God but consists in it altogether.*[38]

The interesting doctrine with which Spinoza begins the passage – that knowledge of an effect through its cause is nothing but knowledge of a property of the cause – provides the ground for the identification of God and nature. The essence of God is the cause of all things. An effect is a property of the cause. Hence, all things are just God's properties that follow from his essence. As a result, Spinoza can say that whatever we know is nothing but God (or properties of God).[39]

The second passage in which Spinoza clearly alludes to the identification of God and nature appears in Chapter 14 of the *TTP*. In this chapter, Spinoza sets out to "propose the separation of faith from philosophy which, indeed, has been the principal purpose of the whole work."[40] The separating line between the two is drawn very clearly: faith and philosophy have different aims. Philosophy attempts to discover the truth, while the aim of faith is not truth but obedience: "faith requires not so much true as pious dogmas, that is, such tenets as move the mind to obedience, even though many of these may not have a shadow of truth in them."[41] Thus, the dogmas of faith must be such that belief in them is conducive to obedience. Obviously, the believer must believe that the tenets of faith are true, but those who disseminate and teach faith should not be much bothered by the truthfulness of the doctrines, but rather by their usefulness. Spinoza even suggests a detailed list of the tenets of faith, each of which is necessary, and all of which are sufficient to secure obedience. These doctrines are (1) that there is a God, (2) that he is one, (3) that he is present everywhere and all things are manifest to him, (4) that he possesses supreme right and dominion over all things, (5) that the worship of God consists solely in justice and charity, (6) that all who obey God, and only they, are saved, and finally, (7) that God forgives the repentant their sins. Spinoza did not hold many of these beliefs (e.g., divine forgiveness), but more interesting is the way he

---

[38] G III 60. Emphasis mine.
[39] Spinoza makes a very similar claim in the *Ethics* in E1p16d. See my "Spinoza's Metaphysics of Substance," pp. 66–69.
[40] G III 174.   [41] G III 176.

formulates some of the beliefs in a manner that could be interpreted in two ways: one consistent with popular, traditional, religion, the other being in agreement with philosophical truth.[42] Indeed, immediately following the enumeration of his seven principles of faith, he adds:

No one can fail to recognize that all these things absolutely need to be known, so that all men without exception may be able to love God. By the command of the Law explained above, for if any of these is removed, obedience too is gone. But what God, or the exemplar of true life, is, e.g., whether he is fire or spirit or life or thought, etc. is irrelevant to faith [*fidem*], as are questions about the manner in which he is the exemplar of the true life; for example, is it because he has a just and merciful mind? Or is it because all things exist and act through him [*vel quia res omnes per ipsum sunt, & agunt*] and therefore we understand them through him and see what is true, right and good through him? Whatever one's views on these questions it makes no difference.

Furthermore, it has nothing to do with faith whether one believes that God is everywhere[43] in essence or in potential [*secundum essentiam, vel secundum potentiam ubique sit*], whether he issues edicts like prince or teaches them as eternal truth, whether man obeys God of his own free will or by the necessity of the divine decree, or whether reward of the good and punishment of wrongdoers takes place naturally or supernaturally.[44]

What is interesting in this passage is that here Spinoza gives clear indications as to his own philosophical views. A reader of the *TTP* could hardly fail to comprehend that for Spinoza God is not just, since "just" is decried by Spinoza repeatedly as an anthropomorphic way of talking about God.[45] Hence, the true meaning of God's being the exemplar of true life is clearly "because all things exist and act through him." Similarly, given Spinoza's harsh critique of the anthropomorphic conception of God as judge or prince,[46] and of the illusory belief in free will,[47] it is clear that Spinoza's

---

[42] Cf. Pines ("Spinoza's TTP," p. 33): "The true philosophers . . . can unhesitantly give their assent to the dogmas . . . the dogmas can be interpreted in accordance with [the adequate knowledge of God]."

[43] In Annotation 6 to the *TTP* (*G* III 253), Spinoza asserts again that once we conceive of God's nature it becomes evident that "God is everywhere [*ubique esse*]."

[44] *G* III 178

[45] "[Paul] spoke 'in human terms', expressly admitting this when he calls God 'just'. Likewise, it is undoubtedly due to this 'weakness of the flesh' that he attributes pity, grace, anger etc. to God" (*G* III 65). Cf. *G* III 42 and *G* III 64. For Spinoza, even ascribing "mind" [*mens*] to God is an act of anthropomorphism (*G* III 25).

[46] "Thus [Moses] perceived all these things not as eternal truths but as precepts and teachings, and prescribed them as decrees of God. That is why he imagined God as ruler, legislator, king, merciful, just etc., despite the fact that all the latter are merely attributes of human nature and far removed from the divine nature" (*G* III 64).

[47] "Nor did Moses adequately grasp that God is omniscient and directs all human actions by his decrees alone" (*TTP* Ch. 13; *G* III 38, cf. *G* III 33 and 42–43).

philosophical truth is that God teaches morality as eternal truth, and that men obey him "by the necessity of the divine decree." Spinoza's claim that for faith it does not matter whether "God is everywhere in essence or in potential" should be understood along the very same lines. One of the disjunctives indicates a belief that is conducive to obedience, but not precisely true, while the other indicates the precise philosophical teaching. The claim that God is everywhere *secundum potentiam* means simply that God's power extends everywhere. This is clearly a very traditional belief, and in fact Spinoza should have no reason to reject it, apart from noting its being a certain understatement of God's ubiquity. Indeed, the other disjunct makes the bolder, and for Spinoza more precise, claim that God is everywhere *secundum essentiam*; but to say that God is *essentially* everywhere is just to claim that physical nature is not and cannot be distinct from God.

4 THE GOD OF THE *TTP*: GOD'S ESSENCE IS EXISTENCE

In the course of his discussion of the different aims of faith and philosophy, Spinoza also digresses into the issue of the meaning of the Tetragrammaton, which, as it will turn out, pertains to the very core of Spinoza's metaphysics. At the beginning of Chapter 13 of the *TTP* Spinoza argues that "biblical teachings contain no elevated theories or philosophical doctrines but only the simplest matters comprehensible to even the very slowest."[48] Yet, it is only a few pages later that Spinoza points out a deep metaphysical issue alluded by the word of God.

In order to show that true knowledge of God is not necessary for piety and faith, Spinoza brings forth the case of the Patriarchs, about whom, he claims, Scripture attests that they did not know the true essence of God, and yet were most pious.

For the first point ["that an intellectual or precise knowledge of God is not a gift generally given to the faithful"], most evidently follows from Exodus 6:3, where in showing Moses the singular grace given to him, God says: "And I was revealed to Abraham, to Isaac, and to Jacob as *El Shaddai*, but I was not known to them by my name Jehova." To clarify this, we must note that *El* Shaddai in Hebrew signifies "God who suffices" because he gives each person what suffices to him; and although *Shaddai* is often used on its own to refer to God, we should not doubt that the word *El* ("God") should always be silently understood. We should further note that no name is found in the Bible other than Jehova to indicate the absolute essence of God [*Dei absolutam essentiam*] without relation to created things. The

---

[48] *G* III 167. Cf. Spinoza's claim that at Sinai God did not reveal to the Hebrews the attributes of his absolute essence, but only roused them to obedience (*G* III 179).

Hebrews therefore claim that this is the only proper name of God and that all the others are forms of address [*appellativa*]; and in truth [*et revera*] the other names of God, whether they are nouns or adjectives, are attributes which belong to God in so far as he is considered in relation to his creatures or manifested through them. An example is *El*, which means simply "powerful" . . . Elsewhere the virtues of his power are given in full, as *El* ("powerful"), great, terrible, just, merciful, [*ut El magnus, tremendous, Justus, misericors*] etc.[49]

Two observations seem to be in place here. First, Spinoza's concurrence ("and in truth") with the claim that only the Tetragrammaton indicates God's essence is not demanded by his polemical objectives. His argument would have held even had he not endorsed the claim of "the Hebrews," i.e., had he just showed that according to the biblical authors God's essence was not known to the obedient and pious Patriarchs. Therefore, I suggest that we should take the "*et revera*" seriously as communicating Spinoza's genuine agreement with this interpretation of the Tetragrammaton, especially if the ensuing view of God's essence would turn out to be in agreement with Spinoza's exposition of his metaphysics in some other texts.

The second observation which we should not miss is the strong similarity between Spinoza's and Maimonides's claims about the meaning of the Tetragrammaton. Although many medieval commentators with whom Spinoza was acquainted adopted similar explanations of the meaning of the Tetragrammaton and of *ego sum qui sum* [*Eheye asher Eheye*] (Exodus 3:14),[50] there is little doubt that Spinoza relates here primarily to Maimonides's discussion in *Guide of the Perplexed* I, 61. Spinoza's claims that the Tetragrammaton is, strictly speaking, God's only name and that "no name is found in the Bible other than Jehova to indicate the absolute essence of God [*Dei absolutam essentiam*] without relation to created things" are just restatements of Maimonides's claims in *Guide* I, 61.[51]

---

[49] *G* III 168–169.

[50] Such as, Ibn-Ezra, Gersonides, and Aquinas. See Ibn Ezra's *Commentary on the Pentateuch*, Exodus 3:14–15, Gersonides's *Commentary on the Pentateuch*, Exodus 3:13–15, and Aquinas, *Summa theologiae*, Ia Q. 13, 11. Cf. Harvey, "Spinoza's Metaphysical Hebraism," pp. 110 and 114 (n. 23). For Christian interpretations of Exodus 3:14, see Gilson, *The Spirit of Medieval Philosophy*, pp. 51f. The view of the Tetragrammaton as indicating God's self-necessitated existence appears also in Avraham ha-Kohen Hererra's *Beit Elohim* [Hebrew: *The House of God*] (1755), p. 33. This is a Hebrew translation (from the original Spanish) by Yitzhak Aboav De Fonesca, who was one of the rabbis of the Amsterdam community at Spinoza's time and might have been one of Spinoza's teachers. The question of Herrera's possible influence on Spinoza is still unsolved.

[51] "All the names of God, may He be exalted, that are to be found in any of the books derive from actions. There is nothing secret in this matter. The only exception is one name: namely, *Yod, He, Vav, He*. This is the name of God, may He be exalted, that has been originated without any derivation, and for this reason it is called the *articulated name*. This means that this name gives a clear unequivocal indication of His essence, may He be exalted" (*Guide* I 61). Cf. "Thus it has

But what then is God's absolute essence which is indicated uniquely by the Tetragrammaton? For Maimonides, the answer is straightforward: God's essence is nothing but simple, unadulterated existence (or rather, necessary existence).[52] Following an initial hesitance to publicly expound the meaning of the Tetragrammaton,[53] Maimonides concludes his discussion of God's unique name with a brief yet unequivocal statement:

He, May He be exalted, has no *name* that is not derivative except the *name having four letters*, which is *the articulated name. This name is not indicative of an attribute but of simple existence and nothing else.* Now absolute existence implies that He shall always be, I mean He who is necessarily existent.[54] Understand the point at which this discourse has finally arrived.[55]

Spinoza's understanding of this issue is not very different from that of Maimonides. In the only other passage in the *TTP* in which the meaning of the Tetragrammaton is discussed, Spinoza writes:

become clear to you that *the articulated name* is the *name having four letters* and that it alone is indicative of the essence without associating any other notion with it. For this reason the Sages have said of it that is is the name *that is peculiar to Me* [*shmi ha-meyuhad li*]" (*Guide* I 61. Italics mine). Interestingly, Maimonides's discussion of the meaning of the Tetragrammaton is cited extensively in the work of Rabbi Shaul Mortera, who was one of Spinoza's teachers in the Jewish community of Amsterdam. See *Giveat Shaul* [Hebrew: *Saul's Hill*], p. 60.

In this context, Spinoza also explains that the name "'*El Shaddai*' in Hebrew means 'the God who suffices' [*Deum, qui sufficit*]" (*G* III 169/4). Compare this with Maimonides's claim that the meaning of the same name is "*He who is sufficient*" (*Guide* I 63). Finally, the examples of "qualities of potency" which Spinoza brings to bear – "the great [*magnus*], the awful [*tremendus*] . . . " are just the attributes which begin the daily Jewish prayer of *Shmone Esre* ("The Eighteen Benedictions"), of which Maimonides says that such anthropomorphic language would have been prohibited were it not inserted into the daily prayer by "the Men of the Great Synagogue" (*Guide* I 59).
[52] This very same view is also suggested by Salomon Maimon (1753–1800), the great modern disciple of both Maimonides and Spinoza: "But the greatest of all mysteries in the Jewish Religion consists in the name Jehova, expressing *bare existence*, in abstraction from *all particular kinds of existence*, which cannot of course be conceived without *existence in general*. The doctrine of the unity of God, and the dependence of all beings on Him, in regard to their possibility as well as their actuality, can be perfectly comprehended only in conformity with a *single system*" (*Autobiography*, pp. 181–182). The "single system" at stake is, I believe, Spinozism. See my "Salomon Maimon."
[53] "There can be no doubt about the fact that this great name, which as you know is not pronounced except in the *Sanctuary* by the *sanctified Priests of the Lord* and only in *the benediction of the Priests* and by *the High Priest* upon *the day of fasting*, is indicative of a notion with reference to which there is no association between God, may He be exalted, and what is other than He. *Perhaps it indicates the notion of necessary existence*, according to the [Hebrew] language, of which we today know only a very scant portion and also with regard to its pronunciation. Generally speaking, the greatness of this name and the prohibition against pronouncing it are due to *its being indicative of the essence of Him, may He be exalted, in such a way that none of the created things is associated with him in this indication* (*Guide* I 61. Italics mine).
[54] By "necessary existence" Maimonides refers here to the Avicennian notion of a thing which exists necessarily and not by virtue of a cause (while all other things – those we call "possible" – are necessitated as they are caused by the thing which is "necessary of existence").
[55] Maimonides, *Guide* I 63.

Anyone who reflects on Moses' opinions without prejudice, will plainly see that he believed God to be a being that has always existed, exists and will always exist, and for this reason he calls him "Jehova" by name, which in Hebrew expresses these three tenses of existence [*quod Hebraice hæc tria tempora existendi exprimit*].[56]

Spinoza agrees with Maimonides that the Tetragrammaton indicates necessary existence, and from Spinoza's brief interpolation that the Tetragrammaton "in truth [*revera*]" indicates God's essence, we can conclude that for Spinoza, as for Maimonides, God's essence is necessary existence.[57] Indeed, in the *Ethics* Spinoza argues and proves that God's essence is nothing but existence.[58] Furthermore, since Spinoza defines eternity (*aeternitas*) as self-necessitated existence,[59] and since eternity is the manner of existence of *natura naturans*, i.e., God's essence,[60] it is clear that in the *Ethics* as well God's essence is self-necessitated existence.[61]

5 SUBSTANCE AND ATTRIBUTES

So far we have seen that on the two crucial metaphysical issues of God's identity with nature and of the essence of God as pure existence, the *TTP* provides important indications as to Spinoza's late views. We may thus be surprised to find that two of the most central concepts of Spinoza's ontology – "substance" [*substantia*] and "mode" [*modus*] – are completely absent in the *TTP*. In fact, it is the only philosophical composition of Spinoza in which *substantia* and *modus* (and their equivalent Dutch terms) do not appear.[62]

When we look at Spinoza's use of *attributum* in the *TTP*, we find that in most cases the term is not reserved, as in the *Ethics*, to God's essential attributes,[63] but is rather used to include also attributes by which various

---

[56] *G* III 38. [57] Cf. Beltrán, "The God of the *Tractatus Theologico-Politicus*," p. 30.

[58] E1p20. [59] E1d8.

[60] "The difference between Eternity and Duration arises from this. For it is only of Modes that we can explain the existence by Duration. But [we can explain the existence] of Substance by Eternity, i.e., the infinite enjoyment of existing, or (in bad Latin) of being" (*Ep.* 12; *G* IV 54–55).

[61] In the history of Western metaphysics we find two competing conceptions of eternity. The one understands eternity as existence in all times, the other as existence that is utterly alien to any temporal existence (a remnant of this second kind of eternity can still be found today in the conception of the existence of numbers among mathematical realists or Platonists). For Maimonides, the existence indicated by the Tetragrammaton is clearly atemporal. One of Spinoza's notes in *TTP* (*G* III 38) might suggest that he understands the meaning of the Tetragrammaton to refer to existence in all time. Yet, in his explanation of the definition of eternity in the *Ethics* he stresses that eternity "cannot be explained by duration or time, even if the duration is conceived to be without beginning or end" (E1p8e). For further discussion of the nature of God's essence as existence, see my "Spinoza's Deification of Existence."

[62] Cf. Curley, "Notes," p. 115.

[63] *G* III 169–170 (discussed above in section 4) and *G* III 179/20–22 are notable exceptions.

people inadequately conceived God.[64] Neither Extension nor Thought is described as a divine attribute. It seems that in the *TTP* Spinoza tried to avoid the use of technical terminology by employing more common and traditional terms instead of the rigid terminology of the *Ethics* (for example, by claiming that God's essence is eternal existence instead of saying that God is a substance, or by insinuating that God is everywhere in essence, instead of claiming that Extension is one of God's attributes). There is one interesting footnote in the *TTP* in which Spinoza clearly refers to the doctrine of the infinity of God's attributes, though intriguingly he does not use the term *attributum* in this place. In this note Spinoza glosses his use of the term "nature" with the following warning:

Note that here I mean not only matter and its affections [*affectiones*], but other infinite things [*alia infinita*] besides matter.[65]

Why Spinoza does not mention the term "attribute" here is somewhat unclear. It could definitely be a coincidence. Yet we would like to point out that in *Ep.* 36, probably dated June 1666, Spinoza expounds expansively on the nature of Extension and Thought without even once mentioning the term "attribute." It is, I think, possible that in this period of time Spinoza was still hesitating as to the precise nature of Extension and Thought. *Ep.* 36, however, survives only in translation, and hence it is hard to clarify this point.

6 THE *CONATUS*

Chapter 16 of the *TTP* begins the part of the book which is dedicated primarily to Spinoza's political philosophy. So it is fitting that Spinoza begins this discussion with the metaphysical principle that grounds much of his politics:

It is the supreme law of nature that each thing strives to persist in its own state [*suo statu*] so far as it can, taking no account of another's circumstances but only of its own.[66]

Following the statement of this "supreme law" Spinoza stresses the exhaustive universality of the law:

Here we recognize no difference between human beings and other individual things of nature [*reliqua naturæ individua*], nor between human beings who are

[64] See, for example, *G* III 48/30, 169/12–13, 170/34–35, 171/23, 172/16.
[65] *G* III 83. I have here corrected the translation of Silverthorne and Israel.   [66] *G* III 189.

endowed with reason and others who do not know true reason,[67] nor between fools or lunatics and the sane.[68]

Spinoza applies the *conatus* doctrine to all individuals in nature: human beings, animals, rocks,[69] and political entities.[70] The *conatus* doctrine is not unique to Spinoza; variants of this doctrine can be found in numerous early modern works, including the sermons of Rabbi Shaul Mortera, Spinoza's teacher in the Jewish community of Amsterdam.[71]

One important feature of Spinoza's discussion of the *conatus* in the *TTP* is that unlike the equivalent discussion in Part Three of the *Ethics* (E3pp4–6), Spinoza does not ground the principle in the impossibility of self-destruction (or self-negation), but rather leaves it as a supreme, most universal, and yet, unexplained, law of nature.[72]

7 CONCLUSION

In this chapter I have attempted to outline the metaphysical views of the *TTP*. I have concentrated on what I consider to be the core of Spinoza's metaphysics. Several important issues, such as Spinoza's conception of laws of nature and his remarks about the love of God and eternity of mind[73] (which may shed light on the enigmatic conclusion of the *Ethics*), were left aside. Each of these two issues deserves a study of its own. We have noticed that in the *TTP* Spinoza avoided his key terminology of substance and mode. Similarly, there seems to be no trace in the *TTP* of the issue of the nature of infinity with which Spinoza was engaged throughout his life. The *TTP* is clearly not a work of technical philosophy. Yet it is a rather precise book, and for the most part, Spinoza seems to be quite cautious not only in trying to avoid political trouble but also in trying to avoid going too far from or being too vague about what he believed to be the exact truth. For these reasons I believe the book is an invaluable resource for understanding Spinoza's metaphysics.

[67] Cf. *TTP* Ch. 5; *G* III 73: "All men do indeed seek their own interest, but it is not from the dictate of sound reason; for the most part they pursue things and judge them to be in their interest merely because they are carried away by sensual desire and by their passions."

[68] *G* III 189–190.   [69] See *Ep.* 58.

[70] On the striving of each state "to be beyond fear, and hence, to be its own master," see *TP* Ch. 3; *G* III 290.

[71] See *Giveat Shaul*, Chapter 18, p. 136.

[72] For Spinoza a law of nature "is one that necessarily follows from the very nature or definition of a thing" (*TTP* Ch. 4; *G* III 57), i.e., it is a proprium which follows from the essence of the things that fall under this law. Presumably, a supreme and most universal law of nature should follow from the essence of *all* things (or all finite things).

[73] See *TTP* Ch. 4; *G* III 60, and *TTP* Ch. 5; *G* III 71.

CHAPTER 8

Spinoza's conception of law: metaphysics and ethics

Donald Rutherford

The God of the Hebrew Bible is a sovereign lawgiver to the Jewish people. God commands his people to act, or not to act, in certain ways and holds them responsible for their actions, punishing disobedience and rewarding obedience. Within the religious traditions that descend from Judaism, divine law is conceived of as a set of dictates or commands that God issues to all human beings – commands that establish inescapable obligations, on the basis of which humans are held accountable for their actions. One of Spinoza's primary goals in the *TTP* is to offer a reinterpretation of the idea of divine law, according to which it is understood not as the literal command of a sovereign being, but as a law taught by the "natural light of reason"[1] and "inferred from the consideration of human nature alone."[2] In the *TTP*, this interpretation is developed against the background of a general analysis of the concept of law that has wide-ranging consequences for Spinoza's philosophy. In what follows I focus on two of these consequences: Spinoza's endeavor to use the notion of law (including divine law) to bridge the divide between the natural and the normative, and the role he assigns to the concept of law in underwriting the systematic unity of his ethical theory.

I GENERAL ANALYSIS OF LAW

Spinoza presents his fullest analysis of the concept of law in Chapter 4 of the *TTP*, "On the divine law." He begins with what I will call his "general account": "The word 'law' in an unqualified sense [*absolute sumptum*] signifies that, in accordance with which, each individual thing, or all or some

---

I am grateful to Yitzhak Melamed and Michael Rosenthal for their helpful comments on an earlier draft of this chapter.

[1] *G* III 10/7. Unless otherwise specified, quotations from the *TTP* are drawn from Jonathan Israel's edition. Quotations from the *Ethics* are drawn from Edwin Curley's edition.

[2] *G* III 61/24–25.

things of the same kind, act in one and the same fixed and determinate way [*certa ac determinate ratione agunt*]."³ The general account highlights the determinacy and regularity of law-governed action, but does not explicitly invoke the notion of necessity, or distinguish between descriptive and pre-scriptive conceptions of law. These ideas come to the fore when Spinoza goes on to distinguish two bases for law: a law may depend either on natural necessity or on "human decision." Let us call these, respectively, type-I laws and type-II laws. A type-I law is a law that expresses a natural necessity, or which "necessarily follows from the very nature or definition of a thing." A type-II law, by contrast, is one that "depends upon human decision [*ab hominum placito*]," and which "men prescribe to themselves and others in order to live more safely and more comfortably, or for other reasons [*ad tutius, & commodius vivendum, vel ob alias causas*]."⁴

Spinoza's general account encompasses two very different notions of law. Type-I laws have no normative content: they are descriptive propositions that state how things necessarily act, and that follow necessarily from the nature of a thing. Spinoza gives two examples of laws of this sort. It is a universal law of body that "when one body strikes a smaller body, it only loses as much of its own motion as it communicates to the other." And it is a universal law of human nature that "when a man recalls one thing he immediately remembers another which is similar or which he had seen along with the first thing."⁵ Type-II laws are distinguished from these laws, in part, by the fact that they do not follow necessarily from the nature of a thing. If it is a law "that men give up their right which they receive from nature . . . and commit themselves to a particular rule of life,"⁶ this law does not follow from human nature alone. By virtue of being human, an individual does not necessarily act in a cooperative manner, though he may prescribe to himself and others that they *should* act in this way. Such

---

³ *G* III 57/23–26; trans. modified.

⁴ *G* III 57/27–31; trans. modified. The phrase *ab* (or *ex*) *hominum placito* presents difficulties. Literally it means "at the pleasure of men," which is to say, as human beings decide it. The phrase appears in medieval debates about whether linguistic meaning is determined by nature or by imposition. See, e.g., Peter Abelard, *Theologia "summi boni"*, III.35: "Priscianus, doctor et scriptor loquendi, in locutionibus maxime usum emulandum esse admonet. Bene equidem, cum locutio significationem non ex natura sed ex placito hominum habeat." For a full discussion, see Meier-Oeser, *Die Spur des Zeichens*; Marenbon, *The Philosophy of Peter Abelard*, pp. 176–184.

⁵ *G* III 57–58. The relativization of type-I laws to kinds or species may prompt concerns about the status of such kinds in Spinoza's philosophy. The universal laws of body present no special problem, since any body is a mode of the attribute of Extension (and similarly for universal laws of mind). The "laws of human nature" are less easily explained, for Spinoza sometimes uses this phrase in a way that does not refer (as it does here) to actions that follow necessarily from the nature of any human being. I return to this point in section 2.

⁶ *G* III 58/4–6.

a requirement would be an example of a type-II law, which depends upon a human decision and involves normative content. In contrast to type-I laws, type-II laws are practical or action-guiding. Their logical form is that of hypothetical imperatives: they dictate how one ought to act, for the sake of a given end.

On the face of it, the account of type-II laws comes closest to capturing our ordinary notion of law. Laws have normative content, and they are action-guiding. Nevertheless, Spinoza holds that type-I laws are metaphysically basic and represent the meaning of "law" in its strictest sense. Given its dependence upon human decision, he says, a type-II law is "more properly called a decree [*jus*]."[7] He acknowledges that this may appear to reverse the correct order of understanding. The word "law" seems (*videtur*) to be applied metaphorically to natural things. Commonly (*communiter*), the word is understood to signify nothing but "a command which men may or may not follow, since a law constrains human powers within certain limits which they naturally exceed, and does not command anything beyond their scope."[8] Yet, for Spinoza, this notion of law is a secondary one, which presupposes the more basic sense of law as the expression of a natural necessity, or a regularity that follows necessarily from the nature or definition of a thing.[9]

Spinoza elaborates his analysis with a further set of observations about how the idea of law commonly functions in political and religious contexts. Taking the operative notion of law to be "a rule for living [*ratio vivendi*] which a man prescribes to himself or others for some purpose," legislators are able (wisely, Spinoza says) to disengage the rule from its true purpose, which is grasped by only a few, and to attach it to "another purpose very different from the one which necessarily follows from the nature of laws."[10] Obedience to the law is now associated with reward and punishment by

---

[7] *G* III 57/29. One might quibble with this rendering of *jus*, which Spinoza (like his predecessors) uses very broadly. As I discuss in the next section, his analysis of natural right (*jus naturale*) in Chapter 16 grounds this right in a natural necessity.

[8] *G* III 58/28–33.

[9] Spinoza may believe that, etymologically, the word "law" is applied metaphorically to natural things, or to "the order of nature itself" (*G* III 162/22). This, however, is consistent with the claim that type-I laws are metaphysically basic, in the sense that the operation of type-II laws is explained in terms of them. Curley ("The State of Nature and Its Law," pp. 108–109) reaches a different conclusion. He argues that what I have called Spinoza's general account is only a "provisional" definition; that the word "law" is used only metaphorically when applied to natural things; and that Spinoza's preferred definition is the one that I have identified with type-II laws: "a rule for living which a man prescribes to himself or others for some purpose" (*G* III 58/33–35). Miller ("Spinoza and the Concept of a Law of Nature") dissents from Curley's view but does not develop the distinction between type-I and type-II laws.

[10] *G* III 58–59.

an authority, as a result of which "the essence of law is taken to be a rule of life prescribed to men by the command of another; and consequently those who obey the laws are said to live under law and are regarded as subjects of it."[11] Spinoza leaves no doubt that he regards this as a superficial understanding of law. One who gives other individuals their due because he is commanded to do so, and fears the consequences of disobedience, cannot be called "just." That title is reserved for the person who acts in the required manner, "because he knows the true rationale of laws and understands their necessity." Such a person acts "steadfastly [*animo constanti*] and at his own and not another's command, and therefore is deservedly called just [*justus*]."[12]

Spinoza's critical remarks on the notion of law as the binding command of a superior make it clear that he sees his own general account – involving the postulation of both type-I and type-II laws – as a revisionary analysis. The principal interpretive problem the account raises is understanding the relationship between these two types of law. Spinoza's last example high-lights the problem. The principle of justice – to give each person his due – seems a prime example of a type-II law: a normative principle that is action-guiding. We know from Spinoza's analysis that this law is not to be construed simply as the command of a superior (who possesses the means to inflict punishment). As a type-II law, the rule of justice is properly regarded as a law that one prescribes to oneself and others, in order "to live more safely and more comfortably." Yet the details of Spinoza's account remain underdeveloped. The just man performs the actions required of him, "because he knows the true rationale of laws and understands their necessity." This underlines the just person's grasp of the necessary connec-tion between the practice of justice and the achievement of a safer and more comfortable life. However, it leaves unaddressed the relation between what the just person understands about the basis of type-II laws and his

---

[11] *G* III 59/8–11.

[12] *G* III 59/14–16. Spinoza offers two distinct accounts of the "just." Philosophically, it is (as presented here) a quality of character exemplary of virtue. This is the notion described in E4p18s: "men who are governed by reason – that is, men who, from the guidance of reason, seek their own advantage – want nothing for themselves which they do not desire for other men. Hence they are just, honest, and honorable [*justos, fidos, atque honestos*]" (*G* II 223/17–18). In other contexts, he restricts the notions of just and unjust to a state governed by civil laws, denying that there can be any wrongdoing in the state of nature. See *TTP* Ch. 16; *G* III 196 and E4p37s2: "in the state of nature nothing is done which can be called just or unjust [*justum, aut injustum*]. But in the civil state, of course, where it is decided by common consent what belongs to this man, and what to that [, things are done which can be called just and unjust]" (*G* II 238–239).

determination (or motivation) to act in accordance with those laws. Fur-thermore, in saying just this, we are no closer to explaining the dependence I have claimed Spinoza assumes of type-II laws on type-I laws.

One thing we do know is that, even if Spinoza is committed to the primacy of type-I laws as statements of metaphysical necessity, he does not believe that we can dispense entirely with type-II laws. This is an important point, because it signals the way in which his philosophy reserves a place for practical, normative laws that depend upon human volition. In *TTP*, Chapter 4, Spinoza affirms his commitment to the thesis that "all things are determined by the universal laws of nature to exist and act in a fixed and determined manner."[13] Given this, type-I laws must be sufficient to explain everything that happens in nature. Nevertheless, he insists that there remains room for type-II laws, and that they play a critical role in human agency.

Spinoza credits the institution, and binding force (*sanctio*), of type-II laws to particular human decisions, as opposed to the nature of the mind in general (or the "mind, so far as it perceives what is true or false").[14] Such laws are not universal principles that can be deduced from the nature of the human mind, but instead depend upon individual human beings pre-scribing "rules for living" to themselves or others. Once decreed, these laws offer significant practical advantages. Knowing that the world is governed by universal necessary laws does not tell us how we should act in particular situations. Such laws give no direction to our efforts to intervene in the world, and they leave us ignorant of "the actual coordination and connect-edness of things,"[15] including the determination of our own power by the power of other things. It is precisely in such circumstances that we are aided by type-II laws, which dictate necessary means to desired ends. When we allow ourselves to be commanded by such laws, we in effect acknowledge our ignorance about how things are "really ordered and connected."[16] We take ourselves to be capable of bringing about the objects we desire by bringing about the necessary means to them. The assumption that we *can* do this may turn out to be mistaken, for other causes may block the efficacy of our actions. Nevertheless, Spinoza observes that "it is better and indeed necessary for the conduct of life, to regard things as possible."[17] This we must do if we are to function as agents, despite its being true that all things

[13] *G* III 58/7–8.
[14] *G* III 58/16–17. On the rationale for translating Spinoza's *sanctionem istarum legum* as "the binding force of those laws," see Bentham, *Introduction to the Principles of Morals and Legislation*, 3, sec. 2.
[15] *G* III 58/23–24.   [16] *G* III 58/24–25.   [17] *G* III 58/25–26.

(ourselves included) are determined by type-I laws "to exist and act in a
fixed and determined manner."[18]

This gives us further insight into Spinoza's position. Type-I laws are
metaphysically basic, yet type-II laws are crucial to human agency. They
guide us in acting in the world, even though they incorporate what is in
effect a fiction about our powers: that, independently of how things are
"really ordered and connected," we are capable of effecting the necessary
means to desired ends. Spinoza's general account, articulated in the opening
pages of Chapter 4, takes us this far. To go beyond this, we must consider
in greater detail some of the specific laws to which he appeals.

2 THE NATURAL AND THE NORMATIVE

Spinoza's general account allows for a wide range of laws of varying scope.
These include type-I laws that express the determinate mode of acting
of all individuals, or of all or some individuals of a certain kind. A clear
example of the first sort of law is what Spinoza calls in Chapter 16, the
"supreme law of nature": "it is the supreme law of nature that each thing
strives to persist in its own state so far as it can [*unaquaeque res in suo
statu, quantum in se est, conetur perseverare*], taking no account of another's
circumstance but only of its own."[19] The *TTP*'s "supreme law of nature"
anticipates a key proposition of the *Ethics* (E3p6): "Each thing, so far as
it can, strives to persevere in its being" [*Unaquaeque res, quantum in se
est, in suo esse perseverare conatur*].[20] The proposition that follows, E3p7,
identifies this striving with the "actual essence" of a thing, which implies
that it depends upon a power proper to that thing (and not a power
belonging to something else). Given this, the import of E3p6 and of the
TTP's supreme law of nature is that, in so far as any thing is determined to
act by its own power, it necessarily acts in ways that preserve its existence.
This is a paradigm case of a type-I law for Spinoza: a law that "necessarily
follows from the very nature or definition of a thing."

---

[18] Compare E4d4: "I call ... singular things possible, insofar as, while we attend to the causes from
which they must be produced, we do not know whether those causes are determined to produce
them." In the present case, the relevant causes are desires to produce effects that may or may not
follow from them. Of course, Spinoza also holds that there is nothing truly contingent in nature
(E1p29). A thing is *called* contingent only because of "a defect in our knowledge." "[B]ecause the
order of causes is hidden from us, it can never seem to us either necessary or impossible. So we call
it contingent or possible" (E1p33s1).

[19] *G* III 189.

[20] For consistency's sake, I have altered Curley's rendering of *quantum in se est* ("as far as it can by its
own power"). The proper translation of this phrase is controversial, and I see little to recommend
the interpolation of the word "power" in it.

The supreme law of nature lacks any prescriptive or normative content. It asserts simply that, necessarily, in so far as each thing acts by its own power, it acts in ways that contribute to its continued existence. One of Spinoza's main goals in Chapter 16 is to argue that this law offers the basis for a correct understanding of the notion of "natural right." Against those who interpret natural right as an inherently normative concept, whose application is limited to rational beings, Spinoza holds that the claims of natural right are grounded in the necessity of the supreme law of nature, as this applies to the actions of any individual whatsoever. Consequently, the scope of any individual's natural right extends to all of the actions by which it strives to persevere in existence, and not just those that are in accord with reason:

Here we recognize no difference between human beings and other individual things of nature, nor between those human beings who are endowed with reason and others who do not know true reason, nor between fools or lunatics and the sane. For whatever each thing does by the laws of its nature, that it does with sovereign right, since it is acting as it was determined to by nature and can not do otherwise.[21]

Spinoza insists that the concept of natural right is to be understood as grounded in a universal type-I law, the supreme law of nature. Consequently, the concept offers no basis for distinguishing between human and non-human individuals, or between humans who act rationally and those who do not. "Each person's natural right," he says, "is determined not by sound reason but by desire and power. For it is not the case that all men are naturally determined to behave according to the rules and laws of reason."[22] Again, he comments:

[A]s long as people are deemed to live under the government of nature alone, the person who does not yet know reason or does not yet have a habit of virtue, lives by the laws of appetite alone with the same supreme right as he who directs his life by the laws of reason. That is, just as a wise man [*sapiens*] has a sovereign right to do all things that reason dictates, i.e., [he has] the right of living by the laws of reason, so also the ignorant or intemperate person possesses the sovereign right to [do] everything that desire suggests, i.e., he has the right of living by the laws of appetite.[23]

The argument of Chapter 16 leans heavily on the idea that from the point of view of the "government of nature" – the order determined by nature's supreme law – all individuals are in exactly the same position: each strives from its own power to persevere in existence, and its ability to do

---

[21] *G* III 189–190.　[22] *G* III 190/13–15.　[23] *G* III 190/3–10.

so marks the limits of its natural right. What is easily missed in Spinoza's argument, however, is the implicit recognition of another class of *prima facie* normative laws. These are the "laws of reason" by which some, but not all, human beings direct their lives. Spinoza is clear that these laws are set against the universal laws of nature, and that they are concerned specifically with the "true interest" of human beings:

[N]ature is not bound by the laws of human reason which aim only at the true interest and conservation of humans [*non nisi hominum verum utile, & conservationem intendunt*] . . . When therefore we feel that anything in nature is ridiculous, absurd or bad, it is because we know things only in part. We wish everything to be directed in ways familiar to our reason, even though what reason declares to be bad, is not bad with respect to the order and laws of universal nature but only with respect to the laws of our own nature.[24]

In interpreting this passage, we must be alert to a systematic ambiguity that infects Spinoza's use of the phrase "law of human nature." In some cases he uses the phrase to designate laws that hold of any human being (or any human mind). In others, he uses it to refer to laws that do not satisfy this condition, but rather hold of only some human beings.[25] The "laws of human reason" are examples of the latter sort of law. Although they are described as "laws of our own nature," they do not follow necessarily from the nature of a human being, for Spinoza acknowledges that many human beings are not governed by them; they live by the laws of appetite alone. Given this, the laws of human reason arguably should be classified as type-II laws: rules of living that "men prescribe to themselves and others in order to live more safely and more comfortably." Supporting this identification is Spinoza's explicit use of normative language in describing the significance of these laws: "no one can doubt how much more beneficial it is for men to live according to the laws and certain dictates of our reason [*leges, & certa nostrae rationis dictamina*], which as I have said aim at nothing but men's true interests [*verum hominum utile*]."[26]

The laws of reason mark the point at which notions of normativity find entry into Spinoza's ethics. How to understand the force and authority of this normativity remains a problem, to whose solution we find at least

[24] *G* III 190–191.
[25] For the first usage, see *TTP* Ch. 4; *G* III 58/3–4 and *TTP* Ch. 16: "it is a universal law of human nature that no one neglects anything that they deem good unless they hope for a greater good or fear a greater loss . . . " (*G* III 191–192). For the second usage, see *TP* Ch. 2 art. 7; *G* III 279/5–6.
[26] *G* III 191/11–13, trans. modified. Strictly speaking, the laws of reason include what Spinoza distinguishes in Chapter 4 as "human law" and "divine law." Here I am concerned only with the former: rules of living "whose only purpose is to protect life and preserve the state [*ad tutandam vitam, & rempublicam*]" (*G* III 59/24–25). I discuss the import of divine law in section 3.

some clues in the analysis of Chapter 4. Most importantly we have Spinoza's description of type-II laws as (1) hypothetical imperatives, which (2) depend upon "human decision." The first of these features identifies the laws of reason as expressing necessary means to a given end: a safer and more comfortable life. Spinoza reinforces this point in saying that the laws of human reason "aim only at the true interest and conservation of humans." The standard account of hypothetical imperatives explains their force in terms of their prescribing rationally necessary means to desired ends. Given that I desire *b*, I ought to do *a*, because I know that *a* is necessary for the production of *b*. If this is the right way to think of Spinoza's laws of reason, then a satisfactory explanation of their normativity, or the sense in which an agent is bound by these laws, must begin with an account of what makes "a safer and more comfortable life" an end for us.

One possible explanation of this being an end for us is that it is something any human being necessarily desires. According to the supreme law of nature, any individual strives, so far as it can, to persevere in existence. Hence, any human being must have as an end the preservation of her life, and the laws of reason are binding on her because they express necessary means to that end.[27] This response, however, is unsatisfactory. The ends Spinoza associates with the laws of reason are not limited to self-preservation, and he makes it clear that individuals are able to persevere in existence governed only by the laws of appetite. Indeed, he is adamant that the supreme law of nature is a universal (type-I) law; it applies equally in the case of individuals who live by the laws of appetite and individuals who live by the laws of reason. Although the actions of the former are often shortsighted and lead to effects that may, indirectly, precipitate their demise, the appetites that motivate their actions are strivings to persevere in existence, which in and of themselves cannot destroy their subject. Given this, the supreme law of nature, which entails that we act only in ways that are consistent with the preservation of our existence, offers no basis for the end specific to the laws of reason. By Spinoza's admission, not all human beings are bound by the laws of reason; yet all human beings (and all other individuals) are determined to act in accordance with the supreme law of nature.

Spinoza associates the laws of reason with the pursuit of our "true interest," that is, a safer and more comfortable life – an end that is aspired to by some, but not all, human beings. In elucidating this point we are aided by his statement that an end is nothing more than "a human appetite

---

27 Curley, "Spinoza's Moral Philosophy," pp. 371–372.

in so far as it is considered as a principle, or primary cause of some thing."[28]
Strictly speaking, the ends that are identified with the "true interests" of
human beings are ends only for those who, in fact, desire to lead a safer
and more comfortable life. Plausibly, we may suppose that many human
beings do desire such a life, and that this desire occupies a central place in
their motivational set. Nevertheless, Spinoza accepts that if anyone were to
lack this desire, then the pursuit of such a life would not be an end for that
person, and the laws of reason would not be binding on him. Individuals
motivated solely by momentary impulses of appetite, he writes, are "no
more bound [*tenentur*] to live by the laws of a sound mind than a cat is by
the laws of a lion's nature."[29]

If the laws of reason are correctly construed as type-II laws, then they
depend, in Spinoza's words, on "human decision" (*ab hominum placito*).
The phrase *ab hominum placito* highlights the point that the existence
of such laws does not follow from general facts about human nature but
depends in addition upon an agent's being willing to limit her actions
to those specified by the law: actions that are necessary means to a safer
and more comfortable life. Spinoza recognizes that even if agents have the
desire to live more safely and comfortably, there is no necessity that they
will limit their actions in ways that are effective in realizing this end. He
is especially concerned with the scenario (made famous by Hobbes) in
which individuals are faced with the choice of giving up "the right they
received from nature" – their natural right to all things – and committing
themselves to "a particular rule of life" (*certae rationi vivendi*),[30] based on
the authority of civil law. His conclusion is that the commitment of human
beings to live in this way – the way that is rational given the desire for a
safer and better life – cannot be derived from human nature alone. That
is, it is not a universal necessary truth (a type-I law) that human beings act
in this way. Instead, "the binding force [*sanctionem*] of these laws can best
be said to depend upon human decision."[31]

Given Spinoza's unconditional rejection of freedom of the will, we know
that the decision leading to the prescription of law to oneself or others
should not be construed as a voluntary act that requires an agent's inde-
pendence from the causal order of nature. On the contrary, any prescription
of law, and an agent's willingness to comply with that law, must be understood as the product of desires that are themselves fully determined within

---

[28] E4pref.; *G* II 207/3–5.   [29] *G* III 190/22–23; trans. modified.
[30] *G* III 58/4–6.   [31] *G* III 58/13–15; trans. modified.

the order of nature.[32] To prescribe a law commanding p (e.g., "Give each person their due") can mean only that one consistently desires that p be done. If this is so, then we find at least one sense in which type-II laws in general are subordinate to type-I laws. Although the former do not follow necessarily from human nature, holding without exception of all human beings, their prescription is explained by additional law-governed facts about the motivations of particular agents. Some agents are so constituted as to prescribe limits on their own and others' actions for the sake of a safer and more comfortable life; others are not. In principle, these are facts that could be known about agents, given a sufficiently detailed knowledge of their mental states and the laws of human psychology. In practice, Spinoza sees such knowledge of how things are "really ordered and connected" as falling outside our comprehension. Nevertheless, the decisions on which type-II laws depend are events that occur in a fixed and determinate manner, in accordance with type-I laws.

Spinoza, like Hobbes, is pessimistic about the natural capacity of human beings to regulate their actions in accordance with their "true interests."[33] For this reason, the political framework of the state is necessary, in order that at least some semblance of those interests be realized. Desiring a safer and more comfortable life, and fearing the consequences of remaining in the state of nature, individuals can be induced to cede their natural right and accept the authority of the state. Thereafter, they live under laws dictated by the state, laws which they obey not because they recognize the necessary connection between the rule of law and their long-term well-being, but because they fear the punishment that is threatened for disobedience of civil law.

In Spinoza's view, the person who *lives lawfully* does more than this. Such a person prescribes a rule of living to himself for the sake of a safer and more comfortable life. In this case, Spinoza believes, the lawgiver must comprehend the connection between the end and the means, and desire the means because of the perceived necessity of the law. Describing the person who lives by the rule of justice, he writes: "he who gives other men what is due to them because he knows the true rationale of laws

---

[32] See E3p2s: "experience itself, no less clearly than reason, teaches that men believe themselves free because they are conscious of their own actions, and ignorant of the causes by which they are determined, that the decisions of the Mind [*Mentis decreta*] are nothing but the appetites themselves, which therefore vary as the disposition of the Body varies. For each one governs everything from his affect; those who are torn by contrary affects do not know what they want, and those who are not moved by any affect are very easily driven here and there" (*G* II 143–144).

[33] E.g., *TP* Ch. 1 arts. 5–7; E5p41s.

and understands their necessity, acts steadfastly and at his own and not another's command."[34]

To say just this, however, is to leave unclear still the precise sense in which the just (or, more generally, lawful) person *prescribes* law to himself – a law that he subsequently takes to command his actions. Does Spinoza envision a situation in which the lawful person understands the relation between end and means, and then forms a desire for the means because he knows it to be necessary for the end he already desires? This would be a common way of explaining the binding force of self-prescribed "rules of living": I desire a safer and more comfortable life, a life of pleasure, without fear of inordinate pain and premature death; I know that certain ways of acting are conducive to achieving this end; therefore, I know that I should act in those ways, and I am motivated to do so, so that I may attain the life I desire.

Spinoza recognizes that many human beings are bound by the laws of reason in only this sense. They know that by observing apt rules for living they can pursue their own true interest, and because of this they (more or less consistently) desire to act in accord with such rules, as a means to that end. Yet this is not Spinoza's deepest account of the binding force of the laws of reason, or of the lawful person's motivation to act in accord with such laws. That Spinoza does not have this picture in mind is confirmed by his frequent use of the phrase "dictates of reason" as a substitute for "laws of reason."[35] His references to the virtuous person acting from the "dictate" or "guidance" of reason (*ex dictamine rationis, ex ductu rationis*) indicate that reason itself has practical force for him. Reason is linked to motivation in such a way that a rational agent is directly bound by the laws of reason. In so far as human beings act from reason, they desire to act in the ways specified by the laws of reason, independently of any consideration of the utility of such laws in relation to the end of a safer and more comfortable life. When we act from reason, Spinoza argues, we necessarily do those things that are most useful to us, as well as those things that are good for human nature, and hence, for each human being.[36] Thus, we consistently act in ways that advance our "true interest," without doing so *because* they have that consequence. The rational person, in so far as

[34] *G* III 59/13–16; trans. modified.
[35] "Dictates of reason" is Spinoza's preferred usage in the *Ethics*. See, eg., E4p18s; E4p35d; E4p37d; E4p50d and c; E4p54s; E4p62; E4p67d.
[36] See E4p18s; and E4p35d: "Therefore, human beings, insofar as they live by the guidance of reason necessarily do those things only which are necessarily good for human nature [*humanae naturae*], and consequently for each human being, that is (by P31C), which agree with the nature of any human being" (*G* II 233/14; trans. modified).

she is rational, simply acts in the way that reason determines her to act, knowing reflectively that such action is conducive to her well-being.

On this way of interpreting Spinoza, the laws or dictates of reason are most fundamentally understood not as normative propositions but as statements of causal necessity.[37] As Spinoza emphasizes in the *Ethics*, we do not strive to understand things, or to act virtuously, for the sake of any other end. Rather, we act in this way, because we are *determined* to do so, by virtue of our own power, or striving to persevere in existence.[38] From this perspective, the laws of reason match Spinoza's description of type-I laws: laws that "necessarily follow from the very nature or definition of a thing."[39] The laws of reason specify actions that necessarily follow from the nature of reason. They do not express merely how any rational agent *ought* to act, but how any agent *must* act, in so far as she is determined by reason.

In fact, we can go further than this. For Spinoza, the power of reason, or understanding, *is* the inherent power of the human mind: the power that the mind exerts by itself and which defines its striving for existence, independently of the influence of external things.[40] Thus, the laws of reason are, in a sense, type-I laws of the human mind: laws that describe necessary patterns of activity of the mind, in so far as it acts from its own intrinsic power. With this we can bring clarity to what I earlier described as a systematic ambiguity in Spinoza's use of the phrase "laws of human nature." In one sense, the laws of reason are indeed type-I laws of human nature, because they describe the lawful effects that follow from the power intrinsic to the mind: the power of understanding. In another sense, however, the laws of reason are *not* laws of human nature, because they do not hold universally of human actions, conceived as determinations of the mind's power. This is because in most situations human beings think and feel in ways that are determined not (just) by the mind's own power of acting, but by the effects of external things on the mind. Consequently, their actions cannot be explained by the laws of reason alone.

It is under this circumstance that we can best make sense of the laws of reason as type-II, prescriptive laws. Human beings are, without exception, imperfectly rational agents, who only rarely, in Spinoza's view, are

---

[37] I defend this conclusion in Rutherford, "Spinoza and the Dictates of Reason."

[38] E4pp21–26.   [39] *G* III 57/28.

[40] See E4p59d: "Acting from reason is nothing but doing those things which follow from the necessity of our nature, considered in itself alone (by IIIP3 and D2)" (*G* II 254/15–17); and E4p35c2: "For the more each one seeks his own advantage, and strives to preserve himself, the more he is endowed with virtue (by P20), or what is the same (by D8), the greater is his power of acting according to the laws of his own nature, i.e. (by IIIP3), of living from the guidance of reason" (*G* II 233/27–32).

determined to act from the dictates of reason. Yet even when they are not determined in this way, they feel the pull of reason in them: they *desire* to act as reason would determine them to act, even if they do not ultimately follow through on those actions. Furthermore, in so far as they are rational, they are able to understand reflectively how the actions determined by reason contribute to the end of a safer and more comfortable life. Consequently, however they end up acting, rational agents understand the benefits of acting according to the laws of reason and they feel the force of reason within themselves. Hence, they consistently desire, or prescribe to themselves, patterns of action that they anticipate will lead to their desired ends. Desiring the things that reason determines them to want, they take those ways of acting as a "law" that commands their action. To the extent that they "obey" this law, they do nothing but act in that way in which reason determines them to act.

Of course, not all human beings are moved by reason even to this extent. In the case of individuals who are led by the laws of appetite alone, another account is needed, one which emphasizes the role of law as a command issued by a superior, who is capable of enforcing the command through the threat of punishment. Spinoza observes that in politics and religion this is often the only conception of law that matters. Nevertheless, he does not believe that it is the conception by which we can best understand the function of law within the life of a reflective rational agent.

3 DIVINE LAW

Spinoza develops his general account of law in Chapter 4 as a prelude to addressing the topic of divine law. Traditional views of divine law equate it with the word, dictate, or command of a sovereign being, who rules over humans with the power and authority of an absolute monarch. God commands humans to act in specific ways, and holds them responsible for their actions, rewarding obedience and punishing disobedience. In this way, God demonstrates his justice, by ruling humanity according to law, as well as his mercy, in forgiving and reconciling to him those who violate his commands.

Spinoza regards such views as deeply confused: "God is described as a legislator or a prince, and as just, merciful etc., only because of the limited understanding of the common people and their lack of knowledge."[41] He allows that there is a sense in which the Hebrew people received through

---

[41] *G* III 65/28–30.

Moses a revelation of divine law, and that by virtue of their reception of this law they can be described as "chosen" by God.[42] Nevertheless, Spinoza's interpretation of these traditional beliefs casts them in a very different light than they are usually seen. To speak of God revealing his will through prophecy is to express oneself on the basis of a "childish understanding" (*puerili captu*)[43] of God.[44] The sense in which the Hebrew people have been chosen relates neither to their superior wisdom nor their superior virtue. With respect to the former, their comprehension of reality, "they had entirely commonplace notions of God and nature"; with respect to the latter, the attainment of "true life" (*verae vitae*), they were "on the same footing as other nations and very few were chosen."[45]

The Hebrew people can be regarded as "chosen" in one sense only: the success and prosperity of the commonwealth built upon their (confused) understanding of divine law. In this they were aided partly by fortune – external causes that favored their collective survival – and partly by the law which commanded their obedience in ways that contributed to the security and prosperity of their state. For this reason, Spinoza insists, the laws propounded in the Hebrew Bible cannot be understood as universal dictates, binding on all human beings. They are laws "revealed and prescribed only to the Jews; for since God chose them alone to form a particular commonwealth and state, they had necessarily to have unique laws as well."[46] In sum, what the Hebrew people have taken as divine law is no more than a specific sort of human law, which they have falsely construed as being directly authorized by God.[47] As human law, the law of the Bible has been

---

[42] *G* III 45.   [43] *G* III 45/24.

[44] In Chapter 1, Spinoza defines "prophecy or revelation" as "certain knowledge about something revealed to men by God" (*G* III 15/5–6). In the most general sense even natural knowledge can be called "prophecy," for "what we know by the natural light of reason depends on knowledge of God and his eternal decrees alone" (*G* III 15/18–20). As conveyed by the Bible, prophecy is knowledge revealed by God to men that "exceeds the limits of natural knowledge," and hence is not known through reason. Such knowledge is revealed in words or images, which are "either true and independent of the imagination of the prophet who heard or saw them, or else imaginary, that is the prophet's imagination, even when he was awake, was so disposed that it seemed to him that he was clearly hearing words or seeing something" (*G* III 17/11–15). In either case, Spinoza conceives of these as natural events (whether or not they can be fully understood by us) (*G* III 28/11–14).

[45] *G* III 48/2–6.

[46] *G* III 48/24–28.

[47] This extends to all "ceremonial laws," governing diet, sacrifices, and feast-days, and morality propounded as a system of requirements on action, reinforced by the threat of punishment. It is certain, Spinoza writes in Chapter 5, that these "do not belong to the divine law and hence contribute nothing to blessedness [*beatitudinem*] and virtue. They are relevant only to the election of the Hebrews, that is . . . only to the temporal happiness of the body and the peace of the state, and therefore could have relevance only as long as that state survived" (*G* III 69/11–16; trans. modified). "Although these Five Books contain much about morality as well as ceremonies, morality is not to

highly efficacious, but this has come at the cost of intellectual error. Biblical law conveys no distinct understanding of God's nature, and it supports no claim for the unique status of the Jews as the recipients of divine law.

In the *TTP*, Spinoza aims to replace the confused and patently anthropomorphic conception of divine law that the Bible presents with a rigorously defined philosophical conception. In fact, he ends up defending two distinct accounts of what can reasonably be meant by the expression "divine law." One account, featured in Chapter 4, construes divine law as a species of type-II law. Another account, prominent in Chapter 6, assimilates divine law to type-I laws. I shall begin with this second conception of divine law and then turn to the position defended in Chapter 4.[48]

In Chapter 6, "On miracles," Spinoza maintains that there is a defensible conception of divine law according to which it is identical with the universal laws of nature. In this chapter he addresses the question of whether it is coherent to suppose the existence of miracles – divinely decreed events – which are exceptions to the laws of nature. He argues that it is not, because the content of God's decrees is just the necessary order of nature:

> But since nothing is necessarily true except by divine decree alone, it most clearly follows that the universal laws of nature are simply God's decrees and follow from the necessity and perfection of the divine nature. If anything therefore were to happen in nature that contradicted its universal laws, it would also necessarily contradict the decree and understanding and nature of God. Or if anyone were to assert that God does anything contrary to the laws of nature, he would at the same time be compelled to assert that God acts contrary to his own nature, than which nothing is more absurd . . . Consequently, nothing happens in nature that contradicts its universal laws; and nothing occurs which does not conform to those laws or follow from them.[49]

On this way of conceiving of divine law, God's decrees are identical with the determinate and necessary ways in which his power is expressed in nature. "[T]he decree of God, his command, his utterance, his word are

---

be found there as moral teachings universal to all men, but only as instructions uniquely adjusted to the understanding and character of the Hebrew nation, and therefore relevant to the prosperity of their state alone" (*G* III 70/16–21).

[48] Spinoza acknowledges this duality in discussing the meaning of the expression "word of God" in Chapter 12: "When 'word of God' is predicated of a subject which is not God himself, it properly signifies the divine law which we discussed in chapter 4, that is, the religion that is universal or common to the whole human race. On this subject see Isaiah 1.10 etc., where Isaiah teaches the true way of living [*verum vivendi modum*], that does not consist in ceremonies but in charity and integrity of mind [*vero animo*], and calls it interchangeably God's law and the word of God. It is also used metaphorically for the order of nature itself and fate – since in truth this depends upon the eternal decree of the divine nature and follows it" (*G* III 162/15–24).

[49] *G* III 82–83.

nothing other than the very action and order of nature."[50] God acts necessarily, or in accordance with law, and since "the power of nature is the very power of God,"[51] the laws of nature and divine law are one and the same. In Chapter 6, Spinoza stresses this point repeatedly:

Since we know that all things are determined and ordained by God, and that the operations of nature follow from the essence of God, and the laws of nature are the eternal laws and volitions of God, we must conclude, unconditionally, that we get a fuller knowledge of God and God's will as we acquire a fuller knowledge of natural things.[52]

There is a legitimate sense, then, in which divine law can be equated with the universal laws of nature – laws that govern all things everywhere in an inviolable manner. On this construal, divine law is represented as a type-I law: a law that "necessarily follows from the very nature or definition of a thing" – that thing being God himself. As Spinoza later expresses the view in the *Ethics*: "all things that happen, happen only through the laws of God's infinite nature."[53]

Yet this is not the only conception of divine law that Spinoza defends. In Chapter 4, he expands his account of type-II laws to include both human law and divine law:

Since law, accordingly, is nothing other than a rule for living [*ratio vivendi*] which men prescribe to themselves or to others for a purpose, it seems it has to be divided into human and divine. By human law I mean a rule for living whose only purpose is to protect life and preserve the country. By divine law I mean the law which looks only to the supreme good, that is, to the true knowledge and love of God.[54]

The twofold distinction of human and divine law tracks the broad structure of Spinoza's *Ethics* (particularly the division between Parts 4 and 5) and allows us to see more clearly the theoretical unity of that work. Spinoza distinguishes divine and human law on the basis of their purpose, or end

---

[50] *G* III 89/34–35.   [51] *G* III 189/20.

[52] *G* III 85/25–29. Spinoza makes the same point in Chapter 3: "the universal laws of nature according to which all things happen and are determined, are nothing other than the eternal decrees of God and always involve truth and necessity. Whether therefore we say that all things happen according to the laws of nature, or are ordained by the edict and direction of God, we are saying the same thing" (*G* II 46/1–6).

[53] E1p15; *G* II 60/10–11. With this Spinoza neatly turns the tables on the defender of miracles as supernatural events: "If therefore something happened in nature which did not follow from its laws, this would necessarily conflict with the order that God established in nature for ever by the universal laws of nature; it would hence be contrary to nature and its laws and, consequently, it would make us doubt our faith in all things and lead us to atheism" (*G* III 86–87). On this sense of divine law, see also E1p17: "God acts from the laws of his nature alone, and is compelled by no one."

[54] *G* III 59/21–26.

(*finis*). Human law is law that is dictated solely for the purpose of protecting life and preserving the state (*ad tutandam vitam, & rempublicam*), whereas divine law is called "divine," because it is concerned with the attainment of our supreme good (*summum bonum*), which Spinoza identifies with the true knowledge and love of God (*Dei veram cognitionem, & amorem*).

Although both human law and divine law consist of laws of reason, they have distinct roles in Spinoza's philosophy. Human laws promote the attainment of goods (our "true interest"), but not the highest good. Significantly, even human law is granted a larger purpose than the preservation of life. Its end includes the preservation of the state, or commonwealth, within which human beings can pursue their talents and prosper. The province of human law, therefore, must include the laws by which a state can be formed and maintained.[55] Nevertheless, living according to human law alone is not sufficient for the attainment of our "supreme good." For this, Spinoza says, we must live by divine law.

Since divine law is defined as the "rule of living" by which we attain our supreme good, its content is fixed by the content of that end. In Chapter 4, Spinoza deploys a cluster of arguments in defense of his conception of our end as the knowledge and love of God.[56] Our highest good and happiness (*beatitudo*) reduce to the knowledge and love of God.[57] From this, he says, it immediately follows that the means to this end can be identified with divine law:

The means required by this end of all human actions, which is God himself so far as his idea is in us, may be called the commands of God, because they are prescribed to us, as it were, by God himself so far as he exists in our minds, and therefore the rule of life which looks to this end is best called the divine law.[58]

Given Spinoza's stated goal of challenging the idea of divine law as the external command of a sovereign being, communicated in Scripture, we must attend to his careful phrasing of his view. Divine law is "prescribed to us, as it were, by God himself so far as he exists in our mind [*quasi ab ipso*

---

[55] See *TTP*, Chapter 16 and E4p37s2. It is worth noting that within the category of human law we can distinguish laws that the rational person prescribes to herself for the sake of a safer and more comfortable life (the dictates of reason, as presented in the *Ethics*), and laws that are prescribed to others, for the sake of the same ends (e.g., the ceremonial laws and morality of the Hebrew people). On the latter, see note 47.

[56] Whether these arguments are sound within the terms of Spinoza's philosophy is a question I cannot address here. In brief, Spinoza maintains: (1) our highest good consists in the perfection of our intellect; (2) the perfection of our intellect consists in the knowledge of God and of all things in so far as they depend upon God; (3) our happiness is greatest when we love and enjoy above all else God, the most perfect being (G III 59–60).

[57] G III/60/18–20.   [58] G III/60.

Deo, quatenus in nostra mente existit]."[59] The double qualification of the sense in which divine law can be regarded as a command of God points us back to the original definition of type-II laws as laws that human beings prescribe to themselves and others for some purpose. Strictly speaking, God does not command anything at all. The command is the prescription of a human being who possesses (as all human beings do) the idea of God.[60]

The content of divine law is fixed by the rule of living which has for its end (*finem spectat*) the knowledge and love of God.[61] According to Spinoza, "it is for universal ethics [*universalem Ethicam*] to inquire what these means are and what is the rule of life which this goal requires, and how the foundations of the best state and the rules for living among men follow from it."[62] This promissory note is made good in the *Ethics*. What is interesting about Spinoza's statement of it, is that he presents the rules of human law as a means to the *summum bonum*. This is not to be read, I think, as implying that the rules of living associated with human law cannot be derived from their proper end, the preservation of life and the state; rather, Spinoza suggests that having fixed our ultimate end as the knowledge and love of God, we are also able to derive the principles of human law from it, as a means to that end.[63]

In Chapter 4, Spinoza says that he will limit himself to speaking of the divine law "in general." His expressions of the law are highly schematic. Given the content of our end, the "sum of the divine law . . . and its highest precept is to love God as the highest good."[64] The crux of the law is that we are to love God not because we fear his punishment or desire his reward; rather, we are to love God from the very fact that we know him, or know that the knowledge and love of God is the highest good.[65] An interpretation of these remarks can be developed from the account of the

---

[59] *G* III 60/22–23.
[60] Curley ("The State of Nature and Its Law," p. 110) also stresses this point. In *TTP*, Chapter 4, Spinoza writes: "natural divine law is inferred from the consideration of human nature alone . . . For the natural light of reason . . . requires only what carries the clearest evidence of being a good or a means to our happiness" (*G* III/61–62).
[61] *G* III 60/24.   [62] *G* III 60/24–29.
[63] In similar fashion, Spinoza interprets the revelation of divine law to include the foundations of morality. In *TTP* Chapter 12, he writes that in one sense only have we "received the divine law, uncorrupted. For we see from Scripture itself, and without any difficulty or ambiguity, that the essence of the Law is to love God above all things and one's neighbor as oneself" (*G* III 165/11–13). See also the Preface to the *TTP*, where he describes the "revealed word of God" as "a pure conception of the divine mind which was revealed to the prophets, namely, to obey God with all one's mind by practicing justice and charity" (*G* II 10/25–28).
[64] *G* III 60–61.
[65] *G* III 60/31–34. In Annotation 34 to the *TTP*, Spinoza stresses the necessary relation between knowledge of God and love of God: "As for the divine natural law whose highest precept we have said is to love God, I have called it a law in the sense in which philosophers apply the word law to

laws of reason presented in the previous section. Divine law is the rule of
living that human beings prescribe to themselves in order to achieve the
knowledge and love of God. Among the "commands" of this law are the
dictates of reason that form the basis of human law. Over and above this,
however, Spinoza conceives of the way of life determined by divine law as "a
rational life" [*vita rationalis*] or "the life of the mind [*Mentis vita*], which is
defined by understanding."[66] Thus, divine law requires a life dedicated to
the pursuit of understanding, specifically knowledge of God, from which
the love of God necessarily follows.[67]

We can speak of divine law as a rule of living that human beings prescribe
to themselves for the sake of the knowledge and love of God. Yet, as we have
seen, the relevant notion of prescription amounts simply to a consistent
desire to act in the way specified by the law. In the case of the laws of
reason, this is a desire to act in the way in which we are determined to
act by reason, conceived as the mind's inherent power of acting. Spinoza is
clear in the *Ethics* that the way of life determined by reason is that specified
by divine law. "What we strive for from reason," he writes, "is nothing but
understanding."[68] Since the "greatest thing the mind can understand is
God, that is . . . a being absolutely infinite, without which . . . nothing can
either be or be conceived,"[69] in so far as we are led by reason, we strive to
perfect the intellect by seeking knowledge of God:

Perfecting the intellect is nothing but understanding God, his attributes, and his
actions, which follow from the necessity of his nature. So the ultimate end of
the man who is led by reason, that is, his highest desire, by which he strives to
moderate all the others, is that by which he is led to conceive adequately both
himself and all things which can fall under his understanding.[70]

To the extent that the affections of the mind are determined solely
by its own power of acting, we necessarily pursue knowledge of God.
However, not all the affections of the mind are determined in this way. More
often they reflect the determination of the mind's power by the actions
of external things, in which case we desire to pursue ends other than the
knowledge of God. Under this circumstance, a conflict may ensue in which,
among other desires, we feel the pull of reason – feel we *should* answer its

the common rules of nature according to which all things <necessarily> happen. For love of God
is not obedience but a virtue necessarily present in someone who rightly knows God" (*G* III 264).
The demonstration of this is given in E5p32c.
[66] E4app5 (*G* II 267/15–17).
[67] For Spinoza, the relevant knowledge includes both knowledge of God *qua* substance (E4p28) and
knowledge of singular things in so far as they follow necessarily from God (E5p24; E5p27d).
[68] E4p26.   [69] E4p28d.   [70] E4app4.

call – and know reflectively that to do so would be in our best interest. Whether or not we answer the call of reason, we take ourselves to be "commanded" or "bound" by divine law to act in ways that promote the end of the knowledge and love of God.

Nothing in Spinoza's position commits him to the thesis that all human beings are bound by divine law in this way. Those whose thoughts are limited to confused representations of the imagination lack an adequate conception of God and of the highest good; consequently, they are led by the teachings of religion to believe that the force of divine law lies, for example, in the threat of eternal punishment. Likewise, the "carnal man" has a "barren" (*jejunam*) conception of God. He has no understanding of the end of divine law, nor is bound by it, for he finds nothing in it "that he can touch or eat or that makes any impression on the flesh in which he takes so much pleasure."[71] In Spinoza's view, only "those who know that they possess nothing more excellent than understanding and a sound mind, will certainly judge that thought and reasoning are the most solid realities." Because of this, they are naturally drawn to the highest good, which "consists in philosophical reasoning alone and pure thought" (*in sola speculatione, et pura mente consistit*).[72] Knowing that the best part of themselves is their intellect, they desire to perfect it; and knowing that the intellect is perfected through the knowledge of God, they desire this knowledge above all else and love God for his own sake. This, in summary, is the path Spinoza charts for his readers in the *Ethics*.

4 RECONCILING THE TWO CONCEPTIONS OF DIVINE LAW

I have argued that Spinoza operates with two distinct conceptions of divine law in the *TTP*: one a principle of natural necessity (a type-I law) and one a "rule of living" (a type-II law). For simplicity's sake, let us call these divine law$_I$ and divine law$_{II}$. We are now in a position to understand better the rationale for this distinction, and how the two types of law relate to each other. The short answer, I suggest, is this: (1) everything we do, including our efforts to act in accordance with divine law$_{II}$, is dictated by divine law$_I$; and (2) we fulfill the requirements of divine law$_{II}$, in so far as we endeavor to understand the world as ordered by divine law$_I$.

It is illuminating to see Spinoza here as responding to the theological tradition, which operates with an analogous dual conception of divine law. There is divine law$_I$, an original decree by which all things are brought into

---

[71] *G* III 61/6–9.   [72] *G* III 61/9–12.

existence and by which the created world develops through time; and there is divine law$_2$, a specific command to human beings, which lays down the range of their responsibilities to God and to other human beings. At the nexus of these two notions of law are traditional worries about divine providence. On the assumption that God is a just ruler, one expects that faithful obedience to divine law$_2$ should be rewarded in a suitable manner. Yet whether this happens is a function of divine law$_1$, which has ordained everything that will ever happen in the created world. The faith of the believer is that God has designed the world such that the natural and moral orders intersect in the appropriate ways. The lament of Job, repeated by sufferers throughout the centuries, is that this does not seem to have happened.

Spinoza's reinterpretation of divine law is intended to alleviate this anxiety. As he writes in *TTP*, Chapter 6:

[I]t was thoroughly obscure to most prophets how the order of nature and human affairs was consistent with the conception of divine providence which they had formed. However, this was always entirely clear to the philosophers who seek to understand things not from miracles but from clear concepts, or at any rate to those [philosophers] who place true happiness in virtue and peace of mind alone, and do not attempt to make nature obey them but rather strive to obey nature themselves. They have certain knowledge that God directs nature not as the particular laws of human nature urge but as its universal laws require and, hence, that God takes account not just of the human race but of nature in its entirety.[73]

Spinoza recognizes that his solution to the problem of providence is by no means original. The basic move of identifying human happiness with the comprehension of the impersonal law of the universe is one he shares with the Stoics – a debt he acknowledges in his own use of the injunction "follow nature."[74] To resist the necessary order of nature, the order dictated by divine law$_1$, is in vain. Consequently, we have no option but to accede to that order. The insight of the philosopher is that there is a way of acceding to God's will that goes beyond mere resignation. To accede because one *understands* the necessary order of things is intrinsically satisfying, both intellectually and affectively. On the path charted by Spinoza, such understanding is constitutive of our highest good. Thus, the best "rule of

---

[73] *G* III 88.

[74] See E4app32: "Nevertheless, we shall bear calmly those things which happen to us contrary to what the principle of our advantage demands, if we are conscious that we have done our duty, that the power we have could not have extended itself to the point where we could have avoided those things, and that we are a part of the whole of nature, whose order we follow [*cujus ordinem sequimur*] ... Hence, insofar as we understand these things rightly, the striving of the better part of us agrees with the order of the whole of nature [*cum ordine totius naturae convenit*]" (*G* II 277/8–21).

living," identified with the content of divine law$_{II}$, is to live in whatever way is conducive to the attainment of that end.

The command to live according to nature, or to pursue the highest good in the knowledge and love of God, nominally takes the form of an imperative that imposes a normative demand on a rational agent. We are inclined to see it as a call that any human being ought to answer, but which he can also choose to ignore. Yet a critic will observe that it is hard to see how this sort of responsiveness to the normative demands of law can be reconciled with the universal causal determination that follows from Spinoza's defense of divine law$_I$. If all is determined by the universal laws of nature, how can human beings be *accountable* to the demands of divine law?

It is here that we find the most radical aspect of Spinoza's reinterpretation of divine law. In the strictest sense, we are not accountable to anyone – ourselves or God – for whether or not we respond to the apparent demands of divine law. Our susceptibility in this regard is, Spinoza asserts, as much a function of the necessary order of nature as any other action we perform. Within this order, some are disposed to obey divine law and some are disposed to live by the laws of appetite. Spinoza can frame his defense of this point in theological terms as a recognition of the universality of God's decrees: If God has decreed everything, then he has decreed how each of us will respond to the demands of divine law$_{II}$. This, he suggests in *TTP*, Chapter 3, is the correct way to understand the concept of divine election: "given that nobody does anything except by the predetermined order of nature, that is, by the eternal decree and direction of God, it follows that no one chooses any way of life [*aliquam vivendi rationem*] for himself nor brings anything about, except via the particular summons of God, who chose this man in preference to others for this task or that way of life."[75]

While Spinoza endeavors to express his views in ways that will be intelligible to adherents of orthodox religion, his underlying message is one in which few believers can take comfort. Normative laws – type-II laws that include both human and divine law – are laws that human beings prescribe to themselves. Yet "prescription," or the laying down of a law for oneself, is an action that is determined by the causal order of nature. Whether one is determined to follow a given "rule of living" is not ultimately within one's power. What Spinoza can claim, and argues for at length in the *Ethics*, is that there are objective reasons for believing that one will be better off – more powerful and better able to sustain one's existence – if one lives

---

[75] G III 46/17–22.

according to the guidance of reason, or the demands of human and divine law. But whether one *can* do that, is not something one can know in advance of the attempt to do so.[76]

5 CONCLUSION

The notion of law plays only a limited role in Spinoza's *Ethics*. By contrast, an analysis of the concept of law, and especially divine law, lies at the heart of his earlier masterpiece, the *Theological-Political Treatise*. The significance of this analysis lies largely in the challenge it poses to orthodox theological understandings of divine law as represented in Hebrew Scripture. Against the conception of law as the literal command of a sovereign being who holds human beings accountable for their actions, rewarding obedience and punishing disobedience, Spinoza interprets divine law as, most basically, nothing more than the necessary order by which all things are connected and determined to occur in nature. This law has not been dictated by a ruler who stands in judgment over human beings; it simply *is* the necessary order of nature, within which human thoughts, decisions, and actions find their inevitable place.

The brilliance of Spinoza's account of law consists partly in the use to which it is put in rethinking the history of the Hebrew people and their religion from the perspective of philosophical reason. Beyond this, however, Spinoza's account addresses general issues concerning the force of law and the role it plays in human action, in a way that goes beyond anything he says in the *Ethics*. While law has its primary philosophical meaning as a principle of necessity rooted in the natures of God and finite things (type-I laws), Spinoza simultaneously develops an account of law as a normative principle that human beings "prescribe to themselves or to others for the sake of some end" (type-II laws). It is an inescapable feature of human practice that we enjoin ourselves and others to act in specific ways. In some cases, the end for which we are to act is explicitly designated; in others, it is left tacit. Spinoza's analysis sharply distinguishes laws that are prescribed by an external authority and bind their subjects through the threat of punishment (or promise of reward) from laws that an individual

---

[76] Compare Spinoza's response to Henry Oldenburg in *Ep.* 75: "this inevitable necessity of things does not do away with either divine or human laws. For moral precepts, whether or not they receive from God himself the form of command or law, are none the less divine and salutary, and whether the good that follows from virtue and the divine love is bestowed on us by God as judge, or whether it emanates from the necessity of the divine nature, it will not on that account be more or less desirable, just as on the other hand, the evils that follow from wicked deeds and passions are not less to be feared because they necessarily follow from them" (*Letters*, p. 337).

prescribes to herself, as a means to a given end. His account of the latter sort of law is a key innovation of the *TTP*, which illuminates central themes of the *Ethics*, particularly the role assigned to the "dictates of reason." These I have argued are best understood not as *sui generis* normative principles, but as principles of natural necessity grounded in the inherent power of the human mind. The upshot of this reading is that, although Spinoza is conscious of preserving the place of prescriptive principles in our lives, as a condition of our agency, he is committed to explaining the normative force of these principles in naturalistic terms: wherever there is a type-II which prescribes a particular course of action as being to our benefit, there are type-I laws that explain why we find a given end valuable and why we are (or are not) motivated to pursue what we are able to understand as necessary means to that end.

CHAPTER 9

Getting his hands dirty:
Spinoza's criticism of the rebel

Michael Della Rocca

Nobody likes to be told what to do. But that doesn't stop Spinoza from making many moral assessments, often harshly negative ones. Thus we find Spinoza branding certain affects as evil or wrong. Indignation, for Spinoza, is "necessarily evil."[1] Hate "can never be good."[2] Pity is contrary to the dictates of reason.[3] Scorn, humility, and many other affects are condemned in similar fashion,[4] and Spinoza offers an especially scathing assessment of people governed by their affects in Chapter 17 of the *TTP*:

Everyone knows what crimes men are often led to by a distaste for the present, and a desire to make fundamental changes by uncontrolled anger and scorn for poverty; everyone knows how much these affects fill and disturb the hearts of men.[5]

At the beginning of the *Treatise on the Intellect* and elsewhere, Spinoza also disparages the all-too-common single-minded pursuit of wealth or power or sensual pleasure. Spinoza first criticizes himself for these pursuits:

I saw that I was in the greatest danger, and that I was forced to seek a remedy with all my strength, however uncertain it might be.[6]

But then he extends his negative assessment to the rest of us too:

all those things men ordinarily strive for, not only provide no remedy to preserve our being, but in fact hinder that preservation, often cause the destruction of those who possess them, and always cause the destruction of those who are possessed by them.[7]

Most of Spinoza's criticisms – indeed all of the criticisms just mentioned – flow naturally from his egoism. As we'll see shortly, Spinoza's is an ethics

For helpful comments and other forms of encouragement, I am especially grateful to Yitzhak Melamed, Michael Rosenthal, Aaron Garrett, Alex Silverman, Justin Steinberg, Ken Winkler, John Morrison, and to the participants at a memorable conference on the *TTP* at Boston University in December 2008.

[1] E4p51s.   [2] E4p45.   [3] E4p50.   [4] E4p48, E4p53.
[5] G III 203.   [6] *TdIE* § 7.   [7] *TdIE* § 7.

of self-interest in which the maintenance and the increase of one's power is the fundamental good and obligation. He makes the above criticisms because the agents in question fail to promote, or be sufficiently attentive to, their self-interest. Scorners are scorned because in scorning they act against their long-term interest. Similarly, the seekers of money, fame, or sex – you know, just about everybody you know – are subjected to Spinoza's invective because their pursuits "hinder that preservation" that all things strive for.[8]

Despite this pleasingly coherent picture – egoism plus moral assessments based on egoism – some of Spinoza's moral criticisms seem to be in tension with his egoism. One apparently anomalous case concerns lying. Spinoza claims that lying is contrary to the dictates of reason and that the free person may not lie – not even to save her life.[9] But how can a moral system that by its very essence promotes self-interest require that one not save one's life by means of a necessary deception? This does not seem to be Spinoza the egoist talking, but then who is it – Spinoza the secret Kantian? I will return to the case of lying briefly later, but I want to train my attention instead on a different seemingly anomalous case, that of the rebel. This case might seem to be as much in conflict with Spinoza's egoism as the case of the liar seems to be. I will argue that the reconciliation of Spinoza's egoism with the case of the rebel requires both a reconceptualization of the way in which the Principle of Sufficient Reason (the PSR) shapes Spinoza's account of normativity and also a deeper understanding of the radically rationalist basis of Spinoza's accounts of action and of the self. These rationalist underpinnings will in turn lead to the perhaps surprising conclusion that *all* moral criticisms – not just the criticisms in the apparently anomalous cases of the liar and the rebel – are problematic and even unjustified by Spinoza's own lights.

I WHO'S A REBEL?

Let's turn then to Spinoza's criticism of the rebel. A rebel is one who challenges the authority of his own sovereign or who seeks to get others to challenge the authority of the sovereign. While Spinoza accords citizens the right to a good deal of freedom of thought and speech, he draws the line at freedom of those actions carried out with the intent to challenge the power of the sovereign. Such action, for Spinoza, is not to be tolerated for it can lead to the destruction of the state and thus either to anarchy or to

---

[8] *TdIE* § 7.   [9] E4p72 and E4p72s.

a more tyrannical and repressive state in which individuals are even worse off than under the old regime. Citing precedents, Spinoza is vividly aware of the hazards of regime change which, he says, cannot occur "without a danger that the whole state will be ruined."[10] For Spinoza, the sovereign must control the actions of the citizens and is right to do so. The one who challenges the authority of the sovereign – the rebel – acts wrongly and "is rightly condemned" [*jure merito damnatur*] to death.[11] Here is Spinoza taking a hard line against the rebel:

[N]o one can act contrary to the decree of the supreme powers without detriment to their right; but everyone, without any infringement of their right, can think, and judge, and hence also speak, provided merely that he only speaks or teaches, and defends his view by reason alone, not with deception, anger, hatred, or any intention to introduce something into the state on the authority of his own decision. For example, if someone shows that some law is contrary to sound reason, and therefore thinks it ought to be repealed, and if at the same time he submits his opinion to the judgment of the supreme power (who possesses the sole power of making and repealing laws), and in the meantime does nothing contrary to what that law prescribes, he of course deserves well of the state, as one of its best citizens. On the other hand, if he does this to accuse the magistrates of unfairness and make them hateful to the people, or if he wants seditiously to disregard that law, against the will of the magistrate, he is just a troublemaker and a rebel.[12]

Indeed, certain beliefs are seditious because of their connection to actions which threaten the state:

[Seditious opinions are] those which, as soon as they are assumed, destroy the agreement by which each person surrendered his right of acting according to his own decision. For example, if someone thinks that the supreme power is not its own master, or that no one is under an obligation to stand by promises, or that each person ought to live according to his own decision, or something else of this kind, directly contrary to the agreement mentioned above, he is seditious, not so much, of course, because of the judgment and opinion as because of the deed which such judgments involve.[13]

Such beliefs, therefore, should not be tolerated in the state.

   This strong indictment of the rebel is puzzling. First, it is not difficult to imagine that the tyrannical actions of the sovereign threaten the life of the not-yet-rebel and prompt him to rebel. The rebellious act may in this way be an act of self-defense, an act certainly in keeping with Spinoza's egoism and the obligation to preserve oneself. Thus, one who rebels because of a threat by the sovereign is much like one who, upon being threatened, lies

[10] *G* III 228.   [11] *G* III 198.   [12] *G* III 241.   [13] *TTP* Ch. 20; *G* III 242.

in order to save herself. In both cases, Spinoza seems to forbid the action taken in self-defense, and this seems out of keeping with egoism.

The second perplexing feature of Spinoza's condemnation of the rebel concerns his attitude towards a successful rebel. The rebel, in rebelling, is only seeking more power for himself and, perhaps, for others. Of course, the rebel may be mistaken in thinking that his rebellious act will lead to his own greater power. And, if he is mistaken in this, one can see why – in the name of egoism – Spinoza would criticize such a rebel. But, of course, the rebellious act may be successful in that the challenge to the sovereign's authority is effective, and the rebel thereby gains more power for himself and for others. This happy outcome may be very unlikely, as Spinoza stresses,[14] but that's not the point. For surely, this is a possibility that Spinoza must acknowledge. Would Spinoza condemn the successful rebel just as he condemns the unsuccessful rebel?

The structure of Spinoza's moral system, based as it is on self-preservation and power, would seem to suggest that a rebel who loses – whose action is unsuccessful – and is thus punished, deserves to lose. After all, for Spinoza, virtue consists simply in power,[15] and Spinoza says we ought to want virtue, i.e., power, for its own sake.[16] And thus a relatively weak rebel thereby seems simply to be wrong.

But by the same token, a successful rebel, a rebel who successfully challenges the authority of the sovereign, is thus more powerful than the sovereign and so *deserves* to win; it is right that the (more powerful) rebel wins against the (less powerful) sovereign who is, thus, in reality, no longer the sovereign.[17] Thus, in power struggles of this kind, whatever outcome comes out seems to be the right outcome. To think that a less powerful opponent *should* win – or that a more powerful opponent *should* lose – is to try to think a contradiction, just as to think that a less powerful opponent *can* win is to espouse a contradiction.[18] Thus, Spinoza's egoism seems to dictate that, when it comes to power struggles, no outcome is wrong or bad, and that a successful rebel is *not* to be criticized.

Spinoza does sometimes seem to take precisely this line. He acknowledges that if a rebel seizes power, the right passes to him.[19] Further, Spinoza seems to endorse the actions of a rebel who has certain revelation from God.[20] It's not clear whether this would entail a blanket approval of

---

[14] *TTP* Ch.18; *G* III 227; *TTP* Ch.19; *G* III 245; *TP* Ch. 5; *G* III 296–297.
[15] E4d8.   [16] E4p18s.   [17] See *TP* Ch. 3 art. 3; *G* III 285.
[18] Compare E1p11d3: "If what now necessarily exists are only finite beings, then finite beings are more powerful than an absolutely infinite Being. But this, as is known through itself, is absurd."
[19] *TTP* Ch. 16; *G* III 194.   [20] *G* III 199, 233–234.

successful rebels. (Would Spinoza say that all such rebels enjoy "a certain and indubitable revelation"?)[21] Nevertheless, Spinoza does, at least on some occasions, seem to see a successful rebel as right.

However, in other passages, Spinoza seems to go out of his way to issue a blanket condemnation of rebels, regardless of whether or not they are successful. Spinoza says that "all citizens, without exception" are bound to uphold the right of the sovereign to govern (*omnes absolute cives hoc jure semper teneantur*).[22] That Spinoza's criticism of the one who challenges the sovereign's authority is independent of the outcome of that challenge is evident in these revealing remarks on treason:

> [T]he crime of treason can be committed only by subjects *or* citizens, who have transferred all their right to the state, either by a tacit or by an explicit contract. A subject is said to have committed this crime if he has tried in any way to seize the right of the supreme power, *or* to transfer it to another. I say "has tried," for if they were not to be condemned until after the deed had been committed, for the most part the state would try this too late, after its right had been seized or transferred to another. Again, I say, without qualification, one who has tried "in any way" to seize the right of the supreme power, for I recognize no difference between the case where the attempt harms the state as a whole and that where it is, as clearly as can be, to the advantage of the state. For however he has tried to do this, he has committed treason and is rightly condemned.[23]

Here Spinoza specifies that, even if it is as clear as possible that benefit to the state would result, the action is wrong. Of course, if the rebel is successful and seizes power, then the right passes to him,[24] and he may, after the fact, decree that the rebellious act was right. Nonetheless, regardless of what the erstwhile rebel may decree later, Spinoza indicates in the passage just quoted that he feels strongly that rebellious actions are wrong independently of the outcome.

But – again – this view seems to be in tension with Spinoza's egoism. Given that the successful rebel is more powerful than the sovereign, why isn't it just plain right that this rebel wins? Isn't that what Spinoza's power-based egoism would lead us to expect?

Of course, this tension may be chalked up simply to Spinoza's reluctance – for prudential reasons – to be seen as condoning rebellions. This kind of explanation must always be taken seriously, but I believe that we can also resolve this tension more straightforwardly, that we can go a long way towards making sense – on Spinoza's own egoistic terms – of

---

[21] For a very helpful discussion of these passages, see Rosenthal, "Toleration and the Right to Resist."
[22] *TTP* Ch. 16; *G* III 197.   [23] *TTP* Ch. 16; *G* III 197; see also *TP* Ch. 4, art. 3; *G* III 292.
[24] *G* III 194.

his often negative assessment of even the successful rebel. To explain how this can be so, I will need to place in high relief the rationalist nature of Spinoza's accounts of normativity, of action, and of the self. And even if, as some passages suggest, Spinoza does ultimately endorse the successful rebel's action, the account I offer will show that there is nonetheless something wrong about the rebel's action even from the point of view of Spinoza's egoism.

2 HOLD THE SAUCE

This is not the place for a full-blown account of Spinoza's use of moral notions. The key point here is that despite disparaging our ordinary moral judgments, Spinoza works hard to arrive at moral notions that are legitimate by his own rationalist standards.

Spinoza's primary complaint against ordinary ways of drawing moral distinctions is that they give rise to assessments of an action or object that are made from one's own perspective and are not reflective of any genuine moral quality in the object itself. As Spinoza says, people judge that

what is most important in each thing is what is most useful to them, and . . . rate as most excellent all those things by which they were most pleased.[25]

He goes on to say in the preface to Part 4 of the *Ethics*:

As far as good and evil are concerned, they also indicate nothing positive in things, considered in themselves, nor are they anything other than modes of thinking, or notions we form because we compare things to one another. For one and the same thing can, at the same time, be good, and bad, and also indifferent. For example, music is good for one who is melancholy, bad for one who is mourning, and neither good nor bad to one who is deaf.[26]

The source of Spinoza's worry is the arbitrariness of ordinary moral judgments. To say that my evaluations are reflective of goodness in the object itself is to make an arbitrary claim: why should my interests be, or be conceived to be, the standard for goodness any more than yours? What is it in virtue of which my interests determine goodness or badness? Nothing about the object itself points to my interests in particular as setting the standard. To the extent that we employ our ordinary evaluative judgments to generate a ranking of objects as good or bad, we are thus positing a brute fact – that a certain thing is good because it is pleasing *to me* (as opposed to

---

[25] E1app.; G II 81. [26] G II 208; see also KV I 10; G I 49–50.

you). And of course, positing a brute fact is illegitimate, for Spinoza who is a big proponent of the PSR.[27]

This arbitrariness in ordinary moral judgments infects certain other judgments made in an apparently more principled way. Perhaps one might say that if (and only if) the object or action leads to a greater overall amount of happiness or pleasure (or whatever) in the world, then that action is good. But this standard of evaluation is arbitrary too. The goodness in this case, as in others, is not a function of the thing to be evaluated in itself; rather it is still a function of the object or action in relation to the interests of certain individuals, here the interests of each person. But, Spinoza would ask, why should the well-being or happiness of people in general be the standard of goodness, instead of, for example, the standard whereby actions are evaluated relative to the interests of all fans of the early 1960s group the Crystals, or all fans of James Dean, or all living beings? The problem is that nothing about the action itself points to any of these standards, including the most inclusive standards, rather than any of the other standards. Each of these standards is arbitrary. For Spinoza, what we need to do in order to arrive at a viable conception of the goodness of actions and of things generally is to find a standard of goodness that derives from the very nature of the thing to be evaluated. Only such a standard – if one could be found – would not be arbitrary and would be in keeping with Spinoza's rationalism.[28]

What Spinoza seeks, in other words, is a standard that is not simply tacked on to the object to be evaluated, a standard that somehow derives from the very nature of the object. Spinoza wants goodness (and other moral features) to be grounded in the nature of the objects exhibiting these features. Goodness, for Spinoza, must not be something special as far as the object is concerned; goodness must not be like a sauce that is spread on the object but is somehow extrinsic to it. As we might put it, Spinoza, in taking his rationalist line with regard to goodness, rejects the view that goodness is a special sauce.[29]

---

[27] See E1p11d2. There are numerous other passages in which Spinoza claims or presupposes that each fact can be explained. For discussion, see Della Rocca, "A Rationalist Manifesto" and *Spinoza*, pp. 4–5.

[28] Parts of this paragraph and the previous one were adapted from Della Rocca, *Spinoza*, pp. 177, 179.

[29] Matheron also makes the point that the standards for evaluation must come from within: "if Reason must formulate ethical evaluations, it could only be guided by a single norm: our individual nature, nothing other than our individual nature, all our individual nature" [*si la Raison doit formuler des appreciations éthiques, elle ne peut s'inspirer que d'une seule norme: notre nature individuelle, rien que notre nature individuelle, toute notre nature individuelle*] (*Individu et Communauté*, p. 245).

To find a standard of evaluation that meets Spinoza's rationalist standards, all we need to do is to look more closely at the nature of the object or action. I will focus for now on actions in particular. Each of my actions is, for Spinoza, fundamentally a striving to preserve myself and to increase my power of acting.[30] Spinoza's reasons for this fascinating and implausible claim (what about suicide, you ask?) are themselves fascinating and plausible. But these reasons cannot be explored here. I do, however, want to note that Spinoza's claims about striving are not inherently psychological: though rocks and chairs – in so far as they are physical or extended – do not have psychological features, they can nonetheless be said in all their activity to strive for self-preservation and increase in power. The striving for self-preservation is, for Spinoza, a universal phenomenon.

With this characterization of each action as a striving for self-preservation, we can arrive at a non-arbitrary standard by which to evaluate the action. An action is good (or otherwise positively evaluated) to the extent to which it is successful in enhancing the power of the agent. An action is bad to the extent to which it leads to the agent's decrease in power. Such an increase in power (when this increase is considered psychologically) is joy.[31] So, for Spinoza, goodness is defined in terms of joy: "By good . . . I understand every kind of joy, and whatever leads to it." Similarly evil is defined as "every kind of sadness."[32] Spinoza ties evaluation to power and essence in the appendix to Part I: "the perfection of things is to be judged solely from their nature and power."[33] This connection also emerges quite vividly in E4d8:

> By virtue and power I understand the same thing, that is (by 3p7) virtue, in so far as it is related to man, is the very essence, or nature of man, in so far as he has the power of bringing about certain things, which can be understood through the laws of his nature alone.

The goodness of an action is nothing but its ability to succeed in increasing the power of the agent. Objects can be evaluated in similar terms: an object's goodness is nothing but its success in increasing its power.

Spinoza can thus be seen as offering an explanation of goodness in general in terms of power. The power of a thing, in turn, for Spinoza is nothing but, is explained in terms of, a thing's ability to cause, i.e., to serve as the explanation of, changes in itself or in other things.[34] Thus goodness is explained in terms of explanation itself. This is an instance of a pervasive move in Spinoza: the two-fold use of the PSR. In this case, as in others, the

---

[30] E3p7d. [31] E3p11s. [32] E3p39s. [33] *G* II 83. [34] E3d2.

phenomenon in question (here it is goodness, elsewhere it is consciousness, causation, inherence, representation, individuality, epistemic justification, rights, existence itself, and, as we will see, identity) must be explained – this demand is the first use of the PSR. And the phenomenon is explained in terms of the notion of explanation itself, is nothing but a certain explanatory connection between things. This is the second use of the PSR. In the case at hand, goodness is *explained* in terms of a thing's *power* which is its ability to serve as the *explanation* of things. Thus goodness is explained in terms of explanation itself, it is made intelligible in terms of intelligibility itself, it is conceived in terms of conceivability itself. If goodness were not accounted for in terms of explanation itself, then it would not be properly grounded in the world, it would be a special sauce.

This account of goodness enables us to see how an action can fail to meet *its own* standard. The action is, by nature, a striving for something, *x*. If the action doesn't lead to *x*, then the action fails to meet the standard dictated by its nature, and so the action is bad. To evaluate the action in this way is not arbitrary for the standard derives from the nature of the action itself.

Further, in this light, we can see that if I simultaneously strive for two incompatible things, *x* and *y*, then I will automatically violate some standard of mine: either I will fail to attain *x* or I will fail to attain *y* (or I will fail to attain each one). In this case, even independently of the outcome of my activity, I will necessarily violate my standards and act badly. The case of striving for incompatible things will be important when we return to the rebel.

My discussion has so far been primarily in terms of the good, but Spinoza offers a similarly rationalist account of what it is for an action to be right. Rightness is just power, just intelligibility.[35] Spinoza accounts for the dictates of reason in similar terms: reason dictates that I act so as to increase my power.[36] I act rationally if and only if I act egoistically. Finally, the rights that individuals enjoy receive the same treatment: I have the right to do whatever is in my power: "each individual has the supreme right to do this, i.e. (as I have said), to exist and act as it is naturally determined to do."[37] In each of these cases – the good, the right, what reason demands, the rights that individuals enjoy – the phenomenon in question is nothing more than power. In keeping with the two-fold use of the PSR, the phenomenon

---

[35] E4p18s.　　[36] E4p18s.
[37] *TTP* Ch. 16; *G* III 189; cf. *TP* Ch. 2 arts. 3–4; *G* III 276–277.

is explained in terms of the notion of explanation itself, in terms of the ability to serve as the explanation of things.

Let's return to the rebel. As I explained, in light of Spinoza's commitment to egoism, it might have seemed that Spinoza would claim that the successful rebel's action is good and right. After all, as the outcome demonstrates, the rebel is more powerful than the sovereign. Thus, given egoism, it might seem that it would be wrong and bad for the sovereign to have won in the conflict with this particular rebel.

But this is not the conclusion Spinoza always reaches. He sometimes sees even the successful rebel as bad. Yet the successful rebel seems to meet the only standard by which his action can legitimately be judged, viz. that of enhancing his power. How then can the rebel be bad? In coming down so hard on the rebel, Spinoza seems to appeal to some standard that is independent of the nature of the rebel and the rebel's action. But any such standard would, by Spinoza's own lights, be an objectionable special sauce. Thus to avoid seeing Spinoza as indulging in special sauce, we must find a way in which, for Spinoza, even the successful rebel violates his own standards.

3 THE FRYING PAN

To find out how, for Spinoza, the successful rebel violates his own standards (and is thus bad and wrong, etc.), I would like to make a foray into one of Spinoza's least successful arguments or, rather, into what is often regarded as one of Spinoza's least successful arguments. By revealing what I think are the previously unexplored underpinnings of this argument, I hope to emerge with a new interpretation of Spinoza's criticism of the rebel and of his account of moral criticism in general.

Spinoza says in E4p31: "In so far as a thing agrees with our nature [*cum nostra natura convenit*], it is necessarily good." And he concludes from this in E4p31c that:

the more a thing agrees with our nature, the more useful, or better, it is for us, and conversely, the more a thing is useful to us, the more it agrees with our nature.

As Spinoza makes clear, for one thing to "agree in nature" with another is just for the first to be similar to the second in a certain respect or respects. In E4p29 and E4p29d, he contrasts something whose nature is completely different from ours with a thing that "has something in common with us" [*commune aliquid nobiscum habeat*]. In E4p30 (which he cites in E4p31d),

Spinoza goes on to speak of a thing that has something in common with our nature. From these passages, we can conclude that agreement in nature is just a matter of similarity. Such similarity comes, of course, in degrees, and so Spinoza's point – as he stresses in E4p31c – is that the more similar a thing is to me, the more useful it is to me.

Spinoza also makes clear that, for him, things similar to me are beneficial to me to the extent that they act from the dictates of reason, i.e., act so as to increase their power, i.e., act so as to benefit themselves, i.e., act solely on the basis of their own nature, i.e., act in a self-determined fashion. As Spinoza puts the point, "There is no singular thing in nature which is more useful to man than a man who lives according to the guidance of reason."[38] By contrast, in so far as those similar to me act non-rationally, i.e., act in a way not determined solely by their own nature, then they can fail to benefit and can indeed harm me. Spinoza thus says: "In so far as men are torn by affects which are passions, they can be contrary to one another."[39]

So, for Spinoza, whether your action benefits me is a function of two separate matters that are matters of degree: the extent to which you and I agree in nature and the extent to which you are rational, the extent to which you act on the basis of your nature. The more it is true both that you and I agree in nature *and* that you are rational, the more your actions also benefit me.[40]

Spinoza's claim is thus that

Simply by being similar to me and acting rationally another individual is beneficial to me.

I will call this view *the frying pan* (and if there's a frying pan, you can be sure that a fire is not far away). The deep implausibility of the frying pan emerges when we ask the natural question: why should your being similar to me and acting in a relatively self-determined way automatically benefit me? Even if you are similar to me and even if you act on the basis of those respects in which we are similar, your action is still *yours*. Why should that action automatically benefit *me*?

To begin to see why Spinoza might hold such a strong view, i.e., why he might accept the frying pan, we need to unpack some of Spinoza's reasoning in E4p31d. To the extent that you and I agree in nature (i.e., are similar), anything that I do that stems from that shared nature also stems from your nature (after all, your nature is, in this respect, the same as my

---

[38] E4p35c1.   [39] E4p34. Cf. *TP* Ch. 2, art. 14; *G* III 281; E4app10.
[40] This paragraph is adapted from Della Rocca, *Spinoza*, p. 199.

nature). So let's say that I am acting in a relatively self-determined way, i.e., acting, to some extent, in a way that is due to my nature and not to the natures of things external to me. Further, let's specify that I act on the basis of those respects in which my nature agrees with yours, those respects in which you and I are similar. To the extent that I act out of my own nature, i.e., in a self-determined way, i.e., rationally, I make things more explicable in terms of me, i.e., I am more powerful. Since increased power is beneficial to me, in acting on the basis of my nature (which I share to some extent with you), I benefit myself. But to the extent that I act out of those respects in which you and I agree in nature, then not only do I act out of my nature, I also act out of your nature. That is, in so acting that I make things intelligible in terms of me, I also make things intelligible in terms of you. And since making things intelligible in terms of you is what it is to increase your power and to benefit you, it follows that in acting out of my nature (which I share to some extent with you), I benefit you. Thus my rational action benefits you, and in the same manner, your rational action benefits me.

Notice that the benefit to me and to you is automatic. To benefit a person who is similar to me, I don't have to recognize the similarity and the other doesn't have to recognize the similarity or that I am acting rationally. It is enough for the benefit to accrue to the other that I am similar to that other and am acting rationally. No awareness of the other is necessary.

From this position, it follows that I have a rational obligation – i.e., it is in my self-interest – to make myself more similar to other rational individuals, other relatively self-determined individuals. In making myself more similar to the other rational individuals, I necessarily – to the extent that I too am rational – strive for what they strive for. In short, I have an obligation, for Spinoza, to strive for the same things that other rational individuals similar to me strive for. Thus, it might be said that I have an obligation to see things and to act from the point of view of rational others who are similar to me.

For this reason, I have an obligation to avoid passions. To the extent that I am motivated by passions, I am determined not from within but by something external, i.e., I am not active, i.e., I am not rational. In this case, despite our similarity, you and I can strive for different things and so can come into conflict.[41]

Again, it's extremely implausible to think that mere similarity can have these wonderful effects. I will return to this problem and show, in

---

[41] E4p34.

section 6, how Spinoza might justify the frying pan. But before doing so, I would like to show how – given Spinoza's claims on behalf of mere similarity – we can see how the rebel violates his own standards and is to be criticized.

4 THE STATE, SIMILARITY, AND POINT OF VIEW

To set the stage for our return to the rebel, consider Spinoza's account of the formation and structure of the state in light of his tribute to the benefits of similarity. Spinoza's framework for understanding the state is in some ways Hobbesian.[42] For Spinoza, it is right and good for each of us to preserve herself, and indeed each of us has the right to seek her own advantage and to seek to control and even kill others if doing so would aid in her preservation. The obvious problem is that, independently of the state, none of us can do a very good job of preserving ourselves and attaining power: too many threats, always someone bigger and more powerful, no one you can trust – a bad scene all around. Each individual comes to see, then, that it is in her interest to lay down the rights she has over other people in return for their laying down their rights against her. But how can she trust others' word that they have given up these rights? Obviously, a mechanism of enforcement is necessary, and that's where the sovereign comes in. So the picture is this: I agree to lay down my rights against you, and you similarly agree to lay down your rights against me. We both agree to transfer these rights to a sovereign who thus agrees to enforce the agreement and to protect us in return for our obedience to the laws the sovereign puts in place to enforce the agreement. Thus Spinoza says,

because we have already shown that natural right is determined only by the power of each [individual], it follows that as much of each [person's] power as he transfers to another, whether by force or voluntarily, so much of his own right does he necessarily give up to the other, and that that person has the supreme right over everyone who has the supreme power with which he can compel everyone by force, and hold them back by fear of the supreme punishment, which everyone, without exception, fears.[43]

This agreement between me and other citizens and between me and the sovereign is, or at least can be, beneficial to me. Because I have agreed,

---

[42] For good treatments of Hobbes's relation to Spinoza, see Curley, "Kissinger, Spinoza, and Genghis Khan," McShea, *The Political Philosophy of Spinoza*, Ch. 9, and Justin Steinberg, "Spinoza's Political Philosophy."

[43] *TTP* Ch. 16; *G* III 193.

at least some others will, *in return*, stop seeking to harm me, and because I have agreed, the sovereign will *in return* endeavor to protect me from others who might seek to harm me (in violation of the agreement). This benefit to me depends on the recognition by these others of me and of my agreement.

But in light of Spinoza's focus on similarity, we can see a more direct benefit to me. The agreement is itself a way of making ourselves more similar to one another, and in particular it is a way of making ourselves strive for the same things (e.g., for the preservation and continued well-being of one another and of the state itself). Further, not only are human beings made more similar by virtue of the agreement, but the agreement brings into existence a new individual – the state – which, like all other individuals, strives to persist. Given the circumstances of its formation, the big individual strives as much as possible for the preservation of the little individuals who entered into the agreement. Of course, this holds only for most cases: Spinoza allows that the big individual may on occasion not strive to preserve some of the little individuals. But in general, the state and the little individuals thus strive for the same things and are similar. So with the agreement that forms the state, a whole lot of similarity between me and other human beings and between me and the state comes into existence.

This similarity is music to Spinoza's ears. As we have seen, other things similar to me, in so far as they are rational, benefit me independently of any awareness these others may have of me. It follows not only that these individuals may be willing to benefit me *in return* for my agreeing to the agreement, but also that the similarity between me and others makes the others beneficial to me automatically, without the intervention of their recognition of me and of my being part of the agreement.

By agreeing in this way, I come to see things and act not only from the point of view of other individuals, but also from the point of view of the state itself, I come to strive for the same things that these others, including the state, strive for. Further, because of the benefits of similarity, we have, for Spinoza, an obligation to agree in this way, to see things and to act from the point of view of the state and other citizens, to strive for what they strive for. Indeed, to the extent that we have agreed, our actions are as much strivings to benefit the state as they are strivings to benefit ourselves. As Spinoza says,

a subject can do nothing contrary to the decree and dictate of his own reason so long as he acts according to the decrees of the supreme power. For it was at the urging of reason itself that he decided without reservation to transfer to the supreme power his right of living according to his own judgment.[44]

Similarly, Spinoza speaks of a situation in which "men have common laws, and are all led as if by one mind."[45]

5 A REBEL WITHOUT INTERNAL COHERENCE

Let's return to the rebel. As we have seen, the rebel threatens the state by challenging its authority (that's part of what it is to be a rebel). At the same time, the rebel is a citizen of that state (that's also part of what it is to be a rebel) and, as such, the rebel has a great deal of similarity not only to the other citizens, but also to the state itself. By virtue of this similarity and to the degree to which the state and its sovereign are rational, the rebel has an obligation to preserve the state and to enhance its power and, in general, to strive for the things the state strives for. In other words, to the extent that the rebel is rational, he strives to enhance the state's power. And so, by one standard that stems from the rebel himself and from his nature as a citizen of the state, the rebel and his actions can be evaluated according to the extent to which he succeeds in enhancing the power of the state. At the same time, the rebel strives to undermine or weaken the state. And so, by the standard that stems from the rebel's nature as rebel, as a threatener of the state, the rebel and his action can be evaluated according to the extent to which the rebel succeeds in undermining the state. Thus the rebel – whether or not he succeeds *qua* rebel – inevitably fails to meet at least one of the standards that arise from his dual nature as a citizen and as a threatener of the state. The rebel will either succeed in undermining the state or fail to do so. Either way, the rebel compromises an internal standard. Either way, he gets his hands dirty: he violates one standard in attempting to satisfy another. As we saw earlier, such internal incoherence is one way to fail to meet one's own standards.

Thus the rebel – even the rebel whose threat to the state succeeds – comes in for justifiable criticism from Spinoza. And even if Spinoza, in the end, endorses the successful rebel's action, Spinoza can legitimately find

---

[44] *TTP* Ch. 20; *G* III 242.
[45] *TP* Ch. 2 art. 16; *G* III 281. See also *TP* Ch. 2 art. 19; *G* III 282–283: "obedience is a constant will to do what by law is good and, in accordance with the common decree, must be done." See also *TP* Ch. 3, arts. 2, 5–7; *G* III 284–285, *G* III 286–287. Cf. Matheron: "we no longer distinguish our perspective from that of the other, because there is not the slightest difference between knowing the joy of another and feeling it" [*nous ne distinguons plus notre perspective de la sienne, car il n'y a aucune différence entre connaitre la joie d'autrui et l'eprouver*] (*Individu et Communauté*, p. 275).

the action wrong in at least one respect, viz. in so far as the action violates one of the rebel's own standards. The criticism makes sense given Spinoza's rationalist account of normativity and his insistence on internal standards of evaluation and also given Spinoza's frying pan – his view that similarity by itself is a source of benefit to me and to others.

In a similar fashion, we can make sense of Spinoza's criticism of lying to save one's own life. In general, as we have seen, I have an obligation to help others similar to me. Also, to the extent that I am rational, I thereby strive to help others similar to me. So, one standard by which to evaluate my action is in terms of the degree to which I help others. In lying to others, I am manipulating them and limiting their power. So I am harming them, and thus – to the degree to which the others are rational and are similar to me – I am harming myself, an activity that Spinoza's egoism classifies as irrational and wrong. Even if I lie in order to save my own life (and this lie is successful), I nonetheless have – by harming someone rational who is similar to me – done something wrong (or at least have done something wrong in a certain respect). I have failed to satisfy my own standards, standards dictated by my own nature.

Here is where I think something might be added to Don Garrett's extremely illuminating account of E4p72s where Spinoza comes down hard on lying to save one's life.[46] According to Garrett, Spinoza thinks that although the perfectly free individual may not lie to save one's life, someone less than free (i.e., each of us finite beings) may permissibly lie in these circumstances. Perhaps that is right, but it follows from my account of Spinozistic moral criticism that we should also say that the less free person, in lying to a rational other similar to herself is thereby doing something wrong in some respect. Thus the less than fully free person who lies to save her own life is not fully off the moral hook.[47]

We can see how Spinoza's criticisms of the rebel and of the liar (not to mention that lowest of all specimens: the lying rebel!) are not out of keeping with Spinoza's general egoism, but rather are dictated by that egoism, by the concern to meet the standards set by one's own nature. Cases of harming another similar to oneself – either a case of lying in order to save one's life, or a case of successful rebellious action, or a case of ordinary murder or robbery – are to some extent cases of harming oneself by failing to promote similarity with others who are relatively rational. Thus it seems that it is not the case, after all, that because of Spinoza's egoism the outcome of any

---

[46] See Garrett, "'A Free Man Always Acts Honestly'" and Garrett's contribution to the current volume.
[47] Diane Steinberg, in "Spinoza's Ethical Doctrine," reaches a similar conclusion.

power struggle is right and good. Even if the rebel is successful, his action is still, and necessarily, wrong in some respect, for in this action he inevitably violates one of his own standards and is, in this respect, subject to criticism.

6 THE FIRE

But what good is my purported solution to the problem of making sense of Spinoza's criticism of the rebel? For to reach this "solution," I have relied heavily on the frying pan – i.e., on the view that similarity is by itself helpful to us. As I've touched on already, there seems to be a deep and fatal metaphysical objection to the frying pan. In thinking that my helping myself is also my helping you to the extent that you and I are similar, Spinoza seems to assume that there is nothing more to you than the qualities that you have and nothing more to me than the qualities I have. But this seems wrong: no matter how qualitatively similar you are to me, helping you doesn't automatically help me (not even to some extent). This is because you and I are each something over and above (or under and below) the qualities that we have. If you and I were nothing more than our qualities (some of which are shared), then Spinoza would be right: to the extent that you and I are similar (have the same qualities) and to the extent that you and I act on the basis of these similarities, then anything that helps you would, to that extent, help me. But obviously there is more to me and to you than our qualities: identity of particulars cannot amount to mere similarity. As Bennett claims,

A thing's being a threat or a help to me depends not only on how it relates to my nature but also on other factors – e.g. on its spatial relation to me. However alike you and I are, the thing in question may relate to us – not to *our natures*, but to *us* – quite differently, and thus bear differently on our welfare.[48]

Or, more pithily: "two things however alike are still two."[49] Because Spinoza misses the obvious point that identity cannot amount to mere similarity, Spinoza is, in the eyes of Bennett and others,[50] obviously wrong in asserting the frying pan.

But what such criticisms of Spinoza fail to appreciate is that Spinoza has reasons for thinking that there is nothing more to identity than similarity, that objects are constituted qualitatively, and thus that the frying pan is true.

---

[48] Bennet, *Study*, p. 301.   [49] Bennett, *Study*, p. 301.
[50] See Allison, *Benedict de Spinoza*, p. 151, and Nadler, *Spinoza's Ethics*, p. 238. Unfortunately, I too jumped on this bandwagon in "Egoism and the Imitation of Affects in Spinoza," p. 132.

As we all know and as I have stressed here, Spinoza accepts the PSR, and, like Leibniz after him, he sees that the PSR dictates that there cannot be *two* distinct but qualitatively exactly alike things. That is, Spinoza (and Leibniz) see that the PSR entails the Principle of the Identity of Indiscernibles (PII).[51] The basic thought here, for both Spinoza and Leibniz, is this: if x and y are distinct, but share all the same qualities, then there would be nothing in virtue of which their non-identity holds, no difference in properties between them that could serve to explain their non-identity. For Spinoza and Leibniz, non-identity of objects must be explained. (This flows straight out of the PSR.) And non-identity of objects is to be explained in terms of qualitative difference. If you think that non-identity is not in need of explanation, then you are not a full-blown rationalist of the kind that Spinoza is and that Leibniz aspires to be. You do not really accept the PSR.

Indeed, I would say that, for Spinoza, not only does perfect similarity entail identity of objects, but also identity of objects just is – reduces to – perfect similarity. For consider: if being identical to a particular object were something over and above (under and below) the qualities that the object has, then what does identity of objects consist in? How could one explain the nature of identity? Identity would under these circumstances be a brute fact, something primitive, and this Spinoza would certainly reject. However, if we account for identity of objects purely in terms of similarity, then we are not treating identity of objects as a primitive, rather we are explaining it in terms of (complete) qualitative similarity. Further, for Spinoza, a quality of an object is just a way in which that object can be conceived or thought of. This is what is behind the equivalence, for Spinoza, of being in or inherence and the relation of being conceived through – an equivalence that figures prominently in the opening stretch of the *Ethics* and that I will return to briefly later. Given that a quality is just a way in which an object can be conceived, it follows that, in accounting for identity of objects in terms of similarity, Spinoza explains identity of objects in terms of conceivability itself. That is, he explains identity in terms of explicability itself. Thus Spinoza's commitment to the qualitative constitution of objects – i.e., to the PII – is yet another manifestation of his two-fold use of the PSR.

So Spinoza's embrace of the PSR dictates his embrace of the PII and of the qualitative nature of identity, and thus enables him to respond in good

---

[51] For Spinoza's commitment to this entailment, see E1p4 and E1p5 and Della Rocca, "Spinoza's Substance Monism." For Leibniz's commitment, see Leibniz, "Primary Truths" and his correspondence with Clarke in Leibniz, *Philosophical Essays*. For a rousing defense of the PII itself, see Della Rocca "Two Spheres, Twenty Spheres."

rationalist fashion to the plausible criticism of the frying pan that Bennett and others make. Perhaps the frying pan is a blunder, but Spinoza – as a rationalist – is right to accept it. You might object that to defend the view that similar individuals automatically benefit one another – i.e., to defend the frying pan – by appeal to the PII and the view that identity is nothing more than qualitative similarity only makes things worse, that this is to jump from the frying pan into the fire. So be it. But this fire is the fire of rationalism, and it is from this fire that Spinoza's philosophy draws its strength. He would not see this move as undesirable at all.

Nonetheless, it would be undesirable if Spinoza had no way to justify the PSR on which the PII is based. Without the PSR, the PII falls. Without the PII, Spinoza's frying pan – the thesis that similarity is by itself beneficial – falls. Without the frying pan, Spinoza's criticism of the successful rebel would be an illegitimate appeal to special sauce. And without being able legitimately to criticize the successful rebel, Spinoza would be committed to the view that the outcome of any power struggle is good. In addition, without the PSR, Spinoza's entire account of normativity and the need for internal standards collapses. Spinoza is thus required to justify the PSR, and I believe he can, but this is a topic for another occasion.[52] Still we can at least see how, on rationalist grounds, Spinoza can legitimately criticize the successful rebel and deny that the outcome of any power struggle is good.

Or can we?

7 SPECIAL SAUCE AFTER ALL?

Problems with this way of understanding Spinoza's criticism of the rebel arise immediately, problems that give us a new window onto the foundations of – and tensions within – Spinoza's metaphysics.

I've shown that for Spinoza, because of the frying pan, we have an obligation to become like rational others and the state and to act and see things from their point of view. Taking this line of thought just a step further, we can see that, for Spinoza, we have at least as much or even more reason to see things and act from God's point of view. In other words, just as we have an obligation to become more and more like the state by striving for the things that the state strives for, so too we have an obligation to become more and more like God by striving for the things that God – from the divine perspective – strives to do and does do.

---

[52] See Della Rocca, "A Rationalist Manifesto" and Della Rocca, *Spinoza*, chapter 8.

You may balk at saying that God strives. I don't want to insist on the term "strives." What I mean here is simply that God does certain things, God acts and has tendencies to act: his being in one state is such that it leads to his being in another state unless external causes intervene. Obviously, there are no external causes to get in the way of God's activity, and so nothing stops God from being in the other state. Thus God tends to be in the other state – in the sense that one state causes God to be in the other state unless external causes intervene. This tendency is always and necessarily successful. It is this tendency on God's part that I am referring to when I speak of God's striving.[53]

Spinoza stresses that reason requires that we see things from God's point of view in E2p44c2: "It is of the nature of reason to perceive things under a certain aspect of eternity." To see things under an aspect of eternity is to see how things follow from an eternal being (E1d8), i.e., from God. So, for Spinoza, reason dictates that we see how things follow from God. Indeed, this obligation is at work in the agreement that formed the state, for in that agreement human beings resolved "to live only according to the dictate of reason."[54] To live by the dictate of reason is to see things, and to act, rationally, i.e., to be self-determined and independent of outside causes. Because only God is fully independent of outside causes, it follows that to live by the dictate of reason is to see things as much as possible from God's point of view. Perhaps Spinoza expresses this view in *TdIE* §13 when he says that the true good for human beings is "the knowledge of the union that the mind has with the whole of nature."

If we have this obligation to see things from God's point of view, then how should we view the rebel's subversive action? We've seen how Spinoza's claim that the rebel's act is bad and wrong can be understood. But from God's perspective, would the rebel's action be evaluated in similarly negative terms?

No, not really.

From God's point of view, the action in question is not fundamentally an action of the rebel, but rather an action of God. This is because all of the rebel's actions and, indeed, the rebel himself and finite things generally, are nothing more than modes or states or actions of God.[55] Given that finite objects have the status of modes, the action in question is really an action

---

[53] For more on God's striving, see Della Rocca, *Spinoza*, pp. 152–153.   [54] *TTP* Ch. 19; *G* III 230.

[55] I will not here defend the view that, for Spinoza, finite things are modes understood as states of God. For an important discussion, see Melamed, "Spinoza's Metaphysics of Substance." See also Della Rocca, *Spinoza*, pp. 58–69. For a vigorous defense of the contrary view, see Curley, "On Bennett's Interpretation of Spinoza's Monism."

of God and, as such, the action is not bad and is, in fact, good. Although the action – seen as an action of the rebel – may be a violation of the rebel's own standards, a violation that makes the action bad, nonetheless the action, as an action of God, can in no way be bad (or wrong, etc.) because God can in no way violate God's own standards or fail to achieve what God is striving or tending towards. So, seen as God's action, the action in question can only be good.

Strictly speaking, none of God's actions can be good because the goodness of an action presupposes the agent's transition to a higher level of power,[56] and, of course, God is already and always maximally powerful and so cannot increase in power. Nonetheless, Spinoza does sometimes apply positive terms of evaluation to God in order to signify that God maintains God's high level of power. Thus, although strictly God is not capable of love because love involves joy and joy is an increase in power, Spinoza says that "God loves himself with an infinite intellectual love."[57] Spinoza specifies that God has this love, this joy, because God "enjoys infinite perfection."[58] As Don Garrett puts the point, "because God eternally has the greatest perfection and capacity for action, he has a kind of eternal analogue of joy."[59]

So, returning to the rebel's action we can say that to see the action from the divine point of view is to see it from the point of view of eternity, i.e., as following from the nature of an eternal being, i.e., as following from God's own nature. In seeing the action as following from God's own nature, God views the action as *God's*, and, as we've just seen, God's action must not be bad and is instead good. So the action, seen as the rebel's action, appears bad, but, seen from the more rational point of view of God or eternity, appears not bad, but good. Given that we have an obligation to see things, as much as possible, from God's point of view, we have an obligation to see the action as good and not – as Spinoza sees it in criticizing the rebel – as bad. Thus, by Spinoza's own lights, his pronouncement of the rebel's action as bad is unjustified: the action can be seen more rationally from the point of view of God and from this point of view is not bad, but good.

You might say, however, that seeing the *rebel's* action as bad is, for Spinoza, perfectly justified, perfectly rational, even though we might see *God's* action as good and even though the rebel's action and God's action are, in some sense, the same. *Qua* action of the rebel, the action is wrong and bad, and *qua* action of God it is right and good. If the action, seen as

---

[56] E3p39s.   [57] E5p35.   [58] E5p35d.   [59] Garrett, "Spinoza's Ethical Theory," p. 283.

the rebel's action, really is bad, then how has Spinoza failed to be rational, failed to be justified, in seeing the rebel's action as bad?

Good question. In response, I would say that, for Spinoza, badness and wrongness are features that cannot properly be located in the world. To attribute such features to objects or actions is to appeal to a special sauce. This emerges from some of Spinoza's central metaphysical principles. As I have argued elsewhere, Spinoza treats as coextensive – and indeed identifies – the relation of being-in or inherence and the relation of causation. And Spinoza sees both of these relations as nothing more than the relation of being conceived through. Thus x is caused by y if and only if x inheres in y if and only if x is conceived through y. At work here are fascinating two-fold uses of the PSR: inherence and causation are each explained in terms of explanation itself.[60]

Given the coextensiveness of inherence and causation, any action, any state, that is not caused from within a given object cannot be fully in, cannot fully inhere in, or be a state of that object. Now take the badness of the rebel's action. What does the badness inhere in? It might seem to inhere in the rebel's action. But it can't fully inhere in the rebel's action because the badness is caused from outside the rebel or at least it is not fully caused from within by the rebel. Indeed, the badness cannot fully inhere in any collection of finite objects because, again, the badness is not fully caused from within any such collection. What, then, can the badness inhere in? It seems that it can inhere only in God, because it seems to be caused by God and nothing is caused from outside God. But when we turn to God as the subject of inherence, the badness does not at all show up: God's action is, as we saw, not bad at all. So the badness of the action cannot fully inhere in anything: not in the rebel's action, not in a broader collection of finite objects, and certainly not in God. By contrast, the goodness of the action – when the action is seen as an action of God's – does fully inhere in God (because it is not caused from outside God).

So to see things as bad is to attribute a feature to things that is not fully inherent in anything. Given that inherence is, for Spinoza, coextensive with conceivability, it follows that to see things as bad is to attribute a feature to objects that is not fully grounded in, not fully conceived in terms of, anything. Thus to attribute badness to things is, for Spinoza, to appeal to a brute fact. Thus in attributing badness to the rebel's action, Spinoza is purveying special sauce. More generally, in making any of his moral criticisms, Spinoza has truck with special sauce. However, from

---

[60] See Della Rocca, "Rationalism Run Amok."

God's point of view – the point of view that, according to Spinoza, reason demands that we take up – none of these moral criticisms would apply, nothing can be genuinely bad or wrong, and all is good and right. Badness and wrongness are simply not on God's radar screen and thus do not genuinely exist.[61] And so we seem to be back at the view that, for Spinoza, moral criticisms – finding things to be bad or wrong – are all unjustified.[62]

What's happened? We were trying to make sense of Spinoza's moral criticism of the rebel and of his moral criticisms in general, and we seemed – with the help of the frying pan and the fire – to be able to do precisely that. But further reflection on the frying pan led to the deeper conclusion that moral criticisms are not Spinozistically legitimate after all. Spinoza nonetheless makes moral criticisms in a way that – we can now see perhaps more clearly than before – threatens the coherence of his rationalist system. Spinoza may appeal to brute facts despite his best efforts.

Of course, Spinoza has no choice but to act in this way. For, in criticizing the rebel (and others), Spinoza can be seen as trying to get us to take a broader state-oriented perspective, instead of remaining locked in our narrow individual-human-sized points of view. The assessment of actions from the broader, state-oriented perspective is more rational than the assessment from the narrower perspective. And so, with his criticism, Spinoza encourages us to take a step in the right direction. Obviously, there are even broader, more rational points of view, culminating in God's maximally rational point of view.[63] It is only when we reach the broadest point of view that we no longer appeal to the brute facts with which narrower perspectives are tainted. Spinoza's moral criticisms – though laced with appeals to special sauce – are ways of exhorting us to become more rational and perhaps to gradually wean ourselves from such appeals. So, yes, Spinoza appeals to brute facts in criticizing the rebel and others – but he is willing to get his hands dirty in this way in an effort to get himself and us to a better and more rational place. As a finite, limited being inevitably burdened by a finite, limited perspective, Spinoza is bound to work from within that perspective in order to make himself and us more rational and powerful. Thus there have to be appeals to brute facts along the way, but at the ideal and perhaps unattainable end of this journey, we would be able to kick away the ladder of appeals to brute facts, appeals that help us to

---

[61] For similar reasons, I would say that privation does not exist for Spinoza. Spinoza says in *Ep.* 19 that a "privation can be said only in relation to our intellect, not in relation to God's" (*G* IV 92).

[62] James, "Power and Difference," p. 220, captures this perspective on negative evaluations very well.

[63] Although Spinoza is, I believe, committed, to points of view intermediate between the state's and God's, he does not explicitly discuss them.

become more and more rational. Absent such an achievement, however, Spinoza must – like the rebel himself, though perhaps more valiantly – get his hands dirty.

Thus, the initial worry that the criticism of the rebel is unjustified in Spinoza's system is, after all, right, but only because, as we now see, *all* moral criticisms – even those that Spinoza makes – are unjustified. For Spinoza, "[i]t is of the nature of reason to perceive things under a certain aspect of eternity,"[64] and under an aspect of eternity, moral criticism simply drops out.

---

[64] E2p44c2.

CHAPTER 10

"Promising" ideas: Hobbes and contract in Spinoza's political philosophy

Don Garrett

> Broken promises don't bother me. I just think, "Why did they believe me?"
>
> (*Deep Thoughts*, by Jack Handy)

Like Hobbes, Spinoza prominently invokes promising and contract or covenant[1] in his discussion of the foundations of the state – primarily, though not exclusively, in his *Theological-Political Treatise*. But how does Spinoza understand their nature and significance, and how, if at all, does his understanding of them differ from that of Hobbes? I begin by posing a set of related puzzles concerning the interpretation of Spinoza's claims about promises and contracts specifically as they relate to Hobbes. I then compare the doctrines of Hobbes and Spinoza concerning several key topics: rights and powers, good and evil, reason and passion, and faith and deception. Finally, I appeal to these doctrines to resolve the puzzles about the nature and significance of promising and contract in Spinoza's political philosophy.

I PUZZLES ABOUT HOBBES AND SPINOZA ON PROMISING AND CONTRACT

The similarities between the political philosophies of Hobbes and Spinoza are striking, extensive, and deep. Both philosophers aim to ground a scientific treatment of politics on a fundamental principle of endeavor for self-preservation. Both assign a theoretical role to a pre-political "state of nature," and both ascribe a nearly unlimited "right of nature" to human

---

I wish to thank Yitzhak Melamed, Michael Rosenthal, Aaron Garrett, Susan James, Susanne Sreedhar, Justin Steinberg, John Morrison, and audiences at Boston University and the conference "Thinking with Spinoza" at Birkbeck College, London, for helpful questions and comments on an early version of this chapter.

[1] Unlike Spinoza, Hobbes distinguishes explicitly between contract (*contractus*) and covenant (*pactum*): a covenant is a contract in which at least one party is to perform his or her part at a later time.

beings to do as they will in that state. Both conceive the commonwealth or state as a composite entity instituted through a contract in which its members transfer rights. Both maintain that the commonwealth has a right to determine the form of religion,[2] and both invest substantial effort in the interpretation of Scripture – in large part because of the political significance of scriptural interpretation for European states such as their own. Both are concerned, as part of that interpretation, with explicating the nature and terms of the particular contract reported in Scripture between God and the ancient Hebrews,[3] as well as with understanding the contracts that give rise to commonwealths more generally.[4]

Some striking divergences of view are evident as well. For one, Hobbes argues that the best form of government is monarchy, whereas Spinoza argues that it is democracy. For another, Hobbes proposes that the state exercise substantial control over speech and religion, whereas Spinoza recommends that it generally allow broad latitude in both areas. Yet to a very considerable extent, these disagreements are practical rather than theoretical, grounded to be sure partly in different conceptions of the good but even more in different overall assessments of how best to enhance the prudential quality of public decision-making and prevent civil instability[5] – differing assessments no doubt related to the two philosophers' differing experiences with their own commonwealths.

Evidence of a subtler but potentially more fundamental difference – despite the two philosophers' seeming agreement about the importance of covenant in creating and maintaining a commonwealth – appears in the opposing treatments they give to a stock problem concerning an explicit promise made to a robber in order to obtain one's freedom. In *De Cive* – which Spinoza had in his library – Hobbes writes:

> It is an usual question, whether compacts extorted from us through fear, do oblige or not. For example, if, to redeem my life from the power of a robber, I promise to pay him . . . next day, and that I will do no act whereby to apprehend and bring him to justice: whether I am tied to keep promise or not? But though such a promise must sometimes be judged to be of no effect, yet it is not to be accounted so because it proceedeth from fear . . . It holds universally true, that promises do

---

[2] *TTP* Ch. 16; *G* III 199–200; *TTP* Ch. 19; *G* III 228, 230, 232, 233–234. Translations from Spinoza's *Theological-Political Treatise* are from Edwin Curley (forthcoming).

[3] For recent discussion, see Curley, "The Covenant with God," and Martinich, "The Interpretation of Covenants."

[4] These are all features of Spinoza's *TTP*; they do not all feature in his later but incomplete *Political Treatise*. I will assume that their absence from the later work – written for quite different purposes – does not constitute a renunciation of them.

[5] For example, Spinoza explains his preference for democracy over monarchy in the *TP* (also Curley forthcoming) thus: "The will of a very large council cannot be determined so much by inordinate desire as by reason" (*TP* Ch. 8; *G* III 326).

oblige when there is some benefit received, and that to promise, and the thing promised, be lawful. But it is lawful, for the redemption of my life, both to promise and to give what I will of mine own to any man, even to a thief. We are obliged, therefore, by promises proceeding from fear, except the civil law forbid them; by virtue whereof, that which is promised becomes unlawful.[6]

In his *TTP*, in contrast, Spinoza writes without qualification:

For the universal law of human nature is that no one fails to pursue anything which he judges to be good, unless he hopes for a greater good, or fears a greater harm; nor does he submit to any evil, except to avoid a greater one, or because he hopes for a greater good . . . But from this it follows necessarily that no one will promise to give up the right he has to all things except with intent to deceive, and absolutely, that no one will stand by his promises unless he fears a greater evil or hopes for a greater good. To understand this better, suppose a Robber forces me to promise him that I will give him my goods when he wishes. Since, as I have already shown, my natural right is determined only by my power, it is certain that if I can free myself from this Robber by deceptively promising him whatever he wishes, I am permitted to do this by natural right, to contract deceptively for whatever he wishes . . . From these considerations we conclude that no contract can have any force except by reason of its utility. If the utility is taken away, the contract is taken away with it, and is null and void.[7]

This verdict, and particularly the final conclusion drawn from it, may seem in tension with what he goes on to say almost immediately:

If all men could easily be led solely by the guidance of reason, and could recognize the supreme utility and necessity of the state, there would be no one who would not absolutely detest deceptions; with supreme reliability, everyone would stand by their contracts completely, out of a desire for this supreme good, the preservation of the state; above all else, they would maintain trust, the most important protection of the state.[8]

It seems equally in tension with Spinoza's seemingly more demanding statements in Proposition 72 of Part 4 of the *Ethics* about the model "free man." As Edwin Curley translates the proposition,[9] it reads:

Proposition 72: A free man always acts honestly, not deceptively.

Demonstration: If a free man, insofar as he is free, did anything by deception, he would do it from the dictate of reason (for so far only do we call him free). And so it would be a virtue to act deceptively (by P24), and hence (by the same Prop.), everyone would be better advised to act deceptively to preserve his being. I.e. (as

[6] *De Cive* 2.16; see also *Leviathan* 1.14.27 for a similar passage. References to *De Cive* are to Hobbes, *De Cive: The English Version*; references to *Leviathan* are to Curley, ed., *Leviathan*.
[7] *TTP* Ch. 16; *G* III 191–192.   [8] *TTP* Ch. 16; *G* III 192.
[9] All translations from Spinoza's *Ethics* are from *C*.

is known through itself), men would be better advised to agree only in words, and be contrary to one another in fact. But this is absurd (by P31C). Therefore, a free man etc., q.e.d.

Scholium: Suppose someone now asks: what if a man could save himself from the present danger of death by treachery? Would not the principle of preserving his own being recommend, without qualification, that he be treacherous?

The reply to this is the same. If reason should recommend that, it would recommend it to all men. And so reason would recommend, without qualification, that men make agreements, join forces, and have common rights only by deception – i.e., that really they have no common rights. This is absurd.

In seeking to understand Spinoza's views on promises and contracts as they contrast with those of Hobbes, we might hope for illumination from his own characterizations of his disagreements with Hobbes. Spinoza makes two remarks of this kind, both bearing clearly if somewhat indirectly on our topic; yet each is puzzling in its own way. Thus, he writes in an Annotation to Chapter 16 of the *TTP*:

No matter what state a man is in, he can be free. For certainly a man is free insofar as he is led by reason. But (contrary to Hobbes) reason urges peace in all circumstances; moreover, peace cannot be obtained unless the common rights of the state are maintained without infringement. Therefore, the more a man is led by reason, i.e., the more he is free, the more will he steadfastly maintain the rights of the state and carry out the commands of the supreme power of which he is a subject.[10]

It seems surprising that Spinoza characterizes Hobbes as denying that reason urges peace in all circumstances, since Hobbes states that "the first, and fundamental law of nature" – from which he derives the obligation to keep covenants – is "to seek peace and follow it,"[11] and he characterizes all of the laws of nature as "dictates of reason." Indeed, if anyone questions the universal rationality of peace, it would seem to be Spinoza himself, for no one seems more ready to allow violations of peace contracts, at least between states, than he:

Allies are men of two states which, to avoid the danger of war, or to gain some other advantage, contract with one another not to harm one another, but on the contrary, to come to one another's aid in cases of need, though each retains its own sovereignty. This contract will be valid just as long as its foundation, the principle of danger, *or* of advantage, is present. For no one makes a contract or is bound to stand by a contract, except out of hope for some good, or anxiety about some evil. If this foundation should be removed, the contract is removed of itself. Experience

---

[10] *TTP* Ch. 16 Annotation 33; *G* III 263.   [11] *Leviathan* 1.14.4.

also teaches this, as clearly as one could wish. For though two different states may contract with one another not to harm one another, nevertheless, they strive, as far as they can, to prevent the other from becoming the more powerful, and they do not trust what has been said, unless they have seen clearly enough the end and advantage for which each one contracts. Otherwise, they fear deception, and not without just cause. For who trusts what someone else has said and promised, if the other person has the supreme power and retains the right to do whatever he likes? Who but a fool, who does not know the right the supreme powers have?[12]

While the note just cited constitutes Spinoza's only use of Hobbes's name in work originally intended for publication, he does mention Hobbes once more in his correspondence. Replying to Jarig Jelles four years after the publication of the *TTP*, he writes:

With regard to Politics, the difference between Hobbes and me, about which you inquire, consists in this, that I ever preserve the natural right intact so that the Supreme Power in a state has no more right over a subject than is proportionate to the power by which it is superior to the subject.[13]

Yet this, too, seems at first sight to get the relation between Hobbes and Spinoza exactly backwards. For while Hobbes maintains that the fundamental natural right of self-preservation, at least, is inalienable in the covenant instituting a commonwealth, Spinoza refers repeatedly not only to partial transfers of right to the sovereign power[14] but also of subjects ceding "all their power of defending themselves – i.e., all their right"[15] and "completely surrendering their natural right."[16] Far from "preserving the natural right intact" in the social contract, Spinoza appears to annihilate it entirely.

2 KEY DOCTRINES IN HOBBES AND SPINOZA

In order to understand Spinoza's view of promises and contracts, as well as his differences with Hobbes in this regard, it is necessary to understand some of their central doctrines concerning rights and powers, good and evil, reason and passion, and faith and deception. Let us turn to those topics in order.

Rights and powers. For Hobbes, a right is a "liberty to do or forebear," where a "liberty" is the absence of an impediment to the exercise of one's power. The Right of Nature, in particular, is

---

[12] *TTP* Ch. 16; G III 196–197; see also *TP* Ch. 2; G III 281.
[13] *Ep.* 50. References to Spinoza's correspondence are to Wolf, ed., *The Correspondence of Spinoza.*
[14] *TTP* Ch. 16; G III 193.   [15] *TTP* Ch. 16; G III 193.   [16] *TTP* Ch. 16; G III 195.

the liberty each man hath to use his own power, as he will himself, for the preservation of his own nature, that is to say, of his own life, and consequently of doing anything which, in his own judgment and reason, he shall conceive to be the aptest means thereunto.[17]

To lay aside a right, whether by renouncing or transferring it, is to divest oneself, by sufficient signs of the will, either verbal or non-verbal, of the liberty of hindering another of the benefit of his or her own right to a thing. He defines a contract as a mutual transfer of rights, and a covenant as a contract in which at least one party is to perform at a later time. In the covenant that constitutes the social contract, individuals agree to authorize the actions of "one man or an assembly of men" as their own and to give up their right of governing themselves to this man or assembly on condition that all others do likewise. While this covenant involves giving up the right to be judge for oneself of what is or is not conducive to one's own preservation, it nevertheless has limits: individuals cannot give up their right to defend their own lives or bodies directly, nor can they give up certain other "liberties of subjects," which include resisting physical harm, availing themselves of the necessities of life, and abstaining from executing dangerous or dishonorable offices.[18] These exceptions are grounded ulti- mately for Hobbes at least in part in requirements on the interpretation of actions – no one can be understood, by any word or action, to be willing the loss of these rights in a social contract.[19] Indeed, in the absence of an enforcing power for covenants – a "power to hold them all in awe," in Hobbes's well-known phrase – covenants are generally rendered void by the suspicion that the second party would fail to perform and would instead simply take advantage of the first performance by the other party.

   Spinoza, too, recognizes an extensive "right of nature." Arguing from the principles (i) that God has sovereign right over all things, (ii) that the power of nature is the power of God, and (iii) that the power of nature is the power of individual things taken together, he concludes that each individual's right of nature extends to "everything in its power" without restriction, so that nothing is outside natural right but "what no one desires and what no one can do."[20] His metaphysical doctrine that *all* activity is pursuit of self-preservation[21] renders Hobbes's restriction of the right of nature to action aiming at self-preservation trivial. But he also goes beyond

---

[17] *Leviathan* 1.16.1.   [18] *De Cive* 2.18; *Leviathan* 11.21.10.
[19] Sreedhar, "Defending Hobbes's Right," distinguishes three principles governing what rights can and cannot be laid down in any given contract.
[20] *TTP* Ch. 16; G III 189. For a discussion of this argument, see Curley, "The State of Nature."
[21] E3p7.

Hobbes in claiming explicitly that natural right and power are necessarily coextensive.

In addition to natural right, Spinoza also recognizes what he calls "private civil right": "the freedom each person has to preserve himself in his state, which is determined by the edicts of the supreme power, and is defended only by its authority."[22] In principle, for Spinoza, a social contract creating the state would be one in which individuals cede all of their right to the state, so that private civil right would be limited to what the state in fact allows or protects. In practice, however, things are otherwise. Natural right is originally unlimited in theory, inasmuch as it is unrestricted by a state, but in practice it is extremely meager because human beings without the security of a state have very little power to do anything. Similarly, the right of the state against the individual is in principle unlimited by any restrictions imposed on it in a contract, but it is in fact limited by the inability of a state to acquire complete power over its subjects. Human beings cannot in fact give up the right to pursue their advantage or self-preservation as they see it, nor to believe what seems to them most likely, nor to abstain from dangerous or dishonorable tasks. These limitations on the rights conveyed are not grounded, as for Hobbes, in the alleged impossibility of giving convincing tokens of the will to lay them down; rather, the rights themselves cannot be ceded simply because the corresponding power cannot be given up. While this may seem to be a distinction without a difference, it will prove to be significant.

Given that whatever is done with right is permissible, it may seem that Spinoza's doctrine that right is coextensive with power amounts to a kind of moral nihilism, since it follows that whatever anyone actually does is permissible. In fact, however, it amounts only to a rejection of the framework of *obligations and permissions* as a basis for drawing absolute moral distinctions. (In a parallel way, his necessitarianism, according to which whatever is possible is actual and whatever is actual is necessary, entails the rejection of a particular framework – in this case, a metaphysical framework – as a basis for drawing absolute modal distinctions. And just as Spinoza's necessitarianism still allows him to distinguish what is possible from what is impossible *relative to some restricted set of laws or circumstances*, so too he can still distinguish what is permissible from what is impermissible *relative to some specified body of laws or commands*.) Since Spinoza denies that *indignation* is ever appropriate – both because it is a kind of sadness (*tristitia*) and because it always reflects an inadequate understanding of the

[22] *TTP* Ch. 16; G III 196.

causal history of the behavior in question[23] – there is indeed some point in terms of appropriate moral attitudes to his rejection of the possibility of "impermissible" actions or actions "without right." But this would constitute a rejection of moral distinctions altogether only if he rejected all *other* vocabularies and frameworks for drawing and embracing such distinctions as well – and that he does not do. On the contrary, philosophers, in his view, "follow virtue not as a law, but out of love, because it is the best thing."[24]

Good and evil. According to Hobbes, "whatsoever is the object of any man's appetite or desire, that is it which he for his part calleth good."[25] This designation of something as good is always "relative to the person that useth the terms, since no common rule is to be taken from the nature of objects themselves." We nevertheless construe disagreements in what we call "good" as disagreements in *judgment* because we mistakenly take a projection of our own desires for the discernment of an objective feature of things. It is because ascriptions of goodness follow desire that Hobbes can assert that "of the voluntary acts of every man, the object is some good to himself."[26] Hobbes insists, however, that there is no *summum bonum* or highest good. Rather, felicity consists in "a continual progress of the desire, from one object to another; the attaining of the former, being still but the way to the latter."[27]

Spinoza agrees that, as the term "good" ("*bonum*") is typically used, it cannot be said that we desire things because we see that they are good, but rather that we call things "good" because we desire them.[28] It is with regard to this usage that he writes:

For the universal law of human nature is that no one fails to pursue anything which he judges to be good, unless he hopes for a greater good, or fears a greater harm; nor does he submit to any evil, except to avoid a greater one, or because he hopes for a greater good. I.e., between two goods, each person chooses the one he judges to be greater, and between two evils, the one which seems to him lesser. I say explicitly: the one which seems to the person choosing to be greater or lesser, and not that things necessarily are as he judges them to be. And this law is so firmly inscribed in human nature, that it ought to be numbered among the eternal truths, which no one can fail to know.[29]

In addition to this vulgar usage, however, Spinoza also stipulates in the *Ethics* a more scientific sense for "good" and "evil" ("*malum*"). Thus, in the Preface to Part 4, he defines "good" as "what we know certainly is a means

---

[23] E4p51s.   [24] *Ep.* 6.   [25] *Leviathan* 1.6.7.   [26] *Leviathan* 1.14.8.
[27] *Leviathan* 1.11.1.   [28] E3p9s.   [29] *TTP* Ch. 16; *G* III 191–192.

by which we may approach nearer and nearer to the model of human nature that we set before ourselves," and in Definition 1 of Part 4, he defines "good" – presumably in a way that is meant to be equivalent – as "what we certainly know to be useful to us." It is in this more scientific sense of "good," and not in the popular sense, that it is possible to "see and approve the better, but follow the worse."[30] Propositions 27–50 of *Ethics* Part 4 are largely devoted to demonstrating what is good and what is evil in this sense. Particularly important for present purposes is the following: "Things which are of assistance to the common Society of men, or which bring it about that men live harmoniously, are useful; those, on the other hand, are evil which bring discord to the State"[31] – a sentiment echoed and amplified, of course, in the *TTP*.

Contrary to Hobbes, Spinoza affirms that there is a *summum bonum*, namely, "knowledge of God."[32] Possession of this highest good is not exclusive. On the contrary, one can hardly achieve any considerable degree of it without the cooperation of others who agree with oneself in nature (e.g., who are not pulled in opposing directions by contrary passions) and with whom one can, as it were, constitute "one Mind and one Body."[33] At a minimum, these are fellow citizens in a state; at best, they are fellow philosophers and intellectual co-inquirers.[34] Because one's own advantage must be understood in terms of "persevering in one's being," however, Spinoza must offer an account of how knowledge of God constitutes[35] a kind of persevering in being that is higher and more perfect than merely continuing to exist for a longer period of duration – long life being an outcome that can hardly be guaranteed by any knowledge of God that human beings are likely to acquire. He offers this account in *Ethics* Part 5, where he argues that knowledge of God maximizes the "part of the mind that is eternal." Having a mind the greater part of which is eternal gives one control over the passions and diminishes one's fear of death. And indeed living a short life filled with the blessedness that comes from the knowledge of God (as Spinoza himself did, we may assume) is preferable to a life of longer duration and lesser knowledge.[36]

---

[30] E4p17s, quoting Ovid.   [31] E4p40.   [32] E4p28.   [33] E4p18s.

[34] For a good discussion of issues concerning the rationality of cooperation in Spinoza's philosophy, see Rosenthal, "Two Collective Action Problems."

[35] Given the way in which Spinoza has defined "good," he is not committed, as Aristotle was, to the doctrine that the *summum bonum* is non-instrumental. In fact, however, it is plausible to regard knowledge of God not just as producing but as constituting the highest kind of perseverance in being.

[36] Youpa, "Spinozistic Self-Preservation," has argued that, because the free man guided by reason has a greater part of his mind that is eternal, he would not harm his eternal part for the sake of a lesser

Reason and passion. Hobbes characterizes reason as the "reckoning (that is, adding and subtracting) of the consequences of general names agreed upon for the marking and signifying of our thoughts."[37] Because passions often lead one to act in ways that frustrate the satisfaction of one's desires, reason and passion can come into conflict in motivating human beings. At times, Hobbes seems to imply that self-preservation, as an end, has a particular relation to reason that is not exhausted by its status as the object of the most basic desire and one whose satisfaction is a prerequisite for the satisfaction of almost all other desires.[38] In any case, however, reason is capable of providing general theorems about how to preserve oneself and achieve a more commodious life, and hence to obtain what individuals regard as good. These theorems are "dictates" of reason and constitute what can be called the "laws of nature."

Spinoza, too, ascribes a motivational role to reason, and one that is often in conflict with passions. Because every affect is also an idea, and each singular thing strives to persevere in its being as a matter of metaphysical necessity, to understand some object as genuinely good in the scientific sense is *ipso facto* to have some desire for it, a desire that may conflict with other desires. He identifies reason (*ratio*) as the second of three kinds of cognition.[39] Unlike imagination (*imaginatio*), the lowest kind of cognition, reason is intellectual and consists in ideas that are adequate and true. Unlike intuitive knowledge (*scientia intuitiva*), the highest kind of cognition, it is a way of "perceiving many things at once," and is therefore inherently general. Accordingly, it provides us with general "rules" or "dictates" of reason, and Spinoza seems very insistent on their universal form and high level of generality. Propositions 51–66 of *Ethics* Part 4 are concerned primarily with acting under the guidance of reason and include the key claim: "From the guidance of reason, we shall follow the greater of two goods or the lesser of two evils."[40]

Because reason provides only general rules for action, it alone is insufficient for action in the external world: one must have some awareness of one's immediate situation, and this can typically only be achieved through sensation and memory, which are forms of imagination. Nevertheless, the more powerfully one's reason-produced adequate ideas play the leading role as desires in determining one's actions, the more one is guided by reason. Guidance by reason is thus a matter of degree, as is resemblance

---

good by breaking his word. However, Youpa does not show how breaking one's word would itself be a cause (as opposed to a relatively common effect) of lack of virtue or freedom.

[37] *Leviathan* 1.5.2.   [38] See Bernard Gert's Introduction to Hobbes, *Man and Citizen*.
[39] E2p40s.   [40] E4p65.

to the ideal "free man" – an ideal that is "the model of human nature we place before ourselves" mentioned in Spinoza's definition of "good" and described in the final seven propositions of *Ethics* Part 4. Just as no one can be solely guided by reason, so no one can be a completely free man. To be completely free is to be determined to existence and action by one's own nature alone,[41] and hence to be God, whereas all human beings are to varying degrees subject to external forces. Nevertheless, just as some individuals are more guided by reason and others less, so some individuals are freer and others less. Likewise, to be free and guided by reason is to act from *virtue* – that is, from power to persevere in one's being.[42] Because a virtuous and free individual guided by reason is genuinely the (relatively) adequate cause of his or her own actions, approbation (*favor*) – unlike indignation – can be appropriate; such approbation is itself, in Spinoza's words, "not contrary to reason."[43]

Reason tells us what is good or evil considered independent of the alternatives, but it does not prevent goods from coming into conflict within one another. Rather, it tells us to follow, in such cases, "the greater of two goods or the lesser of two evils." Spinoza gives revealing examples of such conflicts in the *TP*. He begins by noting, as he did in the *TTP*, that contracts between commonwealths are limited by their utility to both parties:

Therefore each State has an undiminished right to break the treaty whenever it wants to; it cannot be said that it acts deceitfully or treacherously because it goes back on its assurance as soon as the cause of fear or hope is taken away, because this condition was equal for each of the contracting parties: whichever one could first be free of fear would be its own master, and would use its freedom as it thought best. Moreover, no one contracts for the future except on the assumption of certain anticipated circumstances. If these circumstances change, then the nature of the whole situation changes. That is why each of the allied States retains the right to look after itself, and why each of them strives, as far as it can, to be beyond fear, and hence, to be its own master, and why each of them strives to prevent the other from becoming more powerful. So, if any State complains that it has been deceived, it cannot condemn the honesty of the allied State, but only its own foolishness, because it entrusted its own well-being to another State, which was its own master and for which the well-being of its own state is the supreme law.[44]

---

[41] E1d7.   [42] E4p8.
[43] E4p51. For more discussion of these matters, see Garrett, "'A Free Man Always Acts Honestly,'" and "Spinoza's Ethical Theory."
[44] *TP* Ch. 3; G III 290.

He continues, however, by giving an example of a case in which a private individual should not keep his or her word, before returning to the case of a state:

> Moreover, what we have said here does not in any way eliminate the honesty [*fides*] which both sound reason and Religion teach us to observe. For *neither reason nor Scripture teaches that every assurance we give is to be honored.* When I have promised someone to guard the money he has given me to be kept in secret for him, I am not bound to make good my assurance once I know, or believe I know, that what he gave me was stolen. On the contrary, I will act more properly if I undertake to restore it to its owners.
>
> Similarly, if the sovereign has promised to do something for someone else, and afterward time or reason has taught, or seems to have taught, that it will harm the common well-being of his subjects, surely he is bound to break his word. Therefore, since Scripture teaches *only in general* that we should keep our word, and leaves the particular cases where exceptions are to be made to the judgment of each person, it teaches nothing which is incompatible with what we have just shown.[45]

These are both cases, cleverly enough, in which one properly (that is, without acting contrary to reason) breaks one's word for the sake of something else that is also good for others: returning stolen property, or safeguarding the welfare of subjects. But given the definitional identity between what is good and what conduces to one's own advantage, reason could hardly allow that one break one's word for a sufficient good to *others* without also allowing that one break it for a sufficient good to *oneself*; on the contrary, it could only allow that one break it for others if doing so thereby brought or constituted a greater good for oneself as well.

Faith and deception. In the Introduction to *Leviathan*, Hobbes criticizes the hearts of men "blotted and confounded as they are with dissembling, lying, counterfeiting, and erroneous doctrines," but he does not list among the laws of nature any general prohibition against lying. He does, in contrast, state as the third law of nature *"that men perform their covenants made,"* and he characterizes violations of this law as "promise-breaking" or "not keeping faith." Since making a covenant involves an act of the will, Hobbes regards the breaking of covenant as a kind of practical contradiction and hence irrationality, in which an agent both does and undoes the same thing. The law of nature requiring performance of covenants applies only to *valid* covenants; and chief among the conditions that prevent or invalidate a covenant is the suspicion of non-performance by a later party that typically results from the absence of a sovereign "power to hold them all

---

[45] *TP* Ch. 3; *G* III 291, emphasis added.

in awe." Nevertheless, Hobbes argues in his famous "Reply to the Fool"[46] that, if the first party to a covenant does perform, the second party is then obliged to perform as well – evidently, at least in part, because signaling in this way the importance one attaches to uniting in cooperative contractual arrangements is highly conducive to self-preservation.

Like Hobbes, Spinoza does not propound any general principle against lying. It may seem that he does so in the previously cited E4p72 – "A free man always acts honestly, not deceptively" – but this appearance is an artifact of translation. The topic of that proposition is not deception generally, in the sense of inducing belief in what is not true. Spinoza would certainly have no compunction about deceiving non-human animals in that sense, and arguably the *TTP* is intended to deceive its less astute readers in some respects. (Indeed, E4p72 itself is arguably intended to have the same effect.) Nor is the topic of the proposition even out-and-out lying generally, in the sense of asserting what one knows or believes to be false. (Note that the *TTP* was published, presumably with Spinoza's knowledge, under a false imprint ["Hamburg"].) Rather, "honestly" translates Spinoza's "*cum fide*" and "deceptively" translates his "*dolo malo*." Hobbes typically uses "*cum fide*" ("with faith") and "*dolo*" ("by trickery or deception") to describe keeping and breaking faith in his sense, which is specific to promises and contracts. Moreover, Spinoza always uses throughout E4p72, including its demonstration and scholium, the more specific term "*dolus malus*" (literally, "evil trickery or deception"), a term that can be readily contrasted with "*dolus bonus*" (literally, "good trickery or deception"). In well-known Roman law, the former term designates fraud with "evil intent," while the latter term designates appropriate shrewdness or trickery of precisely the kind that might be justified in dealing with a robber or enemy.[47] Furthermore, in Annotation 32 to Chapter 16 of the *TTP* Spinoza explicitly recognizes the distinction between *dolus malus* and *dolus bonus*, indicating that the proscription of any deception as *dolus malus* depends on the state.

As we have already seen, Spinoza maintains that "if the utility [of a contract] is taken away, the contract is taken away with it, and is null and void," so that not merely the absence of an enforcing power but equally *any other* cause of a lack of relative utility in keeping faith for one partner or another can invalidate a contract. Furthermore, as we have also seen, he denies in the *TP* that a state breaking its word for reasons of utility thereby acts "deceptively or treacherously" ["*dolo, vel perfidia*"] and insists

---

[46] *Leviathan* 1.15.4–5.
[47] See, for example, Berger, *Encyclopedic Dictionary of Roman Law*, p. 440 (entry for "dolus").

that whoever relies on a promise or contract while recognizing that faithful performance is not useful to the other party has only his only "foolishness," not another's bad faith, to blame.

3 PUZZLES SOLVED

We are now in a position to resolve the puzzles with which we began. Let us take them up in reverse order.

1. Why does Spinoza say that he, unlike Hobbes, preserves the right of nature intact? As we have seen, Spinoza's social contract differs from Hobbes's in that it does not, by its very terms, cede some rights (for example, the right to hold onto whatever goods one can acquire, the right to say whatever one thinks fit) while retaining others (for example, the right to take sustenance, the right to refrain from dangerous or dishonorable tasks). In particular, for Spinoza, one does not cede to the sovereign power the *general* right to judge what is most conducive to one's self-preservation while still retaining the *particular* right to judge whether one is subject to a (relatively?) direct attempt to kill or wound. Rather, right of *whatever* kind is transferred to precisely the same extent that power is actually transferred. Although in becoming a subject one's power is lessened relative to the state, which acquires power over one, one's "right of nature" remains formally just the same: namely, it is still the right to do whatever one can do. Moreover, in practical terms, one's right of nature actually increases in the state, for one is far more able to act and to achieve one's advantage in cooperation with others than one would be able to do outside it. Indeed, were that not true, one could hardly have been motivated to enter into the social contract at all. Furthermore, the general right of nature itself – in the sense of nature's own right – remains exactly as it was before the social contract, simply arranged differently as a different sum of individual powers of things in nature.

2. Why does Spinoza write that "contrary to Hobbes, reason urges peace in all circumstances?" Although Hobbes does formulate the first law of nature as "to seek peace and follow it," he also expresses it disjunctively: "to seek peace, where it may be had, and where not, to defend ourselves."[48] Presumably, Spinoza saw this latter formulation as counseling the cessation

---

[48] *De Cive* 2.1; see also *Leviathan* 1.xiv.4. In *Leviathan*, Hobbes indicates that, when the prerequisites for the successful pursuit of peace are absent, the law of nature requires only that one *intend* to pursue peace whenever they become present. In a note to his translation of the *TTP*, Curley calls attention to the disjunctive character of the passage from *De Cive* as a possible explanation for Spinoza's note concerning Hobbes.

of *efforts* towards peace under certain circumstances. For Spinoza, however, peace considered in itself is always a good in the scientific sense and hence always actually to be pursued. It is therefore a rule of reason that one seek it, and seek it "in all circumstances." It does not follow, however, that engaging in war (even while continuing to seek peace) is never good relative to one's other options – or rather, it does not follow that war is never the lesser evil available under the circumstances, and hence an alternative that reason also counsels that one take. Indeed, Spinoza emphasizes that war may be relatively good (that is, the lesser evil) for a state in some circumstances, and presumably he allows that it can also be relatively good for competing individuals in the state of nature as well. The more one is guided by reason, of course, the more one will act as the model free man would act. And to the extent that one resembles the free man, the less one fears death and the more one values social and intellectual cooperation. Beyond that, however, the more free, virtuous, or guided by reason one is, the more power one has to prevent any need for war and to bring about cooperation instead; the inability to bring about this better outcome is always some kind of failing of one's active power. The fact remains, however: what an ideal model *would* do is not always what it is *good* for someone to do in order to become closer to that model. This is true whether one's model is that of the idle rich (which is not best attained by a poor man through a life of idleness) or the Spinozistic free man who always refrains from war.

   3. Why does Spinoza write, on the one hand, that violating a promise is sometimes permissible, and yet on the other that if all human beings were solely guided by reason, they would stand by their contracts completely? Spinoza's claim that some *promise-breaking* is permissible is not as strong a claim as it may appear, for two reasons. First, we have seen that for Spinoza not all breaking of explicit promises or assurances need constitute either *deception* or the *violation of a valid contract*. Indeed, at least in some actual circumstances, it is not contrary to "the honesty which both sound reason and Religion teach us to observe". Second, the claim that breaking a promise is sometimes *permissible* is simply a direct consequence of the claim that whatever is within one's power is done by right; it does not by itself entail that doing so is either good, in accordance with reason, or an action of the model free man.

   In some cases, nevertheless, it may well be that breaking a promise by deception is not only permissible but the best alternative available – that is, the lesser evil that, under the guidance of reason, one may therefore reasonably choose in a particular circumstance.[49] Yet this is compatible with Spinoza's claim that if *all* human beings were guided *solely* by reason, then they would all stand by their contract completely. For all would have a maximal appreciation of the value of cooperation[50] and would presumably recognize that others did as well, even as they all jointly pursued the mutually acknowledged shareable highest good of knowledge of God in a well-ordered state. Of course, an individual guided *solely* by reason would also be a *completely* free man. Such an individual would never find utility in breaking a promise, since he or she would never fear any harm and would always have the means to bring about the cooperation required for maintaining the shared highest good. Nevertheless, guidance *solely* by reason, like being *completely* free or *perfectly virtuous* is literally incompatible with being a human being. Human beings can only approximate these models without ever fully embodying them.[51] For this reason, some deceptive promise-breaking and renunciation of contracts may always remain the lesser of two evils for actual human beings.

4. *Why does Spinoza reject Hobbes's claim that one is obliged to keep a promise made to a robber to return with ransom in return for a present release?* Hobbes and Spinoza agree that a contract can be valid even if the motivation for entering into it was fear. Hobbes justifies his claim that the robber's contract is valid (unless explicitly forbidden by the sovereign) by appeal to a principle that "promises do oblige when there is some benefit received, and that to promise, and the thing promised, be lawful." First performance, for him, renders even an otherwise invalid contract valid – second performance, following trusting first performance, therefore falls under Hobbes's law of nature "to keep covenants made." He could, of course, regard the robber's contract itself as invalid if it were impossible to interpret the captive as willing to perform his part. But while this might be a tempting suggestion, Hobbes cannot avail himself of it, for the robber's own willingness to release the captive *depends* on the robber's being

[49] It is worth noting that in the demonstration of E4p72, Spinoza does not state that the principle of preserving one's being would *not* dictate treachery (*perfidia*) to save one's life, but only that it would not do so "without qualification" ["*omnino*"], a term that recurs elsewhere in his discussions of rational guidance and the ideal of the free man. See Garrett, "Spinoza's Ethical Theory." In fact, action undertaken to preserve one's own life may never qualify as treachery for Spinoza, but only as deception in the broad sense of *dolus* generally (and not as *dolus malus*).

[50] In fact, anyone promising first performance in a Hobbesian covenant could then generally count on second performers to appreciate the value of cooperation and perform their part as well, leading to general assurance about first performance.

[51] In addition to Garrett, "'A Free Man Always Acts Honestly,'" see also Garber, "Dr. Fischelson's Dilemma."

able to interpret the captive as intending to comply. The captive, having successfully indicated by signs his or her intention to comply, cannot now fail to do so without a practical inconsistency.

Spinoza, on the other hand, has no such commitments. Even if the released captive has successfully convinced the robber of an intention to pay, he retains the right to refrain from paying because he retains the power not to pay. The contract is invalid because the robber failed to provide the captive with an incentive to pay after release. Indeed, although the robber was misled, he has only his own foolishness to blame, at least if the captive's lack of utility in repayment was evident. Of course, one possible incentive for paying the ransom would lie in the value to the captive of signaling his or her willingness to cooperate in other contractual arrangements. But while Spinoza certainly appreciates the value of cooperation, especially as it renders both the state and intellectual friendship possible, and presumably too appreciates the value of signaling to others that one appreciates it, the question of whether it is useful to try to do so by the surprising act of paying *ex post facto* ransom to a robber – who is not likely to be a promising partner for joint ventures – is a matter of judgment.

To be sure, Spinoza does characterize the captive as giving the robber, despite the invalidity of the contract, a promise that is "deceptive" – *dolo*. This is presumably because the captive, in making the promise and winning release, also convinces the robber, contrary to fact, that he will be motivated to return with the ransom, thereby hiding from the robber his own true assessment of the utility of returning. But there is no general obligation in Spinoza not to deceive. Indeed, although Spinoza does not specify whether this deception of the robber is *dolus malus* or *dolus bonus*, it is clearly the latter – and it is only the former that E4p72 and its demonstration claim to be incompatible with freedom or (by implication) to be contrary to reason. Indeed, the passage cited previously from Chapter 3 of the *TP* strongly implies that *dolus bonus* quite generally is not contrary to "the honesty [*fides*] which both sound reason and Religion teach us to observe" and thus is in accordance with the requirement of E4p72 that the free man always act "honestly" [*cum fide*].

4 CONCLUSION

A recent commentator has claimed that the difference between Hobbes and Spinoza in the case of the promise to the robber results from Hobbes's being a contractualist and Spinoza's being a consequentialist.[52] While there

---

[52] See Marinoff, "Hobbes, Spinoza, Kant."

is an element of truth in that verdict, it is much too simple as it stands. Hobbes does exhibit some attraction to thinking of contracts as generating practical obligations even independent of the evaluation of their utility, but his moral and political philosophy remains embedded in a broader context that assigns *values* on the basis of self-preservation and desire satisfaction. Spinoza does employ a scientific conception of the good as the advantageous, or as what conduces to self-preservation. But self-preservation itself proves to consist not just in continued duration nor even in an affective or cognitive state alone, but also in a state of character – virtue – that is equally a matter of being such as to act in accordance with rules of reason, rules that one freely gives oneself. The full philosophical development of that scheme of value is Spinoza's principal aim of the *Ethics*. His aim in the *TTP*, in contrast, is largely to understand and to help bring about the political conditions that can enable each person to live the best kind of life of which he or she is capable – peaceful contentment for the multitude, true freedom and blessedness for the philosophers.

Spinoza's curious defense of toleration

Justin Steinberg

A little more than fifteen years ago an exchange between David West and Isaiah Berlin concerning Spinoza's "positive conception of liberty" was published in *Political Studies*. West aimed to rescue Spinoza from Berlin's procrustean critique of positive liberty by pointing to liberal features of Spinoza's thought, such as his methodological individualism and his defense of toleration. Berlin's response to West seems to reveal an embarrassing lack of familiarity with these liberal features of Spinoza's thought.[1] He claims that, according to Spinoza, "the obstacles to rational thought must be removed . . . all irrationality, heteronomy, passion, which resist or darken reason, must be removed, or at the very least controlled, by rational self understanding, education *and also legislation – that is, if necessary, the sanction of force, of coercive action.*"[2] There can be no question that Berlin is largely mistaken about this last point.[3] However, Berlin's mischaracterization raises an interesting question: why exactly doesn't Spinoza think that we should attempt to snuff out irrationality and dissolution with the law's iron fist?

In this chapter I take seriously the force of this question. I will intensify the problem in the first section below by noting several features of Spinoza's thought that lead him to eschew skeptical, pluralistic, and rights-based arguments for toleration, and make his defense of toleration even more surprising. I follow this by delineating the prudential, anticlerical roots of Spinoza's defense, before turning – in the final section – to consider just how far and when toleration serves the guiding norms of governance, namely,

---

[1] Berlin's treatment of Spinoza in "Two Concepts of Liberty" and elsewhere is careless at best. We ought thus to be suspicious of Delahunty's claim that "no student of Spinoza has done more to illuminate [the relationship between knowledge and freedom] than Isaiah Berlin" (*Spinoza*, p. 256).

[2] Berlin, "A Reply," p. 298, my emphasis.

[3] After all, Spinoza insists that most legislative attempts to make men wise and temperate are futile, at best. See for instance his claim that "simplicity and truth of mind are not instilled in men by the power of laws or by public authority, absolutely no one can be compelled to be happy [*beatus*] by force of law" (*TTP* Ch. 7; *G* III 116).

peace and positive liberty. Once we see how toleration is anchored in these norms, we form a clearer picture of Spinoza as a liberal perfectionist for whom the bounds of political toleration depend on pragmatic and circumstance-specific assessments of what conduces to the flourishing of the state. This will help to illuminate what is peculiar – and, arguably, commendable – about Spinoza's form of liberalism.

I THE ROADS NOT TAKEN

1.1 Why toleration must be justified

It has often been noted that there is something rather odd about the very idea of toleration. We may follow D. D. Raphael here in describing toleration as "species of allowing liberty...[that] implies that you really disapprove of what you are prepared to leave alone."[4] It seems to involve at least following three conditions:

(1) One disapproves of another's activity.
(2) One is capable of, or at least one believes oneself to be capable of, preventing such activity.
(3) One allows – that is, refrains from attempting to prevent – such activity.

What makes toleration odd is that it is not apparent why one should *not* seek to prevent activities of which one disapproves when one is capable, or believes oneself to be capable, of doing so. This becomes a full-blown paradox if one assumes that to disapprove of something is to think that it should be prevented, since toleration would then imply adopting a policy of not preventing that which one believes should be prevented.[5]

Moreover, even if we deny that there is anything paradoxical about toleration, it must be admitted that toleration does not justify itself. On the face of it, it would seem that, other things being equal, one ought to prevent activities of which one disapproves, especially when the consequences of not doing so are thought to be significant. In other words, intolerance would seem to be the default position. It is toleration, then, that stands in need of justification. So how does one justify this, arguably queer, practice?[6]

---

[4] Raphael, "The Intolerable," p. 139.   [5] See Mendus, "Introduction," p. 4.

[6] In what follows I will be exclusively examining philosophical, rather than religious, arguments for toleration. The most prominent Dutch advocates of toleration in the seventeenth century – from Dirck Coornhert and the Arminians in the early part of the century to the Collegiants and other heterodox Christians of mid-century – based their arguments for toleration primarily on scriptural grounds (see Israel, "The Intellectual Debate," and Kossmann, "Freedom"). Indeed, Spinoza himself offers a sort of religious argument for toleration when he uses his interpretation of Scripture to show that philosophy and faith have separate domains, thereby undercutting the grounds for religious

1.2 The argument from epistemic humility

One natural way to defend the practice of toleration is to point to the fact that we are cognitively limited and prone to mistakes. Because of our fallibility, we ought to avoid dictating how others should live.[7] Let us call this the argument from epistemic humility. The extreme, fallibilist version of this view claims that any one of our beliefs could turn out to be false. But one need not embrace this position to make an argument from epistemic modesty for religious toleration, since even if there are some firm, self-justifying beliefs, beliefs about, for instance, what is necessary for salvation are not likely to be among them. Because we are liable to make mistakes concerning the nature of the divinity and what is required for salvation, we ought to refrain from imposing such highly fallible beliefs on others, lest we suppress the true religion. Epistemic humility is also often cited in defense of tolerating the *ethical* beliefs and practices of others. Indeed, Susan Mendus has argued that "twentieth-century liberalism . . . frequently bases its commitment to toleration on moral skepticism."[8]

The argument from epistemic humility was in relatively wide circulation in the early modern period. Many classical skeptical texts, including the works of Sextus Empiricus, had been rediscovered in the sixteenth century, providing philosophers with a new set of tools for combating various forms of dogmatism. During this same period, wars of religion were being waged throughout Europe. It is no surprise, then, that as political thinkers sought ways to resolve religious disputes, skepticism was often used as an instrument for toleration.[9] The works of Castellio and Montaigne, for instance, contain examples of how skepticism might be invoked in support of toleration.[10]

---

persecution. In focusing on philosophical arguments, then, I do not wish to downplay the role of religious arguments in the history of tolerationist thought.

[7] Epistemic humility, or moral skepticism of the sort I am referring to, is to be distinguished from moral non-cognitivism. Moral non-cognitivism – which claims that moral judgments do not have any cognitive content or truth value – does not give one an obvious reason to refrain from imposing one's own non-cognitive judgments on others. The recognition that one's own judgments are not factual would not necessarily undermine one's commitment to these very attitudes. See Harrison, "Relativism and Toleration."

[8] Mendus, "Introduction," p. 2.

[9] It should be noted that, as Richard Tuck has so effectively pointed out, skepticism in the early modern period did not always support toleration ("Skepticism and Toleration"). It often supported acquiescence to an intolerant authority.

[10] In *Concerning Heretics*, Castellio argues that "dissensions arise solely from ignorance of the truth" (p. 132). It is folly, therefore, to persecute others on the basis of something that we ourselves do not understand. And Montaigne, in *Des Boiteux* ("Of Cripples"), argues that "to kill men, we should have sharp and luminous evidence" (*Essays*, p. 789) – evidence that Montaigne believes that we quite obviously lack.

But however popular this mode of argument was, it is clear that Spinoza's defense of toleration is not grounded on epistemic humility. Indeed, one can hardly imagine a less skeptical philosopher when it comes to our knowledge of God's nature and of the prescripts of ethics.[11] The geometric method deployed in the *Ethics* give us demonstrative proof that there is only one substance,[12] God or Nature (*Deus sive Natura*), that everything that exists exists in and through God,[13] that everything follows from the necessity of God's nature,[14] that nature never acts for the sake of some end,[15] and so forth. These tenets, like all truths of reason, are self-certifying; once grasped, they lie beyond doubt.[16] The same can be said of the dictates of reason, or the ethical prescriptions, that Spinoza presents in *Ethics* Part 4, and the cognitive therapy that he lays out in *Ethics* Part 5. The geometric method leaves no room for skepticism or epistemic humility concerning these matters. So, however common skeptical arguments were in the early modern period, it should be apparent that Spinoza rejects them.[17]

1.3 The argument from pluralism

An argument that is sometimes conflated with the argument from epistemic humility is the argument from pluralism. Unlike the skeptic, the pluralist does not necessarily claim that we cannot know the truth about religion or morality; rather, the pluralist claims that there is not a single truth about religion or morality. Strictly speaking, the pluralist does not offer an argument for toleration, since she does not think that activities that deviate from her own conception of what is good necessarily warrant disapproval. Thus, condition (1) from the above account does not necessarily obtain. Nevertheless, since the pluralist whom we will be discussing presents a case *against* intolerance, we may regard her as a tolerationist, at least in a loose sense.

Pluralism is sometimes presented as an argument for *religious* toleration. Gary Remer, for instance, portrays Bodin's defense of toleration in the

---

[11] See Popkin, *History of Scepticism*, pp. 229–248.
[12] E1p14.   [13] E1p15.   [14] E1p29.   [15] E1app.   [16] E2p43s.
[17] Ultimately, we can imagine Spinoza regarding the argument from epistemic humility as too weak. His account helps to point out that most religious conflicts of the day were based on a confusion. The anthropomorphic, providential conception of God that undergirds and animates religious schisms does not exist; immaterial, immortal souls that provide the foundation for disputes about salvation do not exist. The views that drive persecution are not just *probably* false, they are demonstrably false. So, while the argument from epistemic humility allows the possibility that the intolerationist/ persecutor may be right, even if his beliefs are not justified, on Spinoza's account, the intolerationist's beliefs are both false and unjustified.

Colloquium as grounded in religious pluralism: the truth about religion is not monistic, it is "complex" and "multifaceted."[18] The full truth, according to Bodin, can only be ascertained through the expression of a diversity of perspectives.[19] More often, though, pluralism is invoked in the service of *moral* toleration. John Stuart Mill's *On Liberty* contains perhaps the greatest expression of moral pluralism. In this work Mill, under the influence of Wilhelm von Humboldt, makes an impassioned plea for "experiments in living" and the individual pursuit of happiness. Part of his defense of liberty hinges on his belief that there is no single blueprint for a good human life: "Human nature is not a machine to be built after a model, and set to do exactly the work prescribed for it, but a tree, which requires to grow and develop itself on all sides, according to the tendency of the inward forces which make it a living thing."[20]

However, at best, pluralism just shows that we should not interfere with others' affairs *just because* they run counter to our conception of a good life. But a pluralist might have independent reasons for preventing certain activities, for instance if they fall outside of the range of acceptable activities *for anyone*, or if securing a certain degree of uniformity would have salutary social consequences. In order, then, to move from pluralism to toleration, we need an additional argument. One such argument, offered by Mill, would be to claim that we stand in a privileged – though not infallible – epistemic position when it comes to determining what a good life consists in *for us*.[21] The state cannot hope to be in as good a position to determine how we ought to live as we are, so it ought not to restrict our choices, at least in matters that concern only ourselves.[22]

Having suggested how pluralism could be used to support toleration, we may now consider whether Spinoza himself argues in this manner. To answer this question, we must first ask whether Spinoza was, in fact, a pluralist. Some recent commentators think so. For instance, Steven B. Smith has argued that Spinoza rejects a "monistic view of human flourishing, the one-size-fits-all model of the good life. Instead his awareness of diversity

---

[18] Remer, "Bodin's Pluralistic Theory," p. 121.

[19] One could read Gotthold Lessing's *Nathan the Wise*, published in 1779, nearly two centuries after the completion of Bodin's *Colloquium* in 1588, as advancing a similar version of religious pluralism. The famous ring parable in this work seems to exhort us to give up the notion of one true faith and to allow that a plurality of faiths may have legitimate claims to truth.

[20] Mill, *On Liberty*, p. 56.

[21] See Mill's claims that "with respect to his own feelings and circumstance the most ordinary man or woman has means of knowledge immeasurably surpassing those that can be possessed by anyone else" (*On Liberty*, p. 71).

[22] Admittedly, this is, on its own, a rather weak argument for toleration.

both within and between human beings... makes the *Ethics* an important, although frequently unacknowledged, source of moral pluralism."[23] And David West, in his attempt to save Spinoza from Berlin's critique, highlights what he regards as Spinoza's pluralism,[24] citing it as one of the primary grounds for toleration: "the outcome of a rationalized *conatus* is potentially different for every individual and understanding must be exercised by everyone for themselves, so *no one can justifiably impose their interpretation of virtue or the good life on one another.*"[25]

Smith and West ground their interpretation of Spinoza as a moral pluralist on the fact that we each have distinct and complex bodies, with our own ratios of motion and rest, which will lead us to express our striving in unique ways. What preserves and empowers your body/mind may be rather different from what preserves and empowers mine, a point that Spinoza makes in the scholium to E4p45:

> It is the part of a wise man, I say, to refresh and restore himself in moderation with pleasant food and drink, with scents, with the beauty of green plants, with decoration, music, sports, the theater, and other things of this kind, which anyone can use without injury to another. For the human body is composed of a great many parts of different natures which constantly require new and varied nourishment.[26]

While it is evident that Spinoza does think that sensual pleasures and diversions can contribute to one's power of acting, and that he accepts that these restorative sources of pleasure and amusement often vary from person to person, it is far less evident what follows from this.

If moral pluralism amounts to no more than the claim that there is *some* variation in what contributes in *some* way to the flourishing of individuals, it would be a trivial doctrine that seemingly everyone in the history of philosophy accepts. However, I presume that moral pluralism claims that the *central features* of one's flourishing may vary significantly between individuals and that the sources of value between individuals are incommensurable. If this is the case, it is not at all clear that Spinoza would qualify as a pluralist.

For Spinoza, the basic contours of a fully active, flourishing life are the same for all humans. Blessedness, or one's highest flourishing, is achieved when one comes to understand things through God's essence, resulting in an intellectual love of God.[27] The content of this knowledge is the same for everyone. Flourishing also consists in gaining intellectual control over one's

---

[23] Smith, *Spinoza's Book of Life*, p. 149.   [24] West, "Spinoza on Positive Freedom," p. 292.
[25] West, "Spinoza on Positive Freedom," p. 296; my emphasis.   [26] E4p45s; *G* II 244.
[27] E5p32c ff.

affects[28] and in acting from reason.[29] While it is true that the measures that are taken to acquire this knowledge and gain control over oneself may vary a bit between individuals,[30] the actual rational control that is gained is the same for everyone. Moreover, whatever differences exist between human beings, Spinoza insists that human beings share a rational essence.[31] For these reasons, it seems that, *pace* West, Berlin might actually be right in characterizing Spinoza as a monist about truth and goodness; while the procedures for becoming rational and virtuous may be narrowly pluralistic, reason itself, and the virtues themselves, are universal.[32] And even if one admits that the sources of restorative pleasures vary from person to person, the sources of the most durable and important forms of joy are the same for all humans. And, finally, even if there is a meaningful and important sense in which Spinoza is a pluralist, he seems to have no sympathy for the epistemic privilege view advanced by Mill that would enable him to use this pluralism in defense of tolerationism. So, even if Spinoza were a pluralist, which I have suggested he is not, this position does not appear to play a role in his defense of toleration in the *TTP*.[33]

1.4 The argument from rights

Some have supposed that any satisfactory theory of toleration must be able to show not just that intolerance is impractical or harmful in certain

---

[28] Spinoza provides a digest of how such control is achieved in E5p20s.   [29] E4p18s ff.

[30] Spinoza indicates in E5p10s that gaining control over one's affects requires habituation, and one's regimen must be tailored to one's own proclivities, e.g., "if someone sees that he pursues esteem too much, he should think of its correct use" (E5p10s).

[31] See, e.g., E4p35 and its attendant corollaries and scholia.

[32] This same reasoning could be applied to the response that Spinoza gave to his landlady when asked if he believed that she could find salvation in her religion (reported by Colerus), which was: "your Religion is a good one, you need not look for any other, nor doubt that you may be saved in it, provided, whilst you apply yourself to Piety, you live at the same time a peaceable and quiet life" (Colerus, *Life*, p. 41). Let's assume that Spinoza was not being ironic here. On the face of it, the suggestion that salvation could come through leading a good Christian life rather than through Spinozism appears to betray a pluralism that leads Spinoza to tolerate the beliefs of his landlady. But I think a more plausible reading requires noting that for Spinoza salvation (*salus*) may be a graduated concept: it comes in degrees. Spinoza has simply calculated that (1) his landlady already leads a relatively peaceful, content life, and (2) her tranquillity would likely be disturbed by Spinozism. Her best hope of maximizing her power of acting, then, lies in maintaining her religion rather than trying to become a Spinozist.

[33] The closest that he comes to offering an argument from pluralism occurs in the preface to the work, where he writes: "as men's ways of thinking vary considerably and different beliefs are better suited to different men . . . everyone should be allowed freedom of judgment and the right to interpret the basic tenets of his faith as he thinks fit" (*TTP* Preface, p. 7). If we examine this passage in context, however, it is clear that all he is saying is that different people will be moved to obedience on the basis of different beliefs; so we ought not to worry about people's beliefs, provided that they are obedient to the state.

circumstances, but further that it is wrong, *full stop.*[34] Perhaps the most plausible way of providing a principled defense of toleration is to show that intolerance is a violation of the rights of individuals. If it can be shown that at least certain freedoms are actually rights – i.e., "political trumps held by individuals," to use Ronald Dworkin's formulation[35] – then it will be apparent that any attempt at scotching these liberties will be intrinsically and absolutely wrong.

In the opening paragraph of the *TTP*, Chapter 20 Spinoza appears to appeal to something like a right-based defense of freedom of thought or conscience, writing: "any sovereign power appears to harm its subjects and usurp their rights when it tries to tell them what they must accept as true and reject as false."[36] Michael Rosenthal has suggested that this passage reveals a significant juridical dimension to Spinoza's defense of toleration.[37] However, if there is indeed a juridical component to Spinoza's defense, it must be, as Rosenthal himself recognizes, a rather peculiar one, since Spinoza's notion of right (*ius*) is itself deeply peculiar.

Spinoza rejects traditional normative conceptions of right (*ius*). For instance, he explicitly rejects Grotius's notion of right as "a moral Quality annexed to the Person, enabling him to have, or do, something justly."[38] Grotius is here advancing the notion of a subjective right – to have a right is to have a title to something, which entails that others have corresponding duties to respect this right. If this were the sense of right that Spinoza is using in Chapter 20, then one could reasonably conclude that he has principled, normative grounds for opposing toleration. However, Spinoza consciously rejects the notion of right as title. Instead, he adopts the view that one's right is coextensive with one's power (*TTP*, Chapter 16).[39] The whole aim of Spinoza's analysis of right (*ius*) in Chapter 16 is to eviscerate traditional, normative conceptions of rights, rather than to propound a new theory. Once we recognize that the bounds of our power fix the limits of our right, we can see that the reason that the sovereign should not seek to

---

[34] For instance, Mendus claims that it is a mark against an account of toleration if it only shows that intolerance is imprudent rather than morally wrong ("Introduction," pp. 2–3).

[35] Dworkin, *Taking Rights Seriously*, p. xi.

[36] *TTP* Ch. 20; *G* III 239.

[37] Rosenthal, "Spinoza's Republican Argument," pp. 330 and 333. Rosenthal adds that "the importance of this point, that belief cannot be compelled, cannot be overstated" ("Spinoza's Republican Argument," p. 332).

[38] Grotius, *Rights*, 1.i.4. This is one of three senses of right (*ius*) for Grotius. The other two are "that which may be done without Injustice" (1.i.3) and "the Rule and Dictate of Right Reason, shewing the Moral Deformity or Moral Necessity there is in any Act, according to its Suitableness or Unsuitableness to a reasonable Nature" (1.10).

[39] For a helpful discussion of this point, see Curley, "Kissinger, Spinoza, and Genghis Khan."

regulate the minds of its subjects is simply that it does not have the power to do so, for "it is impossible for one person's mind to be absolutely under another's control."[40] The argument, then, amounts to this: one cannot entirely control another's mind, so to attempt to do so is to attempt to do something impossible, which is irrational.[41]

Even leaving aside the peculiarities of Spinoza's conception of right, there are reasons to think that Spinoza's "argument from rights" is not especially strong, certainly not strong enough to support the level of toleration that he advocates. Immediately after pointing to the right that we have over our minds, Spinoza concedes that "a person's judgment, admittedly, may be subjected to another's in many different and sometimes almost unbelievable ways."[42] That is, even if we always retain some right over our conscience, this right may be seriously limited by the power of others to manipulate our beliefs. Spinoza's apparently right-based defense of freedom of thought is thus not only devoid of normative force, it is also deeply limited. Fortunately, this rather brief argument gives way to a battery of other more effective arguments in favor of toleration to which I will now turn.

2 THE PRUDENTIAL, ANTICLERICAL BASIS OF SPINOZA'S TOLERATIONISM

We are now in a position to see the full force of the question with which this chapter began. If toleration in general is puzzling, it is especially puzzling for someone like Spinoza. Why would one who never doubts the correctness and universality of his own ethical and religious views, and who eschews normative accounts of rights, be willing to tolerate activities of which he disapproves? Why doesn't Spinoza believe, as Berlin supposes he does, that the sovereign should try to extirpate irrational and destructive behavior through legislative means? In this section we will consider Spinoza's thoroughly prudential reasons for opposing attempts to use laws to make people virtuous (henceforth: "moral legislation"). But first let us add one last wrinkle to the puzzle by noting that on certain matters Spinoza was actually relatively intolerant.

---

40 *TTP* Ch. 20; *G* III 239.
41 Waldron reads Locke as offering a similar argument for toleration ("Locke").
42 *TTP* Ch. 20; *G* III 239.

2.1 Spinoza's anticlerical intolerance

At the heart of Spinoza's defense of toleration lies a deep anticlericalism.[43] As we shall see it is a distrust of the moral crusades driven by the clergy that underlies much of his general distrust of moral legislation. But before turning to this, I want to consider the intolerant or illiberal features of Spinoza's anticlericalism.

In certain contexts, Spinoza was perfectly willing to countenance a fair amount of intolerance. For instance, with respect to religious liberty, Spinoza was hardly a liberal by contemporary standards.[44] He argues quite forcefully for the Erastian view that "authority in sacred matters belongs wholly to the sovereign powers."[45] Religious injunctions acquire "the power of law only by decree of those who exercise the right of government,"[46] so it devolves on the sovereign to make ultimate determinations in matters of religion.[47] The sovereign is, thus, the sole authority on both civil and religious law. The rationale behind this claim is that piety must be understood as practicing justice, and there is no standard of justice prior to and independent of the will of the sovereign.[48] Thus, Spinoza concludes, "no one can rightly cultivate piety or obey God, without obeying edicts of the sovereign authority."[49]

It is only through curbing the power of the clergy that the sovereign can protect the public from superstition and bigotry. In the preface to the *TTP*, Spinoza warns the reader of zealots who "take the outrageous liberty of trying to appropriate the greater part of this authority and utilize religion to win the allegiance of the common people."[50] And Spinoza's intolerant attitude towards rabble-rousing religious figures reveals itself in even the most tolerant sections of the *TTP*. When, in Chapter 20, Spinoza identifies

---

[43] The first of his stated reasons for writing the *TTP* is to oppose "the prejudices of theologians. For I know that these are the main obstacles which prevent men from giving their minds to philosophy" (*Ep.* 30).

[44] As many have noted, Spinoza's toleration is not fundamentally a defense of the freedom of worship, but rather of the freedom to philosophize. Jonathan Israel writes: "in Spinoza, freedom of worship, far from constituting the core of toleration, is very much a secondary question . . . The gulf separating Locke's and Spinoza's conceptions of toleration, originating in Locke's concern for saving souls and Spinoza's for ensuring individual freedom, is thus widened further by Spinoza's anxiety to whittle down ecclesiastical power" (*Radical Enlightenment*, pp. 266–267).

[45] *TTP* Ch. 19; *G* III 228.   [46] *TTP* Ch. 19; *G* III 228.

[47] *TTP* Ch. 16; *G* III 199–200. The full passage reads: "it follows that the supreme right of deciding about religion, belongs to the sovereign power, whatever judgment he may make, since it falls to him alone to preserve the rights of the state and to protect them both by divine and by natural law" (*TTP* Ch. 16; *G* III 199).

[48] *TTP* Ch. 19; *G* III 229–230; cf. E4p37s2.   [49] *TTP* Ch. 19; *G* III 233.   [50] *TTP* Preface; *G* III 7.

as seditious anyone who would challenge the authority of the sovereign, or recognize an alternative authority,[51] he evidently has in mind the very zealots described in the preface. And just as it would be wise for the state to "restrain the indignation and fury of the common people,"[52] it seems equally wise to limit the activities of religious leaders who promulgate superstition and galvanize this anger.[53]

Understood in this light, we can agree with John Christian Laursen's claim that many of the illiberal features of Spinoza's philosophy can actually be understood as expressing underlying concern for toleration, since his intolerance is, ultimately, an intolerance of intolerance.[54] In order to protect the freedom to philosophize we must curb the power of the religious zealots who spread venomous superstition and persecute freethinkers. By subordinating religious authority to civil authority, and "not allow[ing] religious dogmas to proliferate,"[55] Spinoza hopes to liberate the citizenry from the destructive forces of fear and superstition.

This intolerance of clerical power and religious enthusiasm seems to lend credence to Berlin's assessment: Spinoza *is* seeking to remove obstacles to rational thought through state interference. However, this misses much of what is most important about Spinoza's anticlericalism, which is that it provides him not only with an argument for *limited* intolerance, but also with a powerful argument for toleration. I want to turn now to the anticlerical grounds for toleration.

2.2 Spinoza's anticlerical toleration

One of the primary reasons why Spinoza is distrustful of moral legislation is that, in general, such laws "are not made to restrain the ill-intentioned so much as persecute well-meaning men,"[56] and are promoted by hateful zealots, rather than by compassionate, truth-loving individuals.[57] Moral legislation is advocated only by those who will not brook any challenge to orthodoxy, i.e., those who are opposed to philosophical reflection and open

---

[51] *TTP* Ch. 20; *G* III 241–243.   [52] *TTP* Ch. 20; *G* III 244.

[53] He claims that regulating beliefs is generally not necessary, except in a "corrupt" state, "where superstitious and ambitious people who cannot tolerate free-minded persons, have achieved such reputation and prominence that their authority exerts greater influence with the common people than that of the sovereign powers" (*TTP* Ch. 20; G III 242–243).

[54] Laursen, "Spinoza on Toleration," pp. 188, 191.

[55] *TTP* Ch. 19; *G* III 238.   [56] *TTP* Ch. 20; *G* III 244.

[57] Michael Rosenthal has argued compellingly that, on Spinoza's view, intolerance is a sign of a poor character; a virtuous person, one possessed of *fortitudo*, or strength of character, will always act mercifully, generously, and tolerantly ("Tolerance as a Virtue").

discussion. Spinoza reasonably suggests that these defenders of orthodoxy – chiefly, religious enthusiasts – are the ones who ought to be constrained, not the freethinkers: "the real schismatics are those who condemn other men's books and subversively instigate the insolent mob against their authors, rather than the authors themselves, who for the most part write only for the learned and consider reason alone as their ally."[58] So we should be very leery about campaigns of intolerance because they are usually driven by those who are corrupt and ignorant, and they often target the wise and the good.

Spinoza, of course, had plenty of experience to fuel his distrust of the intolerant. He was cast out of the Jewish community by an intolerant rabbinate.[59] But perhaps more disturbing was the treatment of his friend and fellow freethinker Adriaan Koerbagh at the hands of the magistrates. Koerbagh, who embraced many of the same metaphysical positions as Spinoza, including the view that God is identical with nature and that everything is governed by the necessary laws of nature, was tried and sentenced for blasphemy. While in prison under squalid conditions Koerbagh fell ill; he died soon after being released. This affair is generally believed to have precipitated the completion and publication of the *TTP*.[60]

Also, the conflict between the Arminians and orthodox Calvinists that raged throughout the United Provinces in the first part of the seventeenth century might also have inspired some of this distrust. From Spinoza's perspective, this dispute was a great object lesson about the source of intolerance. The peaceable Arminians regarded faith as primarily a matter of conscience and thus were opposed to expanding the political position of the Church.[61] By contrast, the orthodox Calvinists, with their theocratic ambitions, misunderstood the very nature of religion and religious authority and sought to regulate civic affairs on the basis of these misguided principles. After the Synod of Dort, in 1618, Arminians throughout the United Provinces were removed from their offices and university posts.[62] The Calvinist zealots in this case illustrated for Spinoza that "schisms do

---

[58] *TTP* Ch. 20; *G* III 246.
[59] Perhaps his own experience lies behind his claim that the sovereign alone ought to have powers of excommunication (*TTP* Ch. 19; *G* III 235).
[60] Nadler, *Spinoza*, p. 170.
[61] See Nadler, *Spinoza*, p. 12. Jonathan Israel notes that "in his address on laying down the rectorship of the university, at Leiden, in February 1606, Arminius condemned theological strife between Christians as the worst of ills, a scourge nurturing doubt, atheism, and despair" (*The Dutch Republic*, pp. 422–423).
[62] Israel, *The Dutch Republic*, pp. 452ff.

not arise from an intense passion for truth (which is the fount and origin of amity and gentleness), but from a great lust for power."[63]

Indeed, Spinoza's entire account of the decline of the Hebrew common-wealth (*TTP*, Chapter 18) can be read as a rather thinly veiled warning about the effects of Calvinist fanaticism in the United Provinces. Accordance to Spinoza's account, when the priestly caste gained political power, they not only destroyed peace, they also perverted religion. The final result was inextinguishable conflict.[64] Spinoza directly invites the reader here to consider the degree to which the Calvinists of his time resemble the Pharisees:

Following this example of the Pharisees, all the worst hypocrites everywhere have been driven by the same frenzy (which they call zeal for God's law), to perse-cute men of outstanding probity and known virtue, resented by the common people for precisely these qualities, by publicly reviling their opinions, and inflam-ing the anger of the barbarous majority against them.[65]

One of the greatest reasons, then, for fearing moral legislation, Spinoza suggests, is that it is the corrupt – e.g., the superstitious Pharisean Calvin-ists – who lead the crusades against honest and honorable people (like Koerbagh, Uriel Da Costa,[66] and Arminius). It was the clergy who rec-ommended extensive laws to reform men, including sumptuary laws to prevent decadence and strict laws on blasphemy;[67] such efforts at reform were misguided and motivated by hatred and bigotry. This sociological observation, however, does not give us much reason to oppose moral legis-lation as such. Rather, it just gives us grounds for questioning the motives of

---

[63] *TTP* Ch. 20; G III 246. Spinoza offers the following dramatic story of religious corruption in the preface to the *TTP*: "as soon as this abuse began in the church, the worst kind of people came forward to fill the sacred offices and the impulse to spread God's religion degenerated into sordid greed and ambition. Churches became theatres where people went to hear ecclesiastical orators rather than to learn from teachers. Pastors no longer sought to teach, but strove to win a reputation for themselves while denigrating those who disagreed with them" (*TTP* Preface; G III 8).

[64] *TTP* Ch. 18; G III 224.   [65] *TTP* Ch. 18; G III 225.

[66] Da Costa, a member of the Sephardic Jewish community in Amsterdam, published a book entitled *Examination of Pharisaic Traditions* [*Exame das Tradições Phariseas*], in which he denied the immor-tality of the soul. The work was denounced by Sephardic elders and burned by local authorities. He eventually committed suicide, just days after writing in his autobiography that the Amsterdam magistrates allowed "the Pharisees" – i.e., his co-religionists – to persecute him. See Nadler, *Spinoza*, pp. 66–74.

[67] Sumptuary laws were often proposed by the clergy in the United Provinces, but rarely adopted. Simon Schama writes that "the synod of Dordrecht in 1618 had urged the enactment of sumptuary laws in restraint of extravagant entertainment, but as in so many matters, the message of the clergy went unheeded by the magistracy" (*Embarrassment of Riches*, p. 186). Nevertheless, sumptuary laws were introduced periodically, including in 1672 (concerning the size and lavishness of banquets), prompting criticism from Spinoza (*TP* Ch. 10; G III 355).

the enactors of this legislation. But Spinoza has a second form of argument that deepens his critique of moral legislation.

2.3 Moral legislation as self-defeating

Even if it were the case that moralizing campaigns were led by virtuous people against the genuinely dissolute, Spinoza would still be skeptical about moral legislation on prudential grounds. As Parkinson puts it, on Spinoza's view, "an illiberal policy (Spinoza argues) would prevent the state from functioning properly."[68] In fact, I think Spinoza's claim is stronger than this: it is not just the case that moral legislation undercuts the proper functioning of the state – moral legislation undercuts its *own* aims. What is moral legislation supposed to accomplish? The general goal is to make people virtuous or pious. This is a perfectly noble objective *in abstracto*. If it were the case that moral legislation effectively promoted moral uprightness, or, say, social cohesion, Spinoza would almost certainly support it. However, he gives psychological and empirical reasons for believing that legislation is an unsuitable tool for realizing such ends.

It might seem that moral legislation could promote cohesion by imposing greater uniformity on the populous. The problem is that "there are many men who are so constituted that there is nothing they would more reluctantly put up with than that the opinions they believe to be true should be outlawed . . . they therefore proceed to reject the laws and act against the magistrate. They regard it as very honourable and not at all shameful to behave in a seditious manner."[69] Resistance to legislative interference can be traced back to the affect of "ambition" [*ambitio*], which Spinoza understands as the striving for others to approve of the same objects that we do.[70] Sometimes ambition will lead us to adjust our own judgments to bring them in conformity with others'; however, more often than not, we will seek to foist our views on others and oppose the efforts of others to do the same to us. Because of our natural ambition, outlawing certain expressions of belief will only further alienate offenders and deepen existing schisms. Moral legislation thus generally promotes disharmony and treachery, rather than loyalty and cohesion.

Moral legislation also fails to make people more upright in their dealings or more honest since if people were prohibited from expressing their true opinions, they "would be continually thinking one thing

[68] Parkinson, "Spinoza on the Freedom of Man," p. 53.   [69] *TTP* Ch. 20; *G* III 244.
[70] See E3p29; cf. Rosenthal, "Spinoza's Republican Argument," and "Tolerance as a Virtue."

and saying something else. This would undermine the trust [*fides*] which is the first essential of a state; detestable flatter and deceit would flourish."[71] People cannot be expected to be morally upright and trustworthy if they must devote so much effort to concealing their true beliefs. Moral legislation will thus undercut honesty or uprightness rather than promote it.

Indeed, it is not just cohesion and good faith that are undermined by moral legislation, it is virtue in general: "trying to control everything by laws will encourage vices rather than correcting them."[72] One can attempt to make people virtuous or to prevent "extravagance . . . envy, greed, drunkenness, and so on"[73] by way of sumptuary laws,[74] but in fact such vices are only multiplied by legal intervention: "for all laws that can be broken without injury to another become a laughing stock, and far from restraining the desires and lusts of men, they even stimulate them, because 'we are ever eager for what is forbidden and desire what is denied.'"[75] Rather than making men more virtuous, rational, or loyal, moral legislation actually serves to exacerbate the very ills that it aims to prevent.

We have seen, then, that Spinoza's defense of toleration is based on two general claims: (1) the people who are most inclined to persecute the beliefs or behaviors of others are generally among the most corrupt, so we ought to be wary of acts of political intolerance, and (2) attempts at perfecting others through the enactment of laws are generally self-defeating. Many will regard Spinoza's defense of toleration as unsatisfactory on account of its prudential basis and its restricted scope.[76] In the final section we will further flesh out Spinoza's defense of toleration by considering how it relates to the central norms of governance, suggesting how

---

[71] *TTP* Ch. 20; *G* III 243.   [72] *TTP* Ch. 20; *G* III 243.
[73] *TTP* Ch. 20; *G* III 243.   [74] See *supra* note 67.
[75] *TP* Ch. 10; *G* III 355; cf. *TTP* Ch. 20; *G* III 243. The quote comes from Ovid, *Amores* III. iv, 17.
[76] Some commentators regard Spinoza's rejection of rights-claims as a fundamental weakness. For instance, Feuer bemoans, "there are no reserved rights upon which the individual can insist . . . this is the final weakness in Spinoza's political theory; his doctrine pleads for wisdom but merges into quiescence rather than deed" (*Spinoza and the Rise of Liberalism*, p. 114). Curley shares Feuer's frustration, though he appears less sanguine about the ultimate ground of rights than Feuer: "If we cannot make sense of the idea that people have a natural right to such things, then we seem to be handicapped in the criticism we want to make of the Roman conduct (or of a tyrant's treatment of his own people). That the notion of natural right (not coextensive with power) disappears in Spinoza seems to me still to be a defect in his political philosophy, sympathetic though I may be to the arguments which lead to that result" ("Kissinger, Spinoza, and Genghis Khan," p. 335). Feuer and Curley seem to be particularly distressed by the lack of a right of resistance, but Feuer explicitly points also to the lack of a principled foundation in Spinoza's defense of freedom of speech (*Spinoza and the Rise of Liberalism*, p. 114).

Spinoza's pragmatism might actually be seen as a strength rather than a weakness.

3 TOLERATION AND THE ENDS OF GOVERNANCE

At this point one might wonder about the precise limits and grounds of Spinoza's tolerationism. On the one hand, he argues that most acts of intolerance or interference – even for the sake of some noble end – are to be avoided because they are self-defeating. However, as we have seen, Spinoza does allow for the regulation of outward religious activities to protect the state from seditious and superstitious religious bigots. This leads one to wonder what norm or principle is guiding the pragmatic calculation that allows for toleration in some contexts but not others. To answer this question we must address more squarely what the guiding norm of governance is, according to Spinoza.

Near the beginning of *TTP*, Chapter 20, Spinoza claims that the purpose of the state is to "enjoy the free use of reason, and not to participate in conflicts based on hatred, anger or deceit or in malicious disputes with each other. Therefore, the true purpose of the state is in fact freedom."[77] I have argued elsewhere that this notion of freedom is consistent with the notion of freedom as one's power of acting (*potentia agendi*) that one finds in the *Ethics*. The state's aim is to liberate or empower people as far as it can.[78] At other points in the political writings, Spinoza identifies the primary aim of the state as welfare (*salus*),[79] security (*securitas*),[80] peace (*pax*).[81] Ultimately, I think that, contrary to appearances, these are in fact different ways of describing the aim.[82] The aim of the state is to bring about, as far as possible, concord between citizens and mutual devotion to the laws; this would be a condition of social flourishing that would in turn redound to the power and liberty of individuals. Spinoza must ultimately be claiming then that toleration, in many circumstances, contributes to this aim.

Michael Rosenthal points to yet another norm that is served by toleration, namely, "stability." Rosenthal's argument is worth exploring briefly, as it will, at once, enable us to see one reason why toleration is so important for a well-functioning state, while also helping us to clarify

---

77 *TTP* Ch. 20; *G* III 241.   78 Steinberg, "Spinoza on Civil Liberation."
79 *TTP* Ch. 16; *G* III 194; *TTP* Ch. 19; *G* III 232; *TP* Ch. 3, art. 14; *G* III 290; *TP* Ch. 7, art. 5; *G* III 310.
80 *TP* Ch. 1, art. 5; *G* III 275; *TP* Ch. 5, art. 2; *G* III 295.   81 *TP* Ch. 5, art. 2; *G* III 295.
82 Steinberg "Spinoza on Civil Liberation."

what a well-functioning state consists in. Rosenthal argues that toleration contributes to the goal of stability by promoting participation, which, as I understand Rosenthal's view, is a *constituent component* of stability.[83] The success of this argument depends on how we understand the terms "participation" and "stability." If we understand "stability" simply in terms of the ability for a state to persevere, it is not at all obvious that toleration is the best policy for producing this goal. While Spinoza repeats Seneca's dictum that "no one has maintained a violent government for long" [*violenta imperia nemo continuit diu*] twice in the *TTP*,[84] he notes in the *Tractatus Politicus* that "no state has stood so long without any notable change as that of the Turks, and, conversely, none have proved so short-lived as popular democratic states."[85] The oppressive Turks, who believe that "it is wicked even to argue about religion,"[86] were successful in using fear and awe to restrain their subjects, which suggests that if the aim of the state is stability in the sense of *mere preservation*, intolerance might well be expedient. But as Spinoza makes very clear, the true end of the state consists not in *mere* stability, but in peace, which "consists not in the absence of war but in the union or harmony of minds."[87] Rosenthal, of course, recognizes that the goal of the state is not mere self-preservation; by "stability" he means something more like "peace" as defined above.[88]

The true end of the state, then, is to bring about peace, which is a condition of flourishing that requires a relatively cohesive citizenry bound by rational laws. How is this end promoted through toleration? Rosenthal's answer is that toleration encourages participation, which is internally connected to stability, or peace. In order for Rosenthal's argument to be successful "participation" must mean something more than formal involvement in the governing process, since there is no reason why toleration would lead to participation in this sense;[89] nor is participation in this sense a constituent component of peace. Rosenthal conceives of participation in

---

[83] Rosenthal, "Spinoza's Republican Argument," pp. 333–335; cf. Rosenthal, "Tolerance as a Virtue," p. 549. Rosenthal wishes to maintain that participation and stability are not merely contingently and instrumentally linked, for, if they were, the argument for toleration would be thoroughly prudential, which is an interpretation that Rosenthal expressly disavows ("Spinoza's Republican Argument," p. 320). Instead, participation must be intrinsically connected with stability, apparently as a constituent component.

[84] *TTP* Ch. 5; *G* III 74; *TTP* Ch. 16; *G* III 194.   [85] *TP* Ch. 6, art. 4; *G* III 298.

[86] *TTP* Preface; *G* III 7.

[87] *TP* Ch. 6, art. 4; *G* III 298. Cf. *TP* Ch. 5, arts. 4–5; *G* III 296; *TTP* Ch. 17; *G* III 219.

[88] He explicitly connects stability with the positive freedom of the *Ethics*, "Spinoza's Republican Argument," pp. 334–335.

[89] Autocrats, of course, can and often did adopt policies of toleration without granting participatory rights – for example, when Henry IV of France issued the Edict of Nantes in 1598, which protected the practices of the Huguenots, he did not thereby *democratize* the kingdom in any sense.

terms of one's "active and continual transfer of right to the sovereign."[90] Put simply, one could understand this notion of participation in terms of one's active commitment, or loyalty, to the state. The connection to peace should be clear: the degree of civic commitment of the subjects will be directly proportional to the degree of harmony or peace in the state. Moreover, this also allows us to see why toleration will generally be more conducive to participation than intolerance: preventing the beliefs or activities of others will often breed resentment, which "lessens the desire of citizens to participate in the government through the passive or active transfer of their right/power [and hence] lessens the power of the government."[91]

However, even with Rosenthal's helpful argument in place, the question that we set out to answer in this section remains. For even if toleration *generally* conduces to participation and peace, we have seen that there are cases when it does not. Consider the case of religious bigotry, once again. Religious bigotry ought to be curbed not just because it threatens the continued existence of the state, but also because it results in hostility, resentment, and ignorance, all of which are anathema to peace. So even if we can imagine a perseverant society run by bigots,[92] this will not be peaceful society. We can see, now, how complicated the sovereign's task is. Its primary directive is to promote peace. But peace requires not just perseverance and the absence of war, it requires civil harmony and the cultivation of reason.[93] Under what conditions will toleration promote peace? Here the sovereign will have to make sophisticated, and highly circumstance-relative, pragmatic calculations.

To see just how circumstance-relative these judgments will be, consider Spinoza's insistence that good governance depends on regime form and existing customs. What is good for a people accustomed to living in a monarchy will differ from what is good for a people accustomed to living in a democracy.[94] And what is good for a people who are accustomed

---

[90] Rosenthal, "Spinoza's Republican Argument," p. 335. There is, however, one problem for Rosenthal, as I see it. Once we form a clearer understanding of what participation consists in, it becomes less clear what makes this argument for toleration specifically *republican*. If participation is measured in terms of the transfer of right to a sovereign or in terms of a citizenry's devotion to the state, it is no longer obvious that participation is a unique feature of republics. For a further discussion of the relationship between republican participation and social flourishing, see Steinberg, "On Being *Sui Iuris*."

[91] Rosenthal, "Spinoza's Republican Argument," p. 335.

[92] Indeed, even a society of "rugged individualists," in which there is very little commerce but also very little enmity between individuals, would hardly qualify as harmonious or peaceful for Spinoza (see, again, *TP* Ch. 5, art. 5; *G* III 296).

[93] See, again, *TTP* Ch. 20; *G* III 241; *TP* Ch. 5, art. 5; *G* III 296.

[94] *TTP* Ch. 18; *G* III 227–228.

to oppression is different from what is good for a free people.[95]
The circumstance-relativity of governance is perhaps best illustrated by
Spinoza's discussion of that shrewd statesman: Moses. Because the Hebrew
people were accustomed to slavery and not yet capable of self-rule, Moses
established a state religion that included a great number of laws – ceremonial, dietary, etc. – that brought about social cohesion and efficiency –
that is, he introduced a great deal of moral legislation.[96] Did such legislation backfire in the way that Spinoza supposes it would if adopted in the
United Provinces? On the contrary, these laws enabled a group of uned-
ucated nomads to live in relative material prosperity and peace. For these
men, accustomed as they were to obedience, such legislation "appeared to
be freedom rather than slavery."[97] And, whereas Spinoza reasons that, for
many, forbidding something only increases one's desire for it,[98] among the
Hebrews "no one could have desired what was forbidden, only what was
prescribed."[99] The major lesson that we can take away from the case of
Moses and the Hebrews here is simply that understanding the customs and
temperament of the subjects will go a long way in determining whether an
act of legislation will be peace-promoting.

So, when calculating whether a particular form of action will promote
or undermine peace, one must consider the receptiveness of subjects to
such legislation.[100] This is an application of Spinoza's general principle of
governance that one must conform one's policies to the actual psychological features of one's subjects, rather than base them on an abstract and
idealized conception of human beings.[101] When tailoring one's policies to
the customs, temperaments, and proclivities of one's subjects, one of the
most important considerations is how much freedom one's subjects are
accustomed to. As Spinoza very astutely notes, "nothing is more difficult
than to deprive people of liberty once it has been granted."[102] The Hebrews,
accustomed as they were to obedience, were well-tempered to receive moral

---

[95] "It remains only for me to remind the reader that the monarchy I here have in mind is one
     established by a free people, for whom alone these suggestions can be helpful; for a people
     accustomed to a different form of government will not be able to tear up the traditional foundations
     of their state, changing its entire structure, without great danger of overthrowing the entire state"
     (*TP* Ch. 7, art. 26; *G* III 319).
[96] *TTP* Ch. 5; *G* III 74ff.   [97] *TTP* Ch. 20; *G* III 216.   [98] *TP* Ch. 10, art. 5; *G* III 355.
[99] *TTP* Ch. 20; *G* III 216.
[100] The source of the command may also go a long way in determining how effective it is. Specifically,
     moral commands are more grating and destabilizing when they come from religious figures than
     when they come from the civil authority: "The prophets, who, of course, were private individuals,
     had more success, it should be noted, in antagonizing than reforming people by means of the
     liberty which they usurped to admonish, scold and rebuke; on the other hand, those admonished
     or punished by kings, were readily corrected" (*TTP* Ch. 18; *G* III 223; cf. *TTP* Ch. 19; *G* III 236).
[101] *TP* Ch.1, art. 1; *G* III 273.   [102] *G* III 74.

laws. However, a people who are accustomed to a wide range of liberties are not likely to take well to new impositions on these liberties.

As noted above, many will regard the absence of a clear principle for delimiting the scope of toleration as a weakness of Spinoza's account. However, the pragmatic, circumstance-relativity of Spinoza's account might actually be one of its virtues. Consider Spinoza's approach in relation to one of the bigger challenges for liberals today, namely, how far we should tolerate hate speech, or speech that vilifies or degrades someone on the basis of their identity (e.g., ethnicity, race, religion, etc.). Like religious bigotry, hate speech may be seen as undermining peace by feeding the zeal of the ignorant and allowing for the stigmatization of members of groups that are often already vulnerable and marginalized. On the other hand, there is some hope that, at least in a relatively enlightened society,[103] permitting hate speech may actually strengthen the resolve of the citizenry in opposing racism and bigotry; and, moreover, restricting speech may well have the consequence of making people who are accustomed to broad liberties more resentful of government. So how far should a sovereign that wants to promote peace tolerate hate speech?

Spinoza would argue that we cannot reasonably take a principled, once-and-for-all, stance on how far such speech ought to be admitted – to do so would be not only naïve, it would be dangerous. Instead, one would have to consider the receptivity of the citizenry to the regulation of such speech, how much general discord is likely to be wrought by the admission of such speech, and how vulnerable the target group is.[104] In countries where there is a dominant ethos of liberty – i.e., where people are accustomed to a very tolerant state with minimal intervention – the regulation of hate speech might be more destabilizing or disharmonizing than it would be in countries where there is, say, a dominant ethos of fraternity.[105] While such circumstance-relativity may well lead to complicated legislative

---

[103] Even Mill claims that the harm principle only applies to those societies that have achieved a certain level of "maturity" and enlightenment (*On Liberty*, p. 11).

[104] See Waldron ("Free Speech") for a helpful discussion of the topic.

[105] In other words, Spinoza's approach might be able to account for some of the differences between the USA and many other Western countries on the issue of hate speech regulation. In the USA, where a certain reading of the first amendment, bolstered by some judicial interpretations, has led many to hold freedom of speech as sacrosanct, there may be reason to be more cautious about regulating hate speech than in other Western countries that do regulate hate speech – such as Canada, France, Germany, and the Scandinavian countries – where there is, arguably, a greater concern for fraternity and a less fetishized attitude towards free speech and so less resistance to such legislation. One concern, however, with seeking to accommodate the customs and psychology of one's citizens is that this would lead to an approach that is too conservative, too acquiescent to prevailing opinions.

determinations, given the complexity of the phenomena, perhaps a little messiness is to be expected.

Let me close by just calling attention to one final, important feature of Spinoza's account. There is a tendency to associate defenses of toleration and liberalism with the adoption of a certain conception of civil liberty, namely, negative liberty, or the freedom of non-interference. But, as we have seen, it is not the norm of liberty as non-interference that is driving Spinoza's defense of toleration, but rather the norms of peace and positive liberty. In his defense of toleration, Spinoza demonstrates that liberalism is not wedded to any particular conception of liberty. One can perfectly consistently endorse both the view that the ultimate goal of the state is to promote positive liberty or power *and* the view that legislation is generally ineffective in promoting this liberty.[106] The failure to see the consistency of these two views might well have been what led Berlin to overlook Spinoza's tolerationism. For those of us, though, who are generally sympathetic to tolerationism, but who do not regard freedom from interference on its own as a particularly robust political norm, Spinoza's ability to reconcile positive liberty with a relatively tolerant state may be seen as one of his greatest accomplishments.

[106] In recent years, a similar position has been advanced by Joseph Raz. After defending a positive model of freedom – freedom as autonomy – and claiming that the state has a duty both to prevent deprivations of this liberty and to promote it actively (*Morality of Freedom*, p. 424), Raz notes that the government's ability to foster such liberty may be rather limited, adopting a pragmatic line very much like Spinoza's: "The extended freedom from governmental action is based on the practical inability of governments to discharge their duty to serve the [positive] freedom of their subjects ... The pursuit of full-blooded perfectionist policies, even of those which are entirely sound and justified, is likely in many countries if not all, to backfire by arousing popular resistance leading to civil strife" (*Morality of Freedom*, pp. 428–429).

CHAPTER 12

Miracles, wonder, and the state in Spinoza's Theological-Political Treatise

Michael A. Rosenthal

I INTRODUCTION

In the *Theological-Political Treatise*, Spinoza seems to offer a purely secular account of sovereign authority, one that has no recourse to God as a source of authority. Chapter 16, which is dedicated to showing the "foundation of the state" [*de republicae fundamentis*],[1] begins with a discussion of the natural right of every person and then shows how the state arises as a consequence of the mutual exercise of these rights. This follows Spinoza's efforts in the first fifteen chapters of the *TTP* to "separate Philosophy from Theology," one of whose key moments is the critique of miracles in Chapter 6. There he points out that there is no such thing as a miracle, if we mean by that a divinely produced contravention of natural law. When confronted by a natural event that they do not understand, men are quick to claim that God is the cause of it and has suspended the natural order to produce it. However, that would lead to a contradiction in God's nature, because God cannot will a law to be universal and at the same time contravene it. But even if miracles have no metaphysical status, Spinoza notes, they still have political uses. Scripture is full of examples in which sovereigns point to some supposed miracle in order to inspire awe and wonder in their subjects. So, the point of the chapter on miracles would be to show that the appeal to miracles is not a sign of actual divine sanction of political authority but merely a human artifice to gain power over the ignorant masses, who are led primarily by their passions. Once this mechanism has been revealed and criticized, presumably politics can leave its divine trappings aside and proceed on a purely mundane, secular, and presumably more rational, path.[2]

---

[1] *TTP* Ch. 16, ¶ 1; *G* III 189. References to Spinoza's political works are to the forthcoming second volume of Edwin Curley's translation.

[2] A good example of this interpretation can be found in Smith, *Spinoza, Liberalism, and the Question of Jewish Identity*.

However, this account is problematic in several respects. For one thing, it is not clear that social contract theory itself can provide a purely rational basis for sovereign authority without violating one of its own basic premises, namely, that if men were all rational there would simply be no need of coercive sovereign authority at all. For another, although Spinoza wants to separate theology from philosophy, it is not clear that he wants to separate all aspects of religion from either philosophy or the state. If religion is useful to found and maintain the state, perhaps his critique of religion is not meant to eliminate all religion from politics. Indeed, in the *TTP* Spinoza distinguishes among three kinds of religion, two of which are political, and one of which is not. The latter is essentially the same as true philosophy, and it has no direct relation to politics, precisely because it deals with the minority of men who are led primarily by reason. The other two are political because they offer guidance to less than rational men who live in a polity. The first of these is founded on theological (read metaphysical) premises that are ultimately unjustified, and Spinoza calls it superstition. The second is founded on the moral and political principles of justice and charity.

Finally, even if we grant that it is possible to develop a secular politics, one that is not informed by religion in either of the forms we have just described, there is still another problem, one that was articulated indirectly by Hobbes in the very title of his most infamous work, the *Leviathan*, and in the engraving on its title page. Of course, the biblical Leviathan is a monster, and the Latin inscription from Job 41:24 on the title page reads, *Non Est potestas Super Terram quae Comparetur ei* ["There is no power on earth which can be compared to him"]. The monster is that which produces wonder and fear. Hobbes seems to suggest that this monstrous artifice, the state, is that which comes to be and is maintained through the production of these passions.[3] Does Spinoza think that for a state to be successful it must simply substitute the earthly powers for the divine in order to stimulate the same passions in its subjects? Would he agree with Hobbes that such a state is itself monstrous in some sense? With these questions we enter into a tangled, but fascinating, thicket of problems about the relation of religion to the state in the modern world.

In this chapter, I shall try to answer these questions. I shall argue that: (1) Collective action problems in Spinoza's social contract theory cannot be

---

[3] On the iconography of the frontpiece see Bredekamp, "Hobbes' Visual Strategies," and on the disputed meaning of the leviathan see Tralau, "Leviathan, the Beast of Myth."

solved via Spinoza's strong sense of reason without begging the question. He knows that. And so (2) all forms of religion are not problematic in Spinoza's view. Religion must be stripped of its metaphysical pretensions. Once that has been done, religion is useful for the passions it produces, in particular those which evoke fear and awe. It may even be the case that, despite Spinoza's critique of them, miracles may still have some political function, precisely because they are a tried and true device to produce fear and awe. And (3) I want to show that even if there is no explicit appeal to miracles and their attendant wonder, there is another way in which the structure of the miracle has been imported into Spinoza's political thinking at a key point. In other words, I claim that Spinoza reestablishes the structure of the miracle in his account of the lawmaker's will. If this is true, then this point has interesting implications for modern social contract theory, in which the sovereign is authorized through the act of will of each citizen.

2 COLLECTIVE ACTION PROBLEMS IN THE SOCIAL CONTRACT THEORY

The collective action problem arises in Spinoza's social contract theory, as detailed in *TTP*, Chapter 16, in the following way.[4] First, Spinoza assumes that all individuals are egoists, who have a natural right to pursue their self-interest, or what is "useful" to the individual.[5] Their self-interest is defined as choosing the greater good and the lesser evil. But it is crucial to remember that each individual has the right to judge what his or her self-interest is, and that judgment itself may be better or worse, i.e., more or less rational.[6] Spinoza thinks that when individuals judge and pursue their self-interest under the guidance of reason, they are led to cooperate without recourse to any other motive. He says that in the *TTP*, when he points out that the laws of reason lead to the true good of man,[7] and in Part 4 of the *Ethics*, in which he argues that in so far as men are led by reason they agree in nature.[8] But Spinoza does not rely on reason in this strong sense to solve the problem of how self-interested individuals in

[4] For a far more detailed account of this problem, see my paper, "Two Collective Action Problems."
[5] *TTP* Ch. 16, ¶ 8; *G* III 190.   [6] *TTP* Ch. 16, ¶ 9; *G* III 190–191.
[7] "If all men could easily be led solely by the guidance of reason, and could recognize the supreme utility and necessity of the state, there would be no one who would not absolutely detest deceptions; with supreme reliability, everyone would stand by their contracts completely, out of a desire for this supreme good, the preservation of the State" (*TTP* Ch. 16, ¶ 21; *G* III 192).
[8] E4p35.

the state of nature can form a sovereign state.[9] The reason for this is the empirical observation that most men are not led by reason but by their appetites coupled with their natural right to act according to their own judgment as far as they can. It could be the case that our natural appetites lead us to cooperate, but Spinoza insists, again both in the *TTP* and in the *Ethics*, that "according to the laws of appetite each person is drawn in a different direction,"[10] and thus to conflict. So while Spinoza thinks that it is rational in the deepest sense to give up some of our rights and form a social contract, that is not the problem of Chapter 16 in the *TTP* (or E4p37s2). For, in a sense, if anyone knew enough consistently to cooperate based on their own judgment, there would be no need of giving anyone the coercive power to restrict the rights of other individuals. In order to avoid conflict among self-interested individuals who are mostly led by their passions, it is necessary to form such an authority.

But why would any self-interested person give up his or her rights to a coercive authority when the coercive power could be used against the individual? Unlike Hobbes, Spinoza does not think that promises as such have any binding power. He says that an individual will only keep a promise as long as it is in that person's interest or utility to do so. The relevant example is that of a robber who extorts a promise to pay him. In Chapter 19 of the *Leviathan*, section 27, Hobbes argues that "covenants entered into by fear, in the condition of mere nature, are obligatory,"[11] and so, on the basis of his promise to pay the robber, the victim would be obligated to pay the robber. Spinoza takes explicit issue with Hobbes's view of this case in the *TTP*. Spinoza writes, "it is certain that if I can free myself from this Robber by deceptively promising him whatever he wishes, I am permitted to do this by natural right, to contract deceptively for whatever he wishes . . . Since, by natural right, I am bound to choose the lesser of two evils, I can, with supreme right, break faith with such a contract, and treat what I have said as if it had not been said."[12] While it might be in an individual's interest to cooperate with others for a while, as soon as circumstances change and the calculation of fear is reckoned otherwise, there is nothing to bind the cooperation, such that the entity formed through the cooperative

---

[9] Spinoza certainly thinks that men who are not rational in the more substantive sense, i.e., in that they know the laws of nature, still calculate and try to figure out what is in their own interest. It is just that they will vary in their judgments in relation to their abilities, knowledge, and particular circumstances.

[10] *TTP* Ch. 16, ¶ 14; *G* III 191.   [11] *Leviathan*, ed. E. Curley, p. 86.

[12] *TTP* Ch. 16, ¶¶ 17–18; *G* III 192.

action – i.e., the state or sovereign authority – would have enough consistent power over the individual to guarantee that the individual's interests (such as avoiding fear) would be consistently satisfied through cooperating with it.

Spinoza does think that the fear and other inconveniences of the state of nature will tend to convince even those less than rational individuals that they would be better off cooperating and establishing a coercive authority. Spinoza claims that the decisions an individual takes to satisfy the striving to preserve oneself are guided by a more minimal, though crucial constraint, which he takes to be inscribed in human nature: "For the universal law of human nature is that no one fails to pursue anything which he judges to be good, unless he hopes for a greater good, or fears a greater harm; nor does he submit to any evil, except to avoid a greater one, or because he hopes for a greater good."[13] But that does not quite explain, given the collective action problems we have described, *how* this transformation takes place. This is precisely where the appeal to a transcendent power is necessary and it is vital to remember that almost everything before and after Chapter 16 of the *TTP* involves an analysis of religion, in particular the history of the Old Testament and its relevance (or lack thereof) to the contemporary Dutch situation.[14] For Spinoza, religion, and particularly one involving the idea of a transcendent God who guides the world providentially, is a natural and widespread means whereby sovereign authority is established and, in the eyes of less than rational men, validated.[15]

Religion can accomplish this task through pointing to a greater power than the state itself, one that has the power to evoke awe and fear of its power to punish. Based on these claims about the supernatural nature of God's providence and its purported relation to the laws of the state, individuals will reckon that their utility is best served through obeying the law and cooperating. In order to explain how religion does this we need to

---

[13] TTP Ch. 16, ¶ 15; *G* III 191–192.
[14] See my paper "Why Spinoza Chose the Hebrews," for more on this.
[15] It should be noted that in the *Political Treatise* Spinoza does not mention the social contract and notes that he agrees in a sense with the notion that man is "social animal" (*TP* Ch. 2, art. 15; *G* III 281). The differences between the *TTP* and the *TP* have been the subject of much dispute. A summary of some of the key positions in the secondary literature can be found in section 5 of the editor's introduction to Shirley's recent translation of the *Political Treatise*. I think that the affective and cognitive mechanisms, which I describe below, rely on the device of a contract in the *TTP*, but we might be able to provide another set of circumstances, one in which the contract itself does not figure, in which some key aspects of the mechanisms are still at work. There may also be means other than the idea of a transcendent God to evoke these affects, but Spinoza focuses on this idea because of his particular historical circumstances.

say something about the affect of wonder itself, and then explain how it functions in Spinoza's account of politics through miracles.

3 SPINOZA'S CRITIQUE OF WONDER

One of Spinoza's most striking departures from philosophical tradition is his relegation of wonder to a minor and even problematic position among the affects.[16] Plato stated in the *Theaetetus* (155d) that wonder is the origin of philosophy, and Aristotle developed this view in the beginning of his *Metaphysics*. We desire by nature to know the world and this is indicated by our delight in our senses, particularly in our sense of sight, which distinguishes between things and prepares the intellect for its task of figuring out why things are different and how they are related to each other (980a). Descartes, in *Les passions de l'âme*, preserves key aspects of this view in his discussion of wonder (*l'admiration*), which he names as one of the six "primitive passions."[17] "Wonder," he says in article 70, "is a sudden surprise of the soul which makes it tend to consider attentively those objects which seem to it rare and extraordinary." Like Aristotle, Descartes thinks that wonder is free of immediate interest and is closely connected to the pursuit of knowledge. Unlike the other passions, which are accompanied by some physiological change, wonder does not "have good or evil as its object, but only knowledge of the thing wondered at" (article 71). The object we wonder at is rare and thus causes us to remember it and seek its cause. But, in good Aristotelian fashion, this passion has its excess and its defect. When it is excessive, that is, when it has become a habit to fixate on the rarity of the event, the individual becomes a mere curiosity seeker. When it is defective, the individual lacks the passion for knowledge. In its proper state, wonder "disposes us to the acquisition of knowledge," and as we acquire knowledge of some object, i.e., explain its causes, then "we should . . . try to emancipate ourselves from it as far as possible" (article 76).

In Spinoza's early writings we see clear evidence of the influence Descartes had on his theory of the passions. In Chapter 3 of Part 2 of

---

[16] In this paragraph I follow the general sketch of Philip Fisher's account in chapters 1 and 3 of *Wonder, the Rainbow, and the Aesthetics of Rare Experiences*. I am also going to use the words "passion" and "affect" interchangeably. For a more general account of wonder, one that situates this debate in a larger historical narrative, see Daston and Park, *Wonders and the Order of Nature*.

[17] Descartes, *The Passions of the Soul*, trans, Voss. The French "l'admiration" is translated in the Latin edition of the *Passions of the Soul* as "admiratio," which is commonly translated as "wonder" in English. For a discussion see Voss, "How Spinoza Enumerated the Affects." The other primitive passions are love, hatred, desire, joy, and sadness (article 69).

The Short Treatise of God, Man, and His Well-Being (*KV*), he follows the basic Cartesian ordering of the passions, but we already see evidence of a systematic critique based on a more Stoic conception of the mind.[18] Although Spinoza does not name them as "primitive," the first passions he discusses in Chapter 3 (through Chapter 6) of the *KV* are wonder, love, hate, and desire, and in Chapter 7 he goes on to discuss joy and sadness. Also like Descartes, Spinoza conceives of wonder as a state of astonishment that arises when a particular case does not correspond to the general rule produced by previous experience. However, rather than seeing the astonishment at some singularity as the basis of curiosity and the search for knowledge, Spinoza thinks that it is a kind of dead-end emotion, one that does not lead to anything further. The peasant who thinks that there are no fields other than his own is astonished to find that there are others. Likewise, the philosopher, who considers that this world is unique, and who, presumably, finds it astonishing to think of any larger world of which ours is only a part, is stuck in his way of thinking. In contrast, Spinoza writes, "there is no wonder in him who draws true conclusions."[19] Knowledge is produced on the basis of true ideas through the explanation of particular instances through the ideas of true laws of nature, and there is no room in the process for the false ideas that cause astonishment.

In the *Ethics* Spinoza settles on a simpler scheme of primary passions, consisting of desire, joy, and sadness, and he relegates wonder to a derivative position. In fact, in the definition of the affects at the end of Part 3 he is clear that he does "not number Wonder among the affects" because it involves a lack of determination to something else.[20] In his systematic exposition of the passions in Part 3 of the *Ethics*, wonder only comes up late in the section, though it plays an important role as the center of a series of related affects. He defines it there as "the imagination of a singular thing, insofar as it is alone in the mind."[21] In contrast to those things that we quickly assimilate to others like it, the singular event stops this natural process of association and we tend to dwell on it in a state of wonder. The singular event does not lead to any systematic relation with other things, whether or not the relation is true or false, and so it does not constitute knowledge of any kind and indeed stands in the way of it. For one thing, it is not

---

[18] In the *KV* Spinoza claims that "the passions arise . . . from opinion" (*C* 99; *G* I 56). This stoic view contrasts with Descartes's insistence that the body also causes passion, except in the case of wonder, and that the will has a distinct role from the intellect in the production of passion.

[19] *C* 100; *G* I 57.

[20] E3, definition of the affects, 4, explication. Susan James discusses the seventeenth-century debate over how to classify wonder in chapter 8 of *Passion and Action*.

[21] E3p52s.

rational but imaginative, that is, it is not derived from some prior true idea but is simply the affect of some idea on us. And for another, unlike some imaginative ideas that lead quickly to associations with others, a person with a singular idea "is determined to consider only that."[22] Hence, wonder keeps a man "so suspended in considering it that he cannot think of anything else."[23]

Although Spinoza does not think wonder leads to knowledge and does not think it changes the power of the body to persist, he does consider wonder to be an important idea or affection in so far as it serves as the center of a series of interpersonal affects. In other words, even if wonder does little or no work in the process of understanding the world, it stands at the center of a variety of personal relations that produce our social world. Wonder has important political implications because it is easily tied to other passions that move us to act. If the object we wonder at arouses fear in us, then the affect is properly called "Consternation [*Consternatio*], because Wonder at an evil keeps a man so suspended in considering it that he cannot think of other things by which he could avoid that evil."[24] When we wonder at someone's personal qualities, that is, we find them incomparable with any we are familiar with, then the Wonder is called "Veneration" [*Veneratio*]. And when we wonder at a person's anger, we call it "Dread" [*Horror*]. And when we join veneration with love then we have "Devotion" [*Devotio*]. What these passions seem to have in common is that wonder, and the suspension of any process of comparison or reasoning at the core of this affect, serves to intensify some existing affective relationship with another person. (As we shall see in the following section, this feature of wonder makes it particularly useful in religion and politics.)

But though wonder does not help produce knowledge, knowledge can dissipate wonder and produce other affects. In the same long scholium in the *Ethics* we find a discussion of the passions produced when, through closer scrutiny or on the basis of some new knowledge, the astonishment dissipates. Spinoza claims that, although Disdain (*Contemptus*) is opposed to Wonder, it depends on it, in the sense that it is caused when the original sense of Wonder is called into question. In Spinoza's words: "if, from the thing's presence, or from considering it more accurately, we are forced to deny it whatever can be the cause of Wonder, Love, Fear, etc., then the Mind remains determined by the thing's presence to think more of the things that are not in the object than of those that are (though the object's presence usually determines [the Mind] to think chiefly of what is in the

[22] E3p52d.   [23] E3p52s.   [24] E3p52s.

object)."[25] Further passions are produced when other passions related to or compounded from Wonder are negated. In this way, Mockery [*Irrisio*] is produced from the contrary of devotion (as disdain causes love to pass into hate), and Contempt [*Dedignatio*] is produced from the contrary of veneration (as prudence is now perceived as folly), etc.[26]

It is worth noting that Spinoza describes this process not in terms of a person coming to question his or her own direct emotional relation to an object but rather in terms of the mechanism of the "imitation of the affects," in which a person wonders at, and then calls into question, something which is like that which he or she normally admires, etc.[27] Again, this only emphasizes the social dimension of wonder. Because wonder is based on ignorance of the relevant chain of causes it is an inherently unstable affection. But it is often easier to see the instability of this affection at some remove from ourselves, when it is experienced first by someone else and then imitated by another. And of course this social dimension of this affect is expressed not only through the spread of wonder from one to another, but also in the spread of disdain. So it is almost like a flock of birds that follow a leader and then as soon as the leader is frightened all turn in another direction. Wonder is a problematic "affect" in that it seems to be primarily cognitive and, at least according to Spinoza, to interrupt our grasp of the chain of causes. And yet, as we shall see in the next section, because it is easily tied to other, more kinetic affects, wonder does tend to play a key role in many social emotions that lead to group action.

4 MIRACLES

Wonder, which he defines in the *Ethics* as "the imagination of a singular thing, insofar as it is alone in the mind,"[28] is at the center of Spinoza's account of the relation between religion and politics, as well as his critique of it, for three reasons, which together we might call the political anthropology of wonder, and which culminate in his critique of miracles.

First, because wonder arises due to their fixation upon or astonishment at singular events, it is related to the systematic anxiety that is at the core of Spinoza's anthropological account of the human predicament that brings

---

[25] E3p52s.
[26] For a fascinating discussion of the political aspect of the relation of passion and error, see the first section of chapter 7 in James's *Passion and Action*, especially the discussion of esteem and *grandeur* in Malebranche on pages 177ff.
[27] The role of the imitation of the affects is made clear by explicit reference to E3p15, E3p15c, and E3p27 in the scholium.
[28] E3p52s.

systematic religion into being. The inability to explain some unusual event may be merely an epistemological quandary or impetus for some, but for most people the ability to explain events in a systematic way is crucial to their ability to survive and thrive. Spinoza makes this clear in the opening paragraphs of the Preface to the *TTP*. Finite individuals in nature all strive to persist. "If men could manage all their affairs by a definite plan, or if fortune were always favorable to them, they would never be possessed by superstition."[29] However, precisely because we are finite, lacking in power, and because nature does not always lend itself to our ends, we tend to vacillate wretchedly between hope that things will turn out our way and fear that they will not. One important symptom of our finite power is our lack of knowledge of our circumstances. Without adequate knowledge of the future, we look for some explanation of events, both as a technique for controlling them and also as a way to manage our hopes and fears. Of course one path to gain control over our circumstances would be for ourselves to gain more knowledge of them, but because the acquisition of knowledge is itself not an easy task, it is often more convenient, especially when in an adverse situation, to defer to the explanation of someone else. Although they might serve a psychological purpose, albeit temporarily, these explanations are usually not epistemologically adequate. They rest on two simple, though important, mechanisms: either they associate an inexplicable event with some past event that they can use to portend some similar one in the future, or they take the inexplicable event and make it part of a pattern of events explained in terms of a supernatural will. As Spinoza writes, "if they see something unusual, and wonder greatly at it, they believe it to be a portent of disaster, which indicates the anger of the Gods or of the supreme God."[30] This is a double or really a triple error. An event we do not understand is explained through the will of God, which itself is understood inadequately in terms of (i.e., as a projection of) our own will, which we do not properly understand either! But the error has a beneficial, though temporary, psychological effect.

It also has a political effect through its association with veneration. The singular event is not properly or adequately explained, i.e., through some other adequately conceived cause, but rather projected onto an equally inadequately conceived projection of a divine will. The prophet, i.e., the person who explains the significance of the event in terms of the imagination, couples the astonishment at the singular event with the figure of all-powerful being, God, and this produces, as we have seen, the affect of

[29] *TTP* Preface, ¶ 1; *G* III 5.   [30] *TTP* Preface, ¶ 1; *G* III 5.

veneration. But as Machiavelli, among others, had shown, Spinoza knows that the use of divine will is really a device for rulers to enhance their own authority.[31] The prophet uses the veneration for God indirectly to bolster his own veneration. Without this cloak of divine authority the ruler's explanation and influence is just one among many. Given the proliferation of competing and inherently unstable (because inadequate) explanations, there is a need "to embellish religion – whether true or false – with ceremony and pomp, so that it will be considered weightier than every [other] influence and always worshipped by everyone with the utmost deference."[32]

Miracles are especially useful not only in producing veneration but also in consolidating and maintaining political power. Once the initial astonishment of a wonder has dissipated, either through its explanation as part of a prophecy or as an instance of the divine will, there is always the possibility that the veneration produced by the wonder coupled with the putative explanation will dissipate as well. Hence there is the need for a renewed sense of wonder and veneration. One way to produce wonder against the background of prophetic explanation is to invoke the miraculous. A miracle is a supposed contravention of the natural order by God for the sake of a divine plan that works through nature but ultimately transcends it. Like any other prophetic explanation the invocation of a miracle serves to cloak our ignorance, and assuage our anxiety, but it also justifies the monarchical political structure through projecting it on nature and the divine being:

The common people therefore call unusual works of nature miracles, *or* works of God, and partly from devotion, partly from a desire to oppose those who cultivate the natural sciences, they don't want to know the natural causes of things. They want only to hear the things they are most ignorant of, and which, for that reason, they greatly wonder at [*admiratur*]. They can worship God and relate all things to his dominion and will only be eliminating natural causes and imagining things outside the order of nature. They wonder most [*magis admiratur*] at the power of God when they imagine the power of nature to be, as it were, subjugated by God.[33]

The prophet-king manages to preserve his authority and power through a highly effective mechanism. Just as his own power seems to be called into question through an apparent inability to explain some event, he points to a higher being whose very greatness and authority is defined by its power to declare exceptions to its own rules in service of some end, which is inscrutable to lesser beings. The earthly authority thus bolsters its own power through a kind of explanation that attempts to preserve the wonder permanently through making it a tangible symbol of the divine authority that shows its power through its ability to make exceptions to its own ordained rules.[34]

However efficacious this mechanism it still suffers from several flaws. A miracle trades on epistemological uncertainty, which can be defeated through some explanation of the events in naturalistic terms. In Chapter 6 of the *TTP*, Spinoza gives a straightforward argument against the possibility of miracles. Such exceptions are metaphysically impossible because, if God is immutable, a miracle would be contrary to his nature. Furthermore, the more people know the less likely they will believe in miracles.[35] There is certainly some evidence that Spinoza, like Hume, thought that there was a history of progress in civilization and that the propensity to believe in miracles was part of an immature stage that would eventually be outgrown as knowledge increased.[36] It was a commonplace of the Enlightenment that a little reason would displace superstition, but short of that, even a competing inadequate explanation, whether naturalistic or supernatural, might be enough to undermine the belief in a miracle. As we saw above, closer scrutiny of either the event or the person may dissipate the singular wonder of a miracle, and what had led to veneration may now just as quickly lead to contempt. If one of the practical functions of a miracle is to produce veneration of some figure and then justify its political authority, then it is also likely to lead to contempt and instability. The zealous attempt of religious and political authorities to maintain the mystery of their exceptional origin through ritual may itself lead to routine and the opposite of wonder. If Spinoza is right, that miracles are impossible because there are no violations of the natural order, and that all individuals strive to persist, then it will often be possible for simple self-interest to check the rampant belief in exceptional events. For all its apparent utility a state will, in the long run, find it contrary to its self-interest to invoke miracles to justify its authority.

So, although the invocation of miracles may have been the way the ancient Israelites and other primitive peoples solved the collective action

---

[34] This mechanism, quite clearly analyzed by Spinoza, has been the subject of a great deal of recent discussion in the domain of political theology. It was Carl Schmitt, who in the first sentence of *Political Theology*, writes "Sovereign is he who decides on the state of exception." See also the recent work by Giorgio Agamben, *State of Exception*.

[35] For a more detailed account of Spinoza's argument see Curley, "Spinoza on Miracles."

[36] Spinoza refers to the ancient Israelites in the *TTP* as "childish" (Ch. 2; *G* III 41), and in his chapter (10) in the *Enquiries* concerning miracles, Hume refers to the prevalence of testimony to miracles found in "rude and barbarous societies."

problem, it has numerous problems. The most important one is its metaphysical impossibility, but there are more practical problems as well. So why is this not enough to conclude that we have become more rational in part through Spinoza's own philosophical critique of the idea of miracle?

5 THE MIRACLE OF THE WILL

We usually think of miracles in relation to God's intervention in the external world. But there is another related kind of phenomenon whose structure is strictly analogous to the miracle in nature though it is far more frequent than something like the parting of the Red Sea, that is, the idea of free will. In the appendix to Part 1 of the *Ethics*, Spinoza makes it clear that teleology – the supposition "that all natural things act, as men do, on account of an end," is at the root of most of our errors about the world, including our mistaken ideas of God and the source of value, and that free will follows from this error.[37] The critique of the Cartesian notion of a sovereign free will is related to the critique of the political system based on the will of the monarch or indeed of the subject.

In the standard Cartesian conception, the mind (*res cogitans*) and the body (*res extensa*) are two substances created by God. Like Spinoza, Descartes was critical of teleological thinking, at least in the domain of extended substance. Bodies, he thinks, are governed by laws of nature that work through efficient causation alone. Minds, on the other hand, are independent of these laws because, as he states in the *Principles of Philosophy*, in addition to the power of intellect, they also have the capacity of a will.[38] There are various modes of willing – desire, aversion, assertion, denial, and doubt – but they all seem to have in common an intrinsic capacity to do otherwise. What characterizes human beings is that they have a will and that "this makes him in a special way the author of his actions and deserving of praise for what he does."[39] Descartes also claims that the freedom of this will, namely, "that we have power in many cases to give or withhold our assent at will," is an innate and self-evident notion.[40] Given the complex nature of the will, this freedom has to be understood in two different ways. It is the freedom to assert or deny an idea but also the freedom to desire or abhor some object outside of our minds. And this brings us to

---

[37] E1app.
[38] CSM 1/204. References to the translation of the *Principles* are to *The Philosophical Writings of Descartes*, ed. Cottingham, Stoothoff, and Murdoch, and abbreviated as CSM with volume and page number.
[39] Principles, 1, article 37; CSM 1/205.   [40] Article 39; CSM1/205–206.

the second remarkable aspect of the Cartesian view. How is it possible for something unextended, the soul, to interact with something extended?[41] And if that is not enough, how is it possible for something regulated by a determined system of efficient causes to be affected by something external to that system? Descartes offers a variety of explanations: to Elisabeth he says that it is the very nature of the mind–body union that allows for this interaction to take place, that it is a self-evident "primitive notion"; or that there is a gland, the infamous pineal gland, that causes the interaction. The Occasionalists take this idea to its logical conclusion and claim that the interaction of mind and body, or indeed any causal interaction, is an ongoing occasion for God's miraculous intervention.

Spinoza's critique of the Cartesian idea runs throughout the *Ethics*, but we find a pointed and scathing summary of it in the Preface to Part 5. There he ridicules the pineal gland as "a Hypothesis more occult than any occult quality," and points out that the only explanation of the mind–body union is the "cause of the whole Universe, i.e., God."[42] Spinoza obviously thinks that the Cartesian solution to the problem of mind–body interaction is nothing more than an appeal to a miracle. That is, instead of explaining an act of will through its place in a determinate chain of causes Descartes fixates on the singular act of will as if that were an explanation in itself. And the astonishment at this power is linked to God, who has given it to us as a gift, and whom, as a consequence, we venerate. But just as the miracle of the will is not really explained neither is the ultimate cause of the will, the divine nature of God, explained. God gives us free will just because he has free will, which itself remains unexplained. Hence the ignorance of the human will is displaced to a higher level, what Spinoza calls the "asylum of ignorance."[43]

Just as Spinoza solves the "problem" of biblical miracles through a systematic effort at placing the wondrous singularity in a determinate chain of causes, so does he solve the problem of the apparently *sui generis* will. On a metaphysical level, the idea of substance, or God, is necessary and cannot stand for any internal exceptions without contradicting its own nature. God does have a will, but it is expressed in the immutable laws of nature as they are eternally expressed. On the level of the human will, any particular will is just another mode of substance under the attribute of thinking. In the system of the so-called parallelism of attributes, any mode of thought

---

[41] Princess Elisabeth asked Descartes this question in her letter of May 6, 1643 (AT III/660) and Descartes attempts to respond in his letter of May 21 with his idea of a "third primitive notion," the union of mind and body (CSM 3/217).
[42] C 596; G II 279.   [43] E1app.; C 443; G II 81/11.

is no less determined than any mode of body, and there is no need for the obscure doctrine of interaction. Descartes had said in the Preface to the *Passions of the Soul* that he was going to study the passions *en physicien*. But when he describes the will as an exception to the regularities of nature, then his attempt at a science of the emotions is flawed. Spinoza has the same ambition in Part 3 of the *Ethics*, but has at least the hope of achieving it. When the will is naturalized as a particular kind of mode of thought in a determinate system, then it in principle becomes subject to a complete explanation in terms of other causes.

This critique of the Cartesian concept of free will would appear particularly important in relation to his political critique. Even in the *Ethics* Spinoza employs political language to discuss the mistaken concept of mind. The Cartesian idea is based on a false analogy. In our ignorance we imagine ourselves as free and then project this inadequate notion of freedom as the power to act outside the chain of determined causes onto God's nature. Because we then imagine that God rules over the world like a sovereign we project back again the political conception of sovereignty into the domain of the mind and say that the mind rules the body like the will of a sovereign.[44] Since Spinoza has exposed this Cartesian error in the *Ethics*, we might suppose that the *TTP* would take this metaphysical conclusion and apply it in the political domain and ruthlessly eliminate any talk of free will. However, in his discussion of law in Chapter 4, we find a quite different story.

6 THE ORIGINS OF HUMAN LAW

The problem is that, in Chapter 4, Spinoza claims that human law originates from an act of sovereign free will, and that this inexplicable act intends to and does produce the passion of wonder among the subjects who then venerate the lawgiving authority. The account of human law seems implicitly to go directly against his double critique of wonder and miracles that we have just seen.

According to Spinoza, "the word law, taken absolutely, means that according to which each individual, or all or some members of the same species, act in one and the same certain and determinate manner. This depends either on a necessity of nature or on a decision of men."[45] Because natural law follows necessarily from God's will, when a finite thing acts in accordance with nature, it acts according to divine law. When a thing

---

[44] See E2p3s and again E5Preface.   [45] *TTP* Ch. 4, ¶ 1; *G* III 57.

follows from an act of law decreed by a king or other sovereign body, it
acts according to human law. Now we could, as the voluntarists might,
read these two kinds of law as fundamentally similar. God acts out of his
free will to create the laws of nature and he has endowed mankind with a
similar power of will that allows the possibility to decree human law. But as
we saw above in the discussion of will, Spinoza does not believe that either
God or man acts from true free will. As his enemies consistently pointed
out, in the *TTP* and in the *Ethics*, Spinoza makes it clear that God acts
out of necessity and that the divine laws could not be otherwise.[46] Human
beings, as finite parts of nature, are likewise subject to these laws and are
not radically free in the Cartesian sense to act otherwise. So why does he
claim that in some sense we are authors of law?

There are two reasons, one of which is consistent with his metaphysics,
strictly speaking, and the other of which is inconsistent with the metaphysics yet consistent with the politics. The first reason is that we can
be described as the "proximate" causes of these acts. So, even if it may
be possible to redescribe the acts as part of larger causal chains, there are
some ways in which we are the salient causes of these acts and so ought to be
held (from the point of view of other humans at least) causally responsible
for them. This leads us to the second reason, which is based on a mistaken
notion of free will, or the notion that things could have been otherwise
and we are responsible in certain cases, such as the decreeing of laws, for
having them turn out one way rather than another. As Spinoza writes, "we
are completely ignorant of the very order and connection of things, i.e., of
how things are really ordered and connected. So *for practical purposes* [*ad
usum vitae*] it is better, indeed necessary, to consider things as possible."[47]
We know that Spinoza does not think things really are possible or contingent. So why does he have recourse to it here as a necessary practical
belief?

It may be that a few individuals are capable of acting in accordance with
the divine law, at least to some extent. To think otherwise would turn the
ethical project of Part 5 of the *Ethics* into nonsense. These individuals would
think of themselves as proximate causes and they would probably attempt
to deduce human laws from their understanding of the natural order. No
passion of wonder would result, since the causes would be known, but

---

46 See, for instance, *Ep.* 74 (p. 335), from Henry Oldenburg, who reports on an objection from some
    readers of the *TTP*: "You appear to postulate a fatalistic necessity in all things and actions. If this
    is conceded and affirmed, they say, the sinews of all law, all virtue and religion are severed, and all
    rewards and punishments are pointless." Spinoza's response is found in *Ep.* 75.
47 *TTP* Ch. 4, ¶ 4; *G* iii 58; emphasis mine.

they would feel joy from acting in accordance with what produced their highest good, i.e., satisfied the strivings of their *conatus*. However, since the masses are incapable of attaining or acting in accordance with this view, they must adopt out of necessity another perspective. And indeed, since the purpose of human law is not to regulate the lives of rational people, who live cooperatively in accordance with divine law, but to regulate those who are passionate and tend to conflict, the laws would fail in their purpose if they did not evoke wonder, which in turn led to veneration of the lawgiver. For that is the very mechanism by which the collective action problem, as we have described it, can be solved.

Again, we see the recourse to ideas and practices based on ideas that are literally false in order to produce states of affairs that are consistent with at least some true, rational ideas of our well-being. And here lurks another problem. In the case of the explicit invocation of religious language to justify political authority, at least we can see how the supernatural is being used in politics. The danger of modern social contract theories, for instance, with their stories of states of nature, original positions, and choices made behind veils of ignorance, etc., is that they are seeking to substitute one transcendent legitimation, the legitimation of the state through appeal to divine providence, with another, the legitimation of the state through the mystery of the human free will. It may be that a secular use of this structure is superior in some respects than a religious use of it, but perhaps, if we think that the critique of it is at all justified, we should be suspicious of how the inexplicable is used even in a non-religious domain.[48] Kant, at least, was clear that we should feel awe and reverence before the moral law, and that the exercise of it was the only way in which God's presence in our lives could be revealed.[49] The question remains whether other more secular versions of these devices can truly free themselves of the religious structure. Spinoza, I would venture to say, would be skeptical. The story of rational agents in the state of nature who autonomously choose to institute a sovereign over them is just that, a story, whose real purpose is to help us

---

[48] This is what Michael Della Rocca would call an appeal to a brute fact and thus a violation of the Principle of Sufficient Reason. See Della Rocca, *Spinoza*, especially chapter 5, section 5 (pp. 199–203).

[49] See Kant's comment in *Religion Within the Boundaries of Mere Reason* in relation to the will and its role in forming moral laws: "The majesty of the law (like the law on Sinai) instills awe (not dread, which repels; and also not fascination, which invites familiarity); and this awe rouses the respect of the subject towards its master, except that in this case, since the master lies in us [i.e., the will], it rouses a *feeling of the sublimity* of our own vocation that enraptures us more than any beauty" (p. 72). See also the famous passage in the conclusion of the *Critique of Practical Reason*: "Two things fill the mind with ever new and increasing admiration and awe [*Bewunderung und Ehrfurcht*] . . . the starry heavens above me and the moral law within me" (p. 166).

understand the mechanisms of the political order (in order to constitute a
more stable one) rather than legitimate a new one *ab novo*.

7 CONCLUSION

It may seem natural to conclude that if anything I have said in the last
section about human law is correct, then Spinoza has simply violated his
own metaphysical doctrines in the most egregious way. But that would be
to ignore the problem with which we began, that is, how less than fully
rational individuals can form a sovereign authority. The logic of Chapter 16,
as I read it, requires that we use reason to discover how to manage the less
than rational aspects of our nature so that we can achieve results that
overall would be better for us individually and collectively. There has
been no better example of these techniques than we find in organized
religions, which have developed over time precisely to this end. This does
not mean of course that religion does not produce its own problems. It
has tried and mostly succeeded, at least up to Spinoza's time, to take over
metaphysics from the philosophers in order to bolster its own authority.
And, even if necessary and unavoidable, any technique to manage the
masses based on their fundamentally instable passions will always have its
shortcomings. (Perhaps the recourse to metaphysics to ground religion is
thus an inevitable temptation.) Nonetheless, all this requires is a constant
attention to focusing on the religious devices wielded by the state, a constant
rational critique of the superstitious in the inevitable theological-political
complex.

However, as I mentioned in the introduction and touched upon at
the end of the last section, there is another problem. An explicit use of
divine authority is one thing, but the implicit use of the structure of
divine authority in a purely secular guise is another. Here we encounter the
problem of whether Hobbes was being ironic or not when he described the
state as a monstrous leviathan. If he had been a religious believer, as some
claim,[50] then perhaps the wonder such an artifice would evoke should lead
to disgust and condemnation. But, if he was not a believer, then he would
have been poking fun at the very idea that the state based on the social
contract could be a monster and a divinely inspired politics supposedly
more natural. Whatever is of value from the old edifice of religion would
have to be mercilessly pillaged and then reused in the construction of a

[50] See Martinich, *The Two Gods of Leviathan*, and the subsequent debate in Curley, "Calvin and
Hobbes," Martinich, "On the Proper Interpretation," and Curley, "Reply to Professor Martinich."

new being, which would be none other than the mundane machine of the state. On this reading Hobbes would have been looking for a new source of wonder in the capacities of human beings to construct their own political orders in the light of reason rather than in the darkness of superstition.[51]

Spinoza, in contrast, at least in the *TTP*, does not conceive of the state in a purely secular way, but always coupled with some manifestation of the religious. (It may be that a pure democracy constituted by purely rational men, as he describes it in Chapter 16, would not have any religion, but that description simply does not fit within the parameters of the political problem as he describes it.) There is an important transition that takes place in Spinoza's critique of religion in the *TTP*, but the transition is not from a divinely ordered world to a secular one. Rather, the transition is from an uncritical notion of religion to a more critical one. The recourse to religion is just as necessary in the modern world as it was in the old. The difference is that we might need to be more vigilant to discover the ways in which the religious – exemplified in the wonder and veneration we have for the lawgiver, be it another person or ourselves as supposedly autonomous agents – has hidden itself in our political lives.

---

[51] In this context it is relevant to note that, although Hobbes was critical of wonder, he used and appreciated curiosity, because it was the chief mechanism by which humans acquired knowledge. In Chapter 6, paragraph 35 of the *Leviathan* says, "*Desire* to know why, and how, CURIOSITY, such as is in no living creature but *man*, so that man is distinguished, not only by his reason, but also by this singular passion from other *animals*" (Hobbes, *Leviathan*, ed. Curley). For a general discussion of curiosity, see Chapter 3 of Daston and Park, *Wonders and the Order of Nature*, in which they point out its morally ambivalent status; for a much more detailed study of this passion in the seventeenth century, see the two works by Neil Kenny: *The Uses of Curiosity* and *Curiosity in Early Modern Europe*. Interestingly enough, Spinoza does not use curiosity as a substitute for wonder. In the few places where he uses this term, mostly in the *TTP*, as far as I can tell, Spinoza uses it somewhat negatively, as in Chapter 7 (*G* III III), where he says that concern for things in Scripture that cannot be known by reason shows more curiosity than regard for our advantage.

CHAPTER 13

Narrative as the means to freedom: Spinoza on the uses of imagination

Susan James

Throughout his philosophical career, Spinoza was concerned with the problem of how the members of societies can be motivated to sustain harmonious and empowering forms of communal life. Given that we need to live together in order to survive, and yet have divergent desires and interests, there is a seemingly ineradicable tension between the urge to cooperate with one another and our wish to go our own ways, both sides of which must be accommodated in any stable political system. If we are to avoid the frustrations and miseries engendered by conflict, we need to be able to reconcile our more individual aspirations with the demands of a shared way of life. But what forms of self-understanding are most effective in helping us to move towards this goal, and in what conditions can they be successfully cultivated?

In developing his response, Spinoza never loses sight of the fact that creating and maintaining a harmonious way of life is a fundamentally practical project, simultaneously made possible and constrained by circumstances. But he nevertheless takes account of the fact that the manner in which the members of a particular society handle the conditions in which they find themselves will partly be determined by their conception of the kind of understanding that is most relevant to resolving their differences. Hence the question, what sort of knowledge is most efficacious in enabling people to reconcile their individual desires with the requirements of their collective life?

Within the history of ethics we can broadly distinguish two lines of reply elicited by this question. According to a universalist approach, we are best served by a systematic and compelling grasp of universal moral principles

Earlier versions of this chapter were given as the Ruth Parcels Lecture at the University of Connecticut and the Benedict Lecture at Boston University, and were also given to several departmental seminars. I am grateful to all my audiences for their probing and helpful comments. I owe a particular debt to Akeel Bilgrami, Aaron Garrett, Moira Gatens, Raymond Geuss, Charles Griswold, Melisssa Lane, Amelie Rorty, Michael Rosenthal, Quentin Skinner, and Daniel Star for invaluable criticisms and suggestions.

that we can then apply to our own situations. By contrast, advocates of a particularist view argue that we need something more specific: an interpretation of ourselves and our circumstances that generates resources for dealing with them.

The opposition between these two stances is venerable and deeply entrenched; but universalism has recently been subjected to a renewed wave of particularist criticism from philosophers who contend that moral reasons are never completely general. One version of this position appeals to the holistic nature of reasons in order to argue that the answer to the question "What do I have best reason to do?" is always determined by features of the specific situation under consideration, and thus varies from one case to the next.[1] A further version contends that we give meaning and value to situations and actions by fitting them into narratives about our place in the world that, while they may express shared values, are less than universal. Only through narratives can we generate the thick descriptions in which moral meaning is conveyed, and provide accounts of what is going on that are sufficiently detailed and focused to explain and justify our actions. So much so that, without this resource, we could not hope to assess possible courses of action as conducive to, or destructive of, a cooperative way of life.[2]

The disagreement between defenders of this latter version of the particularist position and their universalist opponents underlies a range of current debates in ethics, political philosophy, and the philosophy of action. While aspects of the history of their disagreement are often invoked to illuminate one or other position, it is perhaps surprising that Spinoza's distinctive contribution to the argument has not been much explored. Resisting the temptation to opt for one side at the expense of the other, he argues that our capacity to live cooperatively grows out of a situationist capacity for constructing narratives, which in turn explain and justify our actions. At the same time, we realize our highest good when we become capable of acting on the kind of principles that the universalist extols.

This inclusive stance both allows and constrains Spinoza to address the problem of how to reconcile universalism with particularism. How do the narratives that give moral meaning to our collective lives mesh with our commitment to general principles? What contribution can each approach make to our attempts to create the cooperative ways of life on which our ability to live as we wish depends? Rather than trying to keep the two views apart, Spinoza explores their mutual dependence, carefully mapping the

---

[1] Dancy, *Ethics Without Principles.*   [2] MacIntyre, *After Virtue*; Hutto, *Narrative.*

borders at which they meet and tracing the paths that lead from one to the other. Traveling in one direction, we rely on narratives to become capable of being motivated to act on general principles; moving in the other, our principles are made liveable through the narratives that make our individual and collective lives intelligible. There is much to be said about each of these journeys, and about the points at which they intersect as we track from the situational to the universal and back again. Here, however, I shall focus on Spinoza's account of the ways in which we depend on narrative to become more capable of living by universal principles. As I shall try to show, the breadth and subtlety of his analysis opens up a set of possibilities and problems that are not only philosophically rich in themselves, but also add a fresh dimension to contemporary discussion of the kinds of understanding that promote social and political cooperation.

Spinoza aligns the approaches that I have described as universalist and particularist with two distinguishable ways of thinking. We take the universalist approach when we engage in the abstract form of thought that he calls reasoning or understanding, and aim to grasp the unchanging and exceptionless laws governing types of things such as human minds.[3] As we use our reason to extend our knowledge of the laws of human nature, we come to recognize general features of the type of collective existence that is, as Spinoza puts it, most empowering for humankind. For example, so the *Ethics* tells us, everyone has good reason to promote their ability to reason;[4] equally, "a man who is guided by reasoning... desires to maintain the principles of common life and common advantage. Consequently, he desires to live according to the common decision of the state."[5] Furthermore, when reasoning operates as it should, it motivates us to act on our understanding, both by yielding incontrovertible grounds for doing some things rather than others, and by strengthening our desire to put our rationally grounded knowledge into practice.[6]

The true understanding of the world that reasoning provides is in Spinoza's view extremely powerful, but it is not easy to come by. Almost everyone has the capacity to cultivate the practice of reasoning, but few have the opportunity to do so, and still fewer appreciate its benefits.[7] This latter insensitivity is mainly due to the fact that most of us are absorbed in the

[3] E2p44c2.   [4] E4p36, E4p37.
[5] E4p73. All quotations from the *Ethics* are from the English translation by Edwin Curley. Quotations from the *Tractatus Theologico-Politicus* are from Curley's draft translation (sometimes slightly adapted for stylistic reasons).
[6] E4p59.   [7] E4p37s2; *TTP* Ch. 4; *G* III 61.

distinct and wide-ranging kind of thinking that Spinoza calls imagining. Imagining, in this technical sense of the term, encompasses the thinking and behavior that we base on our experience of particular things, situations, and processes.[8] It includes our perceptions and expectations, our memories and fantasies, together with the passions that run through them. It also includes the kinds of informal reasoning that we employ to string these experiences together, such as the means–ends inference that makes me decide to go out for half an hour because the saxophonist next door rarely practices for longer than that, or the inductively based suspicion with which I delete an email offering me a million dollars. In short, imagining is our everyday and favored way of imposing meaning on our experience. "Because deducing a thing solely from intellectual notions often requires a long chain of perceptions, and in addition, supreme circumspection, perceptiveness of mind and self-control – all of which are rare – men would rather be taught by experience."[9]

When an individual imagines, the meaning they ascribe to an event, and thus the way they fit it into their broader interpretation of the world, is determined by their own history.[10] The pattern of our past experiences shapes the way we see and feel about new events and states of affairs, so that the story of what has happened to us in the past remains present, informing our grasp of what is going on and constituting an interpretive standpoint. Spinoza does not describe this process as the creation of a narrative (*narratio*) – a term he mainly reserves for a particular manifestation of imaginative thinking, namely the narratives contained in the Bible and in histories – but I think it is appropriate to see the entire activity of imagining in these terms.

As with any narrative, imaginative thinking expresses the point of view of a narrator and puts together a more or less coherent story about what is going on. And, as with any narrative, later stages of the story may prompt its narrators or audiences to reinterpret what went before, so that the past to which we relate our current imaginings is never fixed. When individuals or groups imagine, they do not construct narratives from scratch, because they are always already absorbed in existing meanings and points of view. To be sure, they may or may not be able to articulate them – for example, one might well be unable to recount the narrative underlying the sudden antipathy one feels for a woman one passes in the street. Nevertheless, when we make use of imagination to describe, explain, or justify, its narrative

[8] E2p17, E2p40s2.   [9] *TTP* Ch. 5; G III 77.   [10] E3post2.

structure comes to the surface as we recount the past experience on which our current judgments are based, or explain how a situation strikes us. Furthermore – and here we come to the point at issue – such narratives, together with the affects they contain, ground our grasp of the things that matter to us, of the means to achieve them, and of the forms of cooperation that will help us to realize them. Amongst many other things, they give us our conceptions of cooperative ways of life, and shape our willingness (or lack of willingness) to live by them.

We therefore have two potential sources of insight into the project of creating ways of life that will accommodate both our desire to pursue individual goals and our dependence on other people. One of them – philosophical reasoning – is universalist. It focuses on unchanging properties of types of things and the atemporal laws that govern them. The other – imagining – is particularist, and charts our individual and collective interpretations of specific things and events. But what contribution does each of these kinds of thinking and acting make to our ability to live together in a harmonious fashion? Spinoza's answer is rooted in his doctrine of the *conatus* – his view that each of us strives to maintain ourselves as the individuals we are, and where possible to increase our power to maintain ourselves.[11] This striving is manifested in every aspect of our existence, including physical processes such as the homeostatic mechanisms governing the temperature of our bodies, and all our thinking. Both through imagining and reasoning, then, we try to get the kind of grip on ourselves and our circumstances that will empower us, by enabling us as far as possible to create a way of life in which we experience high and secure levels of physical and psychological satisfaction.

The role of philosophical reasoning in this process is in outline relatively straightforward. By giving us a true understanding of ourselves and the world, reasoning shows us what we can and cannot achieve, disabuses us of various pervasive errors about the nature of our capacities,[12] and reveals what types of action will and will not be empowering. If we were completely rational, we would follow the dictates of reason and agree on an optimal way of life.[13] As things are, however, we are only somewhat rational. Alongside our efforts to empower ourselves through reasoning, we also strive to maintain ourselves by imagining, and this way of thinking exposes us to various systematic forms of misunderstanding that limit our ability to cooperate effectively.[14]

---

[11] E3p6.   [12] E1app.   [13] E4p35c1.   [14] E4p37s2.

It is important not to exaggerate the dysfunctional character of imagining, as Spinoza conceives it. Despite its deficiencies, it provides us with a largely efficacious grasp of the world and ourselves, and underpins many sensible habits and decisions about what to do and how to live. Indeed, unless this were the case we would not survive. Nevertheless, Spinoza is impressed by the extent to which imagining fails to track the truth as it is revealed by reason, and tends to blur the line between accurate perception and fantasy. We see this above all in a general human disposition to put an empowering interpretation on our experience, thereby making it satisfying and encouraging. As the *Ethics* explains, "the Mind strives to imagine only what affirms or posits its power of acting,"[15] and "avoids imagining things that diminish its own power or that of the body."[16] In our efforts to persevere in our being, we blend realism and fantasy in varying degrees, sometimes taking refuge in projection or denial, and sometimes facing up to disempowering truths with courage or fascination. Contrary to an imaginatively fuelled assumption that we make about ourselves, straightforward observation is extremely difficult to achieve. "Indeed, when men see or hear something new, unless they take great precautions, they will for the most part be so preoccupied with their preconceived opinions that they will perceive something completely different from what has happened, particularly if the event surpasses the grasp of the narrator or audience, and especially if it makes a difference to the narrator's affairs that the event should happen in a certain way." Hence the commonplace observation that two historians or chroniclers may describe an event in such divergent terms that it is hard to believe that they are talking about the same thing.[17]

The central claim here is that, rather than simply recording our experiences, we are disposed to make them affirmative and to resist interpreting them in ways that are physically or psychologically debilitating. In this sense, there is an element of fantasy built into our everyday thinking. The mind strives to imagine what affirms its own power of acting. As interpreters, our narratives are selectively organized to achieve a certain effect, in which truth tracking is subsidiary to empowerment.

In order to appreciate the appositeness of Spinoza's view, it is helpful to remember that the trait he is describing operates at a familiar level. In Joseph O'Neill's novel, *Netherland*, the protagonist, Hans, is a Dutch banker working in New York. On a flight back from London he is given a chocolate bar, and although the bar is frozen he starts to eat it.

---

[15] E3p54.   [16] E3p13c.   [17] *TTP* Ch. 6; *G* III 91–92.

When I took my first bite I felt a painless crunch and the presence of something foreign in my mouth. I spat into my napkin. In my hand, protruding from brown gunk, was a tooth – an incisor, or three quarters of one, dull and filthy.

Dazed, I called over an attendant.

"I found a tooth in my chocolate bar," I said.

She looked at my napkin with open fascination. "Wow . . . "

Then she said carefully, "Are you sure it's not yours?"

My tongue lodged itself in an unfamiliar space.

"Shit," I said.

Hans's striving to conceive of himself as someone with a full set of teeth is not an isolated event. In interpreting what is happening to him, he implicitly draws on a preexisting sense of himself as a competent man who would be ashamed if he thought he was falling apart. This self-evaluation is in turn embedded in a narrative that sustains his conception of the kind of person he is: he is physically attractive, extremely good at his job, a sportsman, and so forth. Here we can begin to see how the narrative that gives Hans a certain orientation to the world also manifests the striving of his *conatus*. It shapes his effort to persevere in his being and, in this particular incident, does so to the point where a wish becomes father to the thought that the tooth in the chocolate bar belongs to someone else. Like Spinoza's historians, Hans and the flight attendant start out by describing their situation in radically different ways, and it is only through their exchange that they arrive at a common account of what has occurred. As it happens, their common account is true: unfortunately, it is Hans's tooth that is broken. But this is not always so. Many of our ordinary beliefs are in Spinoza's opinion profoundly mistaken, so that the scraps and stretches of narrative on which we converge are often only half-truths and are sometimes simply false. The urge to empower ourselves that drives us to interpret our experience in ways that are more or less fantastical will not necessarily be checked by other people; on the contrary, as we shall see, they may equally well corroborate or elaborate our fantasies. Moreover, as Spinoza sees the matter, there is nothing exceptional about this mixing of fantasy with fact. It is what imagining is like.

The fantastical element of imagining can therefore cut both ways. It may bind people together and, as we shall see, can be a potent unifying force. But it is also liable to undermine the effectiveness of the very efforts to cooperate that it engenders. A first and significant difficulty stems from the porous boundary between fact and fantasy that we have just examined. If, for example, a community bases its efforts to cooperate on a narrative that significantly overestimates its capacities, it will run the risk of failure. In addition, however, Spinoza is convinced that imaginative thinking embodies an inherent tendency to generate division and conflict between agents, whether individual or collective.[18] This problem stems from the fact that each of us has our own passions and desires, grounded on our own histories, and strives to persevere in our being in our own way.[19] The narratives we create will consequently embody diverse conceptions of the ends that are worth pursuing and the ways of life that are tolerable, and as we strive to realize them, our aspirations are bound to clash. To make matters worse, some of the psychological laws that are integral to imagining set us at odds with one another. We are naturally disposed, for instance, to want other people to share our desires, and are liable to hate them for failing to do so.[20] But when they do love what we love, and we find ourselves competing with them for scarce goods, we are prone to envy them.[21] Once again, our viewpoints are bound to diverge; and given that we have to live together, they are bound sometimes to give rise to personal and political conflict.

Because the laws governing our affects are an ineliminable part of imaginative thinking and are not easy to offset, the implications of Spinoza's analysis look dark. If imagining is inherently fantastical, it will be unable to correct its own tendency to produce narratives that are erroneous and potentially divisive. If it is inherently antagonistic, it is not obvious how it can make a constructive contribution to the project of creating a stable and cooperative way of life. If it is always prone to generate narratives that collide, surely it is bound to impede rather than promote cooperation. It seems, then, that the version of the particularist approach on which we have been focusing cannot yield the kind of insights that we need in order to build reliable, cooperative forms of existence, so that we would do better to turn to the universalist approach exemplified by philosophical reasoning.

Spinoza agrees that, if human beings were thoroughly rational, this would be the right conclusion to draw.[22] As it is, however, the option is not available. Since the imaginative dimension of our thinking is inescapable, we simply have to reckon with it. However, this state of affairs is not as bad as one might fear because, despite the limitations we have discussed, there are ways in which imagining can enhance our ability to create harmonious and satisfying ways of life. Taking up first the fantastical impetus of imaginative

---

[18] E4p32.   [19] E3p57.   [20] E3p31c.   [21] E3p35.   [22] *TTP* Ch. 5; *G* III 73–74.

258 SUSAN JAMES

thinking, and then its sheer diversity, Spinoza argues that each of these features possesses a productive aspect.

Judging by the historical record, communities have from time to time been strikingly successful in uniting around a narrative that has enabled them to live cooperatively. Moses, for example, generated a remarkably cohesive community by persuading a group of newly released slaves with no experience of the benefits of citizenship to live in accordance with a comprehensive set of laws. He achieved this feat by representing the Jews as the subjects of a divine legislator who could be trusted to reward their obedience. By providing them with a narrative that answered to their beliefs and yearnings, he gave them a largely compelling reason to obey the law. The effectiveness of Moses' narrative was, however, completely independent of its truth since, according to Spinoza, there simply is no anthropomorphic God who imposes laws on individual nations or holds out the prospect of reward and punishment. "Moses imagined God as a ruler, a lawgiver, a king, as compassionate, just, etc., when all these things are attributes only of human nature."[23] In this case, at least, the fantastical element of imaginative thinking was not destructive. On the contrary, it empowered the Jews by enabling them to create a secure state.

If a narrative is to shape the behavior of a particular group of people, they must be motivated to act as it recommends, and this willingness in turn depends on a number of conditions. First, whether or not the narrative is true, the people concerned must believe it to be so. (In the *TTP*, this claim is grounded on the relatively uncontentious assumption that we are generally more strongly motivated to act on claims that we take to be true than on claims we hold to be fictional.[24]) Secondly, Spinoza finds in the Old Testament a number of strategies for creating and sustaining a desire to live in accordance with the values that a narrative extols. One of the less successful ways in which Moses tries to persuade the Jews to conform to the law is to threaten anyone who disobeys with punishment. However, as the Bible indicates (and Spinoza agrees), "harmony born out of fear is without trust,"[25] so that individuals who only cooperate on this basis will "act most unwillingly. They're just trying to save their skins."[26] Since we experience fear as disempowering, our *conatus* ensures that we strive to resist situations that make us afraid, and in the case of the Jewish law this sometimes encouraged people to turn away from God, or to imagine that they were sufficiently powerful to avoid divine punishment.

[23] *TTP* Ch. 4; G III 64.   [24] *TTP* Ch. 14; G III 176.   [25] E4app16.   [26] *TTP* Ch. 5; G III 74.

Moreover, when they acted on these convictions they to some extent undermined the scheme of cooperation on which everyone's mutual benefits depended.

It is therefore more constructive to provide empowering grounds for obedience, and "this was why Moses . . . introduced religion into the body politic, so that people would do their duty not so much from fear as from devotion."[27] According to the *Ethics*, devotion is a kind of love that we feel for people whose capacities far outstrip our own, and who therefore excite our wonder or veneration.[28] To feel this affect for God is, in part, to love him; and because we experience love as empowering, a person who gains satisfaction from loving an infinitely powerful deity will normally seek to maintain this relationship by obeying the divine law. However, as Spinoza's analysis of the passions also allows us to infer, even this strategy is not completely stable, and is liable to be derailed by the element of veneration that devotion contains. In venerating God for capacities that far outstripped their own, the Jews were made aware of their comparative impotence, and were reminded of the extent to which they were dependent on a being who held them in the power of his hand. The sense of vulnerability that they experienced in turn made them anxious. (Can we really trust him? Are we not enslaved to his inexorable power?) As the Pentateuch testifies, a desire to escape this form of subordination intermittently eclipsed their veneration for the divine law, making way for narratives that embodied competing interpretations of their collective experience and recommended other courses of action.

Spinoza's attention to the obstacles that Moses encountered brings us to the second set of problems endemic to any form of cooperation grounded on narrative. Because the narratives to which a community appeals will invariably be diverse, the binding power of any single narrative will be inherently limited. Furthermore, since the balance of power between narratives shifts with the passions that motivate individuals to act on them, a successful narrative must continually adapt to changing times. We see Moses grappling with these only partly superable difficulties as he cajoles, threatens, and bargains, attempting to encourage and amaze the Jews into an enduring condition of steadfast obedience to the law. (It was because he aimed to break their stubborn heart, Spinoza remarks, "that he addressed them, not with arguments, but with the sound of trumpets, with thunder and with lightning."[29]) The story of his attempt to inculcate a level of singlemindend devotion that would guide the actions of virtually all his people

[27] *TTP* Ch. 5; *G* III 75. [28] E3p52s. [29] *TTP* Ch. 14; *G* III 179.

suggests that, at least in some circumstances, such a strategy can work remarkably well. But as we have also seen, it is bound to come up against the labile nature of human affect. Unless an approach to the creation of harmonious ways of life that is grounded on the narrative resources of imagination can accommodate the variety and changeability of our grounds for action, its success is bound to be limited.

Turning to this problem, Spinoza points out that imaginative diversity is not invariably an obstacle to cooperation. For example, communities commonly offer their members a number of disparate interpretations of the benefits of obeying the law, and accept that some individuals conform to it because they fear punishment, others because they hope for gain, still others because they love their country, and so on.[30] As long as most people have a motivating reason for obedience, the goal of cooperation is achieved, and there is no immediate need to achieve greater homogeneity. So although the narratives that constitute imaginative thinking provide an imperfect means of combating political conflict, they are sometimes strong enough to achieve this goal. The Spinozist version of particularism that we have been considering therefore yields an answer to our problem that can in practice be sufficient.

It is clear from Spinoza's outspoken defense of religious pluralism that he appreciates the force of this conclusion. Given that humans interpret their circumstances through many distinct religious narratives, a useful way to generate empowering ways of life is to exploit this very diversity in the name of social unity. Permit people to hold any religious beliefs that strengthen their ability to obey the law. Encourage individuals to interpret the core beliefs on which obedience depends in whatever way makes them easiest to accept. Refrain from inquiring too closely into the particular convictions on which obedience is grounded.[31] Don't worry about the fact that many of these convictions will be false, but judge them solely on the basis of their practical consequences.[32] In short, allow people to generate their own reasons for conforming to the divine law by constructing their own narratives.

This approach to the creation of religious harmony also informs Spinoza's analysis of its political counterpart. Because individuals and sects have different conceptions of what the divine law demands of us, a community needs an authority to pronounce on the matter. In principle, the Scriptures can fulfill this role, since any careful reader can identify their

---

[30] *TTP* Ch. 17; *G* III 202.   [31] *TTP* Ch. 14; *G* III 179.   [32] *TTP* Ch. 14; *G* III 178.

core doctrine;[33] but in practice we know that the biblical account of the law can be interpreted in many conflicting ways. If peace is to be maintained, someone must adjudicate between the claims of competing sects, and the only agent with the power to do so is the sovereign of the state. The interpretation and enforcement of divine law thus becomes a part of the civil law over which the sovereign exercises control. "The supreme power . . . which has the sole responsibility for preserving and protecting the rights of the state, has the supreme right to maintain whatever it judges concerning religion."[34] A sensible sovereign who takes to heart Spinoza's argument for the benefits of religious pluralism will therefore permit a profusion of religious narratives. However, there seems no reason why this strategy should be confined to religion. If it succeeds in generating obedience to the tenets of the divine law that the civil law incorporates, why should it not also generate obedience to other aspects of civil law? A sovereign should surely generalize from the religious case and look kindly on any interpretive narratives, whether historical, personal, political, or cultural, that motivate individuals or groups to cooperate.

While Spinoza recognizes that the promotion of ingenious versions of pluralism is often the most empowering strategy available to a community, he is still not convinced that this conclusion constitutes a satisfactory solution to our problem. His main reservation is the familiar one that, when states ground cooperation on a diversity of narratives, they remain vulnerable to the types of antagonism that the passions engender and will sometimes succumb to conflict or disintegration. Contemporary liberals are liable to regard this risk as a necessary cost of any tolerable political system; but Spinoza remains doubtful. Even where a relatively harmonious way of life exists, the divisiveness inherent in the passionate relationships underpinning it means that its destruction is always in the offing, and its multiple narratives are as likely to become a source of indecision and conflict as of unity. Observing this fact, one may simply resign oneself to living in a political community that falls significantly short of the ideal from which we began. Alternatively, one may decide to look again at the nature of imaginative thinking to see whether it contains further resources for building stronger forms of cooperative life.

Taking up the second of these options, Spinoza turns again to the Bible in order to reexamine the motivating force of different types of narrative. In general, people are more willing to act on a promise of empowerment

[33] *TTP* Ch. 12; *G* III 165.   [34] *TTP* Ch. 16; *G* III 199.

than on a threat of disempowerment, and the Jews were consequently
more stably motivated to obey a God worthy of devotion than one who
traded on fear of retribution.[35] In both cases, however, they were expected
to conform to the commands of an external legislator with whom it was
impossible to negotiate, and although they had reason to believe that God
would look after them, their subjection to him was nevertheless complete.
Since he alone determined the law that bound them together, they were
unable to fix the terms of their own common life, and a form of cooperation
that was empowering in some respects was consequently disempowering in
others. As well as binding the Jews to the law, the structure of the Mosaic
narrative set an absolute limit to their striving to empower themselves,
and in doing so created grounds for anxiety and resistance. The protection
offered by God in the form of the law could also be experienced as a form
of subjection, waiting to be overcome.

There is, in Spinoza's view, no way of escaping from this tension within
the type of narrative that Moses bequeathed. Its constraints can only be
overcome as changing circumstances create new possibilities, intertwined
with revisionary narratives. The discussion of the constitutional history of
the Jewish state contained in Chapter 15 of the *TTP* charts a process in
which control over the law shifts from one agent to another, thus creating a
demand for narratives capable of legitimating and encouraging new forms
of obedience. But it is in the New Testament that Spinoza locates what
he presents as the most empowering outcome of this process. When the
followers of Jesus Christ represent the law made by God as written on the
fleshly tablets of the heart rather than on tablets of stone – that is to say, as
a set of rules that anyone can understand and legislate for themselves – they
draw on the resources of the Old Testament to construct a narrative that
overcomes the limitations inherent in its predecessors. According to the
outlook they offer, one need not submit to commands set by someone else in
order to obey the law; rather, true obedience lies in obeying commands that
one imposes on oneself. Instead of following the law because God requires
it, one conforms to it because one appreciates that one has good reasons of
one's own for doing so, and acts on this understanding. Needless to say, this
conception of one's relationship to the law will only be compelling if one
can be confident that one does in fact have good reason to obey it, and on
Spinoza's reading the narratives contained in the Bible strive to make this
view persuasive. Both testaments represent conformity to the divine law as
the only means of achieving an unparalleled level of power that benefits

[35] *TTP* Ch. 5; *G* III 74.

us as individuals and as members of communities. According to the New Testament, moreover, the law is universal in the sense that it applies to everyone and takes each person's interests into equal account. "Before the coming of Christ, the prophets were accustomed to preach religion as the law of their own country . . . but after the coming of Christ the Apostles preached the same religion to everyone as a universal law."[36] The Apostles thus offer an image of a rule designed to uphold the common good that imposes the same, manageable demands on each of us, and which one can willingly obey in the confidence that one will receive one's fair share of benefits and not carry more than one's fair share of burdens.

What makes the Scriptures attractive, then, is their resolution of the tension between doing what we ourselves regard as best and doing what the law requires of us. Their doctrine, one might say, presents in the compelling guise of a religious narrative the republican view that the only way to gain political freedom is to legislate for oneself a law that upholds the common good. Spinoza represents the emergence of this strong imaginative basis of cooperation as a significant conceptual transition in the history of humanity. But at a psychological and a historical level the story is of course more complicated. Psychologically, a grasp of the universality of the law is not by itself enough to banish debilitating passions such as fear. The prospect of punishment or the threat of corruption may still cause citizens anxiety, and can be expected to qualify their confidence in any legal system under which they actually live. So the problems posed by conflicting passions and narratives will not be completely resolved, although one might expect the disempowering doubts associated with a narrative about a law that one obeys willingly to be less boundless and enervating than those excited by a narrative about a Mosaic God. The fear that comes with total submission to an unpredictable deity is not the same as the fear that a law upholding the common good may be corrupted or go awry. Although anxiety will remain, its quality will be modified by the narrative of which it is a part, and it will play a different role in individual patterns of motivation.

Historically, the task of creating communities that are capable of living up to the ideal held out by the Bible is, as Spinoza recognizes, immensely taxing. The existence of a narrative in which the ideal is represented does not in itself make it compelling, and in practice its effectiveness depends on a host of factors. For example, some agent must be capable of making the narrative credible to a community, and that community must in turn be capable of using it to strengthen its form of cooperative life. Spinoza seems

---

[36] *TTP* Ch. 12; *G* III 163.

to have thought that the Dutch state had made a certain amount of progress in this direction. The idea that one has good reason to obey the law when one legislates it for oneself on terms that apply equally to everyone had been made concrete in the republican constitution of the United Provinces and in the dogmas of some of its sects. However, despite their potential to empower, these institutionalized narratives remained fiercely contested. So much so that, when Spinoza was writing the *TTP*, it even seemed possible that the Dutch republican regime would not survive.

In such circumstances, a more pragmatically minded theorist might well have taken refuge in the thought that an adequate degree of political unity can sometimes be created out of imaginative diversity. But Spinoza is not yet ready to accept what he regards as a weak conclusion and, as before, the next phase of his argument grows almost dialectically out of the impasse he has reached. If the task of politics is to build ways of life in which cooperation is stably protected and upheld, the United Provinces, as Spinoza implicitly portrays it, has reached a significant point of transition. Pulling in one direction, the narrative that he locates in the Scriptures holds out an image of a strongly unifying form of cooperation, organized around an appreciation of the power that can be generated when the members of a community impose the law on themselves. However, like an oasis glimpsed from the desert, this ideal has so far only flickered into view. The circumstances in which it can be securely realized do not obtain, and recent attempts to establish it have met with limited success. Standing in its way, and pointing in other directions, are a number of competing narratives, offering different accounts of the nature and extent of the commitment to cooperation, and carrying with them the materials for religious and political conflicts that may do irreparable damage to the state.

From Spinoza's point of view, this situation is discouraging. But that very fact contributes to the danger the situation poses. Discouragement is potentially as damaging as the situation on which it feeds, because it is liable to reinforce a spirit of defeat in which the United Provinces may fall back on a less empowering way of life than the one it has already achieved, and resort to terror or devotion in order to enforce the law. Whatever the short-term benefits of such a strategy, it carries with it the likelihood of increased social and political conflict. During the 1660s and 1670s, Spinoza seems to have been convinced that the Dutch were at serious risk of curtailing their liberties by abandoning their republican constitution. In his political and philosophical writings he is trying to resist this outcome by providing a narrative that will inspire his compatriots to continue to struggle for stronger forms of cooperation. The narrative he now goes on to offer is thus a political intervention designed to encourage the citizens of a polity to press forward towards a more stable way of life.

To move towards the ideal of a community in which the law is written on the fleshly tables of the heart, one must provide reasons for obedience that have a general appeal.[37] As Spinoza now goes on to claim, the kind of reasons that can best satisfy this demand are those derived from philosophical reasoning. Unlike imagining, which answers to particular and diverse experiences, reasoning yields truths that are universal, eternal, and guarantee their own certainty.[38] To rationally understand a law about what empowers human beings, for example, is to appreciate that it captures an incontrovertible feature of the human good, and that it applies to you as one human being among others. Like anyone else, you have a reason to recognize it and to give it weight when deciding what to do.[39] Philosophical understanding therefore provides us with a universalist approach to the problem of cooperation. It uncovers general principles such as "Be just," or "Strive to bind yourself to others by love,"[40] and shows us why we have reason to act on them.

This conception of reason is familiar enough; but what concerns us here is its role in Spinoza's argument. Spinoza does not claim that he or his contemporaries currently live in an environment where most people can in fact use philosophical reasoning to work out how they have good reason to live. Nor does he claim that even the most advanced philosophers of his time have enough understanding to give more than a fragmentary account of what these reasons are. And he certainly does not claim to know that his sketch of a rational community can be fully realized. He is not therefore appealing to philosophical reasoning as the basis for an immediate and accessible solution to the problem of creating stable and harmonious communities. Instead, he is offering an image of a way of life devoted to the pursuit of philosophical understanding, which, if we could achieve it, would enable us to contain the diversity of our imaginative outlooks and generate forms of cooperation far stronger than any we have so far managed to devise.

In the *Ethics*, Spinoza defends the need for an exemplar or model of human nature that we can set before ourselves and try to imitate.[41] Putting this approach to work, he offers us a model of a life organized around the pursuit of philosophical understanding, and invites us, his readers, to use

---

[37] This section of my argument is particularly indebted to a paper by Moira Gatens, "Spinoza's Disturbing Thesis: Power Norms and Fiction in the *Tractatus Theologico-Politicus*," *History of Political Thought*, 30.3 (2009), 455–468.
[38] *TTP* Ch. 4; *G* III 62–63.   [39] *TTP* Ch. 4; *G* III 60–61.   [40] E4p46.   [41] E4pref.

it to give meaning and value to what we do. We are meant to internalize his ideal of systematic philosophical understanding and let it shape our lives. But in so far as we follow him, and live by a faith in the existence of reasons that we cannot actually grasp, we rely on our capacity for imagining. We are envisaging a way of life in which we have universalist reasons for cooperating from a particularist perspective in which our reasons for acting are for the most part shaped by the narratives through which we interpret our experience.

What will make the ideal of rationally grounded cooperation compelling to us? As we have seen, a first condition is that we should be able to hold it as true. But this is a tough requirement, particularly if we acknowledge that the claim that reason can ground an empowering form of unity may be as much a fantasy as Moses' conception of a legislating God. Although Spinoza is confident that this is not the case, he is also acutely aware that the philosophical arguments by means of which he demonstrates his conclusion are not within everyone's reach. How, then, is he to make his view persuasive? Presumably the most effective means of enabling people to appreciate the benefits that understanding brings is to teach them how to reason; but before he can take this route, Spinoza first faces the problem of convincing them that they should submit to being taught. Since they are not skilled in reasoning, there is no point in offering them a complex philo-sophical argument, and Spinoza therefore pursues the alternative course of appealing to their imagination. His first, comparatively basic appeal is to their experience, and thus to the narratives in which our grasp of our own capacities are embedded. We already understand ourselves as capable of reasoning and have some experience of the kinds of power to which it can give rise; so the suggestion that it might generate further effective conclusions should not strike us as outlandish. For this consideration to move us, however, we need to be convinced that the benefits of learning to reason will be worth the trouble, and here Spinoza makes a second and more interesting appeal.

As aspirant philosophers, he tells us, we are pursuing a kind of knowledge that will free us from the passionate conflicts of our everyday lives and increase our power. Among the rewards we shall gain from living in a community whose members recognize that they have good reasons to cooperate for their mutual benefit are the confidence and satisfaction that come from knowing that we shall be treated fairly, the ability to pursue our own ends within the limits of the law, and the support generated by enduring friendships. In addition, the project of understanding to which such a community is devoted will diminish our susceptibility to sadness and bring us joy. Here, as elsewhere in his work, we find Spinoza employing the resources of imagination in the service of reasoning, gilding his portrait of a life devoted to understanding with a familiar and empowering passion. Part of what makes the image of a rational life desirable, and encourages us to struggle towards it, is its continuity with the familiar pleasures of forms of existence grounded on imaginative thinking. Our ability to identify with these pleasures can inspire us to promote the forms of cooperation from which we imagine them to spring. But what motivates us here is not so much a grasp of the rational basis of cooperation, which still lies ahead, as a narrative about what we might achieve and the satisfactions it would bring. Here, then, Spinoza gives the last word to the particularist approach.

The central conclusion of the argument I have traced is that the way of life endorsed by reason needs to be brought within imaginative reach if it is to mold our desires and actions. The general principles around which it is organized must be made liveable by being embedded in the narratives that give meaning to what we do and shape our aspirations. If we are unable to see how we could, or why we should, conform to the demands of what Spinoza describes as a rational life, an image of such a life will be no use to us. As he appreciates, it is only through more or less particular narratives that a commitment to cooperation can be brought alive. Universalism therefore cannot get along without the form of particularism that Spinoza defends.

Bibliography

SPINOZA

Spinoza, Benedict de, *Spinoza Opera*, ed. Carl Gebhardt, 4 vols. (Heidelberg: Carl Winter Press, 1925/1972)

The Correspondence of Spinoza, trans. and ed. A. Wolf (New York: Lincoln MacVeigh, 1927)

A Theologico-Political Treatise and A Political Treatise, trans. and intro. R. H. M. Elwes (New York: Dover Publications, 1951)

The Collected Works of Spinoza, trans. and ed. Edwin Curley (Princeton: Princeton University Press, 1985), vol. I

A Spinoza Reader, trans. and ed. Edwin Curley (Princeton: Princeton University Press, 1994)

The Letters, trans. Samuel Shirley, with introduction and notes by Steven Barbone, Lee Rice, and Jacob Adler (Indianapolis: Hackett, 1995)

Tractatus Theologico-Politicus/Traité théologico-politique. Texte établi par Fokke Akkerman, traduction et notes par Jacqueline Lagrée et Pierre-François Moreau (Paris: Presses Universitaires de France, 1999)

Political Treatise, trans. Samuel Shirley, with introduction and notes by Steven Barbone and Lee Rice (Indianapolis: Hackett, 2000)

Complete Works, ed. Samuel Shirley (Indianapolis: Hackett, 2002)

Spinoza's Theologico-Political Treatise, trans. from the Latin with Glossary, Indexes, and Interpretive Essay by Martin D. Yaffe (Newburyport, MA: Focus Publishing, 2004)

Theological-Political Treatise, ed. Jonathan Israel, trans. Michael Silverthorne and Jonathan Israel (Cambridge: Cambridge University Press, 2007)

The Collected Works of Spinoza, trans. and ed. Edwin Curley (Princeton: Princeton University Press, forthcoming), vol. II

MAIMONIDES

Maimonides, Moses, *The Guide of the Perplexed*, trans. Shlomo Pines (Chicago: University of Chicago Press, 1963)

DESCARTES

Descartes, René, *The Philosophical Writings of Descartes*, trans. John Cottingham, Robert Stoothoff, and Dugald Murdoch (Cambridge: Cambridge University Press, 1984)
The Passions of the Soul, trans. S. H. Voss (Indianapolis: Hackett, 1989)

HOBBES

Hobbes, Thomas, *Leviathan*, ed. C. B. Macpherson (Harmondsworth: Penguin, 1968)
Leviathan, ed. Edwin Curley (Indianapolis: Hackett, 1994)
De Cive: The English Version, in *The Clarendon Edition of the Works of Thomas Hobbes*, ed. Howard Warrender (Oxford: Clarendon Press, 1983), vol. II
Man and Citizen (De Homine and De Cive), ed. Bernard Gert (Indianapolis: Hackett, 1991)

OTHER WORKS

Abelard, Peter, *Opera Theologica*, Vol III, ed. E. M. Buytaert and C. J. Mews (Turnholti: Typographi Brepols, 1969)
Agamben, Giorgio, *State of Exception*, trans. K. Attell (Chicago: University of Chicago Press, 2005)
Akkerman, Fokke, "Studies in the Posthumous Works of Spinoza: On Style, Earliest Translation and Reception, Earliest and Modern Edition of Some Texts" (PhD diss. Groningen University, 1980)
"Tractatus theologico-politicus: texte latin, traductions néerlandaises et Adnotationes," in *Spinoza to the Letter: Studies in Words, Texts and Books*, ed. F. Akkerman and P. Steenbakkers (Leiden: Brill, 2005), 209–236
Albo, Joseph, *Sefer Ha-'Ikkarim. [Book of Principles]*, ed. and trans. Isaac Husik (Philadelphia: Jewish Publication Society of America, 1929–1930)
Allison, Henry, *Benedict de Spinoza: An Introduction* (New Haven: Yale University Press, 1987)
Antognazza, Maria Rosa, *Leibniz on the Trinity and the Incarnation: Reason and Revelation in the Seventeenth Century* (New Haven: Yale University Press, 2007)
Aquinas, Thomas, *Summa theologiae*, trans. English Dominicans (London: Burns, Oates, and Washbourne, 1912–1936 [repr. New York: Christian Classics, 1981])
Summa contra gentiles, trans. Anton C. Pegis. 5 vols. (Notre Dame: University of Notre Dame Press, 1975)
Aristotle, *The Basic Works of Aristotle*, ed. R. McKeon (New York: Random House, 1941)
Aubrey, John, *Brief Lives*, ed. Andrew Clark (Oxford: Clarendon Press, 1898)
Bagley, Paul J., *Philosophy, Theology, and Politics: A Reading of Benedict Spinoza's Tractatus Theologico-Politicus* (Leiden: Brill, 2008)

Bamberger, Fritz, "The Early Editions of Spinoza's Tractatus Theologico-Politicus: A Reexamination," *Studies in Bibliography and Booklore*, 5 (1961), 9–33, repr. in Bamberger, *Spinoza and Anti-Spinoza Literature: The Printed Literature of Spinozism, 1665–1832*, ed. L. S. Wolfson and D. J. Gilner (Cincinnati: Hebrew Union College Press, 2003)

Barnes, Timothy D., *Constantine and Eusebius* (Cambridge, MA: Harvard University Press, 1981)

Batalier, Jacob, *Vindiciae miraculorum [. . .] Adversus auctorem* Tractatus Theologico Politici (Amsterdam, 1673)

Bayle, Pierre, *Dictionnaire historique et critique* (1697, 1702²). Facsimile of the 1820–1824 Paris edition (Geneva: Slatkine Reprints, 1969)
  Écrits sur Spinoza, ed. F. Charles-Daubert and Pierre-François Moreau (Paris: Berg, 1983)
  Correspondance de Pierre Bayle, ed. Antony McKenna *et al.* (Oxford: Voltaire Foundation, 2001), vol. II
  Philosophical Commentary on These Words of the Gospel, Luke 14:23, "Compel Them to Come In, That My House May Be Full", ed. John Kilcullen and Chandran Kukathas (Indianapolis: Liberty Fund, 2005)

Beltrán, Miquel, "The God of the *Tractatus Theologico-Politicus*," *North America Spinoza Society Monograph*, 3 (1995), 23–33.

Ben Elijah, Meyuhas, *Perush le-Sefer Debarim* [Heb.: *Commentary on Deutronomy*], ed. M. Katz (Jerusalem, 1968)

Bennett, Jonathan, *A Study of Spinoza's Ethics* (Indianapolis: Hackett, 1984)

Bentham, Jeremy, *An Introduction to the Principles of Morals and Legislation* [first edn. 1789], ed. J. H. Burns and H. L. A. Hart (Oxford: Oxford University Press, 1996)

Berger, Adolf, *Encyclopedic Dictionary of Roman Law* (Philadelphia: The American Philosophical Society, 1953)

Berger, David, *The Jewish-Christian Debate in the High Middle Ages* (Philadelphia: The Jewish Publication Society of America, 1979)

— Berlin, Isaiah, "Two Concepts of Liberty," in *Four Essays on Liberty* (London: Oxford University Press, 1969), 118–173
  "A Reply to David West," *Political Studies*, 41 (1993), 297–298

Blom, H. W., "Lambert van Velthuysen et le naturalisme," *Cahiers Spinoza*, 6 (1991), 203–212

Blom, H. W. and J. M. Kerkhoven, "A Letter Concerning an Early Draft of Spinoza's Treatise on Religion and Politics?" *Studia Spinozana*, 1 (1985), 371–378

Bonfils, Joseph ben Eliezer, *Safenat Pan`eah*, ed. David Herzog, 2 vols. (Heidelberg: Carl Winters, 1911–1930)

Bontekoe, Cornelis, *Brief Aen Johan Frederik Swetzer, Gesegt Dr Helvetius, Geschreven en Uytgegeven: Tot een Korte Apologie voor den Grote Philosooph Renatus Descartes en sijne regtsinnige navolgers* (The Hague, 1680)

Bordoli, Roberto, "Filosofia e teologia in Meyer e in Spinoza," *Il Pensiero*, 33 (1993), 146–176

Ragione e scrittura tra Descartes e Spinoza: Saggio sulla 'Philosophia S. Scripturae interpres' du Lodewijk Meyer e sulla sua recenzione (Milan: Franco Angeli, 1997)

Bostrenghi, Daniela, *Hobbes e Spinoza, scienza e politica: atti del convegno internazionale, Urbino, 14–17 ottobre 1988* [*Hobbes and Spinoza, science and politics: proceedings of the international Conference, Urbino, October 14–17, 1988*] (Napoli: Bibliopolis, 1992).

Boucher, Wayne I., *Spinoza in English: A Bibliography From the Seventeenth Century to the Present*, 2nd edn. (Bristol: Thoemmes, 1999)

Bouveresse, Renée, *Spinoza et Leibniz. L'idee d'animisme universel* (Paris: Vrin, 1992)

Boyle, Robert, *The Works of the Honourable Robert Boyle*, ed. T Birch, 5 vols. (London, 1744)

Bredekamp, Horst, "Thomas Hobbes' Visual Strategies," in *The Cambridge Companion to Hobbes's Leviathan*, ed. P. Springborg (New York: Cambridge University Press, 2007), 26–60

Bredenburg, Johan, *Enervatio tractatus theologico-politici* (Rotterdam: Isaac Naeranus, 1675)

Burman, Frans (the Younger), *Burmannorum pietas, gratissimae beati parentis memoriae communi nomine exhibita* (Utrecht: Vande Water, 1700)

Cardano, Girolamo, *De subtilitate libri XXI* (Lugduni: Apud Gulielmum Rouillium, 1559)

Castellio, Sebastian, *Concerning Heretics*, trans. Roland H. Bainton (New York: Octogon Books, 1965)

Chazan, Robert, *Fashioning Jewish Identity in Medieval Western Christendom* (Cambridge: Cambridge University Press, 2004)

Cohen, Marc, *Under Crescent and Cross*, rev. edn. (Princeton: Princeton University Press, 2008)

Colerus, Johannes, *The Life of Benedict de Spinosa* (The Hague: Martinus Nijhoff, 1906)

Cooperman, Bernard, "Elijah Montalto's 'Suitable and Incontrovertible Propositions': A Seventeenth-Century Anti-Christian Polemic," in *Jewish Thought in the Seventeenth Century*, ed. Isadore Twersky and Bernard Septimus (Cambridge, MA: Harvard University Press, 1987), 469–497

Crescas, Hasdai, *The Refutation of the Christian Principles*, trans. Daniel J. Lasker (Albany: SUNY Press, 1992)

Cristofolini, Paolo, *Cartesiani e Sociniani. Studio su Henry More* (Urbino: Argalia, 1974)

Curley, Edwin, "Spinoza's Moral Philosophy," in *Spinoza: A Collection of Critical Essays*, ed. Marjorie Grene (Notre Dame: University of Notre Dame Press, 1973), 354–376

"Spinoza on Miracles," in *Proceedings of the First Italian Congress on Spinoza*, ed. E. G. Boscherini (Napoli: Bibliopolis, 1985), 421–438

"Homo Audax. Leibniz, Oldenburg and the TTP," in *Leibniz' Auseinandersetzung mit Vorgängern und Zeitgenossen. Studia Leibnitiana Supplementa*, 27 (Stuttgart: Franz Steiner Verlag, 1990), 277–312

"Notes on a Neglected Masterpiece (II): The *Theological-Political Treatise* as a Prolegomenon to the *Ethics*," in *Central Themes in Early Modern Philosophy*, ed. J. A. Cover and Mark Kulstad (Indianapolis and Cambridge: Hackett Publishing Company, 1990), 109–160

"On Bennett's Interpretation of Spinoza's Monism," in *God and Nature: Spinoza's Metaphysics*, ed. Y. Yovel (Leiden: E. J. Brill, 1991), 35–51

"The State of Nature and its Law in Hobbes and Spinoza," *Philosophical Topics*, 19.1 (1991), 97–117

"'I Durst Not Write So Boldly,' or How to Read Hobbes' Theological-Political Treatise," in *Hobbes e Spinoza*, ed. Daniela Bostrenghi, intro. Emilia Giancotti (Naples: Bibliopolis, 1992), 497–593

"Notes on a Neglected Masterpiece (I): Spinoza and the Science of Hermeneutics," in *Spinoza: The Enduring Questions*, ed. Graeme Hunter (Toronto: Toronto University Press, 1994), 64–99

"Calvin and Hobbes, or Hobbes as an Orthodox Christian," *Journal of the History of Philosophy*, 34 (1996), 257–271

— "Kissinger, Spinoza, and Genghis Khan," in *The Cambridge Companion to Spinoza*, ed. Don Garrett (Cambridge: Cambridge University Press, 1996), 315–342

"Reply to Professor Martinich," *Journal of the History of Philosophy*, 34 (1996), 285–287

"The Covenant with God in Hobbes's Leviathan," in *Leviathan After 350 Years*, ed. Tom Sorrell and Lic Foisneau (Oxford: Clarendon Press, 2004), 199–216

Dancy, Jonathan, *Ethics Without Principles* (Oxford: Oxford University Press, 2004)

Daston, Lorraine and Kathleen Park, *Wonders and the Order of Nature: 1150–1750* (New York: Zone Books, 2001)

De Boer, T. J., "Spinoza in Engeland," *Tijdschrift voor Wijsbegeerte*, 10 (1916), 181–200

Delahunty, R., *Spinoza* (London: Routledge, 1985)

Della Rocca, Michael, "Spinoza's Substance Monism," in *Spinoza: Metaphysical Themes*, ed. Olli Koistinen and John Biro (New York: Oxford University Press, 2002), 11–37

"A Rationalist Manifesto: Spinoza and the Principle of Sufficient Reason," *Philosophical Topics*, 31 (2003), 75–93

"Egoism and the Imitation of Affects in Spinoza," in *Spinoza on Reason and the "Free Man"*, ed. Y. Yovel and G. Segal (New York: Little Room Press, 2004), 123–147

"Two Spheres, Twenty Spheres, and the Identity of Indiscernibles," *Pacific Philosophical Quarterly*, 86 (2005), 480–492

"Rationalism Run Amok: Representation and the Reality of Affects in Spinoza," in *Interpreting Spinoza*, ed. Charles Huenemann (Cambridge: Cambridge University Press, 2008), 26–52

— *Spinoza* (New York: Routledge, 2008)

Drake, Harold, "Constantine," in *Late Antiquity: A Guide to the Postclassical World*, ed. G. W. Bowerstock, Peter Brown, and Oleg Grabar (Cambridge, MA: Belknap Press of Harvard University Press, 1999), 389–391
  Constantine and the Bishops: The Politics of Intolerance (Baltimore: Johns Hopkins University Press, 2000)
Dugas, Ludovic, *Le Psittacisme et la pensée symbolique* (Paris: Félix Alcan, 1896)
Duran, Profiat, *"Epistle Be Not Like Your Fathers,"* in *Polemical Writings of Profiat Duran*, ed. Frank Talmage (Jerusalem: Zalman Shazar Center, 1981)
Dworkin, Ronald, *Taking Rights Seriously* (Cambridge, MA: Harvard University Press, 1977)
Feuer, Lewis, *Spinoza and the Rise of Liberalism* (Boston: Beacon Press, 1958)
Fisher, Philip, *Wonder, the Rainbow, and the Aesthetics of Rare Experiences* (Cambridge, MA: Harvard University Press, 1998)
Fix, Andrew, *Prophesy and Reason: The Dutch Collegiants in the Early Enlightenment* (Princeton: Princeton University Press, 1991)
Fletcher, R. A., *The Barbarian Conversion: From Paganism to Christianity* (New York: H. Holt and Co., 1998)
Frankel, Steven, "The Piety of a Heretic: Spinoza's Interpretation of Judaism," *Journal of Jewish Thought and Philosophy*, 11.2 (2002), 117–134
Freudenthal, Jakob and Manfred Walther, *Die Lebensgeschichte Spinozas*. Zweite, stark erweiterte und vollständig neu kommentierte Auflage der Ausgabe von Jakob Freudenthal 1899, mit einer Bibliographie herausgegeben von Manfred Walther unter Mitarbeit von Michael Czelinski. Band 1: *Lebensbeschreibungen und Dokumente*. Band 2: *Kommentar* (Stuttgart: Fromann-Holzboog, 2006)
Friedlander, Michael, *Essays on the Writings of Abraham ibn Ezra* (London: Society of Hebrew Literature, 1877)
Friedmann, Georges, *Leibniz et Spinoza* (Paris: Gallimard, 1975 [1st edn. 1946])
Garber, Daniel, "Dr. Fischelson's Dilemma: Spinoza on Freedom and Sociability," in *Spinoza by 2000: The Jerusalem Conferences. Ethica IV: Spinoza on Reason and the "Free Man,"* ed. Yirmiyahu Yovel and Gideon Segal (New York: Little Room Press, 2004), 183–208
Garrett, Don, "'A Free Man Always Acts Honestly, Not Deceptively': Freedom and the Good in Spinoza's Ethics," in *Spinoza: Issues and Directions*, ed. Edwin Curley and Pierre-François Moreau (Leiden: Brill, 1990), 221–238
  "Spinoza's Ethical Theory," in *The Cambridge Companion to Spinoza*, ed. Don Garrett (Cambridge: Cambridge University Press, 1996), 267–314
Gatens, Moira, "Spinoza's Disturbing Thesis: Power, Norms and Fiction in the *Tractatus Theologico-Politicus*," *History of Political Thought*, 30.3 (2009), 455–468
Gerritsen, Johan, "Printing Spinoza – Some Questions," in *Spinoza to the Letter: Studies in Words, Texts and Books*, ed. F. Akkerman and P. Steenbakkers (Leiden: Brill, 2005), 251–262
Gersonides, *Commentary on the Pentateuch*, 5 vols. (Jerusalem: Mossad ha-Rav Kuk, 1996)

Gibbon, Edward, *Decline and Fall of the Roman Empire*, ed. David Wormersley. 3 vols. (London: Penguin, 1994)

Gilson, Etienne, *The Spirit of Medieval Philosophy*, trans. A. H. C. Downes (Notre Dame: University of Notre Dame Press, 1936)

Goldenbaum, Ursula, "Der historische Ansatz des 'Theologisch-politischen Traktats'. Baruch Spinozas als ein Ausweg aus den religionsphilosophischen Debatten des 17. Jahrhunderts," in *Religionsphilosophie. Europäische Denker zwischen philosophischer Theologie und Religionskritik*, ed. Th. Brose (Wurzburg: Echter Verlag, 1998), 83–112

"Die *Commentatiuncula* de judice als Leibnizens erste philosophische Auseinandersetzung mit Spinoza nebst der Mitteilung über ein neuaufgefundenes Leibnizstück," in *Labora Diligenter. Studia Leibnitiana Sonderheft*, 29, ed. M. Fontius, H. Rudolph, and G. Smith (Stuttgart: Franz Steiner Verlag, 1999), 61–98

"Spinoza's Parrot, Socinian Syllogisms, and Leibniz's Metaphysics: Leibniz's Three Strategies for Defending Christian Mysteries," *American Catholic Philosophical Quarterly*, 76.4 (2002), 551–574

Gottlieb, Michah, "Spinoza's Method(s) of Biblical Interpretation Reconsidered," *Jewish Studies Quarterly*, 14 (2007), 286–317

Grotius, Hugo, *The Rights of War and Peace*, ed. Richard Tuck, 3 vols. (Indianapolis: Liberty Fund, 2005)

Halevi, Judah, *The Kuzari*, trans. Hartwig Hirschfeld (New York: Schocken Books, 1964)

Halivni, David Weiss, *Peshat & Derash* (New York: Oxford University Press, 1991)

Harrison, Geoffrey, "Relativism and Toleration," *Ethics*, 82.2 (1976), 122–135

Harvey, Warren Zev, "Spinoza's Metaphysical Hebraism," in *Jewish Themes in Spinoza's Philosophy*, ed. Heidi M. Ravven and Lenn E. Goodman (Albany: SUNY Press, 2002), 107–115

"Judah Halevi's Interpretation of the Tetragrammaton" [Heb.], in *Dabar Dabur `al Ofanav: Studies Presented to Haggai Ben-Shammai*, ed. M. M. Bar-Asher, S. Hopkins, S. Stroumsa, and B. Chiesa (Jerusalem: Ben Zvi Institute, 2007), 125–132

Hererra, Avraham ha-Kohen, *Beit Elohim* [Heb.: *The House of God*], trans. Yitzhak Aboav De Fonesca (Amsterdam: Immanuel Benvenishti, 1755)

Heschel, Abraham Joshua, *Heavenly Torah*, trans. G. Tucker and L. Levin (New York: Continuum, 2007)

Hessing, Siegfried, ed., *Speculum Spinozanum, 1677–1977* (London: Routledge, 1977)

Hoffmann, George, "Anatomy of the Mass: Montaigne's 'Cannibals,'" *PMLA*, 117 (2002), 207–221

Hood, F. C., *The Divine Politics of Thomas Hobbes* (Oxford: Clarendon Press, 1964)

Huet, Pierre-Daniel, *Demonstratio evangelica* (Apud Danielem Hortemels: Parisiis, 1690)

Hume, David, *Enquiries Concerning Human Understanding and Concerning the Principles of Morals*, ed. L. A. Selby-Bigge and P. H. Nidditch, 3rd edn. (Oxford: Oxford University Press, 1975)

Hutto, Daniel, ed., *Narrative and Understanding Persons* (Cambridge: Cambridge University Press, 2007)

Ibn Ezra, Abraham, *Perushe ha-Torah* [Heb.: *Commentary on the Pentateuch*], ed. A. Weiser, 3 vols. (Jerusalem: Mossad Harav Kook, 1976)

Ibn Motot, Samuel, *Megillat Setarim* [Heb.: *Scroll of Secrets*]. MS. Cambridge Add. 1015 [Institute of Microfilmed Hebrew Manuscripts, Jerusalem, no. 17024]

Israel, Jonathan I., *The Dutch Republic: Its Rise, Greatness, and Fall, 1477–1806* (Oxford: Clarendon Press, 1995)

  "The Intellectual Debate About Toleration in the Dutch Republic," in *The Emergence of Tolerance in the Dutch Republic*, ed. C. Berkvens-Stevelinck, J. Israel, and G. H. M. Posthumus Meyjes (Leiden: Brill, 1997), 3–36

➤ *Radical Enlightenment: Philosophy and the Making of Modernity, 1650–1750* (Oxford: Oxford University Press, 2001).

  Enlightenment Contested: Philosophy, Modernity, and the Emancipation of Man, 1672–1752 (Oxford: Oxford University Press, 2006)

James, Susan, "Power and Difference: Spinoza's Conception of Freedom," *Journal of Political Philosophy*, 4 (1996), 207–228

  Passion and Action: The Emotions in Seventeenth-Century Philosophy (Cambridge: Cambridge University Press, 1997)

Jospe, Raphael, "Biblical Exegesis as a Philosophic Literary Genre: Ibn Ezra and Mendelssohn," in *Jewish Philosophy and the Academy*, ed. Emil L. Fackenheim and Raphael Jospe (Cranbury, NJ: Associated University Presses, 1996), 48–92

Kant, Immanuel, *Critique of Practical Reason*, trans. L. W. Beck (New York: Macmillan, 1988)

  Religion and Rational Theology, ed. trans. and Allen W. Wood and George Di Giovanni, The Cambridge Edition of the Works of Immanuel Kant (Cambridge: Cambridge University Press, 1996)

  Religion Within the Boundaries of Mere Reason, in *Religion and Rational Theology*, The Cambridge Edition of the Works of Immanuel Kant, ed. and trans. Allen W. Wood and George Di Giovanni (Cambridge: Cambridge University Press, 1996), 39–216

Kaplan, Yosef, "Rabbi Saul Levi Morteira's Treatise 'Arguments against the Christian Religion,'" *Immanuel*, 11 (1980), 95–112

  From Christianity to Judaism: The Life and Works of the Converso Isaac Orobio de Castro (Oxford: Littman Library, 1989)

Kenny, Neil, *Curiosity in Early Modern Europe: Word Histories. Vol. 81, Wolfenbuetteler Forschungen* (Wiesbaden: Harrassowitz Verlag, 1998)

  The Uses of Curiosity in Early Modern France and Germany (Oxford: Oxford University Press, 2004)

Kimhi, Joseph, *The Book of the Covenant*, trans. Frank Talmage (Toronto: Pontifical Institute of Mediaeval Studies, 1972)

King, Noel Q., *The Emperor Theodosius and the Establishment of Christianity* (Philadelphia: Westminster Press, 1960)

"Theodosius." *Encyclopedia of Religion*, ed. Lindsay Jones, 2nd edn. (Detroit: Macmillan Reference USA, 2005), vol. XIII

Kingma, Jelle "Spinoza Editions in the Nineteenth Century," in *Spinoza to the Letter: Studies in Words, Texts and Books*, ed. F. Akkerman and P. Steenbakkers (Leiden: Brill, 2005), 273–281

Kingma, J. and A. K. Offenberg, *Bibliography of Spinoza's Works up to 1800*. Corrected and annotated reproduction (Amsterdam: Amsterdam University Library, 1985)

Klazkin, Jacob, *Barukh Spinoza. Hayyav, Sefarav, Shitato* [Heb.: *Baruch Spinoza: His Life, Writings, and System*] (Leipzig: Shtiebl, 1923)

Klever, Wim, "L'erreur de Velthuysen et des Velthuysiens," in *L'Hérésie spinoziste*, ed. P. Cristofolini (Amsterdam: APA-Holland University Press, 1995), 138–146

Mannen rond Spinoza. Presentatie van een emancipeerende generatie, 1650–1700 (Hilversum: Verloren, 1997)

Kolakowski, Leszek, *Chrétiens sans Église. La conscience religieuse et le lien confessionel au XVIIe siècle* [1965]. French trans. (Paris: Gallimard, 1969)

Kossmann, E. H., "Freedom in Seventeenth-Century Dutch Thought and Practice," in *The Anglo-Dutch Moment: Essays on the Glorious Revolution and its World Impact*, ed. Jonathan I. Israel (Cambridge: Cambridge University Press, 1991), 281–298

Krauss, Samuel, *The Jewish-Christian Controversy from the Earliest Times to 1789*, ed. and rev. William Horbury (Tübingen: J. C. B. Mohr, 1995), vol. I

Kuyper, Frans, *Arcana Atheismi revelata, philosophice et paradoxe refutata, examine Tractatus Theologico-Politici* (Rotterdam, 1676)

Lærke, Mogens, "À la recherche d'un homme égal à Spinoza. G. W. Leibniz et la Demonstratio evangelica de Pierre-Daniel Huet," *XVIIe siècle*, 232 (2006), 388–410

"Contingency, Necessity and the Being of Possibility: Leibniz's Modal Ontology in Relation to his Refutation of Spinoza," *Revue Roumaine de Philosophie*, 51 (2007), 39–62

"La storia nell'esegesi biblica in Leibniz e in Spinoza," *Quaderni materialisti*, 6 (2007), 265–280

"Leibniz, la censure et la libre pensée," *Archives de philosophie*, 70.2 (2007), 273–287

"Les sept foyers du libertinage selon G. W. Leibniz," *La Lettre clandestine*, 15 (2007), 269–297

"Quod non omnia possibilia ad existentiam perveniant: Leibniz's Ontology of Possibility, 1668–1678," *The Leibniz Review*, 17 (2007), 1–30

"Apology for a *Credo Maximum*: On Three Basic Rules in Leibniz's Method of Religious Controversy," in *Leibniz: What Kind of Rationalist?* ed. M. Dascal (Dordrecht: Springer, 2008), 397–407

Leibniz lecteur de Spinoza. La genèse d'une opposition complexe (Paris: Honoré Champion, 2008)

"Leibniz et le libertinage: quatre fonctions théoriques," in *Libertinage et philosophie au XVIIe siècle* II, ed. P.-F. Moreau and A. McKenna (St. Etienne: Presses Universitaires de St. Etienne, 2009), 267–286

"The Golden Rule: Charitas/Prudentia. Aspects of G. W. Leibniz's Method for Religious Controversy," in *The Practice of Reason: Leibniz and his Controversies*, ed. M. Dascal (Amsterdam: Andrew Benjamin Publishing, 2010), 297–319

Lagrée, Jacqueline, "Louis Meyer et la *Philosophia S. Scripturae interpres*. Projet cartésien, horizon spinoziste," *Revue des sciences philosophiques et théologiques*, 1 (1987), 31–44

"Louis Meyer et Spinoza devant la lecture de la Bible," *Bulletin de l'Association des amis de Spinoza*, 21 (1988), 1–9

"Sens et vérité: philosophie et théologie chez L. Meyer et Spinoza," *Studia Spinozana*, 4 (1988), 75–92

La Raison ardente (Paris: Vrin, 1991)

Lagrée, Jacqueline and Pierre-François Moreau, "La lecture de la Bible dans le cercle de Spinoza," in *Le Grand siècle et la Bible*, ed. J.-R. Armogathe (Paris: Beauchesne, 1989), vol. VI, 97–116

Land, J. P. N., "Over vier drukken met het jaartal 1670 van Spinoza's Tractatus Theologico-Politicus," in *Verslagen en Mededeelingen der Koninklijke Akademie van Wetenschappen*, Afdeeling Letterkunde, Tweede Reeks, Elfde Deel (Amsterdam: Muller, 1882), 148–158

Lasker, Daniel J., *Jewish Philosophical Polemics Against Christianity in the Middle Ages* (New York: Ktav, 1977 [2nd edn. Oxford: Littman Library, 2007])

"Averroistic Trends in Jewish-Christian Polemics in the Late Middle Ages," *Speculum*, 55.2 (1980), 294–304

"Joseph Albo's Theory of Verification" [Heb.] *Daat*, 5 (1980), 5–12

"Saadia on Christianity and Islam," in *The Jews of Medieval Islam: Community, Society, and Identity*, ed. Daniel Frank (Leiden: Brill, 1995), 165–177

"Karaism and Christian Hebraism: A New Document," *Renaissance Quarterly*, 59.4 (2006), 1089–1116

"Imagination and Intellect in the Medieval Jewish Philosophical Polemics against Christianity," in *Intellect et imagination dans la Philosophie Médiévale. Actes du XIe Congrès International de Philosophie Médiévale de la Société Internationale pour l'Étude de la Philosophie Médiévale (S.I.E.P.M.)*, Porto, du 26 au 31 août 2002, ed. M. C. Pacheco and J. F. Meirinhos (Turnhout: Brepols, 2006), vol. I, 615–624

Lasker, Daniel J. and Sarah Stroumsa, *The Polemic of Nestor the Priest*. 2 vols. (Jerusalem: Ben-Zvi Institute, 1996)

Laursen, John Christian, "Spinoza on Toleration," in *Difference and Dissent: Theories of Tolerance in Medieval and Early Modern Europe*, ed. Cary J. Nederman and John Christian Laursen (Lanham: Rowman and Littlefield, 1996), 185–204

Leavitt, Frank J., "The Christian Philosophy of Benedictus de Spinoza," [Heb.] *Daat*, 26 (1991), 97–108

Le Clerc, Jean, *Epistolario*, ed. M. Sina and M. Grazia, 4 vols. (Florence: Olschki, 1987–1997)

Leibniz, Gottfried Wilhelm, *Opera Omnia*, ed. L. Dutens (Geneva: Fratres de Tournes, 1768)

Sämtliche Schriften und Briefe (Berlin: Akademie-Verlag, 1923–)

Textes inédits, ed. G. Grua (Paris: Presses Universitaires de France, 1948)

Die philosophischen Schriften von Gottfried Wilhelm Leibniz, ed. C. I. Gerhardt (Hildesheim: Georg Olms Verlag, 1978)

Philosophical Essays, trans. Roger Ariew and Daniel Garber (Indianapolis: Hackett, 1989)

Leibniz–Thomasius. Correspondance 1663–1672, ed. R. Bodéüs (Paris: Vrin, 1993)

Le Droit de la raison, ed. R. Sève (Paris: Vrin, 1994)

"Leibniz' Marginalien zu Spinozas Tractatus theologico-politicus im Exemplar der Bibliotheca Boineburgica in Erfurt, also zu datieren auf 1670–71," ed. U. Goldenbaum, in *Labora diligenter. Studia Leibnitiana Sonderheft* 29, ed. M. Fontius, H. Rudolph, and G. Smith (Stuttgart: Franz Steiner Verlag, 1999), 105–107

"J.-G. Wachteri de recondita Hebraeorum philosophia (1706)," ed. Philip Beeley, *The Leibniz Review*, 12 (2002), 1–14

Lemler, David, "Abraham ibn Ezra et Moïse Maïmonide cités par Spinoza," *Revue des études juives*, 168 (2009), 415–464

Levy, Zeev, "Al ha-Reqa' ha-Sefardi ve-ha-Anusi shel Filosofiat Spinoza" [Heb.: "On the Sefaradic and Marrano Background of Spinoza's Philosophy"], *Peamim*, 49 (1992), 84–92

Lewis, David, "Many, But Almost One," in *Papers in Metaphysics and Epistemology* (Cambridge: Cambridge University Press, 1999), vol. ii, 164–182

Locke, John, *Essay Concerning Human Understanding*, ed. P. H. Nidditch (Oxford: Clarendon Press, 1975)

Luzzatto, Samuel David, *Perush 'al ha-Torah* [Heb.: *Commentary on the Pentateuch*] (Padua, 1871 [repr. Tel-Aviv, 1965])

Macherey, Pierre, "Louis Meyer interprète de l'Écriture," in *Avec Spinoza* (Paris: Presses Universitaires de France, 1992), 168–172

Machiavelli, Niccolo, *Discourses on the First Ten Books of Titus Livy* (Harmondsworth: Penguin Books, 1983)

MacCullough, Diarmaid, *Christianity: The First Three Thousand Years* (New York: Viking/Penguin, 2010)

— MacIntyre, Alasdair, *After Virtue* (London: Duckworth, 1981)

MacMullen, Ramsay, *Christianizing the Roman Empire* (New Haven: Yale University Press, 1984)

Maimon, Salomon, *An Autobiography*, trans. J. Clark Murray (Urbana: University of Illinois Press, 2001 [original German 1792–1793])

Malcolm, Noel, *Aspects of Hobbes* (Oxford: Oxford University Press, 2002)

Maréchal, G., ed., *Vervolg van 't Leven van Philopater* (Amsterdam: Rodopi, 1991)

Marenbon, John, *The Philosophy of Peter Abelard* (Cambridge: Cambridge University Press, 1997)

Maresius, Samuel, *Vindiciae dissertationis suae nuperae De Abusu philosophiae Carte-sianae* (Groningen, 1670)

Marinoff, Louis, "Hobbes, Spinoza, Kant, Highway Robbery, and Game Theory," *Australasian Journal of Philosophy*, 72.4 (1994), 445–462

Martinich, A. P., *The Two Gods of Leviathan* (Cambridge: Cambridge University Press, 1992)

"On the Proper Interpretation of Hobbes's Philosophy," *Journal of the History of Philosophy*, 34 (1996), 273–283

"The Interpretation of Covenants in Hobbes's Leviathan," in *Leviathan After 350 Years*, ed. Tom Sorrell and Lic Foisneau (Oxford: Clarendon Press, 2004), 217–240

Mason, Richard, *The God of Spinoza: A Philosophical Study* (Cambridge: Cambridge University Press, 1997)

Matheron, Alexandre, *Individu et Communauté chez Spinoza* (Paris: Les Éditions de Minuit, 1969)

Mayshar, Joram, *In His Image: The Idea of Equality from Ezra to Nietzsche* [Heb.] (Jerusalem: Karmel, 2007)

McShea, Robert, *The Political Philosophy of Spinoza* (New York: Columbia University Press, 1968)

Méchoulan, Henry, "Morteira et Spinoza au carrefour du socinianisme," *Revue des études juives*, 135.1–3 (1976), 51–76

Meier-Oeser, Stephan, *Die Spur des Zeichens: Das Zeichen und seine Funktion in der Philosophie des Mittelalters und der frühen Neuzeit* (Berlin: De Gruyter, 1997)

Meijer, W., *Aanteekeningen van Benedictus de Spinoza op het Godgeleerd-staatkundig vertoog* (Amsterdam: Van Looy, 1901)

Meinsma, Koenraad Oege, *Spinoza et son cercle. Étude critique historique sur les hétérodoxes hollandais*, trans. S. Roosenburg (Paris: Vrin, 2006 [original Dutch edn. 1896])

Melamed, Yitzhak, "Salomon Maimon and the Rise of Spinozism in German Idealism," *Journal of the History of Philosophy*, 42 (2004), 67–96

Review of Michael Ayers (ed.), *Rationalism, Platonism, and God* (Oxford University Press 2008), in the *Notre Dame Philosophical Reviews On-Line* (February 24, 2009)

"Spinoza's Metaphysics of Substance: The Substance–Mode Relation as a Relation of Inherence and Predication," *Philosophy and Phenomenological Research*, 78.1 (2009), 17–82

"From the 'Gates of Heaven' to the 'Field of Holy Apples': Spinoza and the Kabbalah" (unublished manuscript).

"Spinoza's Deification of Existence" Oxford Studies in Early Modern Philosophy, forthcoming

J.M.V.D.M. [= Johannes Melchior] *Epistola Ad Amicum, continens censuram libri cui titulus*: Tractatus Theologico-Politicus (Utrecht, 1671)

Melnick, Ralph, *From Polemics to Apologetics* (Assen: Van Gorcum, 1981)

Mendus, Susan, "Introduction," in *Justifying Toleration*, ed. Susan Mendus (Cambridge: Cambridge University Press, 1988), 1–19

Meyer, Lodewijk, *La Philosophie interprète de l'Écriture sainte*, trans. J. Lagrée and P.-F. Moreau (Paris: Intertextes, 1988 [original Latin edn.: 1666])
  Philosophy as the Interpreter of Holy Scripture, trans. S. Shirley, with introduction and notes by L. Rice and F. Pastijn (Milwaukee: Marquette University Press, 2005 [original Latin edn.: 1666])

Mignini, Filippo, "Données et problèmes de la chronologie spinozienne entre 1656 et 1665," *Revue des sciences philosophiques et théologiques*, 71 (1987), 9–21

Mill, John Stuart, *On Liberty*, ed. David Spitz (New York: Norton, 1975)

Miller, Jon, "Spinoza and the Concept of a Law of Nature," *History of Philosophy Quarterly*, 20 (2003), 257–276

Misrahi, Robert, "Spinoza and Christian Thought," in *Speculum Spinozanum, 1677–1977*, ed. Siegfried Hessing (London: Routledge, 1977), 387–417

Montaigne, Michel de, *The Complete Essays of Montaigne*, trans. Donald M. Frame (Stanford: Stanford University Press, 1965)

More, Henry, *Ad V.C.Epistola altera, Quae brevem Tractatus Theologico-Politici confutationem complectitur*, in *Opera Omnia*. 3 vols. (London, 1675–1679), vol. 11

Moreau, Pierre-François, "Les principes de la lecture de l'Écriture sainte dans le TTP," in *L'Écriture sainte au temps de Spinoza et dans les système spinoziste*. Groupe de recherches spinozistes, Travaux et documents 4 (Paris: Presses Universitaires de Paris Sorbonne, 1992), 119–131
  Spinoza et le spinozisme (Paris: Presses Universitaires de France, 2003)
  "Notice sur la réception du Traité politique," in B. de Spinoza, *Traité Politique*, ed. O. Proietti and C. Ramond (Paris: Presses Universitaires de France, 2005), 77–99

Mortera, Shaul, *Giveat Shaul* [Heb.: *Saul's Hill*] (Warsaw: Israel Alaphin Press, 1902)

Müller, Johann Heinrich, *Dissertatio inavgvralis philosophica de miraculis* (Altdorf, 1714)

Musaeus, Johann, *Tractatus Theologico-Politicus*, quo auctor quidam anonymus, [. . .] *ad veritatis lancem examinatus* (Jena, 1674)

Nadler, Steven, *Spinoza: A Life* (Cambridge: Cambridge University Press, 1999)
  Spinoza's Ethics: An Introduction (Cambridge: Cambridge University Press, 2006)

Offenberg, K. A., "Letter from Spinoza to Lodewijk Meyer, 26 July 1663," in *Speculum Spinozanum, 1677–1977*, ed. Siegfried Hessing (London: Routledge, 1977), 426–435
  ed., *Brief van Spinoza aan Lodewijk Meyer, 26 juli 1663* (Amsterdam: Universiteitsbibliotheek, 1975)

O'Neill, Joseph, *Netherland* (New York: Pantheon Books, 2008)

Osier, Jean-Pierre, *Faust Socin ou le christianisme sans sacrifice* (Paris: Cerf, 1996)

Otto, Rüdiger, *Studien zur Spinozarezeption in Deutschland im 18. Jahrhundert* (Frankfurt: Peter Lang, 1994)

Parkinson, G. H. R., "Leibniz's Paris Writings in Relation to Spinoza," *Studia Leibnitiana. Supplementa* XVIII (1978)

"Spinoza on the Freedom of Man and the Freedom of the Citizen," in *Conceptions of Liberty in Political Philosophy*, ed. Zbigniew Pelczynski and John Gray (London: St. Martin's Press, 1984), 39–56

Pautrat, Bernard, ed., "Dossier: la bibliothèque," in B. de Spinoza, *Éthique* (Paris: Éditions du Seuil, 1999), 635–695

Petuchowski, Jakob Josef, *The Theology of Haham David Nieto: An Eighteenth Century Defense of the Jewish Tradition* (Welch: Congregation Emanuel, 1954)

Pick, Bernhard, "Spinoza and the Old Testament," *The Biblical World*, 2 (1893), 112–122

Pines, Shlomo, "Spinoza's TTP, Maimonides, and Kant," *Scripta Hierosolymitana*, 20 (1968), 3–54

"Spinoza's *Tractatus Theologico-Politicus* and the Jewish Philosophical Tradition," in *Jewish Thought in the Seventeenth Century*, ed. Isadore Twersky and Bernard Septimus (Cambridge, MA: Harvard University Press, 1987), 499–521, repr. in Pines, *Studies in the History of Jewish Thought [The Collected Works of Shlomo Pines]*, ed. Warren Z. Harvey and Moshe Idel (Jerusalem: Magnes, 1997), vol. V, 712–734

Plato, *The Collected Dialogues of Plato Including the Letters*, ed. E. Hamilton and H. Cairns (Princeton: Princeton University Press, 1980)

Poiret, Pierre, *Cogitationum rationalium de Deo, anima et malo, libri quattuor.* 3rd edn. (Amsterdam, 1715)

Popkin, Richard H., *The History of Scepticism from Erasmus to Spinoza* (Berkeley: University of California Press, 1979)

"The Deist Challenge," in *From Persecution to Toleration: The Glorious Revolution and Religion in England*, ed. O. P. Grell, J. I. Israel, and N. Tyacke (Oxford: Oxford University Press, 1991), 195–215

"Spinoza and Bible Scholarship," in *The Cambridge Companion to Spinoza*, ed. Don Garrett (Cambridge: Cambridge University Press, 1996), 383–407

Popkin, Richard H. and Michael A. Signer, eds., *Spinoza's Earliest Publication? The Hebrew Translation of Margaret Fell's* A Loving Salutation to the Seed of Abraham among the Jews, wherever they are scattered up and down upon the Face of the Earth (Assen: Van Gorcum, 1987)

Quinn, Philip and Kevin Meeker, *The Philosophical Challenge of Religious Diversity* (Oxford: Oxford University Press, 1999)

Rankin, Oliver Shaw, *Jewish Religious Polemic* (Edinburgh: Edinburgh University Press, 1956)

Raphael, D. D., "The Intolerable," in *Justifying Toleration*, ed. Susan Mendus (Cambridge: Cambridge University Press, 1988), 137–153

Rappolt, Friedrich, *Opera theologica* (Leipzig, 1693)

Rashbam, *Perush ha-Torah* (Breslau: S. Schottlaender, 1881)

Ravven, Heidi M. and Lenn E. Goodman, eds., *Jewish Themes in Spinoza's Philosophy* (Albany: SUNY Press, 2002)

Raz, Joseph, *The Morality of Freedom* (Oxford: Clarendon Press, 1986)

Remer, Gary, "Bodin's Pluralistic Theory of Toleration," in *Difference and Dissent: Theories of Tolerance in Medieval and Early Modern Europe*, ed. Cary J. Nederman and John Christian Laursen (Lanham: Rowman and Littlefield, 1996), 119–137

Robinet, André, *Le Meilleur des mondes par la balance de l'Europe* (Paris: Presses Universitaires de France, 1994)

Romeu Ferré, Pilar "A New Approach to the Polemical Work 'Fuente Clara,'" *Journal of Jewish Studies*, 55.1 (2004), 118–130

Rooden, Peter T. van, "Constantijn L'Empereur's Contacts with the Amsterdam Jews and his Confutation of Judaism," in *Jewish-Christian Relations in the Seventeenth Century*, ed. J. Van Den Berg and Ernestine G. E. Van der Wall (Dordrecht: Kluwer, 1988), 52–72

Theology, Biblical Scholarship and Rabbinical Studies in the Seventeenth Century: Constantijn l'Empereur (1591–1648), Professor of Hebrew and Theology at Leiden (Leiden: Brill, 1989)

"A Dutch Adaptation of Elias Montalto's Tractado sobre o principio do capitulo 53 de Jesaias. Text, introduction and commentary," in *The Contribution of the Jews to the Culture in the Netherlands*, ed. Hans Bots and Jan Roegiers (Amsterdam: APA-Holland University Press, 1990), 189–238

Rosenthal, Michael, "Why Spinoza Chose the Hebrews: The Exemplary Function of Prophecy in the Theological-Political Treatise," *History of Political Thought*, 18.1 (1997), 207–241

"Two Collective Action Problems in Spinoza's Social Contract Theory," *History of Philosophy Quarterly*, 15.4 (1998), 389–409

"Toleration and the Right to Resist in Spinoza's *Theological-Political Treatise*: The Problem of Christ's Disciples," in *Piety, Peace and the Freedom to Philosophize*, ed. P. J. Bagley (Dordrecht: Kluwer, 2000), 111–132

"Tolerance as a Virtue in Spinoza's Ethics," *Journal of the History of Philosophy*, 39.4 (2001), 535–557

"Spinoza's Republican Argument for Toleration," *Journal of Political Philosophy*, 11.3 (2003), 320–337

"Spinoza on Why the Sovereign Can Command Men's Tongues But Not Their Minds," *Nomos*, 48, "Toleration and Its Limits," ed. Melissa S. Williams and Jeremy Waldron (New York: New York University Press, 2008), 54–77

Rutherford, Donald, "Spinoza and the Dictates of Reason," *Inquiry*, 51 (2008), 485–511

Saadia ben Joseph Gaon, *Book of Beliefs and Opinions*, trans. Samuel Rosenblatt (New Haven: Yale University Press, 1948)

Schama, Simon, *The Embarrassment of Riches* (New York: Knopf, 1987)

Schmitt, Carl, *Political Theology: Four Chapters on the Concept of Sovereignty*, trans. G. Schwab (Chicago: University of Chicago Press, 2005 [original edn., 1922, rev. 1934])

Schröder, Winfried, "'Die ungereimteste Meynung, die jemals von Menschen ersonnen worden' – Spinozismus in der deutschen Frühaufklärung?" in

Spinoza im Deutschland des achtzehnten Jahrhunderts, ed. E. Schürmann, N. Waszek, and F. Weinreich (Stuttgart-Bad Cannstatt: Frommann-Holzboog, 2002), 121–138

Scribano, E., "Johannes Bredenburg (1643–1691) confutore di Spinoza?" in *The Spinozistic Heresy*, ed. Paolo Cristofolini (Amsterdam: Holland University Press, 1995), 66–76

Secretan, Catherine, "La reception de Hobbes aux Pays-Bas au XVIIe Siecle," *Studia Spinozana*, 3 (1987), 27–45

Seidler, Meir, "Barukh Spinoza – Me'azev Tadmit ha-Yahadut Avur ha-Haskalah ha-Eiropit" [Heb.: "Baruch Spinoza: The Designer of the Image of Judaism in the European Enlightenment"], *Daat*, 54 (2004), 20–45

Shapiro, Marc B., *The Limits of Orthodox Theology: Maimonides' Thirteen Principles Reappraised* (Oxford: Littman Library, 2004)

Shoshan, Orly, "Rabbi Eleazar ben Mattathias" [Heb.] (PhD diss., Ben-Gurion University of the Negev, Beersheba, 2009)

Simon, Uriel, "Interpreting the Interpreter: Supercommentaries on Ibn Ezra's Commentaries," in *Rabbi Abraham ibn Ezra: Studies in the Writings of a Twelfth Century Jewish Polymath*, ed. I. Twersky and J. M. Harris (Cambridge, MA: Harvard University Press, 1993), 86–128

Smith, Steven B., *Spinoza, Liberalism, and the Question of Jewish Identity* (New Haven: Yale University Press, 1997)

Spinoza's Book of Life: Freedom and Redemption in the Ethics (New Haven: Yale University Press, 2003)

Spitzel, Gottlieb, *Felix literatus ex infelicium periculis et casibus* (Nuremberg, 1676)

Sreedhar, Susanne, "Defending Hobbes's Right of Self-Defense," *Political Theory*, 36.6 (2008), 781–802

Stark, Rodney, *The Rise of Christianity: A Sociologist Reconsiders History* (Princeton: Princeton University Press, 1996)

Steenbakkers, Piet, "Les éditions de Spinoza en Allemagne au XIXe siècle," in *Spinoza au XIXe siècle*, ed. A. Tosel, P.-F. Moreau, and J. Salem (Paris: Publications de la Sorbonne, 2007), 21–32

"The Textual History of Spinoza's Ethics," in *The Cambridge Companion to Spinoza's Ethics*, ed. Olli Koistinen (Cambridge: Cambridge University Press 2009, 26–41)

Steinberg, Diane, "Spinoza's Ethical Doctrine and the Unity of Human Nature," *Journal of the History of Philosophy*, 22 (1984), 303–324

Steinberg, Justin, "On Being Sui Iuris: Spinoza and the Republican Idea of Liberty," *History of European Ideas*, 34.3 (2008), 239–249

"Spinoza on Civil Liberation," *Journal of the History of Philosophy*, 47.1 (2009), 35–58

"Spinoza's Political Philosophy," Stanford Encyclopedia of Philosophy (Spring 2009 Edition), ed. Edward N. Zalta, http://plato.stanford.edu/archives/spr2009/entries/spinoza-political/

Strauss, Leo, *Persecution and the Art of Writing* (Chicago: University of Chicago Press, 1988 [original edn., 1952])

Stroumsa, Sarah, "The Signs of Prophecy: The Emergence and Early Development of a Theme in Arabic Literature," *Harvard Theological Review* 78 (1985), 101–114, rev. in *Freethinkers of Medieval Islam* (Leiden: Brill, 1999), 21–36

Thijssen-Schoute, C. L., *Nederlands Cartesianisme* (Utrecht, 1954 [repr. 1989]).

Tralau, Johann, "Leviathan, the Beast of Myth: Medusa, Dionysos, and the Riddle of Hobbes's Sovereign Monster," in *The Cambridge Companion to Hobbes's Leviathan*, ed. P. Springborg (New York: Cambridge University Press, 2007), 61–81

Tuck, Richard, "Skepticism and Toleration in the Seventeenth Century," in *Justifying Toleration*, ed. Susan Mendus (Cambridge: Cambridge University Press, 1988), 21–35

Twersky, Isadore and Bernard Septimus, eds., *Jewish Thought in the Seventeenth Century* (Cambridge, MA: Harvard University Press, 1987)

Van Bunge, Wiep, "Johannes Bredenburg and the Korte Verhandeling," *Studia Spinozana*, 4 (1988), 321–328

  "On the Early Dutch Reception of the *Tractatus Theologico-Politicus*," *Studia Spinozana*, 5 (1989), 225–251

  "Johannes Bredenburg (1643–1691). Een Rotterdamse Collegiant in de baan van Spinoza" (Dissertation, Erasmus Universiteit, Rotterdam, 1990)

  From Stevin to Spinoza: An Essay on Philosophy in the Seventeenth-Century Dutch Republic (Leiden: Brill, 2001)

  "Velthuysen, Lambert van (1622–85)," in *The Dictionary of Seventeenth and Eighteenth-Century Dutch Philosophers*, ed. Wiep van Bunge *et al.* (Bristol: Thoemmes, 2003), 1017–1020

Van der Wall, Ernestine, "Til, Salomon van (1643–1713)," in *The Dictionary of Seventeenth and Eighteenth-Century Dutch Philosophers*, ed. Wiep van Bunge *et al.* (Bristol: Thoemmes, 2003), 981–983

Van der Werf, Theo, "Klefmanns exemplaar van Spinoza's Tractatus theologico-politicus," in *Limae labor et mora: opstellen voor Fokke Akerman ter gelegenheid van zijn zeventigste verjaardag*, ed. Z. von Martels, P. Steenbakkers, and A. J. Vanderjagt (Leende: Damon, 2000), 206–211

  "Klefmann's Copy of Spinoza's *Tractatus Theologico-Politicus*," *Studia Rosenthaliana*, 39 (2006), 247–253

Van Gelder, H. A. Enno, *Getemperde vrijheid* (Groningen: Wolters-Noordhoff, 1972)

Van Heenvliedt, Simon [Simon Oomius], *Theologico-Politica Dissertatio, ofte Discours over dese Vrage: Of den Pausgesinden in dese vereenighde Nederlanden, niet en behoorde toe-gestaen te worden, d'openbare exercitiën van hare Religie*. S.l.: Landelijke Stichting ter bevordering van de Staatkundig Gereformeerde beginselen, 2004. Facsimile repr. of original ed. (Utrecht: Waterman, 1662)

Van Mansvelt, Regnerus [Petrus van Andlo], *Animadversiones ad vindicias dissertationis quas Samuel Maresius edidit De Abusu Philosophiae Cartesianae* (Leiden, 1671)

  Adversus Anonymum Theologico-Politicum, Opus Posthumum (Amsterdam, 1674)

Van Til, Salomon, *Het voor-hof der heydenen* (Dordrecht: Goris, 1694)

Van Velthuysen, Lambertus, *Ondersoeck of de Christelijcke overheydt eenigh quaedt in haer gebiedt mach toe laten* (Middelburg: Ian Effendewegh 1660)

Verbeek, Theo, *Spinoza's Theologico-Political Treatise: Exploring 'the Will of God'* (Aldershot: Ashgate, 2003)

Vernière, Paul, *Spinoza et la pensée française avant la Révolution* (Paris: Presses Universitaires de France, 1954)

Vieira, Mildred E. and Frank E. Talmage, *The Mirror of the New Christians (Espelho des Christãos Novos) of Francisco Machado* (Toronto: Pontifical Institute of Mediaeval Studies, 1977)

Visi, Tamás, "The Early Ibn Ezra Supercommentaries" (PhD diss., Central European University, Budapest, 2006)

Voss, Stephen H., "How Spinoza Enumerated the Affects," *Archiv für Geschichte der Philosophie*, 63 (1981), 167–179

Wachter, Johann Georg, *Elucidarius cabalisticus, sive reconditae Hebraeorum philosophiae brevis et succincta recensio.* (Rome [in fact printed in Halle], 1706), facsimile in *Freidenker der europäischen Aufklärung*, ed. W. Schröder (Stuttgart-Bad Cannstatt: Frommann-Holzboog 1995), Vol. 1-2

Wagenseil, Johann Christof, *Tela Ignea Satanae* (Altdorf: Johannem Hofmann, 1681)

Waldron, Jeremy, "Locke: Toleration and the Rationality of Persecution," in *Justifying Toleration*, ed. Susan Mendus (Cambridge: Cambridge University Press, 1988), 61–86

"Free Speech and the Menace of Hysteria," *The New York Review of Books*, 55.9 (2008)

Walther, Manfred, "Biblische Hermeneutik und historische Aufklärung. Lodewijk Meyer und Benedikt de Spinoza über Norm, Methode und Ergebnis wissenschaftlicher Bibelauslegung," in *Studia Spinozana*, 11 (1995), 227–299

"Machina civilis oder Von deutscher Freiheit," in *The Spinozistic Heresy: The Debate on the* Tractatus Theologico-Politicus, *1670–1677*, ed. P. Cristofolini (Amsterdam, 1995), 184–221

Weber, Immanuel, *Beurtheilung Der Atheisterey wie auch derer mehresten desshalben berüchtigsten Schrifften* (Frankfurt, 1697)

West, David, "Spinoza on Positive Freedom," *Political Studies*, 41 (1993), 284–296

Wielema, M. *Filosofen aan de Maas* (Baarn: Ambo, 1991)

Wilson, John, *The Scripture's Genuine Interpreter Asserted* (London, 1678)

Wolfson, Harry A., *The Philosophy of Spinoza: Unfolding the Latent Processes of his Reasoning*, 2 vols. (Cambridge, MA: Harvard University Press, 1934)

Youpa, Andrew, "Spinozistic Self-Preservation," *Southern Journal of Philosophy*, 41.3 (2003), 477–490

Index

CPSIA information can be obtained
at www.ICGtesting.com
Printed in the USA
LVHW081354120521
687221LV00026B/455